D0908821

BOOTLEGGER OF THE SOUL

BOOTLEGGER *of the* SOUL

The Literary Legacy of WILLIAM KENNEDY

EDITED BY

Suzanne Lance & Paul Grondahl

AN IMPRINT OF STATE UNIVERSITY OF NEW YORK PRESS

Cover: Photograph of William Kennedy courtesy of Tomas Sennett. Photograph of North Broadway is from Albany Institute of History & Art, Main Photo Collection, DI 1214. Unidentified photographer, ca. 1915, gelatin silver print.
Page v photograph: *Nighttown, State and Pearl Streets*, 1922. Albany Institute of History & Art Photo Collection.

Published by
State University of New York Press, Albany

Excelsior Editions is an imprint of State University of New York Press

For information, contact State University of New York Press, Albany, NY
www.sunypress.edu

Library of Congress Cataloging-in-Publication Data

Names: Lance, Suzanne and Grondahl, Paul, editors.
Title: Bootlegger of the soul : the literary legacy of William Kennedy
edited by Suzanne Lance and Paul Grondahl.
Albany : State University of New York Press, Albany, [2018] | Series:
Excelsior editions | Includes bibliographical references and index.
Identifiers: ISBN 9781438473314 (hardcover : alk. paper) | ISBN
9781438473321 (e-book)

Further information is available at the Library of Congress.

10 9 8 7 6 5 4 3 2 1

. . . a bootlegger of the soul, a mythic creature made of words and wit and wild deeds and boundless memory.

—from *Roscoe*

One story is all stories. Sooner or later we're all going to end up on the corner of State and Pearl.

—Colum McCann

Nighttown, State and Pearl Streets

Contents

PART THREE

Scholarly Perspectives: Critical Views of Kennedy's Novels

Preface

Conjuring Ghosts with William Kennedy

> I write this book not as a booster of Albany, which I am, nor as an apologist for the city, which I sometimes am, but rather as a person whose imagination has become fused with a single place, and in that place finds all the elements that a man ever needs for the life of the soul.
>
> —William Kennedy, opening of *O Albany!*

In the fading light of a blustery winter's day, I walked beside William Kennedy through the working-class neighborhood of North Albany where he grew up, an Irish Catholic enclave nicknamed Limerick. It was four days before his ninetieth birthday and Kennedy had spent the afternoon conjuring ghosts in old warehouses, mechanical shops, and alleyways. I was reminded of William Faulkner's famous line: "The past is never dead. It's not even past."

We were joined by David Gersten, an architect and artist, who came of age amid the gritty labor of his family's heavy truck fabrication and brake shop, J. Becker & Sons, on Broadway, in the same neighborhood as Kennedy. The decades peeled away as they studied old black-and-white photos on the wall of Becker's shop, and Kennedy talked about Gersten's grandfather and uncle with affection. We walked back outside, and Kennedy slowly took the measure of rows of modest two-family houses. "This place looks the same," he said. We stopped at a small apartment building at 620 North Pearl Street, which has a plaque that reads: "This was the home of William Kennedy 1932–1935 and 1948–1956. Won the 1984 Pulitzer Prize for the novel *Ironweed* set in North Albany."

Childhood stories reflexively poured out of Kennedy, such as when a dog chased him down North Pearl, bit him in the leg, and bloodied him so badly that when his mother caught sight of him being carried home, she thought her son was dead. He recalled the time a neighbor girl named Alice Moffatt came hurtling down a steep hill on a sled and out into traffic on North Pearl Street and was killed when she struck a car. He remembered the names of neighbors and shop owners and the priest at Sacred Heart Church and his childhood chums and hilarious tales of mischief they caused. He recalled these incidents from eight decades past in vivid detail and with lively description, the hallmark of a natural-born storyteller who knows how to inject tension and pace and color into his stories. Gersten and I stood transfixed on the sidewalk as Kennedy spun these entertaining childhood yarns from the deep recesses of his astonishing memory as a cold January wind reddened our cheeks and caused our eyes to water.

Even at ninety, Kennedy remains a writer at work, practicing his craft with a novelist's eye and a journalist's sense of documentation. He took out the nub of a pencil and an ever-present tiny notebook from a breast shirt pocket and pressed Gersten for details about his long-lost relatives and their truck business. He eagerly jotted down the information, logging it into his vast Albany database, searching for connections. He was starting to do legwork on a new novel set in Albany, and he never knew when a scrap of information or snippet of narrative might create a spark and ignite his creative imagination. Kennedy is never not working.

For Kennedy, this hardscrabble neighborhood was the start of an improbable journey. Kennedy rose from a humble upbringing as the only child of working-class parents to the pinnacle of success as a novelist who won the Pulitzer Prize and every other major literary award. Moreover, he received a prestigious MacArthur Fellowship and was elected to the American Academy of Arts and Letters. His novels were published in three dozen countries. *Ironweed* was adapted into a feature film starring Meryl Streep and Jack Nicholson, and Kennedy brought its world premiere to Albany. Critics hailed him as one of the great American novelists of his generation and he forged friendships with literary lions Saul Bellow, Gabriel García Márquez, and Norman Mailer, who accepted him as one of their peers. He took his literary skills into unexpected directions by writing screenplays for films, plays for the stage, and by collaborating on an opera based on *Roscoe*, his novel about Albany politics. Into each new arena where he carried his craft, he brought the relentless research and dogged reporting of his journalistic training fused with the countless revisions and painstaking polishing of a prose perfectionist. No matter what he is writing, he makes the words move on the page. "There are no dead sentences in his work," Bellow wrote of Kennedy. "He is just a pure writer."

This new volume of interviews, reviews, scholarly essays, previously unpublished speeches, a play, and a short story traces the long arc of Kennedy's extraordinary writing career and makes clear that he succeeded because he believed in his own literary talent and refused to let years of grinding poverty and dispiriting rejections by publishers destroy his ambition. "Rejection at the age of fifty and dragging his family down with him," recalled his longtime friend, the late Tom Smith, an English professor at the University at Albany. "In his mind he had become like one of his characters, a bum, a literary bum. In the middle of it all, he suffered horrendous financial difficulties. But through it all, he would climb up there and just plug away. And then the dam burst, somewhere toward 1981, and he knew that help was on its way."

What Kennedy discovered was a well of inspiration that had been there all along, the ability to animate his deep knowledge of Albany history, lived and learned, by reconstituting the past with his literary imagination. It took a hiatus of several years of living in Puerto Rico to gain a fresh perspective and appreciation for his hometown and to begin to understand the potent alchemy he performed by reimagining his city's rich past. Smith helped Kennedy establish the New York State Writers Institute at the University at Albany in 1983 with a portion of Kennedy's MacArthur grant. They brought the world's greatest writers to his hometown and built a renowned literary organization.

In the pages of *Bootlegger of the Soul,* a full-bodied portrait of Kennedy as a creative artist mastering not only the novel but a variety of genres, emerges through in-depth interviews, insightful reviews, and assessments by critics and fellow writers. "He consistently seeks the edge of his art," novelist Colum McCann writes in an introduction to a British edition of *Roscoe.* "He is one of the great verbal cinematographers of our times. He captures light, transforms it, guides it forward, shifts it around, and burns it down on to the page." The critic Thomas Flanagan writes: "Kennedy's art is an eccentric triumph, a quirky, risk-taking imagination at play upon the solid paving stones, the breweries, the politicos, and pool sharks of an all-too-actual city . . . Faulkner and Kennedy also share old-fashioned themes like honor, betrayal, the foreverness of the past."

"Drawn against a background of flophouses, bars and soup kitchens, Kennedy's winos are dirty, diseased, and depressed, searching for food, bath, beds, and warmth in their agonizing quest for survival; men in extremis—outsiders, outlaws—they struggle against a cold and rejecting world," critic Margaret Croyden writes of *Ironweed.*

The towering achievement of his Albany Cycle of novels has drawn frequent comparisons to the literary universe created in William Faulkner's

Yoknapatawpha County, James Joyce's Dublin, and Gabriel García Márquez's Macondo.

What this retrospective collection of Kennedy's work reminds readers of is that his long, hard climb to literary success traveled through an extended apprenticeship as a journalist, endured through early failures at novel writing, and persisted despite midcareer rejections. And then literary lightning struck at age fifty-five and Kennedy's place in American letters was assured.

"Recognition is everything you write for," he told Croyden for her 1984 *New York Times* article "The Sudden Fame of William Kennedy." "It's much more than the money. You want your books to be valued. It's a basic aspiration of the serious writer."

As Kennedy walked through the gritty urban landscape of North Albany on that January afternoon, with nothing left to prove, notebook in hand, the present merging with his memories of a distant past, the great verbal cinematographer captured an image and burned it down onto the page.

—Paul Grondahl

PART ONE

About Kennedy and His Work

Reviews, Profiles, and Interviews

Introduction to Part One

With a writing career as a journalist, nonfiction writer, fiction writer, screenwriter, and playwright that has spanned seven decades, William Kennedy and his work have been the topic of hundreds, if not thousands, of reviews, articles, profiles, interviews, graduate theses, and academic books. A Google search of "William Kennedy Albany author" identifies 384,000 results. The eleven essays and two interviews presented here were selected to offer an overview of Kennedy's literary career: early days as a journalist, foray into screenwriting, the novels that make up his Albany Cycle, as well as a profile of the man and his creative passions.

The opening piece is "The Sudden Fame of William Kennedy," by well-known critic, commentator, and journalist Margaret Croyden. It appeared in *The New York Times* in August 1984, shortly after Kennedy's meteoric rise over a two-year period in which he was awarded a MacArthur Fellowship; won the Pulitzer Prize and a National Book Critics Circle Award for his fourth novel, *Ironweed*; was hired to work with Francis Ford Coppola on the script for the film *The Cotton Club*; and, on the personal side, welcomed into the world his first grandchild. As Croyden remarks, it was a period that released Kennedy from "artistic anonymity and financial bondage," catapulting him into literary fame.

Kennedy's achievements were celebrated on the first weekend of September 1984, when the City of Albany hosted "William Kennedy's Albany Weekend." The event included panel discussions on Albany's neighborhoods and politicians, historical exhibits at the Albany Institute of History and Art and the New York State Museum, and guided walking and bus tours, all designed to reveal aspects of Kennedy's Albany, both real and imagined. The celebration culminated in a citywide festival in Albany's historic Washington Park. While plans for the celebration began well before the accolades came his way, the citywide festival was a fitting tribute to the author who put Albany on the literary map.

Doris Grumbach, novelist and literary critic, delivered the celebration's keynote address, "O Albany! O Kennedy!," at the Albany Institute of History and Art on September 6, 1984. It appears here as the second piece. She explores Kennedy's use of Albany as the "substance and subject matter" of his work and ponders the ways in which Albany captured Kennedy's imagination. She asks, "Why was Albany rich and fertile for Kennedy and not for me?"

Edward Schwarzschild, fiction writer and associate professor in the University at Albany's English Department, conducted an extensive interview with Kennedy in 2006 while he was in the beginning stages of writing his novel *Changó's Beads and Two-Tone Shoes*, untitled at the time. The interview covers Kennedy's early career as a journalist, friendships with Gabriel García Márquez and Hunter S. Thompson, his conversations with Fidel Castro, interest in bowling, Albany politics, and remaining productive through advancing years. Schwarzschild refers to Kennedy as not only "a world-class novelist, journalist, historian, and screenwriter" but also "an anthropologist of art and politics." The interview appeared in *The Believer*, a bimonthly magazine of literature, art, and culture.

Stefan Beck, critic and essayist, sets the stage for the remaining essays in this section by exploring *O Albany!*, Kennedy's nonfiction chronicle of his hometown and the city that became his muse. "Not one of [Kennedy's books] could have been written absent Kennedy's lifelong project of getting to know the city he once despised," posits Beck. Beck likens Kennedy to his character Francis Phelan in *Ironweed* as an illustration of "how a man becomes magnetized to home, despite compelling reasons to get lost." The essays in *O Albany!* provide a revealing frame of reference on Kennedy's novels as many of the historical references, people, and places appear in his fiction, altered but recognizable.

What follows Beck's essay are reviews of Kennedy's fiction in chronological order of the books' publication dates.

"Violent Places: On Ghosts, Bums, and Redemption in *Ironweed*," by Robert Towers, novelist and critic, focuses on *Ironweed*, with brief looks at *Legs* and *Billy Phelan's Greatest Game*, which were released as a trio in paperback in 1983 and marketed as Kennedy's Albany Cycle, a designation that stuck. Towers notes a "radical shift not only in its angle of vision but also in its style," between *Legs* and *Billy Phelan's Greatest Game*, and *Ironweed*, "from the breezy, quasi-journalistic narrative voice . . . to a more poetically charged, often surrealistic use of language."

In his book *First Paragraphs: Inspired Openings for Writers and Readers*, Donald Newlove examines the literary brilliance of the opening scene of *Ironweed*. Francis Phelan rides through Saint Agnes Cemetery in the back of a truck, first passing by the "fields of monuments and cenotaphs . . . all guarding the privileged dead," and then through the graves of the masses "under simple headstones and simpler crosses," averting his eyes as he passes by "the neighborhood of the Phelans." These descriptions, says Newlove, "disarm and move us. I, for one, enter the heaven of a writer absolutely on top of his material from the first sound of his voice."

Quinn's Book is reviewed from the opposite side of the Atlantic by Fintan O'Toole, an Irish columnist, literary editor, and drama critic. In his review, which appeared in the Dublin *Sunday Tribune*, O'Toole calls Kennedy "one of the few writers who is both a serious novelist and a skillful yarn-spinner." He describes *Quinn's Book*, the adventure-filled chronicle of Daniel Quinn's journey through the tumult of nineteenth-century America, as part penny dreadful, part Gothic novel, part romance fiction, and part ghost story, making Kennedy "one of the finest literary ventriloquists since Joyce."

Professor and critic Thomas R. Edwards reviewed Kennedy's fourth novel of the Albany Cycle, *Very Old Bones*, for *The New York Review of Books*. The story of five generations of the Phelan family is told through the eyes of Orson Purcell, the unacknowledged bastard son of Peter Phelan. Orson slowly unearths the tragedies, obsessions, and tightly held secrets of the family, much like "an archeological dig." Edwards says, "It may take an outsider to see such matters clearly" and to piece together the family history "from the fragments of life and feeling" that are available. Family relationships can be nurturing and supportive, or—in the case of the Phelan family—rigid, stifling, and even cruel. Edwards suggests that Kennedy's treatment of the complexity of family relationships "may be what measures the human worth of kinship, as this complex, eloquent, absorbing novel powerfully suggests."

Roscoe is explored in three separate essays. The first is the foreword of the British paperback edition of the novel, written by award-winning Irish fiction writer Colum McCann. McCann points to Kennedy's Albany Cycle of novels as "one of the most exuberant literary feats of the past half-century." Much like the character Roscoe Conway, McCann labels Kennedy as a "gambler, a crapshooter, a card shark. He likes the risk. He does nothing to avoid it. . . . There is the daring of the high-wire artist about him."

The second essay on *Roscoe* is an in-depth review by Thomas Flanagan, professor and novelist, which appeared in *The New York Review of Books*. Flanagan's review, the last essay he wrote before his death in May 2002, also includes commentary on Kennedy's entire Albany Cycle of novels. While Kennedy's fictional Albany has often been compared to James Joyce's Dublin, Flanagan suggests, "It is quite possible that [Kennedy's] knowledge of Albany's geography, its nooks and crannies and their histories, is wider than Joyce's knowledge of Dublin."

The third essay on *Roscoe* is not specifically about the novel, but a review by Anthony P. Radford on the world premiere of the opera *Roscoe*, based on Kennedy's 2002 novel. The opera, with music by Evan Mack and libretto by Joshua McGuire, had a four-performance run August 3–6, 2016, at the Seagle Music Colony, the oldest summer vocal training program in the United States, located in Schroon Lake, New York. Radford, a professor of voice and opera, wrote that *Roscoe* "should be considered the model of what a good American opera is in the twenty-first century." He also commented on the adaptability of Kennedy's storyline in opera: "Good opera should have a good story and here Roscoe delivers." The adaptation of *Roscoe* the novel into *Roscoe* the opera is a prime example of how artists working in different art forms can be inspired by each other's work.

In his review for *The New York Times Book Review*, John Sayles calls Kennedy's most recent novel, *Changó's Beads and Two-Tone Shoes* "his most musical work of fiction . . . a jazz piece unafraid to luxuriate in its roots as blues or popular ballad or to spin out into less melodic territory." He describes the "familiar music that runs through the story" and compares it to Kennedy's writing style. "It goes on," says Sayles, "as the best live music always does, never losing us but keeping us guessing about just how we're going to get there." Published in 2011 when Kennedy was eighty-three years old, "[t]his is not a book a young man could or would write. There is the sense here of somebody who has seen and considered much, without letting his inner fire cool," Sayles notes.

The final piece in this section is an extended interview with Kennedy, conducted by Albany-area writer and creative writing teacher William Patrick, which focuses on Kennedy's experiences as a screenwriter. It includes details on Kennedy's collaboration with Francis Ford Coppola on *The Cotton Club* (1984) and writing the screenplay for the film version of *Ironweed* (1987). In the interview Kennedy describes his early fascination with the movies, the fickle nature of the film industry, what he learned from Coppola about writing film scripts, the difference between writing for the screen and writing novels for the page, and the limitations of mid-1980s technology that he and director Héctor Babenco faced during the production of *Ironweed.*

This opening section provides revealing appraisals of his work by the author himself, as well as a wide-angle view of Kennedy's multifaceted career as a writer in multiple genres across seven decades. The broad range of perspectives from reviewers underscores Kennedy's relentless drive to remain a fresh and original voice in each successive book, while repeatedly reconstituting the city of his birth in the Albany Cycle of novels.

—Suzanne Lance

The Sudden Fame of William Kennedy

Margaret Croyden

> Kennedy's novels are inexorably linked to his native city. . . . This sense of place, one of the most important factors in his books, gives Kennedy's work a rich texture, a deep sense of authenticity.
>
> —Margaret Croyden
>
> When fiction closes in on a subject, you know more about what it means to be alive than you can in any other way.
>
> —William Kennedy

As he sits in his study in the countryside near Albany, New York, William Kennedy is surrounded by photographs: William Faulkner, Samuel Beckett, Robert Penn Warren, and Saul Bellow on one hand, and Louis Armstrong, Frank Sinatra, and Mae West on the other. This eclectic array of heroes is indicative of Kennedy's personality: the serious novelist who reveres literature, and the ebullient Irishman who enjoys pop music, movies, and American mythic figures such as Sinatra, whose recording of "New York, New York" filters in from another room. That Kennedy—winner this year of a Pulitzer Prize and the National Book Critics Circle Award for his novel *Ironweed*, which evokes the psychic life of an alcoholic bum—is fascinated by, and apparently lives in, many contradictory worlds may be a source of his imaginative powers.

At home with drinkers and losers as well as with writers and professors, Kennedy is a mixture of earthy manliness and boyish naïveté. Drink in hand, he rocks back and forth in an old office chair, smiling, his eyes mischievous but intense, looking younger than his fifty-six years despite a slight balding of the brown hair. The chin is strong, the face full of vitality and vigor.

Surrounded by stacks of newspaper files and clippings and large framed photographs of the covers of his now-celebrated Albany Cycle—*Legs, Billy*

Phelan's Greatest Game, and *Ironweed*—Kennedy sends out a clear triumphant message: He is free, free at last from the artistic anonymity and financial bondage that had plagued his life as a writer.

"Well, how does it feel to be rich and famous?" I ask. He leans back and smiles again, this time with a tinge of sardonicism.

"I like it. I like it a lot," he replies. "Being poor and unknown is difficult. But this—this is easy. Why wouldn't a writer like it? Recognition is everything you write for; it's much more than the money. You want your books to be valued. It's a basic aspiration of the serious writer."

Kennedy is recognized, all right. Major critics have lauded him for the power and beauty of his writing. Christopher Lehmann-Haupt, in *The New York Times*, said of *Ironweed* that "it is almost Joycean in the variety of rhetoric it uses to evoke the texture and sociology of Albany in the 1930s." Robert Towers in *The New York Review of Books* called it "original . . . full of energy and color."*

Honors and offers poured in. The MacArthur Foundation announced it was giving Kennedy a $264,000 tax-free grant. Movie producer Gene Kirkwood bought the film rights to two of Kennedy's novels and hired him to write the scripts. Francis Ford Coppola signed him to work on a movie script about Harlem's famous Cotton Club. *O Albany!*—a collection of Kennedy's essays about his native town—was published. *Ironweed*, published by Viking Press in 1983, has sold more than 100,000 copies in the United States and is to be published in at least seven other countries. Kennedy's first novel, *The Ink Truck*, will be reissued in both hardcover and paperback. A new novel, *Quinn's Book*, another Albany story, was bought on the basis of just two chapters. In addition, Kennedy received New York State's Governor's Arts Award, and the State University of New York at Albany, where he had been an overlooked part-time instructor for eight years, granted him tenure as a full professor.

Kennedy has decided to make use of an additional contribution—$15,000 annually for five years—available under the MacArthur grant. With the initial sum, he created The Writers Institute at Albany, where aspiring authors can attend lectures and workshops given by well-known writers. Saul Bellow has already appeared, and John Updike and Toni Morrison are scheduled to follow. This month Governor Mario Cuomo signed into law a bill that made the institute a state-supported establishment [New York State Writers Institute] with a $100,000-a-year grant. Kennedy has been asked to serve as the director.

So impressed are the citizens of Albany with the newfound Kennedy fame and the attention it has brought to their city that they have banded with the University at Albany to host a "William Kennedy's Albany" celebration from September 6 through 9. The combined sponsorship of the event includes local

* Editors' Note: See the complete Towers review in this volume, 53–57.

newspapers, businesses and cultural organizations, and the New York Council for the Humanities. There will be a walking tour of Kennedy's Albany, a photographic exhibit of the neighborhoods and individuals that figure in his work, a talk by Kennedy on the city's influence on his writing, and to cap it all off, an old-fashioned "Sunday in the Park" party. Such a testimonial to a living novelist by his hometown is all but unprecedented, even more remarkable when the town happens to be a quiet, sleepy place rarely celebrated for its culture or intellectuality.

Although he is enjoying all the attention, Kennedy has not forgotten the oversights of the past. He says he is neither angry nor resentful about *Ironweed* having been rejected thirteen times, but he remembers that period well.

"Just before *Ironweed*, I hit rock bottom," he says. "I felt the world had been taken away from me. When I made a speech at Russell Sage College, I spoke about 'the stolen world'—the world of writing I knew when I was aspiring to be a writer. Publishing fiction was very tough then; there were the magazines, but, little by little, they began to vanish, too. Because *Billy Phelan*, my third book, didn't sell well, I found it difficult to get a book published again. I had to convince the world that they were wrong.

"I love writing. I couldn't see any other life for me. I love words. The act of writing, in itself, is a pleasure. Of course, there were money problems. But you remember the fun we had at the lake house and how much it meant to me. I wrote *Legs* there in the afternoons when the house was empty. I remember the feeling of ecstasy I had when I finished a real page of writing."

I did indeed remember the house on Crooked Lake, outside Albany, where I first met Kennedy. He was a young writer then, published but unrecognized, and it seemed that the lean years would never end. It was a magical place, the lake house, with its long lawn leading down to the sparkling water and tiny boats bobbing on the horizon, an exceptional haven for weary writers and poets from Albany and New York who gathered there on weekends in an atmosphere of uncommon warmth and high spirits. The house belonged to Ruth Tarson, a New York writer and the best friend of Kennedy's wife, Dana. Kennedy was free to use the house as a writing studio. It was there that he wrote *Legs*, a fictional account of a gangster-bootlegger; *Billy Phelan*; and an exquisite short story, "The Secrets of Creative Love," which used aspects of the lake house as background (complete story appears in this volume on pages 215–225).

The lake house brought out the best in all of us: a rare sense of communion, an unspoken commitment to friendship, an intense excitement for life. There we could forget entirely notions of status, success, and fame, and be wholly ourselves. There we would dance till all hours, skinny-dip on hot nights, gorge ourselves on bushels of corn and tomatoes, drink pints of booze, and recite from poets and writers of the 1920s and 1930s.

Kennedy, with his lively sense of play and his generosity of spirit, was the magnetic force. One moment he would be plucking out "Happy Days and Lonely Nights" on his ukulele, the next playing a tape of Frankie's "One for My Baby" or old Satchmo recordings; the next, he would be eulogizing Faulkner and Kafka, or quoting Joyce and James, or arguing the merits of Nathanael West and F. Scott Fitzgerald. With his inexhaustible energy, Kennedy could electrify the group and keep the party going all night. Whether he was discussing high or low art, or dancing his crazy Charleston routines with Ruthie, or singing nostalgic "golden oldies," Kennedy, reluctant to give up the night, was a life-bringer—a supreme original.

But the Kennedy of those sweet summer nights had another life that I barely perceived. He was never too undisciplined not to put in regular hours in his workroom. On the sunniest of days, he would disappear indoors to write his stories about the bums, winos, gamblers, and gangsters he encountered during the course of his journalistic career, "the archetypes lurking in Ruth Tarson's lake house," as he noted in his dedication to *Legs*. Obsessed with writing, he kept the world of his imagination intact, and few people ever intruded. Writing was for Kennedy a mystique, a calling. But he never spoke of himself in those terms, only of other writers and their gifts. Did he know in those days that he, too, had the gift? Looking back, I can see that he did, but this knowledge of himself was like a secret treasure, not easily revealed.

Now, many years later, we sit in his Averill Park family home, talking about the remarkable changes in his life. His household seems almost the same, but not quite. Prosperity has brought a microwave oven to the kitchen, a giant television screen to the living room and—as soon as the workmen banging away outside finish—a swimming pool to the grounds. Kennedy is not very impressed by these new acquisitions. His constants are Dana, his wife of twenty-seven years, and his children. Living nearby is Dana, twenty-six, who gave birth to a son the night Kennedy received his Pulitzer. Kathy, twenty-five, who acts as her father's secretary and cares for his new word processor, lives at home, as does fourteen-year-old Brendan, who between doing yard chores makes videotapes of the family with a recently acquired camera.

When we settle down around the luncheon table, Dana Kennedy tells me about her more than one hundred cousins in Puerto Rico, where she grew up and where she met Kennedy, who was working there as a journalist. She talks about their wedding within a month after they met and about the financial support they received from her big clan and from friends during their "awful" years.

"I knew that Bill had to keep on writing," she says, "no matter what. I understood his artistic drives because I remembered my own when I was a young dancer. I knew he had to live with his passion to write, and I had to live with it, too, or I wouldn't have a marriage."

After lunch, Kennedy and I drive around Albany, a place he had rejected as a young man with ambitions beyond the confines of his hometown but that he has come to see as "various as the American psyche itself, of which it was truly a crucible." In *O Albany!* he says that though he is a booster of his birthplace, he wrote the book "as a person whose imagination has become fused with a single place, and in that place finds all the elements that a man ever needs for the life of the soul" (3). As a result of the books he has written about it, Albany—a symbol to New Yorkers of provincialism and arcane politics—has suddenly become an integral part of the literary world.

Kennedy's novels are inexorably linked to his native city, particularly during the Depression years, when Albany was a wide-open city, run by Irish bosses and their corrupt political machine. This sense of place, one of the most important factors in his books, gives Kennedy's work a rich texture, a deep sense of authenticity.

Kennedy shows me the old neighborhood in North Albany where he was born and bred, the only child of Irish working-class parents whose ancestors settled in the city more than five generations ago. Is he nostalgic for that vanished world? I ask. "Up to a point," he replies, "but I'm aware of all the negative elements, the power that some had to destroy lives, the vote-buying and the election-stealing."

We pass the old, now-deserted Albany *Times Union* building where Kennedy was a reporter in the 1960s and got to know the people of the city from the inside—the politicos, the ethnics, the working people, the saloonkeepers, the bookies, and the bums. In 1965, he was nominated for a Pulitzer Prize for a series he did on city slums.

His father, William Sr., was a deputy sheriff who often took his son with him to political clubs and gambling joints where young Bill Kennedy, with his eye and ear for detail and for the tone and temper of Irish Americans, listened and watched and remembered.

Albany became Kennedy's Dublin, his Yoknapatawpha, the one "element without which my inspiration cannot do," he says. "All the stories I imagine flow from an environment—this environment," he says, pointing to the old houses that line a quiet residential street, "not a nebulous private domain. Albany provides the verifying elements for me, a verification that life was lived in a specific way. And once you have that you have everything.

"Writers I have valued," Kennedy continues, "always drew upon the specifics of their experience, not free-floating value judgments but the specific of Algeria in Camus, for instance, or the war in Hemingway, or Babylon in Fitzgerald, or the Southern aristocracy in Faulkner.

"The specifics in *Ironweed*—the traction strike, professional baseball, Irish immigrant experiences, a vast Irish cemetery, an Irish neighborhood, the Erie

Canal, and so forth—are elements of life in Albany. Some people say that *Ironweed* might have had any setting, and perhaps this is true. But the values that emerged are peculiar to my own town and to my own time and would not be the same in a smaller city, or a metropolis, or a city that was not Irish, or wasn't large enough to support a skid row. Actually, whether *Ironweed* could come out of another city is irrelevant. The point is that it did not."

Although *Ironweed* takes place in Albany, and that city forms the substructure of the novel, the book is more a depiction of someone trying to make peace with his soul. The hero, Francis Phelan (Billy's father), an ex-ballplayer, after a series of tragedies, including his killing of a scab during a trolley workers' strike, deserts his family for the life of a bum. He wanders through the wasteland streets of Depression-era Albany, talking to the dead, remembering and forgetting the past, wondering why some win and others lose, futilely searching for explanations for inexplicable events. Kennedy's derelicts, like the Beckett bums who are waiting for Godot, are stripped of artifice and social veneer to become ruined pieces of nature, unaccommodated men, ragged heroes, reliving their failures, hoping to make sense of their lives in a nightmare world of outcasts. Drawn against a background of flophouses, bars, and soup kitchens, Kennedy's winos are dirty, diseased, and depressed, searching for food, baths, beds, and warmth in their agonizing quest for survival; men in extremis—outsiders, outlaws—they struggle against a cold and rejecting world. Their hands bitten by dogs, their shoes gone, their feet swollen, their underwear in shreds, yet they fight on until, exhausted, they succumb. But not Francis Phelan.

"The trick was to live, to beat the bastards, survive the mob . . . and show them all what a man can do to set things right, once he sets his mind to it," says Francis. He was a warrior, "[a]nd a warrior, he was certain, was not a victim. Never a victim" (207, 216).

As we drive down Broadway, I remember *Billy Phelan's Greatest Game*, in which a rejected and isolated Billy walked alone down this old main street thinking about his predicament. That book, based on the kidnapping of the nephew of Dan O'Connell, then Albany's most powerful political figure, is about the world of crooks, con men, gamblers, and gangsters during Albany's Depression years. Billy, a small-time gambler caught up in corrupt politics, refuses to play the political game according to the machine's rules. So he pays the price: rejection, isolation, and ostracism. But Billy, like his father, Francis, is stubborn. As he wanders through nighttime Albany, though treated like a pariah, he finds his own kind of integrity and strength.

As we stop for a beer at Kennedy's favorite place, Cafe Capriccio on Grand Street, he says: "Albany in Billy Phelan's time was a city politically dominated and politically controlled. It was also Irish-controlled, and Irish attitudes as they prevailed in that era stirred my imagination. Like Billy, everyone played the numbers, everyone was involved in some kind of gambling, including me when I was a kid. As soon as you were old enough to go to a candy store by yourself, you could play the punchboard. If you had an extra penny, you took a chance and you won something—a nickel, a dime, a quarter. Baseball pools were one of the biggest enterprises; I ran a football pool when I was in college. It was an accepted part of life. It was normal."

It was also "normal" for Albany, and the country, to accept the romantic image of the notorious gangster-celebrity Jack "Legs" Diamond, who drifted in and out of the Albany area and was murdered in a Dove Street rooming house. Now a landmark, it has recently been purchased by the Kennedys and film producer Gene Kirkwood. Kennedy was fascinated with Legs, not only because he was an American mythic figure but because, as Kennedy noted, he "became an impious presence in the city" (*O Albany!* 201). His days and nights were filled with uncommon sensuality and intense drama. In *Legs*, his loyal, cultivated lawyer called Diamond the "underside of everybody's life" (290)—the quintessential American gangster-hero.

Diamond's legal maneuverings and social doings were in the Albany papers every day, Kennedy says, "and we were also frequently aswarm with out-of-town newsmen, particularly the New York tabloid crowd, which claimed Jack as its own and regularly gave him pages of space in order to deplore his depredations. A serious effort at deploring Jack was as good for circulation as a kinky Hollywood sex murder" (*O Albany!* 201).

"When you were researching Legs, weren't you revolted by his life?" I ask as we stand looking at the boarded-up old Kenmore Hotel on North Pearl Street, where Legs threw some grand parties.

"Yes, I was. But I do think that any human being is worthy of the poetry that one can achieve. I don't think of gangsters as animals, beyond redemption, or inarticulate, or that they have no soul. I chose Legs because he was a character who had galvanized the imagination of America. Legs is another version of the American dream—that you can grow up and shoot your way to fame and fortune. On the other hand, the people that live this kind of life are human beings like you or me. People did love Legs Diamond."

"Why did you endow Legs's love life with so much romance?"

"You don't think Legs Diamond was romantic?"

We drove to the old lake house to see Tom Smith, one of the "four good men" to whom *Ironweed* is dedicated, and who now rents the house. A professor of literature at the University at Albany, Smith recalls Kennedy's struggle and his determination to write.

"This was a man who felt deeply rejected," Smith says, "but he had an energetic stubbornness, which is at the bottom of all his characters. Some other guy would just give it all up. But he continued to write.

"When I think of it objectively, I'm awed by it. Rejection at the age of fifty and dragging his family down with him. In his mind he had become like one of his characters, a bum, a literary bum. In the middle of it all, he suffered horrendous financial difficulties. But through it all, he would climb up there and just plug away. And then the dam burst, sometime toward 1981, and he knew that help was on the way."

Help came in the form of Saul Bellow. Viking had published *Billy Phelan's Greatest Game* in 1978—"admittedly it was published badly," says Corlies (Cork) Smith, Kennedy's editor at the time—and it sold very few copies. Nevertheless, Viking initially accepted the first one hundred pages of *Ironweed*. But Smith knew that Kennedy had no real marketing backing at the house and that *Ironweed* could very well suffer a fate similar to that of *Billy*.

"Considering all this," Cork Smith says, "I thought he would be better off making a fresh start with a new house, and so I advised Viking against publishing the book." It was submitted elsewhere and was repeatedly turned down. "A book about bums," Smith says, "was not easy to sell." It looked as if it would never be published. Then Saul Bellow, who had been familiar with Kennedy's work, entered the picture. He wrote to Smith admonishing Viking for not sticking with Kennedy. "These Albany novels will be memorable, a distinguished group of books," Bellow said. "That the author of *Billy Phelan* should have a manuscript kicking around looking for a publisher is disgraceful." Bellow offered to help.

"Now there was a big difference," Cork Smith says. "Of course it was the same book; Kennedy didn't change anything. But now it had been kissed by a Nobel Prize winner. I also knew that Saul did not do this casually: he doesn't puff things. Nobody takes a Bellow quote casually. So with a Nobel Prize winner in my pocket, and with Bellow's offer to help, I thought, 'Let's take a chance.'"

Smith was still not convinced that he could sell *Ironweed* successfully by itself, but Bellow had spoken about "these Albany novels," so Smith got the idea to reissue Kennedy's earlier books, *Billy* and *Legs*, for simultaneous publication with *Ironweed* as "The Albany Cycle" and make of it a publishing event.

"In other words, you would not have published the book if Saul Bellow hadn't written that letter?" I asked.

"You might say so," Smith replied.

Saul Bellow is modest about his role. "Oh, I don't know, someone would have recognized Kennedy—someday. It didn't take long for an old dog like me to know Kennedy was the real thing, even in 1960, when he was a student of mine in Puerto Rico. He could take material from skid row and write about these people as fully human as anyone else. The people he wrote about didn't know they had become pariahs. He wrote about them from the inside. And it was very touching. I was moved by the characters, by their naive but human frailties.

"Kennedy's books show some very original insights," Bellow continues. "His treatment of the characters is very far from the usual hackneyed treatment. There are no dead sentences in his work. His language is vigorous, full of energy. He's just very gifted. At a time when so much cold porridge is served up in the literary world as hot stuff, here is the real hot stuff. In his books, nothing is being put over on the public. He doesn't latch on to subjects so that the book can be sold. He's just a pure writer. What happened to him is going to fill a lot of writers with hope and enthusiasm."

Does this incident raise some fundamental issues about the publishing world? "At fault," Bellow says, "are the slack publishing houses who don't have skilled readers; they give some of their books to receptionists to read. The publishing world counts on an old image of themselves, when they saw themselves as part of the intellectual literati. They were never like that, and are even less now. They're just a bunch of hustlers; they have to submit balance sheets, you know."

Kennedy's reaction to the publishing world was to quote Francis Phelan: " 'I don't hold no grudges more'n five years.' I was never much impressed by the powers who some thought were the arbiters of artistic work," Kennedy says. "Some were saying the book had too many bums. But then I thought, 'Why are they in power, why do they know so much about literature and I don't?' Some said, 'The book is unpublishable; plus, it can't possibly make any money.' And that was the prevailing attitude. From all the best people. There's a grand measure of hypocrisy that goes on in the publishing world."

Despite a tradition in American literature of outcasts and vagabonds, a great deal has been made of Kennedy's focus on bums and the underworld. The use of the life of derelicts and gangsters as a literary vehicle to express the author's perceptions is clear enough to the discerning reader, but the question keeps coming up: Why does Kennedy choose such heroes?

"I'm interested in the human being concealed within a bum's or a gangster's life. When you take a character into his most extreme condition, you get extreme explanations, and you begin to discover what lurks in the far corners of the soul. I really do believe that that's the way a writer finds things out. I love the surrealistic, the mystical elements of life. There is so much mysteriousness going on in everybody's life." *The Ink Truck* is a good depiction of the mystery of human behavior. The book is about an eccentric newspaper reporter, Bailey, one of the last holdouts in a long and bitter newspaper strike. As in all Kennedy's works, the plot is secondary to questions of life and death and the actions of people under duress. A character of extreme individuality and integrity, Bailey, like Kennedy's other crazy, hopeful Irishmen, is a fighter who responds to the world with unusual force.

As for *Quinn's Book*, on which Kennedy has been working all summer, "[i]t is the story of two adolescents who shared a common experience of Albany and of America in that age," Kennedy says, "and the effects of the Irish famine, the cholera, life on the Erie Canal, on the Hudson River, the rabid partisanship of the nineteenth-century press, the theater of that age, the Civil War, and so forth." But these are no more the main subjects of the new book than baseball and flophouses are the subjects of *Ironweed*.

"One doesn't get a sense of deep suffering from Kennedy's personal life, and yet all his books are about suffering and pain," says his current book editor, Gerald Howard. "If you grow up Irish, the sense of sin, death, and suffering is in your bones," says Howard, himself an Irish Catholic. "If you grow up Irish, you have a gloomy view of the possibilities of people. His Irishness is a real key to who he is and what he is thinking. I recognized the Irish link immediately. I'm certain he was an altar boy." (In fact, he was.)

Kennedy's vagabonds have a kind of innocence, blended with a harsh, penetrating sense of reality. As characters from the demimonde, they are elevated to art by Kennedy's sense of poetry and imagistic language.

From *Ironweed*:

> The new and frigid air of November lay on Francis like a blanket of glass. Its weight rendered him motionless and brought peace to his body, and the stillness brought a cessation of anguish to his brain. In a dream he was only just beginning to enter, horns and mountains rose up out of the earth, the horns—ethereal, trumpets—sounding with a virtuosity equal to the perilousness of the crags and cornices of the mountainous pathways. Francis recognized the song the trumpets played and he floated with its melody. Then, yielding not without trepidation to its coded urgency, he ascended bodily into the exalted reaches of the world where the song had been composed so long ago. And he slept. (90)

From his forthcoming novel, *Quinn's Book*:

> The wall of ice grew from a relatively small, fencelike structure, say five feet high, across the thawed center of the river, continued building upon that fence a pyramid, a mountain, an instant Albany iceberg that never was before and probably never will be again. It rose to what some calculated as the height of ten men. Others said twenty. It grew swiftly upward

> with boundless force, brilliant chaos, and just as we thought it would never cease to grow, it was struck from within and below by some central power we could neither see nor understand, even now, but which exploded that mountain into a Vesuvius of crystal, showering the shores of both Albany and Greenbush with fragments, wounding an unsuspecting half-dozen people, killing two horses and a pregnant cat on the quay, and loosing a tidal wave that swept every object storehoused on the Great Pier, including barrels of coffee, piles of lumber and staves, and another dozen men, tumbling them into the torrent as if they were the river's own algae, which they would very soon become. (10–11)

With his ability to write such prose, some people wonder why Kennedy is now writing for the movies.

"Movies are something I wanted to do since childhood," Kennedy says. "When I was broke, I tried desperately to sell a screenplay as a means of paying the mortgage and keeping my car on the road. This time around, I didn't need the money. It's a world that gives me pleasure."

What did he find attractive about working on *The Cotton Club* with Coppola?

"I liked Coppola's work. I liked him as a person as well," Kennedy says. "Our tastes and attitudes toward the subject matter of *Cotton Club* and our exchange was more than just a couple of people working together on a project; it became a friendship. I know he has a reputation for being mad. If he's mad, okay, I can adjust to that. His kind of madness is not really a negative quality. It's very often a sign of vitality and refusal to accept the norm."

Besides, the milieu of *The Cotton Club*—the 1920s gangland, the life of black people, black entertainment, Irish gangsters in the Jazz Age—is all very familiar to Kennedy.

But probably the most important reason for getting involved with the movies, Kennedy says, is "my reluctance to turn my back to new experience."

Kennedy's work on the lively film contrasts sharply with the dark, brooding style of his novels. Although people perceive him as an easygoing, jovial Irishman, full of life, a good party-giver and a good partygoer, friends know there is another side to Kennedy that comes out only in his writing.

"It is a dark, morbid side," says his friend Tom Smith, "haunted by annihilation, by life making you inconsequential, by the tremendous desire to have all of life and not being able to. He seems to be haunted by the fragility of life, how to get through the next twenty minutes, how to redefine life when you're on the skids, when you're dying, when you have terminal cancer. All his characters are one eyelash away from oblivion, in one way or another. But they have all got an overpowering wish to live."

And so has Kennedy. But he believes that everyone exists in two worlds. "Everyone who explores human behavior explores his own, obviously," he says. "And you find that you have very strange and dark elements in your life. The idea of conviviality with other people doesn't preclude the possibility of other things. I'm very much a person who perceives the possibility of tragedy, despair, and darkness around the corner. Yes, my work is about some dark characters, but not all. Not Billy Phelan. It's about a man who has a problem and encounters death and isolation. But he's resilient. His way of life is such that however down one gets, he's able to come up again. It's been my own pattern in life. I can't represent life as some kind of glorious event that's full of parties and drinking and fun, because that's not the case. Socially, I have appeared to live like that for a long time, but I have not been like that privately."

First and foremost, Kennedy believes in the power of fiction. He continues to see writers, and perhaps himself, as different from others because they can divulge the secrets of "the human heart in conflict with itself," to quote Faulkner, and he continues to see writing, and his love of it, as the unshakable anchor in his life. Those who have known him through the years and watched his struggle believe that regardless of success, money, or celebrity, Kennedy's writing impulse will not diminish. Nor will his drive to experience all worlds. He will probably continue to produce finely wrought stories of passion and sensibility, for fiction remains his first love.

"When fiction closes in on a subject, you know more about what it means to be alive than you can in any other way," Kennedy says. "I think fiction has the concreteness of expression that other art forms do not have. It identifies life, it singularizes life. When you think of *The Sound and the Fury* or *Ulysses* or *Billy Budd*, you have the feeling of the complexity of being alive, of being singular. That's what all the great writers have given to me. And that's certainly what I would love to give to someone else."

REFERENCES

Kennedy, William. *O Albany! Improbable City of Political Wizards, Fearless Ethnics, Spectacular Aristocrats, Splendid Nobodies, and Underrated Scoundrels*. New York: Viking, 1983.

———. *Ironweed*, paperback ed. New York: Penguin, 1984.

———. *Legs*, paperback ed. New York: Penguin, 1983.

———. *Quinn's Book*, paperback ed. New York: Penguin, 1989.

This essay was originally published in *The New York Times* on August 26, 1984. Reprinted with the permission of the author's estate.

O Albany! O Kennedy!

Doris Grumbach

> This is the business of the writer of talent: to send the surveyor of his imagination to stake out a parish for his fiction, to populate the fields and valleys and tenements and vacant lots with the pioneers and homesteaders of invention and history.
>
> —Doris Grumbach

I began to compose this ode, with two intentions: to understand why I have always found William Kennedy such an eminently readable and attention-holding writer, and second, to understand why it was possible for him to find in this city more than enough substance and subject matter to fill a continuing series of novels, while I, with the usual equipment a novelist brings to the acquisition and use of material, found nothing. Why was Albany rich and fertile for Kennedy, and not for me? How did the Phelans and the Quinns, the Daughertys, Diamonds, and Gormans rise, full-blooded and glowing with recognizable life, out of what, to my vision, had always seemed a sterile and pallid landscape? How did parochial history become, under Kennedy's pen, invention? And invention: how did he convert it to myth?

I want to answer the easier question first, for it seems obvious that, to the first-rate literary imagination, everything and everywhere are material. Henry James urged the young novelist to try to be someone upon whom nothing is lost. Nothing about this "improbable city of political wizards, fearless ethnics, spectacular aristocrats, splendid nobodies, and underrated scoundrels" (as Kennedy subtitled his recent book [*O Albany!*]) has been lost on Kennedy, neither the dank atmosphere of Saint Agnes Cemetery in Menands where the dead, in Kennedy's invention, talk about the living, nor Keeler's, nor the Kenmore Hotel, nor the sights and smells of the South End and the Salvation Army soup kitchen, nor the old rented houses on Herkimer and Orange

Streets, nor the streetwise ways and talk of the citizens of North Albany. I have walked these same streets, worked for a while along Herkimer and South Pearl and sat in the Pilgrim Baptist Church with the old Better Homes group but, given the same streets and bars and houses and stores and weeds, I did not conjure up Francis and Billy Phelan, or Martin and Mary Daugherty, or Bailey and Grace Bailey. I saw the degrading poverty and noisome halls and porches and steps of South End houses, but to me they spelled little but what they were. And what they were was not enough to make fiction out of, I thought. One must, like Kennedy, be able to raise the dust, the dry clay, and the ironweed to vital, even visionary heights. One must invigorate the lost and desperate souls of the South End with the light and fire and passion of a new reality, stirred into fictional life by a writer's love. Kennedy's wild Irish humor gave the Phelans and the Daughertys heightened existence. His wry compassion converted that existence to the perpetuity of paint. He raised the dust, as I said, and resurrected the dead persons and places in a city's history into fleshed-out, warm-hearted characters, laced with liquorish, guilt-ridden, suffering blood of lives lived in the shadows of Old Albany.

This is the business of the writer of talent: to send the surveyor of his imagination to stake out a parish for his fiction, to populate the fields and valleys and tenements and vacant lots with the pioneers and homesteaders of invention and history. The stiles and fences and walls set in place, the lordly creator then places, within or outside them, by a process of budding from the real into the imagined, his protagonists, made from the real and metamorphosed in fiction to the more real, a synecdoche of magical proportions. Given an arm, he makes a body. Given the grim and sordid, he endows it with dignity, worth, and even glory. Given a body he produces a community. Provided with the local community, he constructs a universe, an extra-territorial fiction, embroidered with the eternal truths of human character and the human condition. And he titles these creations with earthy, noncosmic names like *Legs, Billy Phelan's Greatest Game* and, most mundane and most celebrated of all, the name of a wildflower with a tough stem called *Ironweed*.

The best writers of fiction have been parochial. We know Dublin, not because we have read Michelin or Baedeker, but because James Joyce sent Stephen Daedalus and Leopold Bloom out into the gray stone streets of that Gaelic city on one historic day and night. Ever since, we see that city as reconstructed out of the pages of *Ulysses* and written in the miraculous and playful prose of a fictional magician. We know Oxford, Mississippi, because a conjurer named William Faulkner, a Houdini at liberating fact into fantasy, made Yoknapatawpha County from courthouse records and the artifacts of an age and a region gone to ground and seed. We know the Lublin ghetto because

Isaac Bashevis Singer saved it from historic destruction and raised it to a place where nothing short of total global nuclear annihilation can ever affect it again. We know the inner geography and the mythic history of Prague from Franz Kafka's fevered psychic architecture, which erected a fictional superstructure over the dark streets and empty avenues of the real city. Saul Bellow has created Chicago for the reader of his fiction.

And what of Albany? Is the city of Albany, the one described in *O Albany!* in sometimes moderate and sometimes fanciful and fevered prose, the city to be found in Kennedy's Albany Cycle of novels? Not at all. Albany in the novels is a city of air and mist, floating over and parallel to the real place, both better and worse, bloodier and more pallid, duller and more picturesque, cleaner and more polluted politically, a city of words, not steel and brick and rock and cement and wood. It perches high above an enchanted river, seeing its contradictions in its dark waters. It sits on a towering hill of imagination, both real and unreal, bigger and more unchanging than the place called Albany. Kennedy's Albany turns bricks and cement into unsubstantial streets of the imagination, substitutes all the embroidery of the creative spirit, the crewel work of invention, the tapestry of inspiration for the flat-planing and leveling of statistics, road maps, newspaper accounts, and chronicles in the New York State Library. Albany, Kennedy's Albany, is a state of mind in the conditional tense and, as he wrote, it is "centered squarely in the American and the human continuum, a magical place where the past becomes visible if one is willing to track the multiple incarnations of the city's soul" (7).

So it is that the novelist's Albany, like all cities, regions, nations, and continents filtered through the metamorphosing air of the imagination, exists only on the page and then, by magic, in the mind of the reader. Ultimately it will appear in the literary imagination of a generation, a thing of beauty and elegance, of fancy and transcendence, but hardly, thank God, the real thing. Kennedy's parish of Albany is enchanted and charmed, the way Louie's pool parlor is said to possess "dismally magical dust." The political and social history of this enchanted city is henceforth to be known to us through Kennedy's account of the life and bloody death of Jack Diamond, the athletic triumphs and defeats (by chance) of Francis Phelan, the long journey through the nighttime city, down through North Albany and Broadway, of Billy Phelan, and the sexually pulsating lives of Kennedy's legendary women: Alice, Kiki, Katrina, Flossie, Mary Daugherty.

The names of these women bring me to the second question I asked myself at the start: What precisely is Kennedy's unique quality that provides every reader with a visa into his magical city and keeps us captive there until we have satisfied our appetite for and our curiosity about his place and his people?

Not every pleased reader—and there must by now be many thousands in this country—cares a damn about the answer to this question. The experience is enough. Pinning the quality of fiction to the page is the presumption and the business of the dissecting critic. Something in me, some inquisitive demand to see how it is done, how the magician brings off his trick, requires that I try to run this sorcery down.

First of all, there is Kennedy's clear, unsullied romanticism, a literary coloration that sees the lives of bums and drunks, gamblers and gangsters, knights of the road and ladies of the night as, somehow, purer, more original, and more honest than the lives of privileged and respectable folk. Bonded to his rosy view of them is his compassion for their plight. It could be said, of course, that all pity for man's plight is romantic, that the only confirmed modern attitude is irony, or scorn, or pitiless sarcasm, or removed dispassion. Whatever is the customary stance toward the human wrecks of society, Kennedy has not taken to it. He regards his people as simple, plain, self-deprecating, and, in most ways, virtuous. He admires their humor and their long memories, their fidelity to their own histories. They are virtues and minor vices made flesh.

Personal histories, constantly present in the minds of his characters, are part of the secret of Kennedy's compassion. Often these pasts are conveyed to us through the hard eyes and soft hearts of knowledgeable, educated narrators: Marcus Gorman, lawyer and historian in *Legs*, Martin Daugherty in *Billy Phelan*, who, like Kennedy, has "the gift of tongues." We discover the tragic past of Jack Diamond is really confusion. Marcus Gorman says: "I've often vacillated about whether Jack's life was tragic, comic, a bit of both, or merely a pathetic muddle. . . . Here he was, refocusing his entire history, as if it had just begun, on the dream of boundless empire" (*Legs* 166). Jack's tragedy is his inability to learn from his past, his dogged drive toward success despite the lessons of past failures. But not so with Francis Phelan in *Ironweed*. His past is the bugaboo of his present. He is hounded by the memory of innocent accidents that turned inexplicably into murders: a baby son dropped and killed, a scab killed during a strike by a stone thrown by Francis with his old baseball skill, the killing of Rowdy Dick in self-defense.

As Kennedy advances in his fiction, his toughness (in *The Ink Truck*, in *Legs*) softens. Lyricism sets in, a tendency to see the simple act, the small object, the obscure place, in tender and universal terms. In *Billy Phelan's Greatest Game*, Kennedy describes Edward Daugherty, Martin's father, as "cosmically beyond manual labor" (40). Martin himself is a visionary, and Louie's pool hall is not sordid but has been metamorphosed into the heroic: "a place where even serious men sometimes go to seek the meaning of magical webs, mystical coin, golden birds, and other artifacts of the only cosmos in town" (282), Louie's poolroom, into which the magician, Billy Phelan, disappears in the last paragraph of the book. Allied to Kennedy's vision of the ordinary raised to the cosmic is his universal compassion. Like Martin Daugherty, Kennedy feels "sympathy for them all, has a fondness for them all, gave allegiance to none" (111).

In *Ironweed* Kennedy moves full circle into Martin's all-embracing fondness for his characters. Of Sandra, the old drunk freezing to death in a grassless vacant lot, Rudy says to Francis:

> "She looks like a bum."
>
> "She's been a bum all her life."
>
> "No," said Francis, "Nobody's a bum all their life. She hada been somethin' once . . . A little kid's somethin' that ain't a bum or a whore." (31)

It is the sweetness of these pasts—of Sandra, of Francis, of Helen—that endears Kennedy's bums to him and to readers. Francis's youthful love for married Katrina Daugherty burns with lyricism, as he reviews the past:

> When his torso was naked, Katrina stunned him with a kiss, and with an exploration of the whole of his back with her fingertips. He held her as he would a crystal vase, fearful not only of her fragility but of his own. When he could again see her lips, her eyes, the sanctified valley of her mouth, when she stood inches from him, her hands gripping his naked back, he cautiously brought his own fingers around to her face and neck. Emulating her, he explored the exposed regions of her shoulders and her throat, letting the natural curve of her collar guide him to the top button of her blouse. And then slowly, as if the dance of their fingers had been choreographed, hers crawled across her own chest, brushing past his, which were carefully at work at their gentlest of chores, and she pushed the encumbering chemise strap down over the fall of her left shoulder. His own fingers then repeated the act on her right shoulder and he trembled with pleasure, and sin, and with, even now, the still unthinkable possibilities that lay below and beneath the boundary line her fallen clothing demarcated. (*Ironweed* 113)

Helen's early ambitions are remembered in melic words:

> Oh the lovely power of music to rejuvenate Helen. The melody returned her to that porcelain age when she aspired so loftily to a classical career. Her plan, her father's plan before it was hers, was

> for her to follow in her grandmother's footsteps, carry the family pride to lofty pinnacles: Vassar first, then the Paris Conservatory if she was truly as good as she seemed, then the concert world, then the entire world. If you love something well enough, Grandmother Archer told Helen when the weakness was upon her, you will die for it; for when we love with all our might, our silly little selves are already dead and we have no more fear of dying. Would you die for your music? Helen asked. And her grandmother said: I believe I already have. And in a month she was very unkindly cut down forever. (*Ironweed* 118)

Willingly we are snared by the goodness of the past, in the romantic tension created between the worth of the past and the sordid present, in the tug between the degraded details of the lives of bums and the high hopes, the splendid romance of their memories. These pasts provide an unexpected glamor to the present, making it, somehow, lovable, majestic, and even, in Kennedy's favored word, "cosmic."

Kennedy's people—Jack Diamond, Marcus Gorman, Billy, Francis—are endearing not only because they come so well outfitted with benign pasts, but also because they possess the American virtues. Beyond and above all their acts, there is their great innocence. Jack Diamond's henchman, Fogarty, has "an innocence about him that survived all the horror, all the fear, all the crooked action . . ." (*Legs* 33). Flossie, the whore, "was pretty back in those days, like a canary, all yellow-haired and soft and with the innocence of a birdsong" (*Legs* 14–15). They are all individuals, never copies. Marcus says of Jack Diamond: "It wouldn't matter if he'd sold toilet paper or milk bottles for a living, but he was an original man and he needs an original epitaph" (*Legs* 14). They are American heroes because they possess a kind of fierce energy, an extraordinary vitality that triumphs over adversity and the human inclination to sloth.

Francis tells his son Billy why the sportswriters liked him. "I did crazy things. I was good copy for them. And I had energy. Everybody likes energy" (*Ironweed* 173). To Marcus, Jack Diamond is "a moving glob of electricity, a live wire snaking its way around the porch. I knew then that this man was alive in a way I was not. I saw the vital principle of his elbow. . . . He hit you, slapped you with his palm, punched you with a light fist, clapped you on the shoulder, ridding himself of electricity to avoid exploding" (*Legs* 36). Jack's explosive energy is so great that it lends to his person a kind of luminosity. Kennedy's people are, at least at the start, winners, persons afraid of losing or failing. During Billy Phelan's greatest game of pool his competitor, Scotty, is called by Martin the "nervous sportsman. Did saying what he had just said mean that the man lacked all character? Did only relentless winning define his being? Was the fear of losing sufficient cause for him to try to foul another man's luck? Why, of course it was . . ." (*Billy Phelan's Greatest Game* 9). Finally, these winners, these highly charged and, somehow, pure men, are honest. They tell the truth, but not because of mindless devotion to virtue. When Rudy complains that "you never tell me nothin' that's true," Francis replies: "Hell, it's all true. Every stinkin' damn thing you can think of is true" (*Ironweed* 191).

We take these American heroes to our hearts, and to them we add what might be called Kennedy's beatific vision of women. To him a woman is what Norman Mailer, in describing Marilyn Monroe, called "the sweet angel of sex." These heroines exist in the lyrical mode. Every one of them, in their youth, is the epitome of rhapsodic desire. It is as though Kennedy's gift for sonorous prose is at its ripest and most exalted when Mary Daugherty and Alice and Kiki and Helen and Flossie and Katrina are his subjects.

Marcus looks at Jack Diamond's wife:

> Alice bulged out of her pink summer cotton in various places, and my feeling was that she was ready instantly to let it all flop out whenever Jack gave the signal. All love, all ampleness, all ripeness, would fall upon the bed, or the ground, or on him, and be his for the romping. Appleness, leaves, blue sky, white sheets, erect, red nipples, full buttocks, superb moistness at the intersection, warm wet lips, hair flying, craziness of joy, pleasure, wonder, mountains climbable with a stride after such sex. (*Legs* 42)

Jack's mistress, Kiki, looks like this to Marcus:

> She wore rolled silk stockings with frilly black garters about five inches above the knee, the sheerest pair of lace panties I'd theretofore seen, and areas of the most interesting flesh likely to be found on any mountain anywhere, and I also include the valleys.
>
> I see her there yet. I see her also crossing and uncrossing her silkiness, hinting at secret reaches, dark arenas of mystery difficult to reach, full of jewels of improbable value, full of the *promise* of tawdriness, of illicitness, of furtiveness, of wickedness, with possibly blue rouge on the nipples, and arcane exotica revealed when she slips down the elastic waistband of those sheerest of sheers. They infected my imagination, those dark, those sheer, those elasticized arenas of that gorgeous girl's life. (*Legs* 68)

And the prostitute Flossie is glorified in this way:

> But now Flossie's breasts rose and fell beneath her little cotton transparency in a way that had been inviting all of us all night long, and when she had half turned to leave, when my words of invitation stopped her, I caught a vision of her callipygian subtleties, like the ongoing night, never really revealed to these eyes before.
>
> She came toward me as I lay flat on my back, ever so little bounce in the splendid upheaval of her chest, vision too of calf without blemish, without trace of muscular impurity. (*Legs* 273)

At breakfast, at the beginning of *Billy Phelan*, Martin Daugherty's attention is caught by Mary: "his wife and her behind, jiggling while she stirred the eggs. Those splendid puffs of Irish history, those sweet curves of the Western world, sloping imagistically toward him: roundaceous beneath the black and yellow kimono . . ." (19).

Kennedy saves his most soaring words for the mad Katrina who bares herself to young Francis, who saw in her face "lunar majesty, a chilling fusion of beauty and desolation." But earlier, when first he sets eyes on her he is stunned:

> . . . her blond hair swept upward into a soft wreath, her eyes a dark and shining brown, the stately curves and fullness of her body carried so regally, her large, irregular teeth only making her beauty more singular. This goddess, who had walked naked across his life, and whom he had carried in his arms, now sat on the sofa and with eyes wide upon him she leaned forward and posed the question: "Are you in love with anyone?" (*Ironweed* 105)

Kennedy's women attain heroic status by being impossibly beautiful and infinitely desirable. But there is more: Men and women alike are granted the gift of eternality. Jack Diamond lives on after his death. Years later Marcus tells his old friends, "I don't really think he's dead," and in the final chapter, there Jack is, sitting on his bed in the brick house at 67 Dove Street in Albany, "incipiently dead," (*Legs* 315) as Kennedy says, fading away. Jack assures Marcus: "Honest to God. I really don't think I'm dead" (*Legs* 317). When Francis returns to Albany, his dead are all living again, in the cemetery, on the streets, in bars, and houses, and poolrooms, not ghosts but presences, arrived on the scene to accompany his present.

No one in Kennedy's Albany mythology disappears or is forgotten. Everyone is part of a history that flows everlastingly into the long and loving memory of the present. Some will call this a device, or fantasy, an imaginative incursion into the unreal. Some even term it literary hallucination. William Kennedy would, I believe, say it is true and real. "Every damn thing you can think of is true" (*Ironweed* 191), as Francis Phelan taught us.

REFERENCES

Kennedy, William. *Billy Phelan's Greatest Game*. New York: Penguin, 1983.

———. *Ironweed*, paperback ed. New York: Penguin, 1984.

———. *Legs*. New York: Penguin, 1983.

———. *O Albany! Improbable City of Political Wizards, Fearless Ethnics, Spectacular Aristocrats, Splendid Nobodies, and Underrated Scoundrels*. New York: Viking, 1983.

This essay was delivered as a speech at the Albany Institute of History and Art, in Albany, New York, on September 6, 1984, as part of "William Kennedy's Albany Weekend," a celebration of Kennedy's work that included lectures, panel discussions on Albany's neighborhoods and politicians, historical exhibits at the Albany Institute of History and Art and the New York State Museum, guided walking and bus tours, and a Sunday citywide festival in Washington Park. Twenty-five thousand people turned out for that final event in the Park. Major funding was provided by the New York Council for the Humanities (now Humanities New York), the Albany *Times Union*, the City of Albany, and the Capital District Humanities Program at the University at Albany. Reprinted by permission of Doris Grumbach.

William Kennedy

Interview

Edward Schwarzschild

These characters are always lurking there in the back of my mind, like old friends or family we don't see for years; and suddenly they turn up, and chaos, or joy, or trouble ensues.

—William Kennedy

It's commonplace (and accurate) to observe that William Kennedy has done for Albany what Joyce did for Dublin, Bellow did for Chicago, and what, in different ways, Faulkner did for Yoknapatawpha County and Gabriel García Márquez did for Macondo. But it's not only Albany that comes alive when you're in the company of the seventy-eight-year-old author of the ongoing Albany Cycle [including *Legs* (1975), *Billy Phelan's Greatest Game* (1978), *Quinn's Book* (1988), *Very Old Bones* (1992), *The Flaming Corsage* (1996), *Roscoe* (2002), and *Ironweed* (1983), which won both the Pulitzer Prize and the National Book Critics Circle Award]. The longer you talk with Kennedy, the more you begin to feel as if you're in conversation with an artist who has somehow gained direct access to all the significant creative projects of the last two hundred years, and then some. In addition to being a world-class novelist, journalist, historian, and screenwriter, he is also, essentially, an anthropologist of art and politics. A typical conversation with Kennedy moves from Hunter S. Thompson to Fidel Castro to Louis Armstrong to Ingmar Bergman to Diane Sawyer to Francis Ford Coppola (with whom he worked on *The Cotton Club*) and Meryl Streep (who starred in the film version of *Ironweed*). The subtitle of *O Albany!*, the stunning work of nonfiction Kennedy published in 1983, described New York's capital as a city full of "political wizards, fearless ethnics, spectacular aristocrats, splendid nobodies, and underrated scoundrels." Kennedy knows that cast of characters personally, and he writes about them better than anyone else.

When Kennedy received a MacArthur Foundation "genius" award (also in 1983), he used some of the award money to start a writers' program at the University at Albany, part of the State University of New York system. "It is my longstanding feeling," Kennedy said at the time, "that literary conversation is the best conversation in the world." With that feeling in mind, Kennedy has served as founder and executive director of the New York State Writers Institute, which has brought close to two thousand writers to Albany, and has sponsored numerous workshops, film series, and conferences, all free to the public and full of conversation.

This interview took place during two evenings of conversation and dining in early 2006. I had been hoping to lure Kennedy out to bowl while we talked—he's had a storied career as a bowler, in addition to his better-known career as a writer—but I happily settled for a few games of pool. Kennedy trounced me in game one, then kindly scratched on the eight ball as he was trouncing me in game two.

—Edward Schwarzschild

"I DECIDED I COULD MAKE A DECENT PIECE OUT OF ANYTHING."

The Believer: Your career as a writer started with journalism, and you've done scores of interviews over the years. How did you learn to become a good interviewer?

William Kennedy: I started out very hesitant about interviewing and even about being a reporter. I wondered whether I'd even recognize a news story when I came across one. I had nightmares about going out on a story and missing it entirely. I started as a sportswriter on the Glens Falls *Post-Star*, writing an occasional column, and when I was drafted during the Korean War the *Post-Star* gave me a column—"This New Army"—three dollars a pop and write whenever I wanted. Everything I wrote they published and sent three bucks home to my family and they put it in the bank. I probably made a hundred dollars in the two years I was in the army. Sumptuous beginning.

Believer: What were the columns about?

Kennedy: My first column was about how lousy the food was at Fort Devens. Then we were sent to Fort Benning to form the Fourth Infantry, which I later found out was a division Hemingway had attached himself to during World War II. The Fourth came home after World War II and disbanded and now they were reconstituting it from scratch. We thought we were going to Korea, but they sent us to Germany, the first American troops to go to Europe during the Cold War. At Benning, I was in a heavy weapons company and writing columns for the *Post-Star*. What I didn't know was that a recruiting sergeant in Glens Falls, New York, was clipping them and was very pissed off that I was making fun of the army, especially one about a general. I thought it was funny, but the sergeant didn't. I got a call from a Major Zimmerman and he said, "That was a good column you wrote in the *Post-Star* about the general." I said, "Well, thank you, Major." And he said, "Don't write any more. But come up and see me and maybe I'll give you a job." Major Zimmerman was putting together a Public Information Office for the division, and after basic training he had me transferred out of the heavy weapons company.

I went to PIO, working with visiting newsmen, writing, and when we got to Frankfurt we started a weekly division newspaper, about sixteen pages, and I became sports editor. I spent the Cold War covering golf and baseball and home run hitters, and a fellow who pitched a perfect game and whose wife turned out to be a spy. You asked about interviewing and I remember an Italian private in the Eighth Regiment who had been a club fighter in New York. I drove up to Bad Nauheim, Germany, where the Eighth was headquartered, and watched this fellow teaching guys to box. There was no real story, but I wrote it anyway and decided I could make a decent piece out of anything.

Believer: Did any of your interviews go badly?

Kennedy: I remember one with Arthur Miller when *After the Fall* was about to open in New York. Miller had an apartment in the Chelsea Hotel. We talked and talked and talked and it seemed all right, but nothing extra. I wanted to sit with him during a rehearsal but he wouldn't let that happen. He was keeping the play a secret. I tried to get him to tell me what it was about, and he evaded the question and said, "It's a lot of fireworks going off all over the place." At no time did he hint that it was, in good measure, about Marilyn Monroe. It was a vapid interview—what he said and didn't say, and also what I wrote.

I'd rather remember the day in 1956 in Albany when I went to see Louis Armstrong at the Kenmore Hotel. I didn't know what to expect but I was a fanatic about him and he was a sensational interview—so open, so original. He had great verbal talent on top of being a musical genius. When I was walking down the corridor to his room, he was practicing a tune he said was called "Nevada." He stopped, let me in, and then said, "Wait till I hit the high note." Here's what I wrote about that moment: [Kennedy consults his collection of selected nonfiction called *Riding the Yellow Trolley Car* (1993).]

> He blew some low notes, then a few higher ones, and finally he hit the high one and held it for about a week and turned it like a corkscrew and flattened it out two or three ways and sharpened it up and blew it out the window. Then he put down the horn and smiled. "Solid," he said. (350)

I drove up to Glens Falls after the army to a high school prom so I could hear Duke Ellington. I remember leaning on the piano as the Duke played and talking to him. I don't know what he said or I said, and I never wrote a line about it, but it was a great moment.

"A FUN CONVERSATION WITH FIDEL ABOUT SPORTS."

Believer: It seems like sports has been one of the passions you've had your whole life—it runs through your work, from *Billy Phelan's Greatest Game* to *Roscoe*. I suppose it's an American trait on some level, but your devotion seems deeper than that.

Kennedy: I was more passionate at a younger age when I followed everything, but then I realized that I wanted to write about the larger world and I left sports, but always came back to it. I didn't want to write about politics either, and I can't stop writing about it. The passion for sports was from my family. My father and my uncle were rabid baseball fans, and Hawkins Stadium, where the Albany Senators played in the Eastern League, was in my backyard. We also had an open field across the street from my house where we played baseball all the time. I played first base because I had a first baseman's mitt. I hit a home run over the fence one day and the next week they moved the diamond to the other end of the field and I could never hit another one. The fence was a mile away.

Believer: There's always someone moving the fence, raising the bar. Or are sports more of an escape from our lives?

Kennedy: No, it's absolutely a segment of life that is very valuable—the idea of gaming, that's the theme of *Billy Phelan*. The urge to play, the element of play in the life of the human being. [Kennedy reaches for a copy of *Billy Phelan's Greatest Game* and quotes the epigraph, which is from Johan

Huizinga's *Homo Ludens*.] "The great archetypal activities of human society are all permeated with play from the start." That became clear to me at a later date. I didn't have it in mind when I was hitting that home run. I also had a hole in one and a 299 game. I had a great career in sports and then I retired. The hole in one was up at the Schroon Lake Country Club. I was twelve. A par three and I hit it with my junior driver—off the tee and into the cup. My father was with me and one of my uncles and a friend from New York, and they couldn't believe it. The 299 game I wrote about in *Billy Phelan*.

Believer: It's only the best bowling scene in American literature!

Kennedy: I told that 299 story when I went to Cuba. I was in García Márquez's house and Fidel Castro came in just after we had lunch. Norberto Fuentes, a writer who had invited me down, and Gabo [Gabriel García Márquez], who knew my work because I'd interviewed him, had both mentioned me to Fidel, so he came by to say hello. And he said, "I have your books." We talked a long time and then he visited again the night we were leaving Cuba. He said he had read the books and loved *Ironweed* and said I should write another book about Francis Phelan, which I did. He'd also read *Billy Phelan* and couldn't understand this game, how it was even possible. He said he bowled now and then and had access to any bowling alley in Cuba. "But my high game is 169," he said. So, I told him the story, how it happened.

Believer: How did it happen?

Kennedy: It was 1938, 1939 maybe, and my uncle Pete McDonald was bowling at the Knights of Columbus, a five-dollar-a-head match game, and my father was on his team. Pete rolled 299 but another man on the team rolled 143 and they lost the match. It got into the newspaper and Pete used to tell me, "When you roll 300, kid, come around and talk to me." He was keeping score one night, about 1948 or 1949, and we were bowling in Thorne's Alleys in Watervliet and I was hot. I had something like a 215 average for four or five games, and then I rolled eleven strikes in a row, and on the twelfth I had a perfect hit, one of the best hits of the night, and the four pin never moved.

Believer: I hope nobody hexed you the way Scotty hexed Billy Phelan—

Kennedy: I don't think anybody hexed me, not like in the book, but who knows what kind of voodoo is ever going on behind your back? Pete putting the hex on me? No, he wouldn't. Anyway, I pulled even with him, both of us with 299 from then on. And Fidel couldn't get over that. And when I told him that not only had Billy Phelan done it, but I had done it, he seemed really awed and he changed the subject. He told me what a great shot he was. He invited me to go duck hunting with him in the south of Cuba. He said he shot ducks in competition—millions of ducks go to Cuba for the winter—and he won the prize for marksmanship—101 ducks with 99 shots—

Believer: The equivalent of a 301 game, I guess.

Kennedy: A fun conversation with Fidel about sports. It was telling.

"AGE MAKES THE WORK MORE DIFFICULT."

Believer: I've been rereading the pieces you've written about García Márquez and they seem particularly important to me. You were working as a journalist and you were writing your novels and then *One Hundred Years of Solitude* came across your desk in 1970. You read it, loved it, and raved about it in one of the earliest reviews of Márquez in the U.S. [The opening line of the review is: "*One Hundred Years of Solitude* is the first piece of literature since the Book of Genesis that should be required reading for the entire human race."] Then you arranged to interview Márquez in Barcelona in 1972. When I read that interview, it feels like I'm eavesdropping on a separated-at-birth reunion. You were both born in the same year, you both moved from journalism to fiction, and you both pushed against the boundaries of traditional realism. It wasn't like he was doing something that then inspired you to do something. Instead, it was as if you were both doing similar work simultaneously in different parts of the world and you finally crossed paths. Was it like meeting a kindred spirit?

Kennedy: It certainly was. And because of all the things you say. He was a journalist and we were the same age and he aspired to write literature and we shared a love of the movies and the Surrealists. It was enlightening to see how he viewed himself and explained his work, and the great wit with which he wrote and conversed. He was a funny guy and he loved to tell stories. So we got along and we've kept up a casual friendship over the years.

Believer: I read recently that Márquez didn't write last year. He said it was the first year he could remember not having written and he didn't know if he would write another novel, though he felt he could if he were inspired.

Kennedy: Gabo has had a lot of physical trauma in recent years, but the last we talked he seemed to be past that. Bill Styron was silenced by his depression and never went back to his war novel. And ego can do it, as it did to

Ralph Ellison, who couldn't publish a second book that might be compared negatively to his masterpiece, *Invisible Man*. Gabo never had the ego problem, even after *One Hundred Years of Solitude*. But for most writers I do think age makes the work more difficult.

Believer: Is that how it feels for you these days?

Kennedy: I don't think it's entirely the aging with me. After floundering around for years with two unpublished early novels, then writing *Legs* over six years and finally publishing it, I said, "Maybe I know how to do it now." I wrote *Billy Phelan* in two years and *Ironweed* in seven or eight months. That was unbelievable, and I thought I was home free; but then it was four or five years with *Quinn's Book*, which was interrupted by the movies. *Very Old Bones* and *The Flaming Corsage* were both tough, and *Roscoe* was a killer. This book I'm involved in now seems endless. I wrote a page and a half today, which took me forever; but it's always that way, and you don't seem to carry over certain elements of your experience. You learn craft, but creating out of nothing is still like building the Tower of Babel every day. You get up so high, but without a clue where it's going; and you'll never get to the top. How high is up?

Believer: That's a tough question to answer.

Kennedy: I remember one night in the newsroom up in Glens Falls, the composing room foreman, Jimmy O'Neil, was listening to two reporters talking about how tough it was to be a writer. And Jimmy said out of the side of his mouth, "Yeah, the guys up in the slate quarry in Granville got it tough, too." You can't pity yourself. If Gabo can't figure it out, who can? Hemingway couldn't figure it out. Fitzgerald, for years and years, couldn't make his second act work. Finally, he had the Hollywood novel going and was on his way to something pretty good when he died. Whether he could have pulled a *Gatsby* off again nobody knows.

Believer: You've said more than once that one way in which you got your education as a writer was by talking to other writers.

Kennedy: When I left Puerto Rico in 1963 and came back to Albany, I felt totally isolated. I had no friends who cared about literature. I also had to do something on the side to pay some bills. So I started to freelance and I connected with the *National Observer*. Because I'd been in Puerto Rico [working as managing editor of the *San Juan Star*] they sent me Latin American novels, as if I were an expert. That's how I got *One Hundred Years of Solitude*. After a while I connected socially with some university people who were writers or teachers of literature and finally there was somebody to talk to. I was the apprentice in those years, trying to learn how it was done, and I sought out established writers to profile, and pick their brains. "How did you do this?" "Why this way?" I also remember the importance of making it all real—the world of publishing and writing—because it was only a fantasy world for me when I was in Europe and Puerto Rico. I had no real connection to New York City.

Believer: Were there any particular revelations that you remember from those early days?

Kennedy: I got by osmosis from these writers what was essential in their attitude toward their work—their seriousness, their commitment, how they confronted the problem of creativity. I couldn't conceive of anybody being more committed than I was then, but I wasn't at all secure. I might never write a book that anybody would care about. That's the early nightmare. Bernard Malamud was up the road in Bennington and I was a great fan of his writing, especially his dialogue, and I got to know him over the years. Granville Hicks lived nearby in Grafton and he'd been a character of great complexity and influence in the 1930s as editor of the *New Masses*. I did a long piece on him and his history and on his attitudes toward contemporary writers, which was illuminating. I talked to Norman Mailer and James Baldwin in New York; Saul Bellow and John Cheever were down the river. Saul was brilliant as usual, and I remember him saying that the sources of real power in America will never be revealed to innocents and underdogs.

Believer: Hunter S. Thompson was a writer you were in touch with back then, as well.

Kennedy: Well, I knew Hunter when we were both very young people. He was younger than I was, but I was still young and new to fiction. We spent a lot of time talking. Hunter was a very smart guy and very committed to literature. Ultimately, he didn't do that. He found a way to live as a journalist, and he was so successful at it that he stopped writing fiction, though he returned to it late in his life. But I give him very high marks for something else—for extending the boundary of literature into the new dimension of gonzo. Some of what he wrote is as good—as fiction—as anything written by any number of established high-level fiction writers. I keep arguing on behalf of his being considered a great comedic fiction writer, but people will probably always consider him a journalist.

I think he was extremely gifted both as a user of the language and as an inventor of himself, and that self-invention was the raw material of his work.

You could say the same of any number of first-person writers in our century. Hemingway and Mailer immediately come to mind. Mailer broke ground using his own persona as the narrator. Bellow was probably our most brilliant first-person fiction writer and even when he uses third person it seems like first person. His capacity to invent an individual almost full-blown on half a page with his insights is extraordinary. I go crazy with Bellow's prose; how could anybody write that well? His language and his intellect are endlessly astonishing. I've been rereading *Humboldt's Gift*—wonderful, wonderful prose, he's a maestro on every page.

Believer: Could Thompson have done that in fiction if he'd stayed away from journalism?

Kennedy: Not like Bellow, who was all by himself. But there's no telling what Thompson might have accomplished if he had gone directly into fiction and stayed there; but he didn't. The originality of what he did speaks for itself. The way of life he entered when he wrote *Hell's Angels* changed him forever. He was already on the way to becoming the maximum extrovert, and once he presented his bizarre persona to the world, he felt he had to keep it up ever after—extending his imagination into wilder and wilder feats of outlandishness, often dangerous and self-destructive. The incredible abuse of drugs, the willingness to create very wild public scenes—he carried this to extreme degrees until the end of his life. His later years are full of horror stories about what happened with his body as well as his mind. Nevertheless I always thought him, in some compartment of his strange brain, to be one of the sanest people on the planet, and as smart as they come, and extremely funny. There was always great conversation with Hunter, even during his most dire final days. He was a great friend for a long time, a man worth knowing.

"GENRES MOVE IN CYCLES, AND ONLY NEED A WRITER WITH NEW VISION."

Believer: Hearing you describe Hunter S. Thompson makes me wonder how writers manage to remain inspired and excited and productive without veering into destructive behavior. Thompson went his way, and Fitzgerald went his way; and other people have gone other destructive ways. Maybe this question is too innocent or naive, but how does a writer exist in our society in a healthy, productive way?

Kennedy: I make no claims to mental health but I am still producing work. I had a vision of what I wanted to write, and it was fiction. And I kept at it in solitude, teaching myself what I knew was the work of my life. It started consuming me after college and when I was in the army. I was devouring everybody on the shelf, and even into the sixties I would have thirty or forty books out of the library and I wanted to read them all. I wish I were a better reader but I'm very slow, methodical, and I get bored easily. But I'd found writers of incredible value this way, and when I did find one I'd go through the whole shelf: Graham Greene or Borges or Nathanael West or Camus, so many. It's as if I were sketching a rough draft of what I was going to imagine—and this was early on. It then became my obsession, my assignment to myself, to flesh it out, to discover the use of language, dialogue, structure, suspense, discover how people think and then behave or misbehave, a learning process that's always changing. And for many it doesn't seem ever to be easily done.

Self-destruction happens often, when the writing ceases to be central and the life takes over. Remember Yeats's famous line, "The intellect of man is forced to choose perfection of the life, or of the work."* Sometimes when the work becomes difficult the only way forward is to repeat yesterday's success, and then the game is over. It always has to be new. I hear about this ongoing struggle over and over again, even from the most achieved writers. I just saw an interview with Orhan Pamuk where he said that in the novel he was writing he was having a problem about how to bring a person into the room [laughs]—this at a stage of life when he's considered the greatest writer of his country.

Mario Vargas Llosa, after four decades of creating a shelf of very distinguished novels, said he has a tormenting lack of confidence about writing. He doubts himself, and it gets worse with time. Hemingway certainly underwent that in his late years, really lost his gift. It's precarious, what we go through, but it's also not something to be surprised about. The imagination gets you into this novel you're working on, using all the knowledge of craft, design, theory, character, structure that you've been learning all your life, and then you grapple with the unknown, an endless struggle to find the way, and you finish, at long last. And when you start over it's a brand-new game. You don't forget how to ride a bicycle, but you might forget how to get from Albany to Troy on a bicycle. [Laughs.]

Believer: Do writers lose touch with their assignments? Is that why some writers are unable to continue to create?

Kennedy: When you get older I suppose one thing you lose is the adventurousness of the quest and the great feeling of having done something

---

* Editors' Note: From "The Choice," by William Butler Yeats.

absolutely original. Emerson wrote about the wisdom of the man who utters his own thought with a divine confidence that it must be true if he heard it there. In your late years that's difficult, but it surely is the way to proceed. The question is always the same: what's new about this subject? When I was writing *Legs*, about Jack Diamond, the gangster novel and gangster movie were clichés; the genre was a cliché. But it came back with *The Godfather* and again with *The Sopranos*. Genres move in cycles and only need a writer with new vision. I believed there was something new to be found in the story of Diamond's life, and in how the world looked at him, and I think I found something. I've changed much since those early days, but I still have that assignment I gave myself so long ago. I haven't finished, haven't given up. I'm still here, still writing. So far, so good.

Believer: Another potential danger for writers is their relationship to politics. How have you come to think about that over the years?

Kennedy: I've always been very leery of it. Not of politics as a subject, but a political point of view as a theme or argument. There are writers who would not exist if they did not have that political point of view—literature as a vehicle for social change. A writer like Camus was an incredibly political man with intense moral fervor in his life and his work; but he separated himself from partisan commitment to pursue a larger dimension. In his allegorical novel of 1947, *The Plague*, he was faulted for being insufficiently engaged—should have been tougher on Fascism, the Nazis, the French collaborators. But he was after a subject that transcended even those horrendous war politics—which is the defining of the human behavior that begets such plagues. He wrote in one of his notebooks, "Everyone wants the man who is still searching to have reached his conclusions."

I keep coming back to Camus as an inspiration toward an attitude that is political but that does not strangle on its own politics. He said something to the effect that if you weren't able to write about . . . wait a minute. I want to say this right. [Kennedy picks a book off his shelf and finds the Camus quote he's looking for.]*

> It would appear that to write a poem about spring would nowadays be serving capitalism. I am not a poet, but I should have no second thoughts about being delighted by such a poem if it were beautiful. One either serves the whole of man or one does not serve him at all. I like men who take sides more than literatures that do. (92)

* Editors' Note: Albert Camus's *Carnets 1942–1951: Camus' Diary and Working Notebooks*, trans. Philip Thody (London: Hamish Hamilton, 1966).

That idea has been a guiding principle for me from very early on, long before I read Camus. I came to it, I suppose, by rejecting novels that were dated either because of their politics or because of facile manipulation of history. In service of what? The cause or the theory of the moment? Proust said that a work with theories in it is like an object with the price tag still on it.

Some element of me always wants to be political and I think much of my writing has been that—*Ironweed*, for instance. But I never intended that as the politics of any moment, or any movement. That was never what literature was about for me. The struggle is always the revelation of the individual spirit that you're creating. That's the mystery that prevails throughout the quest. And if there is a political theme, it should be woven into the fabric of that spirit. *Roscoe* is all about politicians but it's not an argument. It is, I hope, a personification of political power in an ambiguously moral rascal. There are a lot of those out there, and *Roscoe* illuminates one of them.

Believer: But aren't you still tempted, occasionally, to put an explicit political position in your work?

Kennedy: Well, yes. I have a great urge right now to write something that would help get rid of the Cheney-Bush administration, the most secretive in our history, which is relentlessly hacking at the established rights the nation has so carefully nurtured for so long. The press is their enemy and is targeted as such; we're mired in a hateful war, and in the rape of the environment, and we're subsidizing incredible plunder. Many American writers feel this, and it's come to be comparable to what European writers felt in the oppressive days of communism and fascism. The dangers in this country now will surely find their way into our literature, but whatever I write on such matters will be carried through obliquely. I write speeches about it all, but not novels.

"I WANTED TO TAKE ALBANY THROUGH THE AGES."

Believer: When did you have a sense that you were going to be deep in Albany with your novels for a long time?

Kennedy: I would say that it started in the early sixties. I came back here to work in Albany because my father was sick, and I got an assignment to do a history of the neighborhoods in Albany for the *Times Union*. And in doing it I discovered how much Albany had to offer. I knew it had a great history and I'd heard about it for years, and I loved that about it. But I didn't think it was necessarily my turf, because when I left Albany I didn't want to come back. I figured I'd roam the world and do the expatriate number. That's what I did, in a sense, for six years in Puerto Rico. Then I got my belly full and came home. I remember somebody saying, "You don't really know why you're going back to Albany, but you'll find out when you get there." And I did.

Believer: Did your Albany Cycle start soon after that?

Kennedy: I came across a note to myself from 1964 about writing this big book on Albany, long before I ever thought about such a thing as a cycle of novels. I didn't know what it would be like and I didn't have a model. But I wanted to take Albany through the ages and cover all the wars and the presidents and the railroads and the Erie Canal and the gangsters and all the immigration and the church and the wacko politics, and in my imagination it was a single book, which was absurd. When I came across that note I realized I'd forgotten totally how far back that idea went for me.

The reality set in when I started to write a novel on modern Albany politics, and put Legs Diamond in as a secondary character. But he took over the book and shoved out the pols, and I saw the unmanageable immensity of my old plan. And I settled for one novel at a time. I was tracking Diamond through all the newspaper morgues of Albany and New York City, and I knew that the ancillary stories I kept finding would be part of future novels—the kidnapping of the political boss's nephew, Thomas E. Dewey trying to bust the political machine in 1938 and again in 1942 when he became governor, the city as a transportation hub, the Erie Canal as the way west, the vast fortunes made in railroads and lumber—in my neighborhood—all the arrests for gambling, which was so intimately tied to politics—and I had gamblers in the family. One of my buddies put himself through college running a horse room in the back of a barbershop. I grew up betting horses there. That convergence of worlds galvanized my imagination and Billy Phelan came into existence.

Believer: But how did you get to the specific Albany families? The Phelans, the Quinns, and so on?

Kennedy: The first novel I wrote was terrible and I destroyed it. The second was gloomy and episodic but not bad. I called it *The Angels and the Sparrows* and in it I established the whole Phelan family. It didn't work, but those people were very alive to me, and the manuscript received some serious attention. I'm glad it wasn't published, but it did form the foundation for much of my future work; and eventually I rewrote it entirely as *Very Old Bones*. When I was writing *Billy Phelan*, I had to give Billy a family, so I brought in those old Phelans. In *The Angels*, Francis Phelan was a bum on the road, unmarried, coming home for his mother's funeral. He was in his thirties, and mean-spirited, but when I put him into *Billy* I improved his disposition. He drops his infant son Gerald while changing his diaper and the baby dies, and Francis, in shame, abandons the family for twenty-two years. He comes home in 1938, meets his grown son, Billy, and finds out that his wife, Annie, never told anybody he dropped the baby; he is baffled and amazed and becomes a different character. That incident of dropping the baby and running away gave me the forces that shaped the man's personality; and in time I knew I could take Francis forward into a novel of his own. That was *Ironweed*.

By this time I had also invented other families—the McCalls and the Conways, who held the Irish-Catholic political power in Albany for decades, along with the Fitzgibbons, wealthy Protestants who also coveted political power and achieved it for more than a century; and the Daughertys who had an artistic and religious bent, and, like the Quinns, also had journalism in their genes, and so on. I saw ways of structuring these lives so I could talk about the forces that move them, and how such inheritances pass on generationally.

I felt that with these characters I could frame a historical panorama—which was part of what I had wanted to do early on. Also, as I went along, I saw that I would always have more and more people in a complex social framework to move through time. But even with all this there's still the vexing question of writing it—personifying it—which is a very mysterious process. Creating unknown people out of your imagination is a ridiculously difficult procedure. And why I have to do it, I don't know.

Believer: Calling it a "procedure" makes it sound almost systematic.

Kennedy: I wish it were. The procedure is to talk to yourself every day as if you're solving a mathematical problem. I have no comprehension of mathematics, but I know it's fairly difficult to arrive at $E=mc^2$. It's also difficult—less difficult—to arrive at Francis Phelan. Right now, I'm again in the midst of a mystery, not at all sure where I'm going. I keep telling myself I'll figure it out, but it's a faith-based pursuit. And if you don't have faith in a breakthrough, you'll go crazy or stop writing.

Believer: Are you still surprised by the way things come back? I'm thinking, for example, of how you worked on *Legs* for six years more than thirty years ago. You couldn't get that book out of your head, but then you finally did. And yet, decades later you wind up working on *Roscoe* and Legs Diamond reappears in that story. Is that kind of reappearance something that catches you off guard, or is that part of the faith as well?

Kennedy: These characters are always lurking there in the back of the mind, like old friends or family we don't see for years; and suddenly they turn up, and chaos, or joy, or trouble ensues. The imagination is equivalently random. It's as if you have an imprint of a cosmos and suddenly something urges you to focus here—like those magnifying glasses on the internet when you're looking at a painting—the *Death of Socrates* or *Las Meninas*; something in the corner grabs your attention—Plato is off-scene so you zoom in; Velázquez's gaze is telling, but it's small, so you zoom in. Staring at anything long enough reveals the unexpected. It's the way I've always worked, going back in time and finding old characters who still seem valuable. I keep an eye on them, hoping for something new, and when I get lucky they come to life.

"IF I KNOW TOO MUCH TOO SOON, I'LL STOP WRITING OUT OF BOREDOM."

Believer: Can you talk about what you're working on now?

Kennedy: I can talk about it up to a point. I'm not exactly sure how much I want to say because I know it's going to change. Everything is fluid. What's your question?

Believer: It takes place outside of Albany for the most part, right?

Kennedy: Somewhat. But the civil rights era in Albany is a dominating element. The Bobby Kennedy assassination, for instance; there are allusions to it, to that whole horrible string of assassinations and never a satisfying resolution to any of them, or to the veiled purposes behind them. But I also touch on the Cuban Revolution and events before and after it within Cuba. For years I wanted to write about that. The book is emerging slowly, and I feel I'm on the way, but it's a peculiar journey, and it may not be like any of my other books. The voice will be my own. I can't change that. But I seem to have a different narrative structure. The end is not in sight, so who knows? Maybe it will turn out to be like all the rest.

Believer: Is there a working title?

Kennedy: I wish I had one. Have any ideas?

Believer: I need to know a little more about it.

Kennedy: I'm not going to tell you any more. You've got enough. Just give me an idea, out of the blue.

Believer: How about *Out of the Blue*?

Kennedy: [Laughs.] It's been done. I asked my son Brendan the other night and he said, "Don't worry about it." "That's a good title," I said. And I went up and I made a title page, *Don't Worry About It*, and I showed it to Brendan and then threw it out. [Laughs.] I don't know what the title is because I still don't know what the book is about.

Believer: I don't believe that.

Kennedy: I know a few things. But if I know too much too soon, I'll stop writing out of boredom. Tracking the mystery is what keeps me going. *Tracking the Mystery*—rotten title.

REFERENCES

Camus, Albert. *Carnets 1942–1051: Camus' Diary and Working Notebooks*. Trans. Philip Thody. London: Hamish Hamilton, 1966.

Kennedy, William. *Billy Phelan's Greatest Game*. New York: Penguin, 1983.

———. *Riding the Yellow Trolley Car*. New York: Viking, 1993.

Yeats, W. B. *The Collected Poems of W. B. Yeats*. England: Wordsworth Editions, 1994.

This interview originally appeared in *The Believer* 4, 8 (October 2006). Reprinted by permission of Edward Schwarzschild.

Human Capital

O Albany! Pays Homage to the Hard-to-Love City That Is the Greatest Hero of Kennedy's Novels

Stefan Beck

> Nothing in Kennedy's Albany is sentimentalized, trivialized, romanticized, or demonized. He confers dignity on vagrants and prostitutes without turning them into glowing unfortunates. He can mull the causes and effects of political corruption without assuming the mantle of a thundering reformer.
>
> —Stefan Beck

On January 16, 1928, William Joseph Kennedy suffered a misfortune of birth only slightly preferable to bastardy. Having drawn his first breath, he studied his surroundings and found himself a newly minted Son of Albany. The gravity of his situation may have been lost on him, but not for long. By the age of reason, in the Catholic sense, he must have accepted the sordid truth of his paternity. Albany was a bookie and a gambler, a bootlegger and a dipso, a pimp and a john, a boss and a stooge. "Of all the miserable, wretched, second-class, one-horse towns," wrote the architect Stanford White, "this is the most miserable" (3).

Albany was far from the action, halfway between Manhattan and the Canadian border. Where its political climate was strictly *smoke-filled backroom*, its actual one, much of the year, was *walk-in meat locker*. A youngster like Kennedy might don a cassock and surplice in the morning, quaking for his soul as an altar boy; survive a pointless fistfight at midday; bring his robes to the "Chinaman" for laundering in the afternoon; and at night hang around street corners or grocery stores, looking for a good chance to sin. It would have been a decent enough life, growing up in the shadow of Irish Catholicism and political corruption—but for a kid with ambition, who needed it?

In 1956 Kennedy lit out for Puerto Rico, taking a position as assistant managing editor of the *Puerto Rico World Journal*. In 1959 he became a founding managing editor of the *San Juan Star*, where he refused to hire the young reporter Hunter S. Thompson. In Puerto Rico, Kennedy found himself engrossed in a picture book of nineteenth-century Albany. He had to face it: "[San Juan] was not engaging my soul, and that Albany picture book was." In 1963, he went back to Albany for good.

Ironweed, the 1983 novel that made Kennedy's name—it won the Pulitzer Prize the next year—is about a man returning to Great Depression–era Albany at Halloween. Though he bears no resemblance to Kennedy, Francis Phelan, a guilt-wracked alcoholic hobo, illustrates how a man becomes magnetized to home, despite the compelling reasons to get lost. As the story begins, Francis, "[r]iding up the winding road of Saint Agnes Cemetery in the back of the rattling old truck . . . became aware that the dead, even more than the living, settled down in neighborhoods" (1). The neighborhoods of men and memory, the ever-changing anima of a city, are Kennedy's perennial subjects, and never more explicitly than in the other book he published in 1983, the essay collection *O Albany! Improbable City of Political Wizards, Fearless Ethnics, Spectacular Aristocrats, Splendid Nobodies, and Underrated Scoundrels*.

Kennedy's remarkable project began in 1963, when an Albany *Times Union* editor, Walter Hawver, asked Kennedy for a series showcasing the city's neighborhoods. This Kennedy completed between 1963 and 1964. Later, revisiting those pieces at the request of Albany's Washington Park Press, he "found them all misshapen by time and their prose as flat as Mesopotamian root beer." Thanks to his insistence on revising them, what might have been a very minor, parochial pamphlet—the sort of thing you fan yourself with at the Historical Society—became a detailed portrait of America in microcosm, and proof that a penetrating eye can turn a one-horse town into a metropolis deserving of its place in posterity.

In his overture, "Albany as a State of Mind," Kennedy calls his project "an attempt to strike a balance as to Albany's legend. Even iniquity has its charms: consider what Milton did with Satan." (4) Nothing in Kennedy's Albany is sentimentalized, trivialized, romanticized, or demonized. He confers dignity on vagrants and prostitutes without turning them into glowing unfortunates. He can mull the causes and effects of political corruption without assuming the mantle of a thundering reformer. He was, after all, a reporter before he was a novelist, and the essays in *O Albany!* are products of a fact-finding mission that transformed into a newspaper position and in turn into a life's work. Here, then, are some of the things he demanded to know:

> Why was I an only child in a vast family of brothers and sisters and untrackable cousins? . . . Why did my uncles marry so late or not at all? Was there such a thing as culture in Albany? Could you get rich without being in politics? Who was this Van Rensselaer fellow? Why was Eddie Carey called the Squire of North Albany and what precisely was a squire in Albany's lexicon and why did Eddie live at the top of Van Rensselaer Boulevard and why had I always lived at the bottom in one of his houses? Why was the North End, my neighborhood, almost exclusively Catholic, and Irish, and Democratic? (4–5)

Kennedy's intention was to answer a few of those questions—to learn more about "the city's ethnic blueprints, its political history and the nature of its peculiar people"—but probably not to be consumed by them. Fate, and Albany, had other plans.

O Albany! is divided not chronologically but into six sections of loosely associated essays. The first and last, "The Magical Places" and "Closing Time," are the loosest in this regard. The former serves to familiarize the reader with Kennedy's avowed Albany boosterism; the latter consists of acknowledgments and parting reminiscences. The middle sections get right to the point. "The Neighborhoods" is a thorough guided tour. "Nighttown" is a trio of essays about the fine distinctions between a "sport" and a "swell"; how Albany negotiated Prohibition; and the murder of Jack "Legs" Diamond, Albany's favorite gangster. The "fearless ethnics" who appear in part 4, "Some of the People," are Jews, Italians, Germans, and Blacks—the Irish being segregated in part 5, "Long-Run Politics: Wizardry Unbound."

This patchwork is a vastly more interesting way to learn about a city than the traditional chronological history, but it presents two difficulties. One is that the individual essays tend to jump around in time, and not just because Kennedy is writing about neighborhoods and institutions down through the decades. Almost as often, it is a function of his style, which is pleasingly torn between the journalistic and the literary, the present-day and the poetically historical. This tension of styles and techniques means that everything in *O Albany!* happens out of anything like order, and however vivid a *sense* of Albany the reader walks away with, he will never have a prayer of explaining the city's chaotic progression from a "primeval and savage wilderness" opened up by "those agents of the first Patroon, and the Dutch West India company pioneers" to whatever shape Kennedy found it in, in 1983.

The second difficulty is related, and similarly forgivable on the grounds that a great book is preferable to a merely educational one. As Kennedy has eschewed a chronological trudge, he is free to allow his own preoccupations, literary and personal, to guide his investigations. His account leans heavily on three famous Albanians: Erastus Corning 2nd, Daniel Peter O'Connell, and Jack Diamond. To know these names and what they mean is to know, perhaps, enough about Albany—and certainly enough about Kennedy's Albany—even if they belong to just one century of its long history.

It is not unusual to hear in 2012 about machine politics, though the preferred phrase, for obvious reasons, is "Chicago-style politics." Whether the latter term endures because Albany has been overlooked or because it has been let off the hook is a matter of speculation. The fact is that Chicago's Mayor Richard J. Daley served from 1955 to 1976, and Albany's Mayor Erastus Corning 2nd was first elected in 1941 and made it to 1983, the auspicious year of *O Albany!*'s publication. That's eleven terms. Though the record never made it into Guinness, it did wind up in Ripley's, in July 1982, alongside "nineteen wingwalkers and a chicken that laid eggs for 448 straight days, believe it or not" (*O Albany!* 326).

The boss of Albany's Irish Democratic political machine was Dan O'Connell, who had grown up with Mayor Erastus's father, Edwin, making Dan and Erastus's "eventual union in politics. . . . really an extension of a long friendship" (330)—a family friendship, in any case, or even an existing alliance. Kennedy's essays "The Democrats Convene" and "They Bury the Boss: Dan Ex-Machina" form an operating manual for machine politics. What did the machine provide? "[T]he job, the perpetuation of the job, the dole when there was no job, the loan when there was no dole . . ." (43). O'Connell got his start in politics after being elected tax assessor in 1919, and abuse of the assessor's office played a major role in the machine's control: Back a non-Democratic candidate for any office and one might find the assessment on his property higher than expected. Electoral fraud was, naturally, in the natural order of things as Kennedy writes:

> One city water inspector was arrested passing out envelopes to voters at a polling place, and when searched he had 45 envelopes in his pocket, each containing $4. This looked rather like a man purchasing votes. But he said he was contributing to a charity fund to buy food and shoes for needy folks and the polling place was the best spot to find them. He was released, probably because such ingenuity could not go unrewarded. (286)

At Dan O'Connell's funeral, "only if you were seventy-nine years old . . . could you have voted for a Democratic candidate for mayor of Albany who hadn't been of Dan's choosing" (271). He and his longest-serving mayor had survived Governor Thomas Dewey's corruption investigations. Corning had survived service in World War II—during a mayoral term. If these men had a lock on Albany politics, it was in part because Albanians encouraged it.

It is easy enough for a journalist to loathe corruption, even corruption that keeps the peace or keeps the people happy. It is harder for a novelist. The journalist Kennedy "[wrote] stories that complicated [the mayor's] life." The novelist Kennedy was delighted when the mayor approached him to collaborate on a book in which Kennedy would be able to say whatever he liked, as would Corning. The book never came to fruition, but an essay, "Erastus: The Million Dollar Smile," did. The result is an excellent example of Kennedy's candid, psychologically astute, and above all *sympathetic* portraiture. The essay gets to the heart of Kennedy's essentially novelistic journalism. Whether because he retains some vestigial sense of Original Sin, or simply because he grasps human folly, he is capable of regarding any man as an equal, a potential friend, and certainly a fascinating subject for study—no matter how wicked.

Kennedy never met the gangster Jack Diamond, but one guesses he would have held his own there, too. Diamond, a Prohibition-era rumrunner, hijacker, and bootlegger, was killed under mysterious circumstances inspected carefully by Kennedy in "The Death of Legs Diamond." Diamond's criminal career, romantic life, and death are also given a monumental treatment in Kennedy's novel *Legs*. The novel, narrated by Diamond's lawyer, is a valuable study of how seductive a legendary figure can be, even if he is evil. The Diamond of Kennedy's essay is a much smaller and uglier character, albeit still fascinating. To read the two treatments side by side is a lesson in how facts may undergird a novel, but, more important, in how to take the shine off a legend when dealing in reality.

Nowadays, rare is the work of nonfiction without a subtitle chugging across its jacket as long and noisy as a passenger train. *O Albany!*'s is as long and noisy as the worst of them, but it may be forgiven—partly because Kennedy was something of a pioneer in this, and partly because nobody would buy a book with "Albany" in its title unless it bore a subtitle promising the sensational. The trouble with Kennedy's *Political Wizards, Fearless Ethnics, Spectacular Aristocrats, Splendid Nobodies, and Underrated Scoundrels* is that it omits an important class of characters. Albany's great buildings, in Kennedy's telling, have a life of their own.

Take Union Station: In "The Romance of the Oriflamme," Kennedy writes that it "was magical because it was more than itself, which is how it is with any magical man, woman, or building" (17). Kennedy ponders it from the vantage of a "child of modest means": "The child knew only that trains passed over the Van Woert Street trestle and chugged up the Cut to the West, knew railroads had magic all right because in his kitchen there hung a sepia print of a grandfather and two granduncles standing beside Engine 151 on a clear day in the century's teens . . ." (18).

This rhapsody continues for two hundred words. Suddenly, Kennedy goes journalistically deadpan. The Station, "a gift of munificence from the New York Central to Albany" (*O Albany!* 18), is made of pink Milford granite, by the architectural firm "organized to complete the work" of Henry Hobson Richardson, a principal architect of the new State Capitol and also Albany's City Hall. The station opened its doors on December 17, 1900. A *Times Union* reporter remarked upon its magnificent ceiling, chandeliers, mosaic floors. The inaugural ticket transaction is described, down to the denominations of coins given in change. Of his facts, Kennedy asks: "Trivial?" and answers, "As trivial as a day in December 1968 when Union Station's closing was only days away" (19). He makes the reader fall in love with the place, only to reveal that he has been eulogizing it all along.

Many of the buildings celebrated in *O Albany!* are gone. Their impermanence fascinates Kennedy as much as their greatness does. The John Van Schaick Lansing Pruyn branch of the Albany Public Library, where Kennedy endured the "hallowed trauma" of reading profanity in *Of Mice and Men*, was also leveled in 1968, by a wrecking ball. If one is alarmed, in 2012, to find that public libraries resemble homeless shelters, he will be chastened to learn that the Pruyn, back in young Kennedy's day, was a haven for "winos and vagrants, crazies and shopping-bag ladies, and ordinary knights of the road of the Depression years" (10). Perhaps encountering books and the low life under one roof was a tonic, enabling Kennedy to write books about the low life without sentimentalizing or trivializing it.

It is especially painful to read about Albany's lost restaurants. Keeler's (56 State Street) satisfied the appetites of John Philip Sousa, Grover Cleveland, Thomas Edison, and August Busch, among others. How many others?

> . . . 1,500 patrons were served daily by 178 employees—48 waiters, 6 busboys on every shift, 27 cooks and assistant cooks: fry cooks, broil cooks, sauce cooks, roast cooks, fish cooks, vegetable cooks, oystermen, pantrymen, a meat butcher, a fish butcher, bread chefs, pastry chefs, topped off by the head chef, bottomed off by the potwasher and dishwasher. There were 14 dining rooms, a laundry on the third floor to handle table linen by the ton, a full-time seamstress to repair rent linen, a complete bakery, a printing plant for the daily menus and souvenir postcards, a machine shop, and a carpentry shop. (183)

There was the Kenmore Hotel, whose famous Rain-Bo Room hosted such musicians as Tommy Dorsey, Duke Ellington, Cab Calloway, and Bix Beiderbecke. There were saloons and bars that only seemed innumerable, except during Prohibition, when Albany boasted speakeasies that were actually uncountable: "All you needed to create a speakeasy was two bottles and a room" (193). Many, of course, were anything but humble. O'Connor's, which Kennedy identifies as the largest, boasted a massive and ornate bar that came to be preserved in a Cohoes, New York, restaurant. The more common fate of such places was to be preserved only in booze-addled memories. The same goes for the houses of ill repute described in "The Gut: Our Boulevard of Bluest Dreams," an essay about a vice-driven neighborhood that has passed out of existence.

Because Kennedy is obsessed with change, with the passing of great eras—Ozymandias is forcefully invoked in his farewell to Union Station—the structures he describes are, in their ability to accumulate history, to become vulnerable, and to pass away, every bit as human and sympathetic as the people who inhabit this history. They also serve as an oblique warning. The completion of the imposing South Mall (now generally known as Empire State Plaza) in the 1970s, a boondoggle Kennedy describes in "Everything Everybody Ever Wanted," leveled an entire neighborhood and transformed much of Albany's downtown into a featureless concrete office park. The old Albany gave birth to colorful, larger-than-life men like O'Connell and Corning. The coldly functional, modernist expanse of Empire State Plaza incubates dull bureaucrats and grim-faced clock-watchers. Though he never says it outright, Kennedy seems to believe not that a city gets the buildings it deserves, but, funny as it sounds, that buildings produce the people they deserve.

By the time *O Albany!* appeared in 1983, Kennedy had already written four novels, *The Ink Truck*, *Legs*, *Billy Phelan's Greatest Game*, and *Ironweed*. He has written five novels since then—his most recent, *Changó's Beads and Two-Tone Shoes*, an astonishing late-life critical success. Not one of these could have been written absent Kennedy's lifelong project of getting to know the city he once despised. Many of the real people described in *O Albany!* resurface, wearing disguises and assumed names, in Kennedy's novels. Yet it is a missed opportunity to treat *O Albany!* as a guidebook to the fiction. One wants to compare it to the New York chronicles of Joseph Mitchell, but Kennedy's task was more difficult than Mitchell's. He had to make us care about a place most could live without. If *O Albany!* is a guide to a mostly vanished place, it is also a blueprint for how other fallen, forgotten cities might be reinvigorated by the right kind of attention. It may be fascinating to view the "ruin porn" of places like Detroit, but it is anything but inspirational.

A book cannot save a city, but it can prove that a city is worth saving. It would be a fine thing if more writers and observers shared Kennedy's magnetic attraction to home and his ability to transfigure it. It is easy, if one has talent, to ride it out of town and to laugh at those unlucky peasants left behind. Yet often one is forfeiting an incredible inheritance, a wealth of history and poetry unknown to outsiders. *Ironweed*'s Francis Phelan is a man tormented by ghosts of Albany past; he is doomed to wander Albany, despite himself. Phelan's creator, however, collected ghosts as boon companions, and learned everything they had to tell. This is how a writer should honor his birthplace—by giving life and voice to the dead, for their good and for all of ours.

References

Kennedy, William. *Ironweed*, paperback ed. New York: Penguin, 1984.

———. *O Albany! Improbable City of Political Wizards, Fearless Ethnics, Spectacular Aristocrats, Splendid Nobodies, and Underrated Scoundrels*. New York: Penguin, 1985.

This essay first appeared in the *Columbia Journalism Review* in the November/December 2012 edition. Reprinted by permission of *Columbia Journalism Review*.

Violent Places

On Ghosts, Bums, and Redemption in *Ironweed*

Robert Towers

> What Kennedy has written is a kind of fantasia on the strangeness of human destiny, on the mysterious ways in which a life can be transformed and sometimes redeemed.
>
> —Robert Towers

William Kennedy's new novel, *Ironweed*, is accompanied by outriders—in this case two earlier works that have been simultaneously reissued as Penguin paperbacks. These are *Legs* (1975) and *Billy Phelan's Greatest Game* (1978), both of which belong, as does *Ironweed*, to Kennedy's Albany Cycle. They are to be welcomed, for together they form an impressive body of work by an entertaining and inventive writer who is by no means as well known as he should be. Collectively—and from strikingly different angles—the three novels reconstruct a time and a place and a population: the little world of Irish Americans living in Albany, New York, as Kennedy imagines it to have existed five and more decades ago.

Legs is a fictional account of the career of Jack "Legs" Diamond, the notorious Prohibition-era gangster who was shot to death in an Albany rooming house in 1931 just after he had been acquitted (to the tumultuous cheers of his fans) of kidnapping charges. Though less centered in Albany than the other two novels, *Legs* throws its own distinctive light on the Irish American ethos of that city through the ambivalent self-revelations of its narrator, Marcus Gorman, a rising Albany lawyer with political ambitions who, like millions of tabloid-reading Americans, allows himself to be seduced by the glamorous aura surrounding a psychopathic criminal of ability, daring, and reckless brutality. Not a profound work, *Legs* is fast-moving and absorbing, expert in its documentation of the period.

In *Billy Phelan's Greatest Game*, a more thickly textured novel set in 1938, the focus is upon the interconnections of Albany's Democratic machine, run by the McCall brothers, and a colorful, low-life collection of poolroom sharks, poker players, bartenders, bookies, and assorted night crawlers who run errands for the bosses and depend upon them for handouts, protection, and patronage. Here the ethical point of view is supplied chiefly by a middle-class journalist, Martin Daugherty, while the action itself centers upon a sharply dressed and resourceful petty gambler, Billy Phelan, who has his own peculiar standards to uphold.

Ironweed, also set in 1938, reveals a radical shift not only in its angle of vision but also in its style. In it Kennedy largely abandons the rather breezy, quasi-journalistic narrative voice of his previous fiction and resorts to a more poetically charged, often surrealistic use of language as he re-creates the experiences and mental states of an alcoholic bum, Francis Phelan, who, after a long absence, is once again in Albany, lurching around the missions and flophouses of the city's South End. Owing fifty dollars to Marcus Gorman for keeping him out of jail on a charge of falsely registering to vote (twenty-one times, at a fee of five dollars for each registration), Francis sobers up enough to find work shoveling dirt in a Catholic cemetery. There he is observed by various ghosts from his past, ghosts whose characterization provides a good example of the hallucinatory mode that Kennedy frequently employs in this novel:

> Francis's mother twitched nervously in her grave as the truck carried him nearer to her; and Francis's father lit his pipe, smiled at his wife's discomfort, and looked out from his own bit of sod to catch a glimpse of how much his son had changed since the train accident.
>
> Francis's father smoked roots of grass that died in the periodic droughts afflicting the cemetery. He stored the root essence in his pockets until it was brittle to the touch, then pulverized it between his fingers and packed his pipe. Francis's mother wove crosses from the dead dandelions and other deep-rooted weeds; careful to preserve their fullest length, she wove them while they were still in the green stage of death, then ate them with an insatiable revulsion. (1–2)

From another pair of ghosts—two brawny young brothers "skewered by the same whiskey bottle in 1884, dumped into the Erie Canal in front of the Black Rag saloon in Watervliet, and then pushed under and drowned with a long stick"—we get our first physical description of Francis:

> The brothers looked at Francis's clothes, his ragged brown twill suit jacket, black baggy pants, and filthy fireman's blue shirt, and felt a kinship with him that owed nothing to blood ties. His shoes were as worn as the brogans they both had been wearing on the last day of their lives. The brothers read also in Francis's face the familiar scars of alcoholic desolation, which both had developed in their graves. (3)

The dead keep appearing, fully characterized, throughout the book, and with their aid the reader can fill out the saga of Francis Phelan, the finest baseball player ever to come out of Albany, a man, capable of both tenderness and violence to an exceptional degree, who is fated to kill and to run—and to kill again and keep running until he has reached the mucky bottom-side of degradation where the only question a man asks is, "How do I get through the next twenty minutes?"

His first killing stemmed from his talent as a ballplayer: a smooth round stone, pitched with consummate skill by Francis during a transit strike in 1901, laid open the skull of a strikebreaker, causing the militia to fire into the crowd and kill two innocent bystanders. The second killing occurred in 1916 when Francis accidentally dropped his thirteen-day-old son while lifting the baby to change his diaper; not even waiting to attend the baby's funeral, the grief-stricken, guilt-stricken Francis fled, abandoning his family forever. The third occurred in 1930 when Francis—by now a derelict—defended himself against a crazed wino who tried to cut off his feet (for the sake of his shoes) with a meat cleaver. The fourth takes place during the Albany visit that forms the current action of *Ironweed*.

The story of Francis is balanced by that of Helen, his companion in drink and homelessness during the past nine years. Outwardly, Helen is "a drunken old douche bag" with a tumor-swollen belly and spindly legs who will submit to the sexual fumbling of a fellow derelict in order to sleep in his wheelless wreck of a car; within, she is still a nice Catholic girl, musically inclined, who was well brought up by an adoring father. She is an innocent who can't be trusted to cross the street on her own, someone whom Francis loves and tries to protect even while he drunkenly reviles her at times with outbursts of pure hatred. The peregrinations of the unsteady couple as they search for shelter on a chilly night (hoping always to avoid the fate of sleeping in the weeds of a vacant lot) form one of the movements of this musically composed novel. Another is based upon the wagon trip that Francis makes with a crusty old junk dealer, a journey that takes him through all the old neighborhoods before depositing him near the home of his long-deserted wife and grown children.

Throughout the novel Kennedy plays with the contrast between sordid event and exalted illusion, between remembered past and threadbare present, between precise description and blunt colloquialism on the one hand and on the other a style so heightened as to become rhapsodic. At times he flirts perilously with Irish sentimentality—and for the most part gets away with it. Here is the account of Helen's final moments in a fleabag hotel:

> And so when crippled Donovan knocks again at eleven o'clock and asks if Helen needs anything, she says no, no thank you, old cripple, I don't need anything or anybody anymore. . . . And after he goes away from the door she lets go of the brass and thinks of Beethoven, Ode to Joy,
>
> And hears the joyous multitudes advancing,
>
> Dah dah-dah,
>
> Dah dah-de-dah-dah,
>
> And feels her legs turning to feathers and sees that her head is floating down to meet them as her body bends under the weight of so much joy,
>
> Sees it floating ever so slowly
>
> As the white bird glides over the water until it comes to rest on the Japanese kimono
>
> That has fallen so quietly,
>
> So softly,
>
> Onto the grass where the moonlight grows. (138–139)

Thus quoted in isolation, the passage seems shameless in both its sentimentality and its poetic inflation. But in the context already established of Helen's deluded self-image, one sees that Kennedy is, so to speak, allowing her one final aria, an aria to cap the sentimental songs she had earlier sung—to imagined applause—in a sleazy skid-row saloon.

Though there is much shrewd observation of both conscious and unconscious motivation, *Ironweed* was not intended to be read as a psychologically realistic portrayal of alcoholic degradation and its causes. Did or did not Francis, the glorious ballplayer, mean to kill the strikebreaking trolley conductor? At one point he contemplates "the evil autonomy of his hands." At another he believes himself to be "a creature of unknown and unknowable qualities, a man in whom there would never be an equanimity of both impulsive and premeditated action" (216). A few sentences later he reaches the "unutterable" conclusion that his guilt is all that he has left: "If I lose it, I have stood for nothing, done nothing, been nothing" (216). But Kennedy never allows the issue to be closed. What he has written is a kind of fantasia on the strangeness of human destiny, on the mysterious ways in which a life can be transformed and sometimes redeemed. As such, *Ironweed* seems to me a work of unusual interest, original in its conception, full of energy and color, a splendid addition to the Albany Cycle.

Reference

Kennedy, William. *Ironweed*. New York: Viking, 1983.

This essay first appeared in *The New York Review of Books* on March 31, 1983. Reprinted by permission of the author's estate.

The Literary Brilliance of the Opening of *Ironweed*

Donald Newlove

> These "flowing masses" and Kennedy's black Irish wit disarm and move us. I, for one, enter the heaven of a writer absolutely on top of his material from the first sound of his voice.
>
> —Donald Newlove

First paragraphs are written on Olympus. White-hot shoes from the forge, they glow and ring on the anvil as a god batters them into shape. But even Vulcan's shop has its perils. Great writing is dangerous. It singes the eyeball and wants to change our lives.

William Kennedy's *Ironweed* takes place in the demonic underworld of Francis Phelan, at a depth of soul not too distant from that of *To the Lighthouse* and struck instantly in the first paragraph:

> Riding up the winding road of Saint Agnes Cemetery in the back of the rattling old truck, Francis Phelan became aware that the dead, even more than the living, settled down in neighborhoods. The truck was suddenly surrounded by fields of monuments and cenotaphs of kindred design and striking size, all guarding the privileged dead. But the truck moved on and the limits of mere privilege became visible, for here now came the acres of truly prestigious death: illustrious men and women, captains of life without their diamonds, furs, carriages, and limousines, but buried in pomp and glory, vaulted in great tombs built like heavenly safe deposit boxes, or parts of the Acropolis. And ah yes, here too, inevitably, came the flowing masses, row

> upon row of them under simple headstones and simpler crosses. Here was the neighborhood of the Phelans. (1)

This paragraph's high purpose and manner of statement is a variation on the noble Augustan march of Samuel Johnson's prose and the theme of his great poem "The Vanity of Human Wishes," as well as on the theme of Sir Thomas Browne's great essay "Hydriotaphia, Urn Burial." From high seriousness Kennedy veers into sheer novelty when the next paragraph shows us dead Phelans alive and grumbling in their graves, with the mother twitching nervously and eating dead dandelions and weeds that give her ghost-stomach waves of nausea, the father smoking dried roots of grass he grinds to dust in his fingers and packs into his pipe. Do we want to go along with this strange, almost mocking, stuff about buried Phelans? Slowly we accept this graveyard's laws, for this is Francis's real world, the Irish Catholic's limbo, a stage of the afterlife. These living dead hold in their auras the deepest values of Francis's life, laws he still measures himself by, and yet these are dream folk of his hallucinating alcoholic brain.

Francis, a once-heroic ballplayer who has slaughtered two men and, after only a couple of beers, accidentally killed his own baby Gerald by letting him slip from his diaper and fall to the floor, has been paying for his sins for twenty-two years on the bum. Saul Bellow writes a skillful thumbnail of Francis, which can hardly be bettered and is worth quoting despite coming from the novel's dust jacket: "Francis is also a traditional champion, the fated man, a type out of Icelandic or Irish epic. To kill is his destiny, and he kills American style, with techniques learned in play, throwing a rock like a baseball and, again in Hooverville, hitting a man with a baseball bat. He considers himself a man of sin."

Again and again in *Ironweed*, Kennedy's power to bring light into dark places and to write tragic dialogue ringing with a Shakespearean blackness strikes me as the happiest art. I have a fellow writer who calls this phantasmal dead-baby stuff corn. But for me it's bliss, as when Francis prays above Gerald:

> In his grave, a cruciformed circle, Gerald watched the advent of his father. . . . Gerald's grave trembled with superb possibility. Denied speech in life, having died with only monosyllabic goos and gaahs in his vocabulary, Gerald possessed the gift of tongues in death. His ability to communicate and to understand was at the genius level among the dead. He could speak with any resident adult in any language, but more notable was his ability to understand the chattery squirrels and chipmunks, the silent signals of the ants and beetles, and the slithy semaphores

> of the slugs and worms that moved above and through his earth. He could read the waning flow of energy in the leaves and berries as they fell from the box elder above him. . . . His body had not only been absolved of the need to decay, but in some respects—a full head of hair, for instance—it had grown to a completeness that was both natural and miraculous. Gerald rested in his infantile sublimity, exuding a high gloss induced by early death, his skin a radiant white-gold, his nails a silvery gray, his cluster of curls and large eyes perfectly matched in gleaming ebony. . . . He was neither beautiful nor perfect to the beholder but rather an ineffably fabulous presence whose like was not to be found anywhere in the cemetery, and it abounded with dead innocents. (17–18)

In this reader's heart, Kennedy will have a hard time getting upriver of his success in *Ironweed*. And yet, as we said about McInerney's success in *Bright Lights, Big City*, and Fitzgerald's in *The Great Gatsby*, authors must not be asked to repeat perfect works. One *tour de force* in a career—all stops pulled on his mighty Wurlitzer and every phrase shaped to his fingering—is enough. Could Dickens match himself with a second *A Christmas Carol*?

What is so attractive about Kennedy's voice in this opening paragraph? Perhaps it's the subject matter—the social grid Kennedy finds in the fields of death, his ironies hitting bull's-eyes phrase after phrase—as much as his way of speaking. First we are taken in by Francis's sense of the gravestones falling into neighborhoods, with monuments and cenotaphs marching by in noble Latin, and then Kennedy undercuts the illustrious dead with an amused commonplace, that they are vaulted in "heavenly safe deposit boxes . . ." Then irony fades before "the flowing masses, row upon row of them under simple headstones and simpler crosses. Here was the neighborhood of the Phelans" (1). No granite Latin diction for the Phelans.

So the author's voice follows an arc, rises from the rattling old truck to the august and glorious, spreads to acres of the illustrious, then falls to the familiar and sweepingly sad. These "flowing masses" and Kennedy's black Irish wit disarm and move us. I, for one, enter the heaven of a writer absolutely on top of his material from the first sound of his voice. Please, none of that moldiness that writing's all work and slavery. His undercurrent of unkillable laughter that carries us safely through sudden upwelling sadness: Can that come from a mere factifying stonemason and bricklayer of words sweating under a fluorescent desk lamp? Mr. Kennedy's no hod carrier. His load is light, every page. Pure light. And surely he changes our lives, enriches our understanding of the madness of one drunk in a fellowship of rock-bottom boozers during the Great Depression. It's not just historical understanding he gives us. We become Francis Phelan, a deep-witted walking grave, lighted up with family ghosts like fireflies in twilight.

> "Hey, bum," he called to Rudy. "Let's find that truck driver."
>
> "Whatayou been up to?" Rudy asked. "You know somebody buried up there?"
>
> "A little kid I used to know."
>
> "A kid? What'd he do, die young?"
>
> "Pretty young."
>
> "What happened to him?"
>
> "He fell."
>
> "He fell where?"
>
> "He fell on the floor."
>
> "Hell, I fall on the floor about twice a day and I ain't dead."
>
> "That's what you think," Francis said. (20)

Reference

Kennedy, William. *Ironweed*, paperback ed. New York: Penguin, 1984.

Rattling Great Yarn

Quinn's Book

Fintan O'Toole

> Kennedy is one of the few writers who is both a serious novelist and a skilful yarn-spinner.
>
> —Fintan O'Toole

The American novelist William Kennedy is above all else a chronicler. In his trilogy of novels set in his native city of Albany, New York State, the best known of which, *Ironweed*, is now a film with Jack Nicholson and Meryl Streep in the leading roles, he uses Albany to tell the story of his times, the tide of history coursing through the veins of the most ignominious of people. Kennedy's power is not a provincial charm in the detailing of parochial eccentricities. He used Albany to give us a sense of the texture of history, how it is seen and felt in a real place, by real people. His new novel *Quinn's Book* shifts back in time, and in style, to the nineteenth century, but it remains very much a chronicle.

It is a mark of how sterile much modern fiction has become that phrases like "a rattling good yarn" have become shorthand for a bad book, useless clichés about useless fictions. Kennedy is one of the few writers who is both a serious novelist and a skilful yarn-spinner. *Quinn's Book* is as full of incident as a book by Dickens and it rattles along initially at a fearsome pace. In the first few chapters alone there are several major disasters—fires, floods, drowning—some remarkable couplings and a resurrection from the dead. If the rest of the novel doesn't quite live up to this opening, it still has maimings, riots, lynchings, bare-knuckle boxing, a horse race and a Civil War. Kennedy clearly is not afraid of action.

Quinn's Book begins as a formal chronicle—"I, Daniel Quinn, neither the first nor the last of a line of such Quinns, set eyes on Maud the wondrous on a late December day in 1849 on the banks of the river of aristocrats and paupers, just as . . ." (5)—and it retains its nature throughout. Its hero, Daniel Quinn, who begins as an Irish orphan working on a down-at-heel skiff on the Hudson River, becomes a journalist, a famous war correspondent, literally a chronicler of his times. And at the same time the book is full of formal, almost Biblical genealogies, of who begat whom and whom they in turn begot, except that in this case the Garden of Eden is replaced as a starting point with the arrival in America of the first family member, reminding us all the time that Kennedy is dealing with an unformed country, a country with a dramatically short history where nothing is yet fixed.

But within this formality, Kennedy sets out to appropriate to serious fiction much of what has been lost to popular genres. *Quinn's Book* takes its incidents and styles from all the popular forms:

> —penny dreadfuls (horrible, gory, murders);
>
> —Gothic novels (Hillegond's rambling mansion that becomes, for a time, Quinn's home);
>
> —romance fiction (Quinn rescues the wondrous Maud from drowning, falls immediately in love with her and pursues her through the rest of the book);
>
> —ghost stories (Maud's psychic powers);
>
> —*Boy's Own* stories (Dirck's secret alphabet, Quinn's buried treasure);
>
> —and journalism (a long description of a boxing match involving Quinn's erstwhile employer John the Brawn).

Together with letters, snatches of songs, descriptions of historical incidents, *Quinn's Book* becomes the kind of cacophony of competing stories, voices and genres that the postmodernist professors dream about.

It is Kennedy's genius that all of this bravura stylistic display, showing himself to be one of the finest literary ventriloquists since Joyce, is kept at the service of the story. Though the focus from 1849 to 1864 remains on the same surprisingly small group of characters, Kennedy's narrative sweep is epic. The lives of Quinn, Maud, Maud's aunt, the great courtesan Magdalena Colón, John the Brawn, and the black ex-slave Joshua (all except Joshua are Irish) are touched at every point by the forces of history. The struggle against slavery, the battles between the Famine Irish and the more established immigrants who saw them as cheap labour and unfair competition in the struggle for jobs, the rise of American capitalism, and, of course, the Civil War, are what give shape to the individual lives with which Kennedy is concerned. Through it all, Quinn, seemingly doomed to be forever a witness, struggles to become a protagonist.

What makes *Quinn's Book* such a joy to read is Kennedy's extraordinary vividness. As a writer, he doesn't so much use images as create them. Instead of using metaphors and similes to charge his language, he creates situations and incidents of such striking proportion that they become images. He doesn't need to use metaphors because the whole book is a metaphor—for the struggle with history, for the unknown that haunts us. Writers like Kennedy, and they are few indeed, give the art of yarn-spinning a good name again.

Reference

Kennedy, William. *Quinn's Book*, paperback ed. New York: Penguin, 1989.

This essay appeared in the Dublin *Sunday Tribune* on June 19, 1988. Reprinted by permission of Fintan O'Toole.

Family Values

William Kennedy's *Very Old Bones*

Thomas R. Edwards

> Our possible mutuality in sorrow, guilt, and loss, may be what measures the human worth of kinship, as this complex, eloquent, absorbing novel so powerfully suggests.
>
> —Thomas R. Edwards

In making the case for restoring "traditional family values," politicians imply that there have always been "traditional" families, which were beneficial to their members, and that their supposed disappearance has created much of the misery observable all around us. William Kennedy's *Very Old Bones* is a family novel that puts this rhetoric in its place. The fourth of Kennedy's Albany Cycle, it returns to the Phelan family of *Billy Phelan's Greatest Game* (1978) and *Ironweed* (1982). (The first book in the series, *Legs* [1975], does not have to do with the family.)

The Phelans came from Ireland in the 1820s to help dig the Erie Canal, work as lumbermen and railroaders, and gradually enter the lower middle class. In *Very Old Bones* Kennedy is concerned with the seven children born of the marriage of Michael Phelan and Kathryn McIlhenny in 1879, and that generation's own, less bounteous issue. In 1895, after siring his family and building the house on Colonie Street that some of the Phelans still inhabit in 1958, the year in which *Very Old Bones* purports to be written, Michael had died. Kathryn survived him for another four decades and brought up their children harshly and piously.

Of their daughters, Julia died young and single, Molly was married in her mid-forties and widowed two years after, and Sarah, a devout and tyrannical spinster, has kept house for her mother and siblings as her father had commanded her to before he died. Chick Phelan, a feckless linotypist who had failed at the priesthood and school teaching, left home in 1954 after a bitter quarrel with Sarah, married the woman he had desired but not slept with for seventeen years, and settled in Florida. Shortly later, Tommy, a mental defective, drowned at the water filtration plant where he worked.

The other two sons had talent. Francis, the oldest child and the tormented central character of *Ironweed*, fathered three children and killed one of them accidentally, played professional baseball (three years in the majors), and left home for good in 1916, to spend the rest of his life as a drifter and wino—"Artist of the open road. Hero of Whitmanesque America," as his brother Peter describes him with fond irony (118). Francis died during World War II, after his brief return to Albany and baseball, as a coach.

Peter, the second son, also ran away, in 1913, to become a painter. He had a long liaison with his landlady in Greenwich Village, who bore a son, though possibly not his son, in 1924. Peter began to make a small reputation as an artist in the late 1930s with his *Itinerant* series of paintings, inspired by his remorse and pity for Francis. In 1954, after Sarah's death, he returned home with his putative son, Orson Purcell, to take care of Molly and Tommy, and live rent-free. The novel, which takes in these events, is written as Orson Purcell's memoir of his family.

Orson Purcell's self-questionings are at the center of *Very Old Bones*. He is unsure of his parentage and his "credentials" as a Phelan; his life is shadowed by an episode of madness that he suffered during and just after his service in Germany during the Korean War. He is afraid of losing his attractive French wife, Giselle, a *Life* photographer who is often away on assignments; he yearns to be a writer, not just a manuscript-fixer for the publisher he works for. An accomplished card shark who dreams of an imaginative magic that could reveal some radical innocence within his fallen life, Orson writes this book in the hope of reconstructing and making endurable the sources of his being.

But Orson's firsthand experience of the Phelans is limited. In 1934, as a boy of ten, going with Peter to Albany for the funeral of Kathryn, he met for the first time Peter's siblings, including the long-lost Francis, for whom the reunion was almost fatal. Orson has seen the family occasionally during his college days in Albany, but he got to know them and their history closely only when Giselle took him to them in 1953 to recover from his second breakdown. Most of what he learns or imagines comes from the stories Molly then tells him and from witnessing the creation of Peter's *Malachi Suite*, pictures based on a long-forgotten family tragedy that bring Peter a major reputation and some money at last.

Orson is an outsider not just among the Phelans but within the fictional territory Kennedy's earlier novels claimed so impressively. The "Albany" of those books was a powerfully and closely detailed scene of provincial and ethnic American life during the 1920s and the Depression, and the solidity of their realistic materials tended to obscure the technical subtlety of their management. *Very Old Bones* seems at first to be almost all technique, sophisticated time-and-perspective games, and tricky, self-referring narrative.

Orson might seem, for example, an unlikely interpreter of Albany's "Broadway," the crossroads of local pols, bettors, tin-horn sports, gunmen, and ordinary barflies, a world of cunning, nerve, and blarney through which Orson's cousin Billy Phelan still moves hopefully in the late 1950s, when urban renewal is making it harder and harder to bet a horse, shoot some pool, find a comfortable saloon, or even get arrested. Broadway is "the playground of that part of the soul that is impervious to any form of improvement not associated with chance," and "playground" seems the right word here. Broadway affords habitués like Billy a free zone for masculine ego in a life otherwise dominated by do-gooders, priests, and female moralists. It bravely claims to know a fraudulent world for what it really is, as a saloon-keeper suggests when a Scout troop parades by on the Fourth of July; a stranger remarks: " 'What a fine bunch of boys,' " but "Sport took his cigar out of his mouth to offer his counterpoint: 'Another generation of stool pigeons,' he said" (36).

Yet free spirits like Billy, in his fifties an unemployable bachelor unable or afraid to marry his mistress of many years, are, as Orson can see, the victims of the stronger, if subtler, constraints of routine family loyalties and animosities, sexual repression and guilt, the general mutability of things to which illusions of personal freedom are particularly vulnerable. Francis, the athlete ruined by the independence his spirit and grace demand, and Tommy, the middle-aged moron who gets arrested for lifting a woman's skirt with his cane as he saw Chaplin do in the movies and is crippled by the beating Sarah gives him for it, show in their own ways the futility of hoping for autonomous satisfactions.

It may take an outsider to see such matters clearly, and the book's technical intricacies reflect Orson's learning—or inventing, who can say?—how a story, or history, can be assembled from the fragments of life and feeling that may be available. Early in the book Orson and Billy (his broken ankle in a cast) speak idly of some "elephant" bones recently unearthed near the filtration plant Tommy worked and died at; on Broadway Billy makes what Orson thinks a foolish bet that they are *not* elephant bones, despite their size and the tusks found with them. At the end Billy confesses that he had previously heard from one of the excavators that they were really the bones of a mastodon, "whatever the hell that is." In between these moments lies a variety of suggestions that Orson's memoir is a kind of archaeological dig, and not just metaphorically speaking. He learns, for one thing, that his Aunt Molly, whom he had known until then only as a warm and generous single woman, was married and widowed in the 1930s, that she experienced sexual delight as frank and intense as his own with Giselle, and that she secretly bore a stillborn child before her marriage, whom she named Walter and buried in the cellar of the family house.

Orson and Molly fall in love in a strong though hypothetical way, as surrogates for her dead husband and his absent wife; in a lovely scene, alone at a resort hotel on Saratoga Lake, they dance tenderly together to an old Ray Noble record of "When I Grow Too Old to Dream," just before she tells him of her dead baby. And just before the funeral of the grim and righteous Sarah, Orson agrees to dig up the child's remains and conceal them in Sarah's coffin, so that they may be buried in hallowed ground.

Bones are, of course, not just physical evidences of the past but relics of its spiritual and emotional content. Other, less literal relics of the past haunt the story: Giselle's photographs capturing key moments in Orson's own hard life; his discovery of the dead Tommy's "treasure," the underclothes he bought to give to women whose looks he liked; Molly's discovery of the scandalous old news stories Sarah had hidden, which inspire Peter's *Malachi* paintings; Molly's revelation of the hoard of gold pieces, given her by a bootlegger's widow, that has provided many of the family's little luxuries for three decades.

But the major trove, which Orson gradually uncovers and reveals to us, is the appalling story of Malachi McIlhenny, Kathryn Phelan's brother, a shanty Irishman who in 1887, crazed by drink, whoring, superstition, and his own general incapacity, tortured and burned to death his young wife Lizzie and buried her naked and mutilated body, in the conviction that she was a witch. Kathryn, then pregnant with Peter, was a helpless witness to this horror, which Peter has recreated with ugly meticulousness in his *Malachi Suite* paintings.

Art recreates the familial for the Phelans who survive. When Peter gathers them together at lunch in 1958, he gives them the money the *Malachi* paintings will bring him as well as the future proceeds of his other works. Seeing the pictures teaches them, if not exactly forgiveness, then at least some understanding and compassion for Kathryn, the frigid, repressive matriarch who has so awfully damaged her children. And Peter at last acknowledges Orson, familially and legally, as his "true and only son," to bear the Phelan name and bequeath it to the child that Giselle is now carrying, whose paternity Orson himself has had some doubts about.

But if Peter has turned history into art, the "truth" of any history is undeterminable, as Orson's assemblage of the past has continually had to acknowledge. Only in the imagination, perhaps, do biological and emotional relations become fully a family, at best an ambiguous entity with no promise of permanence. Near the end (if 1958 can seem an "end" in 1992) Orson, contemplating his uncertain future with the elusive and perhaps opportunistic Giselle, grants that she at least "was responsible for my being here . . . and therefore obliquely responsible as well for this day of reunification, this time of our dawning into unity (as Keats put it), if indeed it was unity, if indeed it was dawning" (283). To imagine the Phelans as a family is to come close to the madness that has dogged his life—his vision of them as members of one body is as a grotesque "skeleton that would have Lizzie's ribs and fingers, Tommy's chipped backbone, Francis's all-but-gangrenous leg with the bone showing, Billy's broken ankle, Sarah's near-fleshless arms with bones pushing through skin and with tubes dangling, Peter's arthritic hips, Walter Phelan's partial skull" (291). Not the wholesome family values invoked by politicians, but our possible mutuality in sorrow, guilt, and loss, may be what measures the human worth of kinship, as this complex, eloquent, absorbing novel so powerfully suggests.

Reference

Kennedy, William. *Very Old Bones*. New York: Viking, 1992.

This essay originally appeared in *The New York Review of Books* on August 13, 1992. Reprinted by permission of the author's estate.

Bootlegger of the Soul

An Introduction to *Roscoe*

Colum McCann

> . . . while his work is aligned with Albany, he, like all serious writers, is really examining the territory of the mind and the heart, what happens to them when they are hung out there in the harshest human weather.
>
> —Colum McCann

William Kennedy's cycle of Albany novels may be one of the most exuberant literary feats of the past half-century. When he first wrote *Legs* in 1975, Kennedy didn't set out to create a themed cycle. That degree of consciousness might well have brought a numbing familiarity or an ease to the work. Instead the novels feel as if they have grown out of a fluid imaginative necessity—he is a writer working at the coalface of language, examining the present by delving into the past. Over the last four decades the Albany stories have begun to weave and interweave so that they, in Kennedy's words, have become an "open-ended set of non-sequential tales." Be thankful for them. They show us who we are.

Stepping into a Kennedy novel is like stepping into all available art forms. He's a historian, a journalist, a critic, an essayist, a poet, a philosopher, a playwright. He consistently seeks the edge of his art. He is one of the great verbal cinematographers of our times. He captures light, transforms it, guides it forward, shifts it around, and burns it down onto the page.

And while his work is aligned with Albany, he, like all serious writers, is really examining the territory of the mind and the heart, what happens to them when they are hung out there in the harshest human weather.

One story is all stories. Sooner or later we're all going to end up on the corner of State and Pearl. Take a jaunt down the street and you might end up in Yoknapatawpha County. Turn left and there's Eccles Street. Pop down the alleyway and you might be in Macondo. Kennedy's work has earned him a rightful place alongside Faulkner, Joyce, and Márquez. In terms of contemporary American writers his reputation sits comfortably alongside those of Roth, Morrison, DeLillo, and Doctorow.

Roscoe was published first in 2002, the seventh novel in Kennedy's Albany oeuvre. He has always demanded as much from his novels as they can give, and all of Kennedy's strengths are on display here.

It is 1945. The war is over. Roscoe is overpaid, overweight, oversexed, and over here. He is "a bootlegger of the soul, a mythic creature made of words and wit and wild deeds and boundless memory" (71). As a fixer within the Democratic Party, he spends his days at Keeler's and the Ten Eyck. He is contemplating getting out of the game, but finds himself drawn into the election, a paternity suit, a brace of feuding brothers, and a widening spiral of memory and desire. A new wave of the American "morality plague" is resurgent, and Roscoe's soul, though he himself does not yet know it, has been getting him ready for an encounter with death.

Still, life and all its vulgar vagaries won't let him go. Neither will the police, the politicians, the porkheads, the prostitutes, the pool sharks, or the poker parlor Petes.

Roscoe is large in every sense of the word: verbally exuberant and imaginatively hyperactive. He is a man of immense spirit, "a man of loss." Kennedy invents out of a confluence of known facts and fictions plucked from his wonderfully promiscuous imagination. There's the raunchy aside, the serious set piece, the scrupulous accuracy, the linguistic flourishes, the pertinent questioning. One of Kennedy's projects is to identify just exactly where fiction shapes itself into the world of fact. Facts are mercenary. They can be shipped off to wherever you want. Fiction—or texture—is far more honest. "Truth is in the details," says Roscoe, "even when you invent the details" (250). He believes that "fraudulence is the necessary modality for human existence" (221). And he allows for all realities, "including those that do not exist" (275).

For Roscoe, "it's a short walk from politics to hell" (14). He lives in a world of extortion and subordination. American novels about politics are relatively rare to begin with, but *Roscoe* goes to the heart of the matter. It could very well apply to the elections of the 1970s or indeed the high jinks of 2012. It's a terrifying landscape for a literary writer to enter, but there is an intense political savvy here.

And where there's politics, there's sex. At fifty-five years of age, Roscoe's libido still clouds his good senses. Kennedy writes about sex, "the sweetest of pressures," just about as brilliantly as anyone.

As the novel progresses we begin to recognize that Kennedy is a literary gambler, a crapshooter, a card shark. He likes the risk. He does nothing to avoid it. A sentence often stays up in the air way longer than it should. A word has the weight of a stone in his hands. A vowel has colour. There is the daring of the high-wire artist about him. Kennedy knows that if you fall you most likely won't fall halfway. In one of the novel's finest literary set pieces you can feel Kennedy truly enjoying himself. A cockfight becomes a lesson in blood and brotherhood:

> His neck will swell with blood and he'll be cyanotic, presumed dead. The savvy handler will quickly massage the blood out of his neck in the ring and revive him before he goes into irreversible shock, then will do it again at the first-aid bench, and the bird will recover, but now be known as a loser. Take him off the coumadin and fight him again, with long odds against him now as the loser; but this time he'll be wearing proper-length spurs to kill, he will have fought and lived, and he will think with the serrated edge of a survivor. (103)

The serrated edge of a survivor indeed. It's a line that could apply to Kennedy's career. He has always been there, ready to lift the skin raw.

In 1989 Kennedy told an interviewer, "I don't think there's any rule that you can't supersede your own early work. . . . I am fond of insisting that I'm not in decline, that the next book is going to be better than the last. It may or may not be, but I have no doubt I know more about how to write a novel, more about what it means to be alive, than I ever have."* In *Roscoe*, which he wrote in his early seventies, Kennedy shows a novelist still at the height of his imaginative powers.

But perhaps Kennedy's greatest gift is his sheer decency and humility. He finds grace in the enormous human mess. He is a writer of deep empathy and soul. He is well aware that we must endure this earth because we just don't have another one. His characters are spectacles of honest dilemma. He gets in under their skin. Nobody gets off scot-free. Even the bums on the street are a collision of complications. It's not a very fashionable term to bring up here in the front end of the twenty-first century, but Kennedy's work is deeply *moral*. His words have weight. He is not afraid of the big emotion. Our lives matter. So too do our deaths. He believes in redemption, even if we have to crawl down into the gutter to find it. He is emphatic that, even despite the evidence,

* Editors' Note: From William Kennedy, "The Art of Fiction No. 111," interviewed by Douglas R. Allen and Mona Simpson, *Paris Review* 112 (Winter 1989).

we cannot afford to give up our delight in the world. He gets at the old verities and truths of the heart, without which, as Faulkner said, any story is ephemeral and doomed: "love and honour and pity and pride and compassion and sacrifice."

As Roscoe himself suggests at the end of his novel: love or death, it doesn't matter, either way he could use a little music. In William Kennedy's hands, it's symphonic.

References

Kennedy, William. "The Art of Fiction No. 111." Interviewed by Douglas R. Allen and Mona Simpson. *Paris Review* 112 (Winter 1989): https://www.theparisreview.org/interviews/2391/william-kennedy-the-art-of-fiction-no-111-william-kennedy

———. *Roscoe*. New York: Viking, 2002.

This essay originally appeared as the foreword to the London edition of *Roscoe*, republished in paperback in 2012.

O Albany!

Roscoe and the Triumph of Kennedy's Albany Cycle

Thomas Flanagan

Kennedy's deepest allegiance is to language, and in return it lets him say just about whatever he wants to say.

—Thomas Flanagan

THE ALBANY CYCLE

Roscoe is the seventh in William Kennedy's cycle of Albany novels, which began with *Legs* in 1975. This was followed by *Billy Phelan's Greatest Game* in 1978, and *Ironweed* in 1983. They were spoken of then as a trilogy, partly because they shared a setting and some characters and partly because the third of them, a harrowing narrative of pain and a possible redemption, seemed to bring certain shared themes to resolution.

But then came *Quinn's Book* in 1988, which reaches out from Albany to an impressionistic nineteenth-century America, a land of slavery and warfare and haunted rivers. There followed *Very Old Bones* in 1992 and *The Flaming Corsage* in 1996, set solidly in Albany, but bearing down not on the public scene but on erotic and creative energies within highly untypical (I trust) families in the city's Irish Catholic community. Now, with *Roscoe*, he returns to the larger city, a model, so he has persuaded us, of urban corruption.

Taken together, the cycle, which surely has not ended here, is one of the triumphs of recent fiction, uneven but audacious in its ambition and dazzling in its technical resources. Two Albanys exist within its pages, superimposed upon each other. The "actual" Albany is a middle-sized state capital on the Hudson River, with a patrician Dutch past. In the nineteenth century it glowed with the oyster-and-beefsteak opulence of the Gilded Age, its restaurants and music halls resting upon the shoulders of an exploited and chiefly Irish immigrant population. By the new century, though, it had become complacent, unguarded, and after World War I it came under the control of an Irish political machine almost comic in its organizational thoroughness. In the 1920s, it was in competition with the downstate gangsters who ran the distribution and sale of bootleg liquor, the Legs Diamonds and Dutch Schultzes who had moved northward from Manhattan.

Bookie operations, prostitution, poker parlors existed at the pleasure of the machine, whose decisions were enforced by the police. In this, Albany was probably no worse than Trenton or Philadelphia, and may even have been a bit better than Kansas City, but those cities have lacked chroniclers with Kennedy's voracious appetite for fact and local mythology, his journalist's strong net for detail. Like Crane and Hemingway, he is both reporter and artist, one of the central defining traditions of American fiction.

The Albany of his novels, though, is not one of those great cities that have given modern literature its characterizing images, not the London of Dickens and Eliot, nor the Dublin of Joyce nor the Chicago of Dreiser and Bellow. It does not resemble the cameos carved by Runyon and Chandler out of New York and Los Angeles. These cities, in art as in life, overwhelm by their immensity, their unknowability. In Kennedy's Albany, everyone knows everyone else, even if they do not know themselves. They have been cheating and screwing one another for decades, one way or another. They know each other's bloodlines, alliances, vices, secret lyricisms, schemes for survival or success. The bosses and their lieutenants and goons know what buttons to press, what feudal loyalties to exploit. Ordinary people, the poor and the obscure and the homeless, can make themselves useful stuffing ballot boxes, or, like Francis Phelan of *Ironweed*, voting early and often. Their masters use power and triumph as counters to buy the best food and the gaudiest women. But they also cherish power for what in itself it is, a mysterious, self-justifying energy and delight.

Kennedy creates this setting with scrupulous accuracy, a Joycean reverence for street names, urban legends. It is quite possible that his knowledge of Albany's geography, its nooks and crannies and their histories, is wider than Joyce's knowledge of Dublin. It is displayed with flourishes not only in the novels but in *O Albany!*, the combined history, street guide, and memoir that he published in 1983, and which is based on wide reading, a childhood and youth lived there, and long experience as a reporter at the *Times Union*. He speaks of himself, in the preface to that book, as "a person whose imagination has become fused with a single place, and in that place finds all the elements that a man ever needs for the life of the soul" (3). He is not quite Dante, and Albany is not quite Florence, but the principle is the same.

It is a city not without its detractors. "Misery, wretchedness, ennui, and the devil," the architect H. H. Richardson wrote in 1870, "I've got to spend another evening in Albany."* And Kennedy himself calls it "a pinnacle of pork-head bossism, Wasp and Irish" (3). But is quick to add that he is fond of things "beyond the city's iniquity. I love its times of grace and greatness, its political secrets and its historical presence in every facet of the nation's life, including the unutterable, the unspeakable, and the ineffable" (4).

Like Joyce, he employs his surface of precise naturalistic detail to move beyond it, to hint at shapes, destinies, states of being that are alien to naturalism if not hostile to it. His Albany of gravy-logged meals at Keeler's and Bruegelesque hijinks in the whorehouses is also a city of spiritual mysteries and metaphysical illusions. The barrier between death and life is thin and permeable. *Roscoe* is restrained in this regard: on occasion, Roscoe's dead father sits in his familiar chair in the lobby of the Ten Eyck, and long-dead wraiths cling to a mountain resort. He creates his two Albanys and thrusts them against each other, balancing them with a zest that is out of fashion these days.

Kennedy plays for high stakes. *Ironweed*, a harrowing presentation of life in the hobo jungles and freight cars of the derelict, is at the same time an exploration of guilt and the tangles of loyalty, told entirely without condescension toward its battered characters. In *The Flaming Corsage*, a range of literary modes—prose narrative, drama, journalism, workbooks—disputes the meaning of the story's "facts." Its subjects are as extreme as its methods—lust, incest, paternity, sexual exploration. In that novel, he may have demanded more from fiction than the form can accommodate.

Like Joyce, Kennedy emerged from an Irish Catholic background and education with a skeptical, modern-day intellect and a strong residual sense of miracle, mystery, magic. And the social world that he creates is almost entirely Irish American; that is to say, Catholic with trimmings of clan loyalty, deep-banked feelings of caste hostility unassuaged by good meals in the best restaurants. The most attractive of the novel's political figures, Elisha Fitzgibbon (clearly based on the "real-life" Erastus Corning), is a Protestant, but we do not enter his world. Otherwise, Protestants, rarely glimpsed, are like unicorns, comely, but delicate of bone.**

In the world of the novels, as in much of America in those years, religion set people apart from one another to an extent that is likely now to seem

* Editors' Note: This sentiment was actually expressed by architect Stanford White. Kennedy corrected the attribution in *O Albany!* in subsequent editions.

** Editors' Note: Kennedy clarifies that the Elisha Fitzgibbon character was somewhat of an invention, but part of him was based on Edwin Corning, the "real-life" Erastus's father, who ran a steel mill and was a founder of the Democratic political machine, like Elisha.

improbable. Not a hostile separation much of the time, but severe, weighable. Kennedy's world is that of the Knights of Columbus, the Legion of Decency, Father Coughlin's broadcasts from the Shrine of the Little Flower, parochial grade schools and high schools, and, beyond that for the lucky ones, colleges maintained by the Christian Brothers and the Jesuits.

Things were different for me, growing up in Greenwich, Connecticut. Kennedy has described Scott Fitzgerald as the first Irish yuppie, and like John O'Hara I was following in his footsteps. By the time I was moving through the public high school, the very name of Father Coughlin's shrine evoked sickeningly the odor of Easter lilies and candle wax which I remembered (still remember!) from my days as an altar boy. Soon I would be off to my minor Ivy League college in Massachusetts, where I would join my peers in denouncing Boston's Irish boss, James Curley, whose counterpart in Albany was Dan O'Connell, Kennedy's Patsy McCall.

Kennedy takes a far more complex view of that world than I did in those years, though, a view touched with ethnic loyalty and affection, while he does not fail to dramatize the brutality and hypocrisy on which the political machine rested or the parochial narrowness that it expressed. But then back in those years, as he tells us in *O Albany!*, he had believed that "the enemies of the world then were the goddamn Irish-Catholic Albany Democrats" (39). He was detained though, as I eventually would be, by "the Irishness, which was the only element of my history that wasn't organized, the only one I couldn't resign from, and, further, the only one that hadn't been shoved down my throat" (39). Me too. In *Quinn's Book*, his foundation myth of the nineteenth century, young Daniel Quinn carries with him from famine-ridden Ireland a grime- and dirt-encrusted plate said to possess magical powers, and which when scraped down and cleaned proves to be an antique Celtic disc, its power enigmatic and undeniable.

The more immediate foundation myth, its power pervading all of the novels, is the use by the political boss Patsy McCall of the assessor's office in 1919 to pry open the oyster of Albany's political power. From that all else flowed. By the end of the 1920s, the Irish were in full possession, Patsy controlling the patronage and his brother Bindy controlling Nighttown, which meant the speakeasies, the poker parlors, the whorehouses, the police. This night world is most vividly and thickly present for us in *Billy Phelan's Greatest Game*, a world in which Billy moves as a skillful denizen, not of champion class, but able to make a living at poker, billiards, keeping a small book. But when the McCalls put out the word, he is cut off from that world as absolutely as if he had been exiled to Alaska, unable to buy a drink, place a bet. And he knows better than to challenge his fate.

In that novel, as in *Ironweed*, the novel about Billy's father, Kennedy displays a truly impressive ability to write on a level with his characters, to share the way in which Billy, a gambler on the margins, thinks and moves, but he is equally resourceful when it comes to portraying the world of Billy's masters, the masters of city life who pull the strings and jerk the puppets. Kennedy has no master when it comes to the juicy and horrifying story of city and state politics.

Politics is present in all the novels, but it holds center stage in *Legs* and *Billy Phelan's Greatest Game*, and now in *Roscoe*. It is 1945, and the machine is still in power, with the same bosses and the same henchmen carrying out their dark instructions. Times change, though, and as the novel suggests by indirection, it will soon be time for the machine to be taken over by young lions back from Normandy and the Pacific. Not better men, so the novel hints; indeed a bit more sinister perhaps, but different in style.

Roscoe Conway, the machine's chief fixer, is already ready to step aside. He is painfully aware that he is overweight, overeducated for the slippery skills he has perfected, and, for a man in his mid-fifties, oversexed. He spends his days at party headquarters, sweeping rolls of tribute money into a desk drawer, dining on oysters and Chablis at Keeler's or the Ten Eyck, and polishing the curious prose in which his perceptions are expressed, a kind of Henry Adams gravitas jazzed up with a hail-fellow breeziness. "Righteousness doesn't stand a chance against the imagination" (227). Lately, though, these and other pleasures have begun to lose their savor. Roscoe's soul, though he himself does not yet know it, has been preparing him for death.

In *Legs* there is a rough sketch of what Roscoe may have been like as a young man. Marcus Gorman, the narrator, might have had a bright political future, but threw it away to become the upstate attorney for Jack "Legs" Diamond, the notorious bootlegger and gangland killer. Gorman is a student of Rabelais and a knockout speaker at Knights of Columbus communion breakfasts. For him too, as for the aging Roscoe, if for different reasons, life has something lacking, some essential cocktail sauce of danger. Diamond supplies it, for reasons made clear to us by the story, "pieced painfully together from Joe, Jack, and a half-dozen others," of how Jack Diamond had dealt with a couple of noisy troublemakers at Manhattan's Hotsy Totsy Club one night in 1929, after the fights:

> Standing then, Jack fired into Tim's forehead. The head gave a sudden twist and Jack fired two more bullets into it. He fired his last two shots into Tim's groin, pulling the trigger three times on empty chambers. Then he stood looking down at Tim Reagan.

> Billy opened his eyes to see his bleeding brother beside him on the floor. Billy shook Tim's arm and grunted "Timbo," but his brother stayed limp. Jack cracked Billy on the head with the butt of his empty pistol and Billy went flat.
>
> "Let's go, Jack, let's move," Charlie Filetti said.
>
> Jack looked up and saw Elaine's terrified face peering at him from the checkroom. The bartenders' faces were as white as their aprons. All faces looked at Jack as Filetti grabbed his arm and pulled. Jack tossed his pistol onto Billy's chest and it bounced off onto the floor. (*Legs* 28)

A fine piece of Hammett pastiche, but the credit goes not to Kennedy but to Gorman, our narrator. It is Gorman who has pulled the facts painfully together and shaped them into a narrative, which impresses us with its studied lack of affect. Like much hard-boiled prose, though, it is really not neutral but expresses a covert admiration. "Tossed," for example, would not be the word chosen by Joe Vignola, who is one of the Hotsy Totsy witnesses. Rather, it expresses Gorman's sense of a man who can kill in blind fury and then not give a damn. Dumbfounding, but rather stylish.

Poor Joe, a family man with children, winds up in the Tombs prison, a material witness. At night he begins to see Jack Diamond, disguised as a Boy Scout, coming through the bars of the cell window, sometimes accompanied by another underworld figure, Herman Zuckman. "The night the dead fish jumped out of Herman's tuxedo Joe finally won his straitjacket" (66). For Joe, Legs was now a figure out of legend, out of nightmare, and Gorman sees the comedy of telling it to us this way. And so, God help us, do we.

Jack Diamond was a real person, of course, a tough kid out of Philadelphia who had somehow acquired the nickname Legs, although never called that by his friends, but only by the tabloids and the columnists and eventually by the general public. He got very famous very fast, a hijacker of trucks and distilleries, ready to use torture and to leave henchmen in the lurch, a dispenser of random, casual favors, and brutalities. He worked with the most powerful of the New York bosses, Owney Madden and Arnold Rothstein, and at the time of his death was in a volatile competition with Dutch Schultz and Lucky Luciano. Luciano did not share Jack's love of the limelight, which allowed him to live into old age. He was a creature of the 1930s and 1940s.

Crime and celebrity fed upon each other in the 1920s. Their common theater was nightclubs like the Hotsy Totsy, all of them mob-owned and peopled by the types that form our cultural memory of the decade—reporters and racketeers, show people, chorus girls, shysters, boys down from Harvard and Princeton, enforcers. Every reader of Winchell knew that Diamond's wife was named Alice and that his latest girlfriend was Kiki Roberts, a showgirl with the tawdry good looks then in vogue. The posters for the movie *The Public Enemy*, which opened shortly before Diamond was suddenly killed in 1931, hinted at the resemblance between the Jimmy Cagney character and a certain celebrated desperado. Cagney played a highly specific type—violent, trigger-tempered, impudent, swaggering, with the charm and magic of a young roughneck on the way to riches but not breaking into a sweat about it. And very Irish. Diamond too had a certain charm and also good looks, especially when the competition was Dutch Schultz and a psychopath named Mad Dog Coll. Not even Jimmy could boast of having limped away from four murder attempts. But Legs, like the Cagney character, was doomed to die young: everyone knew that. Unless, of course, he was immortal.

This was also the celebrity decade in the world of letters, stars of the columns and the rotogravure, Hemingway and Fitzgerald. Fitzgerald met Arnold Rothstein and used him as the model for Meyer Wolfsheim in *The Great Gatsby*, the man with cufflinks made of human molars. The brilliant economy with which he creates Wolfsheim is made possible because everyone had heard about bosses like Rothstein.

Critics have seen a resemblance between the two narrators, Nick Carraway and Marcus Gorman, but as Kennedy himself has remarked, Nick, like his creator, is too much the yuppie. At critical moments he breaks into purest yuppiespeak. "Gatsby, who represented everything for which I have an unaffected scorn," nevertheless "turned out all right at the end." (2) There is, though, a more profound difference between the two characters. For Gorman the foul dust that trails in Diamond's wake is part of his glamour—the violence, the swift rages, even the vulgarity. They beckon Gorman toward his exciting new life. Like Jack Burden, the narrator of *All the King's Men*, he shares his leader's corruption.

On Gorman's first visit to Diamond's Catskill hideout, Legs and Alice offer a trial of a new machine gun, their equivalent, perhaps, of a fast set of tennis. "I smiled at Alice to imply I was her friend, and Jack's too. And I was then, yes I was. I was intuitively in sympathy with this man and woman who had just introduced me to the rattling, stammering splatter of violent death. Gee, ain't it swell?" (41). He's a goner. Like every true New Yorker, though, he uses slang and self-mockery to let us know he realizes what is happening to him.

Diamond spent his final months in Albany. On the night of December 18, 1931, after celebrating a courtroom victory that Gorman had won for him, he was shot to death, alone, in a back-street rooming house. "Who shot Legs Diamond?" is still a lively subject of discussion in Albany's better bars, or so Kennedy assures us. With *Legs*, he himself had made certain that this would be the case. But the novel asks a second question, which holds more interest for Gorman and for Kennedy. Diamond, Gorman tells us, has passed from life into legend and from legend into myth. And as myth, he has been granted immortality, hasn't he?

Parts of the Legs Diamond legend had begun to accumulate even while Jack was alive. He was aware of the process and tickled by it, if puzzled. Birds fall silent at his approach, it was said, and the story goes that he could tie both his shoes at once. Years after his death, an old whore swears that he could turn on the lights by snapping his fingers. Gorman has an explanation out of popular science for that one, as Leopold Bloom would. "Jack had a luminous quality at certain moments, when he stood in shadow" (105). The luminosity is pure energy.

One time the tabloid headlines had read: "Jack Diamond Shot Five Times by Gunmen in 64th Street Hotel." Lew Edwards the impresario visits him in the hospital and promises him a publicity campaign that could make him the biggest thing since Billy Sunday and Aimee Semple McPherson, with the help of speech coaches. He could found a new religion. Only in America. The reader remembers that in the same years, Zelda Fitzgerald was telling friends that Al Jolson was greater than Jesus. She may have been onto something. The transformation of celebrity into legend into myth in specifically American terms is the real subject of *Legs*. The final, surreal image is a bit like the Ascension in a Renaissance painting, Gorman and Arnold Rothstein helping Jack out of his body through his bullet-shattered skull. " 'Honest to God, Marcus,' he said going away, 'I really don't think I'm dead' " (317).

ROSCOE

Jack Diamond makes his final appearance in *Roscoe* in one of its flashback chapters. The real Legs, out of luck and out of money, unprotected by goons or crooked cops, is sitting in his underwear on the side of his bed, pleading for his life. His killers, of course, are the cops themselves, O.B. and Mac. O.B., the chief of police, is Roscoe Conway's compliant brother, and Mac is a thick-witted brute. Jack's fate, though, had been decided at the highest Albany level.

In the spring of the year, Governor Franklin Roosevelt was preparing his run for the White House, and people like Legs Diamond operating on his doorstep did not look good, especially now that Legs had added kidnapping and torture to his repertoire. Roosevelt sent his troopers over to "rupture Jack's empire up the middle and sideways." Jack, though, had never been one to listen to reason, and instead he proposed to Roscoe, the machine fixer, a scheme to make Albany his headquarters in exchange for cheap beer. Roscoe agreed to pass the question along to Patsy and Bindy McCall, out of politeness, but he never doubted their reaction. Diamond, Coll, and Schultz had been leaving corpses all over Manhattan in the beer wars, and newsmen reckoned that Diamond was ahead in the corpse count. "Did Albany need beer that came in coffins?" Patsy's response was mild, as words go: "That fella's going to be a serious nuisance if they don't put him in jail" (161).

"Roscoe *at that moment*" (161), so the narrative tells us, making a rare use of italics, became the outsider in future Jack talk: Patsy trusting him like nobody else apart from certain cosmic decisions. You run the party, Roscoe, I'll run the Nighttown—as if they could be separated. But Patsy believed in separate realms of power, pitted even his closest allies against one another when it suited him. Like pitting chickens. Competitive truculence. See who survives.

But of course Roscoe understands Patsy's decision as clearly as his murderous knights understood the words with which Henry II ordered the death of Becket. "Probably we'll never know the truth," the narrator tells us. "So many out there who wanted vengeance on the man. Whoever did it, give him a medal, one cop said" (163). Kennedy's use of third-person narrative in *Roscoe* is deliberately disingenuous. At times it seems to be recording Roscoe's thoughts—shrewd, artful, cynical, yet often and fundamentally large-minded and chivalrous, especially in matters of the heart. But at other times, as here, it is the wised-up voice of wised-up Albany itself talking *at that moment* off the record. Kennedy's deepest allegiance is to language, and in return it lets him say just about whatever he wants to say.

It may be that Kennedy takes it a bit too easy on Roscoe in this account of his twilight years, giving him as problems to solve the suicide of his aristocratic friend Elisha Fitzgibbon, his unconsummated love for Elisha's wife, and a deadly feud between the chief bosses of the city, Patsy and Bindy McCall, a feud over their fighting chickens. The first and third of these problems seem unworthy of the worldly wisdom and skill with which we are asked to credit him. These are tasks better left to Scattergood Baines in the old *Saturday Evening Post* stories or David Harum in the old Will Rogers movie. But theirs, come to think of it, is the world in which Roscoe has grown up and which one day soon, rueful and reflective, he will join.

The plot earns its keep though. Kennedy has never written a more vivid and sanguinary chapter than his description of a cockfight at a pit in neighboring South Troy, "in the opinion of cockers east and west, north and south, the most famous cockpit in the Northeast, maybe in all of America" (103). That chapter captures it all—the birds themselves, their owners and handlers, the circular dirt pit with its three-foot-high canvas wall, the surrounding crowd of gamblers and lovers of bloody murder. Here is Kennedy describing how to rig a fight with the help of a little anticoagulant:

> His neck will swell with blood and he'll be cyanotic, presumed dead. The savvy handler will quickly massage the blood out of his neck in the ring and revive him before he goes into irreversible shock, then will do it again at the first-aid bench, and the bird will recover, but now be known as a loser. Take him off the coumadin and fight him again, with long odds against him now as the loser; but this time he'll be wearing proper-length spurs to kill, he will have fought and lived, and he will think with the serrated edge of a survivor. (103)

"To Roscoe," we are told by that eerie, unstable (to use a word in vogue) narrative voice,

> . . . spectating at cockfights was a lifelong education in tension, cowardice, unpredictable reversals, and courage. The birds, bred for battle, fought for neither God nor glory, neither to eat nor for love. They fought to conquer the other, to impose death before it was imposed. Just like politics, Roscoe decided, but without the blood. Well, sometimes there's blood. (101–102)

Ask Legs. *Neither to eat nor for love*. Now the unstable voice can quote Shakespeare, as Roscoe can. Whose voice it is now is beyond me.

The richest sections of *Roscoe* are the ones that move backward in time to the machine's seizure of power and to its full, flowering existence ten years later, when the book deals with Jack Diamond. But that story pauses with a shadow of the future on it, with the Democratic gubernatorial convention in the autumn of 1932. It is then that the boys learn that Jimmy Walker, the pride of Tammany Hall and the Albany machine, will be thrown to the wolves by FDR and Al Smith himself, the prince of Irish Catholic pols, himself denied the presidency in 1928 by a nation of Protestant bigots. Not only that, but FDR and Smith, unlikely allies, are throwing the governorship not to Elisha Fitzgibbon but to Herbert Lehmann, partly for political reasons and partly because the country is experiencing one of its recurring morality epidemics, as Roscoe calls them. Roscoe has consoling words for Patsy. "Pat, we are Democrats, remember? And we are steeped in Democracy. We own the city, the county, the state, and the nation. Things could be worse" (242).

Kennedy's art is an eccentric triumph, a quirky, risk-taking imagination at play upon the solid paving stones, the breweries, the politicos, and pool sharks of an all-too-actual city. The collisions of setting and stance, if nothing more, bring Yoknapatawpha County to mind, despite the vast distances, geographical and cultural, which separate the Mississippi and the Hudson. But Faulkner and Kennedy also share old-fashioned themes like honor, betrayal, the foreverness of the past.

References

Fitzgerald, F. Scott. *The Great Gatsby.* New York: Scribner, 2004.

Kennedy, William. *Legs.* New York: Penguin, 1983.

———. *O Albany! Improbable City of Political Wizards, Fearless Ethnics, Spectacular Aristocrats, Splendid Nobodies, and Underrated Scoundrels.* New York: Penguin, 1985.

———. *Roscoe.* New York: Viking, 2002.

This essay first appeared in *The New York Review of Books* on April 25, 2002. This is the last essay Thomas Flanagan wrote before he died on March 21, 2002. Reprinted by permission of the author's estate.

World Premiere of *Roscoe*

American Opera at Its Finest

Anthony P. Radford

> Good American opera should have a good story and here *Roscoe* delivers.
> —Anthony P. Radford

American opera came with the European settlers and was a transplanted art form until the beginning of the twentieth century. It was then that a new art emerged that could be called distinctly American. That was one hundred years ago, so one could really say that American opera is entering its second century. Today, opera's cousin musical theater draws more audiences, has a larger budget and better production values in the U.S., so it is no wonder that opera would like to match that relative success in its second century. My summer has been, quite accidentally, an examination of American opera during which I have asked, Where is American opera heading in this century? Is opera a relevant creative force able to tell and sound like an American story?

There are a few items on my checklist for whether an opera is creatively interesting and relevant. First, it has to have a good story—and that story should be uniquely American. Second, it should incorporate the sounds of American music and dance. Third, it should involve young American talent: Americans telling our story. Disclaimer and perhaps a buzzkill for the patriots: I am Canadian, but I know a good American opera when I see one.

I saw an opera last weekend in the Adirondacks of upstate New York at the Seagle Music Colony that I think should be considered the model of what a good American opera is in the twenty-first century. Seagle is a venerable festival and training program for young singers tucked in the mountains and woods with the rustic feel of a visit to your friend's cottage. Artistic Director

Darren K. Woods assembles a cast of thirty-two singers to perform four shows over a summer season that spans July and August. This season offered something for everyone, including the world premiere of a new American opera entitled *Roscoe*, by composer Evan Mack and librettist Joshua McGuire. This particular performance was the Saturday night finale of a four-show run, and a good word had obviously spread as this performance was packed to the rafters (literally) with audience members.

Good American opera should have a good story and here *Roscoe* delivers. *Roscoe* is an opera adapted from a novel of the same name by Albany writer and Pulitzer Prize–winning author William Kennedy. Roscoe Conway is a political operative in the Albany Democratic Party and in 1945 is fifty-five years old and wants out of politics. The voices of his past, his father Felix, and his recently deceased best friend Elisha are constantly with him as he tries to sort out a messy child custody battle between his ex-wife Pamela and her sister and Elisha's widow, Veronica, all the while trying to fix the mayoral race for Elisha's young, up-and-coming son Alex. We come to find that the now twelve-year-old child Gilby is the biological son of Alex and Roscoe's ex-wife, a scandal that could end Alex's political career as mayor. This all plays as backdrop to what is essentially a love story between Veronica and Roscoe, having been young lovers some thirty years ago. Now in middle age their love has become a simmering lust for each other. McGuire was more than up to the challenges of this plot, having adapted the novel *Secret of Luca* in his first collaboration with Mack. In *Roscoe*, McGuire expertly took on the added challenge of working with an author who is still very much alive and interested in his art. There was an element to McGuire's challenge here that was not unusual for a librettist—how to take a complicated novel and boil it down to its essential pieces so it fits into a comfy libretto, so that it sings, and makes sense on stage. What he did so well was to capture Kennedy's unique style of making the past mix with the present. For example, Roscoe finds his friend Elisha dead, but Elisha immediately starts talking to him.

Good American opera should be well composed and use not only the traditional models of aria and recitative but search out new ways of expression in song and even dialogue. Evan Mack's composition shows great skill in assembling sounds and writing for singers. He also displays a natural sense in the tradition of Mozart, always knowing where the actor is on stage, staging the opera from the score. He never falls into that pitfall of writing "too many notes" (as Emperor Joseph famously and wrongly accused Mozart's *Marriage of Figaro* of harboring) thus leaving the actor hanging in a time-hole-of-acting nightmare situation. The opera is full of the sounds of the first half of the twentieth century and it uses arias, but also has stand-alone songs, duets, and ensemble pieces. This variety in sound and structure helped to orient the audience, essentially helping us to find where they were in Roscoe's memory from the late-nineteenth-century patter of Gilbert and Sullivan to the dance halls of the Roaring Twenties or the post-war Big Band era. Mack's score also featured jazz and scat, and although his day job is as an academic, he doesn't write in the overly complicated style of today's composer-academics. His thoughts are always on melody, and if he likes it he writes it, and in all cases we the audience like it too and actually appreciate a composer who allows us to enjoy his work. I would be remiss not to mention that Mack's *Roscoe* is scored for two pianos and percussion. This "all percussion" pit provided a cornucopia of sound and was meticulously fashioned by the composer who, rather than meeting outlines and dividing them between pianos, actually composed separate piano parts for the first and second pianos. It was a fantastic musical display that was led by Conductor Tony Kostecki and Music Director Jennifer McGuire. Mack's writing and her musical support and good ear guided the singers and moved the story along.

Good American opera should be staged honestly and sung well. Richard Kagey's staging was quite honestly brilliant. The stage incorporated a turntable and a backlit screen. The turntable served to smoothly change the scene, or act as a metaphor for the passage of time and characters that run through Roscoe's life. The screen helped the audience stay in the story, setting the scene and flashing up the odd newspaper headline. The young actors always knew where to go and were rarely caught in awkward situations. This seamless staging was combined with some very good, artistic, and, always important with young singers, healthy singing. On this night Roscoe was played by Scott Purcell. Purcell has a handsome, true, and full baritone voice that warmed into itself as the evening rolled along. Despite his smaller stature, which was obvious next to some other north-of-six-feet cast members, Purcell was able to capture the nuances of Roscoe's character, from confident power player, to lusty pursuer. The aim of his lust, Veronica, was played by Lauren Cook. Cook is the kind of actress who, when she is on stage, you know it. All eyes are on her, and she achieves this not with tricks, flips, mugging, or winks, but with a presence that quietly states, "I am here and you are going to watch me." It was a commanding performance vocally, and she showed that maturity and command of character that is sure to please audiences well into this century. Other notable up-and-comers included the young tenor Michael Vlach who played Alex Fitzgibbon. This young tenor showed he had all the elements of a fine singer and actor and the ability to move his six-foot-four-inch frame around the stage. Texan bass Johnny Salvesen played a cool, refined, and sometimes quirky Elisha. Just as refined was his bass voice, which had an excellent command of the entire vocal range and dynamic.

My conclusion is that this is a major and mature triumph for Mack and McGuire, and with continued refinement this could be a lasting and popular American opera. It was a meticulous production worthy of the finest of professional stages, all played in the woods (no pun intended, Mr. Woods) where there is no cell service and the backstage is basically a screened porch (plans for a new performing arts center are in the works; there are no plans for a cell tower). So where are we in the second century of American opera? I think if companies and festivals hire composers like Mack and McGuire, who have the unique ability to tell an American story through words and sounds, and *also* have the ability to treat every opportunity as one to adapt and change their score, all with an ear to the skill of American singers, then opera has a promising future. This was American opera on display and at its finest.

This essay appeared on the National Opera Association website, http://www.noa.org/2016/08/Review-World-Premiere-of-Roscoe-present.html, August 9, 2016. Reprinted by permission of Anthony P. Radford.

Jam Session

A Review of *Changó's Beads and Two-Tone Shoes*

John Sayles

> Kennedy . . . proves here that he can play with both hands and improvise on a theme without losing the beat.
>
> —John Sayles

William Kennedy's new novel, *Changó's Beads and Two-Tone Shoes*, is his most musical work of fiction: a polyrhythmic contemplation of time and its effects on passion set in three different eras, a jazz piece unafraid to luxuriate in its roots as blues or popular ballad or to spin out into less melodic territory.

Employing multiple storytelling modes, the book always finds its way back to Daniel Quinn, a not-so-young-anymore newspaperman in Kennedy's familiar stomping grounds of Albany, who, given the compromises endemic to that calling (hit too hard and you lose access, get too chummy and you lose self-respect), is gradually drifting toward a cynical, old-pro objectivity as the political machine that has run the city for decades applies dirty tricks and brute force to manage an incipient race riot in the days after the June 1968 assassination of Bobby Kennedy.

But we've met this Quinn before—as a small boy in 1936, deeply stirred as he wakes to a casual jam between the stride pianist Cody Mason and the visiting Bing Crosby (Quinn's father, George, everybody's pal in Albany, provides the piano)—and we know he's got soul. We've also seen him on a wild hayride in the poisonous Havana of 1957, trading quips with Ernest Hemingway at the Floridita bar and falling in love with the wealthy, quixotic Renata Suárez Otero, up to her beautiful neck in a doomed attempt to assassinate the dictator Fulgencio Batista. Renata is educated, connected, and serious in her devotion to Santeria, with its jealous, volatile gods and goddesses.

Much of the stylistic tension in the book results from Renata's relationship with Quinn, whose Irish American fatalism runs counter to her overheated Cuban idealism and produces exchanges of the snappy, 1940s-movie variety. Here's Quinn and Renata in their first real conversation, about the two men she's seeing:

> "The diplomat wants to take me to Europe, but. . . . My mother would kill me."
>
> "You love the anthropologist more than the diplomat."
>
> "He needs me more. He's married." (17)

This is not a book a young man would or could write. There is the sense here of somebody who has seen and considered much, without letting his inner fire cool. By the time the novel reaches 1968, Quinn's father is starting to slip mentally, but he remains the resilient get-along Irishman he has always been, a walking compendium of local street and backroom history, who lives in the moment (though not necessarily this moment) with a smile on his face and a song on his lips. Dressed to waltz, George wanders through the increasingly menacing Albany tenderloin as the riot fever builds, totally lost but at home in his memories. He is so appealingly rendered that one awaits his reappearance with the happy anticipation familiar from listening to Louis Armstrong records—Oh good, you think, here comes Pops with the solo. In one long day George has a romance with a generous former flame, is wounded, fights the good fight without knowing what it's about, cuts a rug and doesn't remember a bit of it even as his heart is always in the right place.

Familiar music runs through the story, Bing scatting around the lyrics to "Shine" (the public's evolving attitude toward that song becomes a leitmotif), George and his Tin Pan Alley standards, the voodoo drums of the *santeros* and the R&B of the struggling African American community. This culminates in a moving fusion that parallels the style (or styles) of the book when Cody Mason, fatally ill, caps off his farewell appearance with a waltz-time version of "Shine" that gradually shifts:

> . . .and he switches keys and ups the tempo, just a little, and ba-boom goes that left hand, the power of it, he's on a ride, six choruses and counting, feel that beat, beat, beat, that goddamn beat, this is stride on high, stride the way it's supposed to be, brilliant invention, the poor guy can't help himself, smothering the song with his gift, exploding it, and Quinn's pulse is up and cantering, those left-handed arpeggios, the glissando that surprises, and he notches the speed upward. (305)

It goes on, as the best live music always does, never losing us but keeping us guessing about just how we're going to get there. Kennedy's time scheme allows him to quit a sequence with a lot of business left hanging, teasing us, leading us through other events with other characters so that plot points mean much more when finally resolved. It's a risky technique, and Kennedy repeats himself more than usual, but given the book's structure this is a welcome bit of orientation, Miles Davis reminding us that the song is, in fact, "My Funny Valentine."

Parallels, more emotional than political, are meant to be drawn between the murderous lead-up to the Cuban revolution and our own racial problems of the late 1960s, with Daniel and Renata's troubled marriage jump-started by the frustration and anger of another desperate, seemingly hopeless situation. (My own strongest memory of Albany in that period, the beginning of the third decade of the O'Connell-Corning machine's reign, is of garbage volcanoes. One day in the South End there would be an unspoken agreement to pile uncollected trash on a random spot on the sidewalk, the heap growing wider and taller each morning till the city was forced to take note.)

Daniel, we learn, is capable of passion, but like Kennedy he is no sap. He still cares enough to file his exposés and character profiles, but as his paper increasingly bows to the will of City Hall he dreams of quitting the newsroom and putting his truths into fiction. He is, however, too practiced to think this is any but a personal liberation, and though an admirer and former acolyte of Hemingway, he ultimately recognizes that "the simple declarative sentence is an illusion."

Daniel and Renata are not the cuddliest of protagonists—Daniel's a little detached at times, and Renata is addicted to drama, whether political or romantic—but you root for them to stay together. Even the easily parodied Hemingway, though self-destructive and badly behaved, appears in flesh and blood and wins our sympathy. The African American and Cuban revolutionaries are seen mostly through Daniel's eyes, and he is a careful, sympathetic observer, attracted by their energy but skeptical of their chances for survival. The scattered, half-accidental incidents that add up to a major racial confrontation (and the role played by a callous, confrontational power structure) are skillfully dramatized here, and when fatal happenings are reported from offstage we've been prepared for them. Kennedy understands that a riot is a block-by-block phenomenon that doesn't necessarily shut down the opera.

Other writers have worked aspects of this territory before with success—I think of José Latour's *Havana World Series*, Jimmy Breslin's *Table Money*, and almost anything by George V. Higgins—but the ambition and ability to pull wildly diverse worlds together in a single story is rare. Kennedy, master of the Irish American lament in works like *Billy Phelan's Greatest Game* and *Ironweed*, proves here that he can play with both hands and improvise on a theme without losing the beat. At eighty-three years old, he remains a writer we hope to hear more from.

REFERENCES

Kennedy, William. *Changó's Beads and Two-Tone Shoes*. New York: Viking, 2011.

An Interview with William Kennedy

From Novelist to Screenwriter

William Patrick

> To work with Coppola was a gift. I can't even evaluate what I learned from him, but the main thing . . . was concision, and the discovery of its power.
>
> —William Kennedy

William Kennedy's *Ironweed* was published in January of 1983. It was his fourth novel, following *The Ink Truck*, *Legs*, and *Billy Phelan's Greatest Game*, and it would go on to win the Pulitzer Prize in 1984. The same week *Ironweed* appeared to critical raves, Kennedy got a call from the MacArthur Foundation, informing him he was being awarded $264,000, tax-free. As he told a *Paris Review* interviewer, "I'd gotten a Chinese fortune cookie that week which said, 'This is your lucky week.' I thought it had to do with the fact that I was getting reviewed in about five different major places in the same week. I thought that was good enough, but then I got the MacArthur. Quite a week!" Later in 1983, Francis Ford Coppola hired him to write the screenplay for *The Cotton Club*, and two of his earlier Albany Cycle novels were reissued in paperback. Quite a year!

Kennedy has been writing screenplays since the 1970s (including one for *Ironweed*, the movie, directed by Héctor Babenco) and plays since the mid-1990s, and much of what he has created is under option. He has added five more novels to his upstate cycle during that time as well—*Quinn's Book*; *Very Old Bones*; *The Flaming Corsage*; *Roscoe*; and *Changó's Beads and Two-Tone Shoes*. As Sam Sacks wrote in the *Wall Street Journal*, "The novels in the cycle overlap and are non-sequential . . . but their connections are so eccentric that it's best to think of them as planets in a common solar system." Whether William Kennedy is writing fiction or screenplays, his characters are always original and his language is rowdy, inventive, and full of energy. As Saul Bellow once noted, there's not a dead sentence or a flat character anywhere in sight. Kennedy has always been the real deal as a writer, with the rest of his rich and compelling stories ready to be developed.

William Patrick: How did you get started writing screenplays?

William Kennedy: I got started writing screenplays because I was fascinated by the movies in the 1960s, and always wanted to do it, and started to teach myself how to write for the movies. I did a lot of film criticism, started a film society, and eventually—it was in the 1970s actually when I began trying to make a living as a screenwriter. And I changed agents. I moved over to William Morris and got myself a movie agent; he was very helpful, and I learned a lot. I wrote one screenplay for a friend of mine where this agent negotiated the deal, and then I wrote another screen treatment on speculation. Not on speculation, I beg your pardon. I wrote a screen treatment on the basis of a conversation I had over lunch with my agent and a producer. I had an idea to do a movie in Puerto Rico, and I needed to go down there and do some research on it, and I needed some option money. I needed some walking-around money. I was broke. In about a fifteen-minute pitch, I got this advance to write the treatment for $10,000—and $5,000 for expenses—to do what amounted to something like a twenty-page treatment.

A friend of mine had written a short story. He was a pilot in Central America, and it was a strange world he got mixed up in, before all the drug smuggling. But it had all the intrigue of Central America, plus a black market, plus just general hauling, and what it was like flying these planes that were ready to fall out of the sky. Anyway, I wrote the treatment and optioned the story from my buddy, and we were going to share and share alike if it ever went forward. But it didn't.

Patrick: What stopped it from going forward?

Kennedy: The usual "No." The usual negative attitude toward anything that you present to folks in Hollywood. They say no all the time; very rarely do they say yes. They're in the business of saying no; they're in the business of not making movies. I thought we could have a good adventure movie, but it didn't happen.

Patrick: Now this was in the time period between *Legs* and *Billy Phelan's Greatest Game*, right?

Kennedy: *Billy Phelan* was just about to come out, and I had sold an option to Warner Brothers on *Legs*, but nobody wanted me to write the script. I wanted to write the script on *Billy Phelan*, and I wanted somebody to option that, too, but I couldn't get the time of day on that either. For *Legs*, Warner Brothers had hired a fellow by the name of Joe Walsh, who had written *California Split* for Robert Altman. Joe, a good guy, wrote the *Legs* script, and we were talking about Jack Nicholson, and that level of aspiration for the film. What happened was a change in the hierarchy at Warner Brothers, and the people who had brought the project in no longer had power. That was the first time that happened. But it happened over and over. You don't know what to believe, and you never know for sure why you're getting turned down, or even why they were interested in you in the first place.

It's intuition, I suppose, that they play with when they buy somebody's pitch. I went out and made a pitch on a sportswriter movie. Mike Medavoy turned me down, and then my agent talked to him and he called me back and he said, "Okay, we'll go ahead and do it." That was a film about two sportswriters on *The Daily News* who were best friends, and they got involved in a feud during a strike. One of them continued to work for the paper during the strike and one of them didn't, and that broke their friendship. It was about personal attitudes and the common ground they shared as sportswriters. It seemed like a very human movie. They hired me and I wrote the script and had a good payday on that.

The screenplay went in and it immediately went down the tubes. It was a movie about the labor movement, and once they saw it down on paper, then they didn't want it. They knew all that going in, so you can't figure. I think there's a careless optimism in the executives' minds when they spend this money. It's pin money to them, these options or development deals they make to get the script, they feel they can throw it away. If it gets done somewhere else then they'll get some of their money back. I don't think that movie went into turnaround—I think they just killed it. It was a funny, interesting story.

Patrick: Did they give it back to you?

Kennedy: I never pursued it. It may have reverted to the producer who first optioned it. I obviously have equity in there if anybody ever makes that movie, and I would also get a screen credit. The deal was a good one. You go in with these extremely high hopes. I don't know why, after a while, that you have those hopes, because it's very hard to continue to be serious about writing screenplays. You get cynical, and you feel the money's the only thing.

Patrick: Let me ask you another question before we move on to *The Cotton Club* and *Ironweed*. When you first started writing screenplays back in the 1970s, how did it feel to make the transition from writing novels to writing in dramatic genres like plays and screenplays—from making art with words to using words to make pictures?

Kennedy: The problem, basically, was the belief in dialogue to tell the story, and that's only partially necessary in movies. You need the dialogue for the intelligence of the film, but you can't think in terms of merely talking heads, or even dialogue in the midst of action. The visual element of the story has to come first, and then you use the natural dialogue that comes out of the action. But without that picture of the motion, the conflict, the whatever it is that's going to keep the story moving—the pacing of the story—you're not going to get anything except a lot of static conversation on the screen. And that was what I learned very slowly. You know that from the beginning, but when you're a novelist, it's hard to stop thinking in terms of dramatic development through conversation, or interior monologue, or the historical narrative that will explain what's going on—you can't do that. This is basic, elementary screenwriting, but it's hard to stop thinking like a novelist.

One of the things that happened to me was working with Francis Coppola, and watching the constant editing that he did on the scripts that we put together, or just on the scenes that I would write. I'd write a five-page scene and he'd cut it to three and a half pages. Then I'd redo it and he'd edit that down to two pages. And we'd still more or less have the same action frame—the same movement forward. That was an unbelievably tight script that we had to produce for *The Cotton Club*, because there was so much music and so much dancing, and so many characters that it was difficult to develop anybody seriously.

Francis was very aware of minimalism in terms of narration. He thinks in visual terms. All good moviemakers do. I grew up believing that movies like *Citizen Kane*, *8½*, *Persona*, *Smiles of a Summer Night*, the Buñuel movies, that they were visual achievements, but at the same time there was a pervasive intelligence, and a remarkably vivid conversation going on in those films. In so many Hollywood movies, especially in the last twenty or thirty years, we have ceased to have writers acting as a dominant force in the making of films, at least not in the way they were a force in the 1930s and in the early 1940s, where you had old newspapermen, and playwrights, and essayists, and novelists coming into Hollywood to become the screenwriters. By the 1960s and 1970s, the visual image had become so dominant that dialogue went out the window.

I saw something the other night about one of these action directors who uses about six or eight writers for each movie—four teams of writers—and that's such a ridiculous way to work from the point of view of a writer. Nor is it very smart. No single intelligence is of any significance in the making of those films, except that you presume that the director's intelligence is there. But when you look at these movies that are written by committees, they're an excuse for another plot departure, yet another action sequence with a veneer of plot line. It's depressing to be a writer and have to cope with that.

Now I'll never have that problem: no one will ever hire me to write an action movie. But what I'm talking about is the way that a writer comes into the writing of a film. A fiction writer becomes a screenwriter and brings all this novelistic baggage with him: the way of telling a story traditionally, which is verbally, through words alone, and orally, through spoken words. And so often that way of telling just clutters a film. I'm sounding like Screenwriting 101 here, but if you—the novelist—don't understand this very early in the game, you're not going to write much of a screenplay. I'm also saying that, at the beginning, I didn't understand it very well, and that I had to learn it quite quickly. I learned it in about six or eight weeks working with Francis.

Patrick: How do you think storytelling in movies affects an audience differently than the way it does in well-written novels? And what does that difference augur for our development as human beings, if we assume that storytelling is one of the activities that differentiates our species from other animal species?

Kennedy: Well, it's a reduction of complexity, obviously. Movies can only rarely approach the density and complexity of one human life. I'm not even speaking of the first-line novels like *Ulysses* or *The Sound and the Fury* or *Moby-Dick*, or novels by writers like Proust and Tolstoy. You don't have such enormous density in the movies—you just can't. There's not enough time. With movies, the process is the opposite of methodical, careful thought, rumination, or synthesis. You're constantly forced into a relentless excitement that the screenwriter, and director, and cinematographer are creating for you, and which is essential to the medium. The assault is terrific. The movies don't need all the nineteenth-century descriptions from Henry James's gardens and tea parties. You do it instantly with one broad dolly shot in a garden. By the same token, you can't get the complexity of a tortured mind unless you have the luxury of time and space, and in the movies you can't keep anybody sitting still that long.

I had this argument with Coppola. I said, "You'll never make a movie out of *Ulysses*, not the way that it really is. You can make one chapter, and that would take six or eight hours." And he said it didn't make any difference, you could make a hundred movies and do *Ulysses*. Yes, but who's going to sit through them?

Patrick: But don't you think that classic films like *Wild Strawberries* or *8½* or *The Pawnbroker*, and many others, come closer to creating the experience we get from good novels?

Kennedy: I do. *8½*, I'm halfway through that right now, again, and I could sit through it over and over. I've seen it fifteen or twenty times. I think it's a great movie, in terms of focusing on one individual and getting the complexity across. It's really a masterpiece of one man's interior life, in ways that most other films never get at.

But to get back to your earlier question, I don't think that just because a new art form exists that complexity is going to disappear, any more than it was lost when the narrative poem died and the novel came along.

Patrick: Can you talk about when you started working with Coppola? How did that come about?

Kennedy: Coppola had read *Legs*, and *Legs* had also been used as source material by the people who had preceded Coppola on *The Cotton Club*, because the real Cotton Club was run by gangsters, and basically an Irish gangster named Owney Madden. Owney Madden was a friend of Legs Diamond, and Legs had his own nightclubs in New York City at various times. He ran the Hotsy Totsy Club on Broadway, and he had a nightclub in the Bronx. It was a way of life for gangsters, and the way they moved their beer and so on. My book, *Legs*, covers that era, and Francis had read it and liked it.

In the summer of 1982 I got a call from Fred Roos, one of Francis's producers who was trying to produce a film on Vietnam. It was about the show people who went over to Vietnam, and he wanted me to write it. That idea became the Bette Midler movie, *For the Boys*, with James Caan. It was going to be an extension of the scene in *Apocalypse Now*, where they helicoptered the Playboy bunnies into the improvisational show for the troops on the front lines. Bette Midler wanted to do it then. Fred and I met with Bette and talked about it, and I had a lot of background. John Mackenzie was going to direct it. It didn't happen when I was involved with it because there was an Oliver Stone film, *Salvador*, that didn't fly. And another that surfaced in 1982, and it bombed. So that Vietnam showpeople movie never got off the ground at that time.

But we were talking about it in 1983, when it was just an idea. Fred invited me to come down and talk about that and he said, "I'll take you in and you can meet Francis." So I said, "Okay." I had heard that they were using my book as a point of reference. Actually, when I got there, I discovered that all the dialogue in my book had been excerpted into a script of its own, and Francis had used that as source material for something that he was planning. He had a machine called a zippy-script, and it turned the pages of a novel, or anything, and it had the sense to scan everything within quotes and eliminate the exposition. So you had this 250- or 300-page manuscript of nothing but quotations from the novel, but he never used it. It was an exercise for Francis. He was shaping *The Cotton Club* in his mind, and orchestrating it with actors, choreographers, musicians, set designers, etc. He had something like 550 people on the payroll when he came into it—he inherited that. Bob Evans was going to direct it, and Mario Puzo was going to write the script. Puzo had already written four scripts, but the film didn't get made on the basis of Evans and Puzo. They brought Francis in to write a script, and he wrote one and they liked it so-so, then he wrote another one and they said, "Great. Let's go."

That's more or less when I entered the scene. Francis had his second script: Legs Diamond was in it a little bit, and he brought me in because he loved *Legs*. Francis had just moved his people into New York from the West Coast, when Fred invited me to come down. I went in to just say hello, and we talked for about an hour, and we got along very well. Then, about two days later, I got another call from Fred, and he said, "Would you like to go to work for Francis and write some dialogue for about five or six weeks, whatever it takes?" And at that point, the project was going to be me filling in the blanks on Francis's second script. He had created a full script but with some scenes having only summaries of the action, or sometimes with a few lines of dialogue taken from *Legs* or from Brecht's *Threepenny Opera*, suggesting a line of talk or a style or a tone he'd like to see developed.

So we went to work (and it wasn't five weeks, but a year and a half), and we talked and talked for days and nights, listening to Duke Ellington tapes. It was mid-July, and our deadline was late August. The details of this are in "The Cotton Club Stomp" in my collection, *Riding the Yellow Trolley Car*. Here, I'll read what I wrote there: "From July 15 to August 22, when shooting began, we produced twelve scripts, including five during one forty-eight-hour, non-stop weekend. We lost track of the total number of scripts we turned out, but it was somewhere between thirty and forty." And before that: "Fourteen-sixteen-hour workdays were not unusual, and once we worked thirty-four hours without sleep. Coppola called this sort of stint 'the death trip.' "*

I've forgotten how long it took us to write the rehearsal draft, which was only eighty pages. It was awful, but it was the beginning of coherence, and it was the beginning of some characters, and some other things that we were both happy with, even though there was so much left to be done. And right up until he went into shooting, the script was still very unfinished. On the eve of the first day of the shoot, Richard Gere was downstairs in his dressing room, waiting for the final version of the script, and when he didn't get it by two o'clock in the morning, he walked. So we didn't have Richard in the film on the first day. He liked the first half of the script, but he thought the second half was chaos, which it was. So, I had to stay over and I was

* Editors' Note: From William Kennedy, *Riding the Yellow Trolley Car* (New York: Viking, 1993), 393–394.

writing as fast as I could type. And as fast as I could type a page, or two pages, Francis's assistant, Anahid Nazarian, would take it and put it into the computer and print it out and begin to circulate it. Francis finally went home about 1:30, because he was supposed to be on the set at six or seven o'clock the next morning. So I worked for another four and a half hours by myself, rewriting the final draft of the script, and I was very arbitrarily deciding on whatever coherence I could bring to this chaotic document. And it was a big improvement over what we had—that forced-feeding of the computer was very valuable. People began to say, "Well, it's beginning to shape up." It finally had some coherence. It was such a slap-dash script, and we had so many scenes that we wanted to use—the conflicts between the black brothers; conflicts with Dixie and Dutch Schultz; Dixie Dwyer, the Gere character and Vera Cicero, the Diane Lane character.

There were a million conflicts, and Francis was always unhappy, always trying to change it and fix it. As usual, he had the storyboards up on the wall in his bedroom. We had this suite of rooms that used to be dressing rooms in the Silent Era. The Marx Brothers had used it; Gloria Swanson had used it. It was at the Kaufman Astoria Studio in Queens, which was in the process of being refurbished into something spectacular, but at that time it was fairly ramshackle. The roof leaked. It was huge, occupied a whole block or two. The Museum of the Moving Image is now in that building. We didn't stay there. I was living at the Park Lane, on Central Park South, and Francis was living across the way, in his apartment on Fifth Avenue at the Sherry-Netherland. But we worked in Queens almost all day long. Very often I would work until three or four in the morning, and then go back and fall asleep for a few hours, get up and have some breakfast, and be back at work at ten in the morning. And Francis would always be there. He lived at the studio in the early days of the production, before his family came in. He had one room set off as his private living quarters.

Anyway, it was a spectacular experience to see the development of a film from scratch, and watching Francis transform everything. He fired a lot of people: the choreographer; the music director; the production staff. The only one he couldn't fire was Bob Evans, the producer, and he would have liked to fire him. He wound up in court with him eventually. There was even a murder involved with this film—Roy Radin, a producer who was raising money in the very early days of the film's development. He got mixed up in a drug deal in L.A., and some woman put out a contract on him. She hired a couple of thugs to kill him, and they picked him up in a restaurant, had a gun in his mouth in the backseat of a car while they were driving him through L.A. traffic, and they took him out into some canyon and offed him. They didn't find him for a while, but one of the hit men got caught on something else and blew the whistle. Evans knew Radin but he wasn't involved in his killing in any way, though he had to testify at the trial. It was a woman who had killed her previous husband. She was a dragon lady. There have been documentary movies made about this case. I don't remember what the titles are—*The Secrets of the Cotton Club*, or something like that. This story will be back, you can be sure of that. There was a very good piece by Michael Daly on the making of *The Cotton Club* in *New York* magazine that brought in for the first time the background on this murder.

Anyway, it was a three-ring circus, and I learned a lot about writing a screenplay. To work with Coppola was a gift. I can't even evaluate what I learned from him, but the main thing that I learned was concision, and the discovery of its power. You have to find the visual element that you're going to tell the story through, and then you find the dialogue that goes with that, and you say it all in the shortest possible way. You keep the story moving.

In a story like my novel *The Flaming Corsage*, where there's as much banter as possible because they're newspaper guys and people talking about history, there's a dimension that allows for rumination and development of ideas in a way that you had no time for in *The Cotton Club*. You might be in the club itself, then suddenly you're in a gangster's conference or a shootout, then a love affair or a dancehall—the movie just kept moving, and there was always music, and wonderful entertainment. There will be a longer version one of these days, and much more of the dialogue will appear, I hope. A lot of great music and dance also vanished when it was cut to two hours and seven minutes because the producers wanted less tap dancing, less black family story, and more of Gere and Lane. Critics faulted this version as an incomplete and illogical story. Francis gave the outtakes to the son of one of his backers, and the young man edited together the video of the film and the outtakes, into about a two-and-a-half-hour movie. It was rough, but I thought it was terrific, and I knew it would be reappraised positively if such a cut was released.*

---

* Editors' Note: Kennedy provided the following update on the film:

In September 2017 at the Telluride Film Festival, without advance notice, Francis released his new cut, which he calls *The Cotton Club Encore*, which has a new twenty-five minutes from the outtakes. He also cut some from the original and the new film is 139 minutes. It's everything I thought it would be: Great songs (Lonette McKee's "Stormy Weather") and tap and specialty numbers restored; the intercutting of the Williams brothers' (Gregory and Maurice Hines) and the Dwyer brothers' (Gere and Nick Cage) stories, has new balance and more logic; and the meaningful fusion of song and dance with the plot line again makes sense. It won a rave review at Telluride. MGM, which owns the rights, didn't want to release the new version, but in the spring of 2018, Francis was hopeful of gaining distribution by year's end.

When the first version came out, everybody was reviewing the money: the story was that it cost $57 million, in the early 1980s. It was maybe the most expensive movie up to that time other than the Russian version of *War and Peace*, which cost about $100 million, they said. In those days, it was enormous, and people were talking about the money and the hoopla surrounding the film. It was Coppola, and Puzo, and Evans, and Evans was advertising it as the three men who gave you *The Godfather*. He kept me secret—I wasn't even listed in the telephone directory on the set, because they were still selling interests in a film from Coppola, Evans, and Puzo, "who gave you *The Godfather*." Puzo wrote four scripts that were not used and had been gone long before I came into the picture.

Patrick: Do you think you've created a distinct style in the screenplays that you've written, as you have in your novels, or is that impossible given the nature of how screenwriters have to work?

Kennedy: I would never think of myself as having created a style. People tell me they recognize my dialogue in *The Cotton Club* or *Ironweed*, of course. *Ironweed* was very close to the book in certain ways. A lot of the book had to be excised, but the basic story was kept, and the dialogue was as close to it as we could make it. Héctor Babenco, the director, wanted that, too, so it was a very harmonious development of that film.

When I write dialogue, I think there's a kind of signature that goes with it, but I wouldn't be able to tell you what that is. I just know that certain writers have it. Two pages of DeLillo dialogue, and I could probably identify it. I could certainly do it with Hemingway, and Cheever's dialogue I could recognize. Writers who use dialogue to a major degree in telling their stories—have a signature. I think that would show up in a screenplay. That doesn't mean that it will show up on the screen, because so much gets edited out. Voice is always intruded upon by the action and by the visuals and by the music and by the sound effects and god knows what else.

Patrick: Do you find yourself writing dialogue for films differently than when you write dialogue for novels?

Kennedy: Tighter. Just tighter. You can't let scenes run on and on. It's counterproductive, and it really doesn't fit with the art form. You can have a whole chapter, or a whole novel, with nothing but dialogue, which some of the French writers have done. Philip Roth did it with *Deception*, and Nicholson Baker did it with *Vox*. But you're not going to put all that dialogue into the movies. I think you would find people getting very restless. They need movement, and they need the action that goes with it. Having said that, Louis Malle directed one of the best pictures of 1981, *My Dinner with Andre*, from a script by Andre Gregory and Wally Shawn, and it was all conversation. So rules are made to be broken.

But it's so difficult to get the interior life on screen. Francis Phelan in *Ironweed* sums up the trajectory of his entire life, from the moment he's conceived—a primal pool squirming into burgeoning matter, then yanked from his mother's womb by his father, who slaps him into being, swiftly molds him into a bestial weed, he sprouts into wildly maturing growth, and then stands clad in the clothes he's now wearing, a bum on the street. And how do you get that on film? Back in the 1980s you didn't, or at least we didn't. The technology with computers is now so advanced, and the capacity for CGI people in Hollywood to do almost anything they want, wasn't there when I was writing *The Cotton Club* and *Ironweed*. I'm not sure we would have used it, but if we had I would have started *Ironweed* under the ground, in the graveyard, with the dead conversing about Francis coming up the road in the truck and so on, and walking to Gerald's grave. I would have loved to do that, and it would have been anticipatory for the scenes with the ghosts in the later scenes. And the ghosts could have been done in a different way.

The way Babenco and I looked at it at that time was we didn't want to do any kind of animation. We didn't want scenes with characters where people were fading in and out of visibility. That was gimmicky, and we wrote it off. But I would have loved a second chance with it to do it in a more surreal way than we were considering in those days.

Patrick: Have you ever extrapolated any of what you've learned from writing screenplays into your methods for writing fiction?

Kennedy: I don't know what I might have learned from writing movies, but I'm sure I learned ten thousand things. I grew up with the movies. I'm a child of the Age of Cinema. I've been going to the movies since I was old enough to sit up in a theater and have the patience to sit through a Buck Jones or a Ken Maynard or a Hoot Gibson movie at the Leland Theater in the 1930s. I couldn't specify, but I know I've always been somewhat of a concise writer—barebones writer sometimes. But I suspect that the movies and screenwriting have forced me into rethinking that. There's more concision possible, at least usually. However, there's no more concision possible, for instance, in a Chekhov story, or in Babel, who were maestros. Hemingway's dialogue is so minimal and so powerful when you read it—you get caught up in his stories. As with Ray Carver. You feel like you're in the hands of some maestro of the dramatic arts with a minimum amount of dialogue, and I love that. I've practiced it almost all my writing career.

I started out writing very short stories full of dialogue. But I would assume I've learned more about pacing and cutting now. I'm always sort of amazed that after writing a screenplay I can go back to becoming a novelist without even thinking about it, you know. It's like I put on another hat and become this other kind of person, with never a thought about concision. I've got nothing but expansion in my future with the novel I've been working on for years, with the accumulation of information and characters, and it's totally anticinematic.

Patrick: Have you ever wanted to blend the two forms, the way Arthur Miller did it in *The Misfits*?

Kennedy: Well, I used to think that would be a way for the movies to develop, but I don't think they will. They haven't so far. On occasions, maybe, and certainly you get into the films made from O'Neill's plays and what are they but dialogue? It's very little action—just people talking to each other for two and a half hours. The other way—making a novel look more like a screenplay—I used to think that the form of the screenplay was workable as a novel, but I don't think so anymore. Sometimes they're very good reading, but usually they're just utilitarian. Not that you can read a great screenplay and not know that it's terrific. When you reread *Citizen Kane* or a Fellini or Bergman screenplay, you realize they're exciting and engaging stories all by themselves, without seeing a single image; but they're not novels, nor should they be. There's no need to fuse them. They're separate forms and they fight each other.

I remember Godard movies that I reviewed in the 1960s, like *Weekend*, and he had so much talk going on—excerpts from philosophical writings and long speeches, some of which you couldn't begin to stay with. I never thought that was a successful form of filmmaking. A lot of people love Godard and think I'm all wet, but I think fewer and fewer think so as time goes on. But Fellini continues, because so much of Fellini is composed of the great images. Even though he has these intelligent characters moving through his stories, their conversations are succinct. They don't interfere with the images; they enhance them. And they're remarkably successful works of art.

Patrick: Let me just ask you one more question, because I know you want to get to work. Can you talk about what happened with *The Flaming Corsage*?

Kennedy: Well, it's not a finished story. Basically, I was approached by a producer who was very excited to make a film from it, and we talked for an hour in a restaurant about it. We agreed that he should come and talk some more about it with me, which he did, and he brought one of his associates in and we sat around for a day and a half and talked through the whole book. Then I began to think about the kind of movie that they thought they wanted, and that they thought they could get through the system out there at

Universal, which was where he was based. We went back and forth on how to approach the novel. I had my ideas and he had his. It took me about a year to decide to really do it, and finally I began to go to work, and we moved ahead on the deal. I was working for some months before I got paid. I knew I was going to get paid, and then it took me another six months to finish the script. Much too long.

But what happened to me in writing this screenplay was that I began to see things that weren't in the novel, and that I knew about the various lives of my characters, and I began to reinvent the story. So there are scenes in the screenplay that don't exist in the novel, but that are in some sense compatible, and alternative possibilities for the behavior of the characters. I thought once that I might even publish the novel and the screenplay together, if the movie ever got made.

Anyway, by the time I got through writing it, everything had changed at Universal. A few honchos saw it and didn't get excited about it, and the project stopped. New people took over and so it ended up in turnaround. It's hardly news that a movie gets turned down by the first three, four, five studios. It can go for years. *One Flew Over the Cuckoo's Nest*, and many other films that were deemed impossible, took years to get made. *The Flaming Corsage* is a period story, for one thing, and it's a tragic love story, and Hollywood isn't crazy about either. Even when they're successful, like *The English Patient*—which was done by an independent producer and was not a studio movie—it's hard to get them done. The producer who wanted to make the *Corsage* called me a few years ago and had an idea to make it with a young woman very much on the rise in films; and she became a young superstar. But even though that film didn't happen, he called me again last month with another starlet in mind. He still loves the novel, twenty years after our first venture, and so we're on the road again, maybe. And why not? Sometimes it actually happens. Mostly it doesn't.

Ironweed, the novel, was the best I could do at the time I wrote it, and I thought it was a finished piece of work; but an awful lot of people turned it down on the grounds that my book before it had not been successful. So much of what becomes popular in this country is the consequence of the cult of personality. It's the image of the writer that's in the popular imagination at any given moment. I'm not saying that that's all that happens, but very often it happens. Success just begets more success. Tom Wolfe sold more than a million copies of *Bonfire of the Vanities* before it was even published—that man could not do anything wrong in the popular mind.

I think that there's a great chance that a film made by somebody who really understands *Billy Phelan's Greatest Game* would be a terrific movie. I think *Legs* could be a sensational movie in the right hands. But it's like everything else—you have to have this confluence of sympathetic minds—and if you don't have it, you're just out there knocking your head against the wall. I remember I wrote to Mario Puzo once and wanted to do a piece on him about his early work. He said at one time he had owed a lot of money and he was deep in debt, and that "it was time to grow up and sell out." So he wrote *The Godfather*. It was a great line and an honest thing to say. But he wrote very good and serious novels, and that was what I wanted to talk to him about, and what it was like for him to make the transition from fiction to screenwriting. He said, "Look, either you go out there and you live and you plug along all your life trying to make it, or else lightning strikes."

Well, for me, lightning struck, and for him, it struck big time. For me, it was the publication of *Ironweed* and winning the MacArthur, all in the same week. Then six months later, I was working with Coppola, and then six months after that, everything was under option. But it was another four years before *Ironweed* got made, and that was really the doing of Babenco and myself. The people who had optioned it had very little to do with the fact that it became a movie. Babenco's desire to make it, my insistence on working with him, his friendship with Jack Nicholson, and his knowing of a producer who convinced Keith Barish to put up the money and pay Jack five million dollars to play Francis—those four elements were what made that film possible.

So that was lightning for me, in the sense that I got into the movie business on a fluke, even though I wanted to get into it and I was ready to go into it. That could have happened to a lot of people and they wouldn't have known what to do with it, or they wouldn't have wanted anything to do with it. I'm sure that John Updike must have had some chances to write for the movies, but I don't think he did. I know Saul Bellow had a movie made from his novel *Seize the Day* and he wrote some TV scripts, and I know Jack Nicholson wanted to make *Henderson, the Rain King*, but Saul didn't really want to write screenplays. I don't think he had the patience or the interest.

I might write another script one day, if it's an adaptation of one of my books or plays. But I'll never do another original screenplay. If I'm going to invent anything from scratch, it will be a novel.

REFERENCE

Kennedy, William. *Riding the Yellow Trolley Car*. New York: Viking, 1993.

This essay first appeared in *The Writer's Chronicle*, in the May/Summer 2017 edition. Reprinted by permission of William Patrick.

William Kennedy's Literary Biography

Bits of biographical information on William Kennedy appear throughout the reviews, articles, and essays in this collection. His literary trajectory is presented here in a series of photographs that traces his career from his early days as a journalist, through his transition to writing fiction, and to his eventual success as a novelist and screenwriter. Also included are photos of some of the literary luminaries Kennedy has welcomed to the University at Albany as founder and Executive Director of the New York State Writers Institute.

Photos, unless otherwise noted, are from William Kennedy's collection and the New York State Writers Institute's archive.

After graduating from Siena College with a bachelor's degree in English in 1949, Kennedy was hired in 1950 by the Glens Falls, New York, *Post-Star* newspaper as a sportswriter and columnist. Later that year, Kennedy was drafted into the U.S. Army and served in the Public Information Office at Fort Benning, Georgia. He covered a visit to Fort Benning by the secretary of the army *(hatless at right)*.

At Fort Benning Kennedy talks with *Baltimore Sun* war correspondent Bill Blair, who went on to work for the State Department in 1959, retiring as deputy assistant secretary for public affairs in 1980.

Kennedy was stationed in Germany during the Korean War, where he worked as sports editor for the Fourth Infantry Division's weekly newspaper, *Ivy Leaves*. At an army show in Frankfurt, Germany, Kennedy *(third from left)* donned a fake mustache and sang with a barbershop quartet.

The army assigned Kennedy to cover the 1952 Summer Olympics in Helsinki, Finland, where he wrote sports columns and feature stories. He wears a signature bow tie and strikes a pose at the rail of a ship en route to Scandinavia.

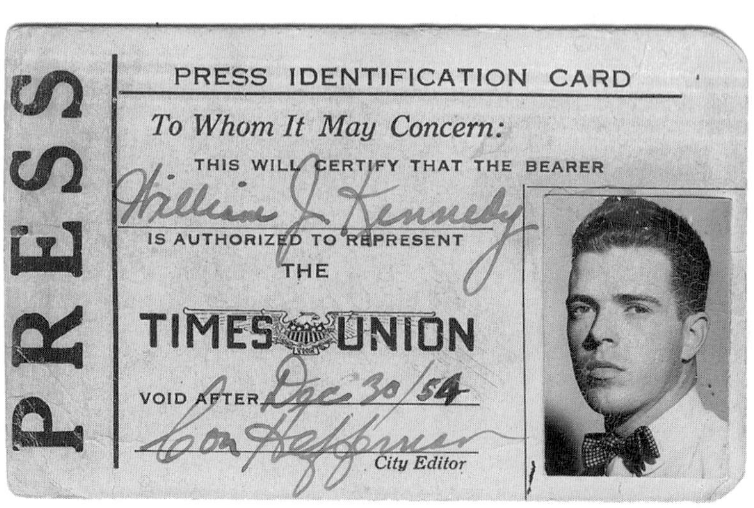
PRESS

PRESS IDENTIFICATION CARD

To Whom It May Concern:

THIS WILL CERTIFY THAT THE BEARER

William J. Kennedy

IS AUTHORIZED TO REPRESENT

THE

TIMES UNION

VOID AFTER Dec. 30/54

City Editor

Upon his discharge from the U.S. Army in 1952, Kennedy was hired as a reporter for his hometown newspaper, the Albany *Times Union*.

In 1956, Kennedy accepted a position at an English-language daily newspaper in San Juan, the *Puerto Rico World Journal*. He interviewed actress Rita Hayworth on her arrival at the San Juan airport. He bought this pair of tinted sunglasses on the island and noted it was the first time he saw the world through rose-colored glasses. He was promoted to assistant managing editor, but the paper folded nine months later.

After a brief stint as a reporter with the *Miami Herald*, Kennedy was hired as managing editor of the *San Juan Star*, a new English-language paper established in Puerto Rico in 1959. He was working as a stringer for *Time* magazine when he covered a 1958 stop in San Juan by then–vice president Richard Nixon, who was returning from an infamous trip to Venezuela where his car was attacked by rock-throwing anti-American demonstrators. *(Left to right)* U.S. Rear Admiral Dan Gallery, Vice President Richard Nixon, Puerto Rico Governor José Luis Alberto Muñoz Marin, and Kennedy.

Kennedy at his desk at the *San Juan Star* in 1960. A year later, he resigned as managing editor and worked half-time as weekend editor in order to devote more time to his fiction writing.

In 1963 Kennedy returned to Albany to care for his ailing father and worked once again as a reporter at the *Times Union*. He and *Times Union* photographer Bernard Kolenberg teamed up for an in-depth story on the homeless who lived on the streets in Albany's South End. This investigative series on the slums of Albany was nominated for a Pulitzer Prize, and Kennedy's experiences also provided inspiration for his Pulitzer Prize–winning novel, *Ironweed*. On leave from the *Times Union*, Kolenberg was on assignment for the Associated Press in Vietnam where he was killed on October 2, 1965, the first American journalist killed in action covering the war.

Photo by Bernard Kolenberg. Courtesy of the Albany *Times Union*.

Kennedy joined the picket line of the Newspaper Guild strike against the *Times Union* in 1964. A Guild strike is a major element in Kennedy's first published novel, *The Ink Truck* (1969).

A magical stretch of recognition during 1983 and 1984 marked a major turning point in Kennedy's literary career. On January 14, 1983, he received a John D. and Catherine T. MacArthur Foundation award of $264,000. He used a portion of the no-strings-attached grant to create The Writers Institute at Albany. Kennedy also celebrated the publication of *Ironweed* in 1983. After thirteen rejections by publishers, Viking published *Ironweed*, at the urging of Saul Bellow, along with a simultaneous release of Kennedy's previous two novels, *Legs* and *Billy Phelan's Greatest Game* as Penguin paperbacks. These three novels were called Kennedy's Albany Cycle. In 1984, *Ironweed* received the Pulitzer Prize for fiction and National Book Critics Circle Award. Hy Rosen, longtime editorial cartoonist for the *Times Union*, marked the occasion by penning one of his signature cartoons. On August 6, 1984, Governor Mario M. Cuomo signed legislation creating the New York State Writers Institute, a state-sponsored agency with Kennedy as director, and a month later on September 6–9, Albany civic and cultural organizations sponsored a citywide celebration of Kennedy and his work. To top off this incredible two-year period, Francis Ford Coppola's film, *The Cotton Club*, starring Richard Gere and Diane Lane, for which Kennedy collaborated on the script, had its world premiere in Albany on December 2, 1984.
Hy Rosen cartoon courtesy of Elaine Rosen.

(Left to right) Francis Ford Coppola, Dana Kennedy, William Kennedy.

(Seated) William Kennedy, *(standing)* Richard Gere, Diane Lane.

New York Governor Mario M. Cuomo signed the legislation that created the New York State Writers Institute, housed at the University at Albany and directed by William Kennedy. Cuomo called the law "one of the best pieces of creative writing I'll ever do." Kennedy looked on with State Senator Tarky Lombardi *(left)* and State Assemblyman William Passannante *(right)*, who sponsored the legislation.

Kennedy *(center)* and Cuba's president Fidel Castro *(left)* talked for hours at the home of novelist Gabriel García Márquez *(right)* in Havana, January 1987. Kennedy was invited by his friend García Márquez, a literary kindred spirit, to visit.

Kennedy poses in front of the Palace Theatre marquee that announces the world premiere of *Ironweed* on December 17, 1987. Proceeds from the premiere screening benefited homeless shelters and other human services and recovery programs in the city of Albany.

Kennedy and his wife, Dana, pose with the stars of *Ironweed*, Meryl Streep and Jack Nicholson, on the movie set. Much of the movie, which was directed by Héctor Babenco and written by Kennedy, was filmed in Albany, Troy, and other Capital Region communities.
Photo by Joel Warren.

In 2003, Kennedy turned over his papers to the University Libraries' M. E. Grenander Department of Special Collections and Archives at the University at Albany. The collection included seventy boxes of manuscripts, film scripts, and memorabilia. *(Left to right)* Dean of Libraries Meredith Butler, Kennedy, University at Albany President Karen Hitchcock and Provost Carlos Santiago. Photo courtesy of the University at Albany.

In 2007, Kennedy visited a class at his old North Albany elementary school, P.S. 20, with his son Brendan, coauthors of the children's book *Charley Malarkey and the Singing Moose*, published by Viking in 1994.

Kennedy's vision for the New York State Writers Institute, and its precursor, The Writers Institute at Albany, was to bring the world's greatest writers to Albany for a series of lectures, seminars, readings, film screenings, and literary discussions that would enliven and inspire University at Albany students and faculty and community audiences from across the Capital Region. The Writers Institute quickly established Albany as a literary crossroads. Saul Bellow, recipient of the Pulitzer Prize and Nobel Prize for Literature, was the first visiting writer of The Writers Institute at Albany on April 26, 1984.

Toni Morrison *(right)*, who later won the Pulitzer Prize and Nobel Prize for Literature, kicked off the New York State Writers Institute's inaugural fall Visiting Writers Series on September 13, 1984.
Photo courtesy of the University at Albany.

William Styron *(right)* visited the New York State Writers Institute on October 15, 1985, and again in fall 1993.

Governor Mario M. Cuomo presented Irish poet John Montague with a citation in 1987 "for his outstanding literary achievements and his contributions to the people of New York." Montague served as Distinguished Writer-in-Residence for the New York State Writers Institute, teaching workshops in fiction and poetry and a class in the English Department at the University at Albany during the spring semester for several years. *(Seated)* John Montague. *(Standing, left to right)* Tom Smith, associate director of the Writers Institute, Kennedy, Governor Mario M. Cuomo.

Seamus Heaney *(left)* delivered the Herman Melville Lecture on the Creative Imagination at the Writers Institute on April 27, 1988. Heaney received the Nobel Prize in Literature in 1996.

Frank McCourt *(right)*, the Pulitzer Prize–winning author of *Angela's Ashes*, visited the Writers Institute on November 20, 1996; April 15, 1999; and January 24, 2006. McCourt and Kennedy were members of the "First Friday Society," a coterie of Irish American authors who met in Manhattan on the first Friday of every month. McCourt called the society "an organization devoted to its own existence. There's no reason for it existing. You can't join, and you can't leave once you're in."

Photo by Paul Buckowski. Photo courtesy of the Albany *Times Union*.

Joseph Heller *(right)*, who visited the Writers Institute on February 22, 1995, to read from *Closing Time*, his sequel to *Catch-22*, chats with Kennedy *(left)*, and former *Times Union* reporter Paul Grondahl *(center)*. Grondahl was named the third director of the Writers Institute in February 2017.

Pulitzer Prize–winning playwright August Wilson *(right)* visited the Writers Institute on April 8, 1996.

Studs Terkel *(right)*, broadcaster, Pulitzer Prize–winning nonfiction author, and recipient of a 1997 National Humanities Medal visited the Writers Institute on May 5, 1998.

Hunter S. Thompson *(right)* and his literary executor, historian Douglas Brinkley *(left)*, visited the Writers Institute on November 4, 1998, to discuss Thompson's book *The Rum Diary: The Long Lost Novel*. Thompson and Kennedy maintained a friendship and correspondence dating back to 1960, when Thompson unsuccessfully applied for a job at the *San Juan Star*, where Kennedy was managing editor.

While he was in Dublin, Ireland, to speak with Joycean scholars, Kennedy knocked on the door of 7 Eccles Street, the house where Leopold and Molly Bloom lived in James Joyce's novel *Ulysses*.

Kennedy celebrated his ninetieth birthday on January 16, 2018, at Cafe Capriccio in Albany by dancing with his wife, Dana. They were joined by family, friends, and fellow writers at a dinner hosted by Friends of Writing, a group dedicated to supporting the programming of the New York State Writers Institute. Chef-owner Jim Rua created a culinary feast and many attendees contributed to the William Kennedy Endowment Fund to sustain and expand Writers Institute programming.
Photo by Joe Putrock.

PART TWO

Kennedy in His Own Words

Essays, Speeches, Memorial Tributes, and Creative Work

Introduction to Part Two

In *O Albany!,* William Kennedy's nonfiction collection on the city of Albany's history, he poses a question to himself: How does a child who grew up in a household without books become a writer? "My grammar school (P.S. 20) had no library," he remembers, "and my high school (Christian Brothers Academy) was one of, shall we say, modest resources. Every student's crutch in my neighborhood was the Albany Public Library system, and so it was that the John Van Schaick Lansing Pruyn branch on North Pearl Street became my personal point of entry into the beauty and magic of books" (8).

In this section Kennedy provides answers to his own question of how he became a writer. He traces his own literary career, describes his early influences, and how and why Albany captured his imagination. He also offers memorial tributes to two fellow writers and personal friends, shares a rare short story, and a one-act play.

"I began my writing career as a newspaperman . . . but along the way something happened to my head and I turned into a novelist," William Kennedy says in the introduction to *Riding the Yellow Trolley Car*, a collection of his journalistic writing. In the first essay in this section, "Why It Took So Long," he describes this transition from journalist to novelist, with stops along the way as a book reviewer, movie critic, screenwriter, interviewer, and teacher.

At Kennedy's ninetieth birthday celebration on January 16, 2018, which included a number of warm appreciations from friends and family, his granddaughter Annabella said she is convinced that her grandfather is a magician. Her assessment is based on the fact that ever since she was very young "he would sneak up . . . and pull a piece of chocolate" from behind her ear. Just when she was starting to figure out that he must already have the chocolate in his hand, "he pulled a banana out of nowhere." Now a teenager, she and Poppy, as she calls her grandfather, are working on a book together about a cat stuck in a tree. And she has that same sense of wonder and amazement about his writing technique as she did about how the chocolate magically appeared. "We still haven't decided why this cat is up in the tree, or how to get it down. But we've talked about things that don't have anything to do with what is actually happening in the book. Does the owner have any kids? Or was she married before she started living alone with the cat? Or does her name have an integral background that the reader has to discover? He comes up with these amazing things that just come out of nowhere and I still don't know how he does it."

Novelist and critic Doris Grumbach shared a similar view of the magical nature of Kennedy's writing in her speech "O Albany! O Kennedy!" (p. 19–27). She asked the question, "How did parochial history become, under Kennedy's pen, invention?" And how do Kennedy's characters "rise, full-blooded and glowing with recognizable life, out of what, to my vision, had always seemed a sterile and pallid landscape?"

In "Reinventing Albany in Fiction: Notes from a Native Son," which the novelist presented at the "William Kennedy's Albany Weekend" celebration, Kennedy answers both his granddaughter's and Doris Grumbach's questions as to where it all comes from. He explains what he sees in the landscape of Albany and its history, and how his "imagination has become fused with a single place, and in that place finds all the elements that a man ever needs for the life of the soul." He presents several photographs and describes how they sparked his imagination. As he says, "It's not quite a *tabula rasa* but it's close to that." He does not, however, reveal where the banana came from.

Kennedy explores his literary influences in the two essays "Learning from Faulkner: The Obituary of Fear" and "Gifts from Joyce." He describes his early fascination with William Faulkner's Yoknapatawpha saga and finding "this intertwining of lives in a single place the most ambitious fictional device I could imagine." What he could not imagine at the time was ever being able to create his "own fictional cosmos." And yet, the "fascination with recurring characters continued . . ."

Kennedy delivered "Gifts from Joyce" as the James Joyce Lecture at University College Dublin on the eve of Bloomsday in 1993. He confesses that after reading *Ulysses* cover to cover when he was recovering from an illness, the book "made me doubt my intelligence, and made me think English was not my native tongue. . . . And yet the reading was a thrilling experience." He notes that the book inspired him to think of "an impossible enterprise: the creation of a book that would leap over my own conventional ambitions, a book that would be greater than what I knew I could do." He valued Joyce's "courage in the face of the rejection . . . and the censorship he encountered," and as with Faulkner, Kennedy was inspired by Joyce's insistence "on the essentiality of place."

Kennedy has had personal and professional friendships with some of the most lauded writers of his generation. He offers memorial tributes to two of them—Saul Bellow and Norman Mailer. Kennedy's connection to Bellow as a professional mentor is well documented in Margaret Croyden's profile "The Sudden Fame of William Kennedy" (p. 7–18). But in his paean to Bellow that he delivered at the American Academy of Arts and Letters members' dinner in November 2005, he reveals the personal side of their relationship, including a remembrance of a lunch he arranged with Bellow and Jack Nicholson in Wilmington, Vermont.

In his memorial to Norman Mailer, Kennedy describes the many faces of the man and the writer. Mailer was known for blurring the edges between fiction and nonfiction, for which he was alternately praised and maligned. He also possessed an often-exasperating personality beyond his writing style. Kennedy first met Mailer in 1969 when he was covering the New York Film Festival as a movie critic for the Albany *Times Union*. Mailer was working on his new film *Maidstone*. Kennedy asked Mailer's film editor, Jan Welt, if he could interview Mailer. The answer came back from Mailer that he couldn't do the interview because it would be like "feeding caviar to spaghetti eaters." Kennedy says, "[Mailer's] life was an open book, opened and written by himself—ego-driven, psychoanalytical, truculent, self-flagellating, coruscating, sometimes fictional, routinely brilliant. . . . the literary phenomenon of his generation." Kennedy poignantly describes a lunch he had with Norman at his home in Provincetown, Massachusetts, in September 2007, just two months before Norman's death, painting a portrait of a man whose sharp mind had outlived his failing body. "We agreed," Kennedy notes, "that without a doubt, this had been one of the great lunches."

Stories about Hunter S. Thompson run throughout this collection. His reputation preceded the iconoclastic journalist, irascible author, and founder of the "Gonzo" journalism style. He was a free spirit who became a notable counterculture figure. Kennedy and Thompson met in Puerto Rico in 1960, and after an inauspicious beginning—Kennedy rejected Thompson's application for a position at the *San Juan Star* newspaper, where Kennedy was managing editor at the time—the two developed a sometimes-rocky friendship that spanned forty-five years. In "A Box of Books," Kennedy offers a skewed portrait of their contentious early relationship through their correspondence about a box of books that Thompson left at Kennedy's home, after he was forced to leave Puerto Rico abruptly. Their hilarious stream of insult-ridden notes and letters underscores not only an unconventional friendship, but it captures in an authentic way their shared struggles in establishing literary careers.

While he is known primarily as a novelist, Kennedy has branched out into other literary genres. Early in his career he wrote short stories, although he says in his essay "Why It Took So Long" that his first attempts were "all derivative and blithering. . . . I came to loathe the stories, as did my family, my friends, and fiction editors from coast to coast." However, his short story "The Secrets of Creative Love" did make it out of the rejection pile and was published by *Harper's Magazine* in 1983. Some of the characters appear in Kennedy's later novels, but this time the locale is Saratoga Springs, rather than Albany. In the story Kennedy describes his main character Daniel Quinn this way: "Quinn remained a writer, obsessed still with the past and its mysteries, and had reaped a few of the rewards and ironies such a life offers." It's hard to resist the temptation to wonder if Kennedy is describing his character or himself.

Kennedy has also ventured into playwriting. Presented here is a one-act play *In the System*. It was commissioned in 2003 for The Technology Plays, an interdisciplinary initiative of The Center for Humanities, Arts and TechnoScience at the University at Albany as part of a project that explored the boundaries between the sciences, the humanities, and the creative arts. It's a zany look at computer hacking, crossed circuits, and the seedier side of the Internet.

In remarks given at his ninetieth birthday party—which in typical fashion he continued to relentlessly revise with a pencil, even as he prepared to step from his seat to the microphone—Kennedy referenced Philip Roth's announcement at the age of seventy-nine that he was finished with writing fiction: "I don't want to read it, I don't want to write it, and I don't even want to talk about it anymore. . . . It's enough!" (n.p.). With wide-eyed disbelief Kennedy said about his own writing, "I haven't quit yet and I'm not sure I ever can. I am writing now what may or may not turn into something, but it will keep me wired with authorial anxiety on into what's left of my foreseeable future." Grateful readers breathed a sigh of relief. And the next day Kennedy went back to his computer keyboard.

—Suzanne Lance

Reference

Remnick, David. "Philip Roth Says Enough." *New Yorker*. https://www.newyorker.com/books/page-turner/philip-roth-says-enough.

Why It Took So Long

> What I had finally come to realize was that I'd learned all I wanted to learn about newspapering, and that I could never learn enough about how to write fiction; for the more I learned, the more difficult writing became. That is still so today.
>
> —William Kennedy

I was working as a newspaperman at the *Post-Star* in Glens Falls, New York, when I was drafted into the Army during the Korean War, and I decided to write a continuing column about it for my paper called "This New Army," which was what everyone was calling that same old army in those days. I wrote about how unbelievably stupid sergeants and corporals were, how unspeakably dreadful army food was, and how very peculiarly the general behaved when he noticed I was marching out of step.

When these columns were published back in Glens Falls, enlistments in this new army dropped to zero, the first time I changed the world with my writing. This change was testified to by the local doomsday recruiting sergeant, who packaged off my clippings, along with a formal complaint, to Fort Benning, Georgia, where I was taking basic training. Because I could type, somebody had made me the company clerk, and so I also got to answer the phone. A call came in one day and guess who it was for? Me. The major who ran the division's public information office was calling.

"Kennedy," he said to me, "that was a funny column you wrote the other day about the general."

"Thank you, Major," I said. "I'm glad you liked it."

"I didn't say I liked it and don't write any more." And then he added, after a pause, "Come up and see me and maybe I'll give you a job."

Well, I did, and he did, and for the next two years I spent my days writing for army newspapers in the United States and Germany. I was also thrown in with the literate and subliterate malcontents who populated the public information section, most of them also draftees and ex-newspapermen, and four, including me, aspirants to writing of a different order: short stories, novels, films, plays—we weren't particular.

These years were seminal to me, the period in which I dived headfirst into literature. One of my great pals was a brilliant newspaperman from Mississippi who had not only seen and talked to Louis Armstrong, he actually attended a lecture by William Faulkner. Closer than that to the empyrean no man I knew had ever ventured. Four or five nights a week we would gather in our enlisted men's club in Frankfurt, arguing, over *heilbock* and *dopplebock*, the relative merits of Sherwood Anderson, Ernest Hemingway, John Dos Passos, John Steinbeck, Erskine Caldwell, F. Scott Fitzgerald, Norman Mailer, Nelson Algren, Katherine Anne Porter, Flannery O'Connor, James Jones, Irwin Shaw, Thomas Wolfe. "Wolfe said it all, but Faulkner said it better," was the youthful anthem from Mississippi.

I also began writing what I thought of as serious short fiction. I had written stories in college, all derivative and blithering, but now I was beginning to match myself against these maestros I'd been reading. At first I was such an amateur I couldn't even imitate them, but in the year or two after I left the army I managed to write dialogue that sounded very like Hemingway and John O'Hara, I could describe the contents of a refrigerator just like Wolfe, I could use intelligent obscenity just like Mailer, I could keep a sentence running around the block, just like Faulkner. But where was Kennedy?

I came to loathe the stories, as did my family, my friends, and fiction editors from coast to coast. Nevertheless, by diving into literature I had baptized myself as a writer. I have since come to look upon this as religious experience—not because of its holiness, for as a profession it is more profane than sacred, but because of its enmeshment with the Roman Catholic Church's supernatural virtues of faith, hope, and charity—as I had learned them.

Charity, of course, is what the writer supports himself with while he is finishing his novel.

Hope is the virtue by which he firmly trusts that someday, somewhere, somebody will publish his novel.

But it is in the virtue of faith that the writer grounds himself or herself in the true religious experience of literature, and faith was defined early on for me as a firm belief in the revealed truths—truths of God as religion would have it, truths of the writing life, as I would have it.

"How may we sin against faith?" the catechism used to ask, and then it provided four answers:

Sin No. 1: "By rashly accepting as truths of faith what are not really such."

I take this to mean that the writer should learn how to tell the difference between literary gold and dross.

Sin No. 2: "By neglecting to learn the truths which we are bound to know."

> *This is a large order. It means you should read the entire canon of literature that precedes you, back to the Greeks, up to the current issue of the* Paris Review. *If you have any time left over, you should go out and accumulate an intimate knowledge of politics, history, language, love, philosophy, psychology, sex, madness, the underworld, soap opera, your cholesterol level, and whether the Beatles will ever have a reunion.*

Sin No. 3: "By not performing those acts of faith, which we are commanded to perform."

> *This means you should write even on Christmas and your birthday, and forswear forever the excuse that you never have enough time.*

Sin No. 4: "By heresy and apostasy."

> *This means writing for the movies.*

My life after the army was a tissue of muddle, a pilgrimage through ignorance, anxiety, and innocence, but a pilgrimage with some discernible milestones. Five years after leaving the army I would get married, write my first and last play (this "last play" notion proved not to be true) and my twenty-fifth short story, then quit journalism to write a novel. I would write the novel and it would be awful. Seven years after the army I would become managing editor of a daily newspaper. After nine years I would quit journalism again to finish another novel. I would be showing improvement in novel writing, but not much. After fifteen years of work as a half-time journalist, half-time fiction writer, I would become a movie critic. After seventeen years I would publish my first novel. After nineteen years I would become a book critic. After twenty-two years I would become a teacher. And then, after thirty-one years, I would write my first movie script, may God have mercy on his soul.

For a time I was a true believer in journalism, lived it passionately, gained entry to worlds I had no right to enter, learned how to write reasonably well and rapidly, was never bored by what I was doing, found the work an enduring source of stimulation, met thousands of the crazy people who populate the profession, and learned madness from most of them. I loved the tension, the unexpected element of the news, the illusion of being at the center of things when you were really at what approximated the inner lining of the orange peel.

Also I learned who I was, in certain small but significant ways. I became, as I mentioned, a managing editor, a position to which I had been obliquely gravitating since the beginning; for in wanting to learn all there was to learn about writing, I also wanted to learn all there was about what you did with writing after you wrote it.

When this happened to me—over the objection of my second self, which had always wanted to be a daily columnist until the seductive muse of fiction took command of my pencil—I contemplated the new condition, especially what H. L. Mencken once wrote, "All managing editors are vermin." I remained verminous for two years. I never worked harder, never found more pleasure in the work, yet always longed to be out of it, for the job had interrupted my novel-in-progress and I yearned to return and see how it would turn out. It took me those two years to accumulate the courage and wisdom to quit a lucrative, fascinating job, live off my savings and a weekend editing job, and work five full days a week on fiction. What I had finally come to realize was that I'd learned all I wanted to learn about newspapering, and that I could never learn enough about how to write fiction; for the more I learned, the more difficult writing became. That is still so today. I don't mean to be simplistic about journalism, which is mired in the complexity of randomness. It was a great training ground for a writer, but I'd reached my limit with it and knew in my soul that I was a committed novelist, whose work is grounded in the complexity of unconscious logic.

The problem then became the quest for the elusive Kennedy voice. I had ceased to consciously emulate anyone in my work, but what I was left with was the voice of literary objectivity—a journalistic virus, an odious microbe that paralyzes the imagination and cripples the language.

The transition from journalism to fiction is always a precarious trip, for journalism foists dangerous illusions on the incipient fiction writer. The daily journalist is trained, for instance, to forget about yesterday and focus on today. There is also a car parked downstairs, ready to carry him off into tomorrow, and so every new day becomes for him a blank sheet of paper. This is deadly. The fiction writer who puts little or no value on yesterday, or the even more distant past, might just as well have Alzheimer's disease. Serious fiction, especially the novel, has time as its principal tool.

The journalist is also under pressure to believe that his presence at the great moments—whether he be first on the scene after a murder of passion, or witness to the fall of an empire—gives him the stuff of fiction. This is true to a point, but the stuff in question is merely raw material. The writer who believes he has a ready-made work of fiction spread out before him in his notes, needful only of a bit of sprucing and spicing, is deluded. He is a victim of the cult of experience, the impulse that sends writers who can find no value in the quotidian off to wars and revolutions to find something to write about. More than experience is called for.

In recent months in this country we have witnessed a rather tub-thumping, hog-stomping, name-calling literary argument on this subject, begun by

Tom Wolfe, a notable tub-thumper and baroque hog-stomper of high journalistic achievement and repute, who moved into the realm of fiction with an extraordinarily successful first novel, *The Bonfire of the Vanities*. Having succeeded, he now would like others to succeed as well by writing novels like his.

The essence of Mr. Wolfe's argument is that American literature in the last half of this century has gone down the tube of navel-gazing, neofabulism, magic realism, absurdism, and so on—that no one is writing about the age we live in—and that the only way to rescue it is through a return to realism of a nineteenth-century order, writing akin to that of Dickens, Trollope, Thackeray, Zola, and Balzac. The means of achieving this movement back to the future, says Mr. Wolfe, is reporting.

I am sympathetic to some aspects of Mr. Wolfe's argument, but I think it is an exercise in audacity to tell a writer what and how to write. The writer, of necessity, is the sole judge of that, for the making of these decisions is evolutionary, a process of trial and rejection, of finally choosing among infinite possibilities the method, and story, and characters that allow the work to be written at all. I could never fault any writer for not writing about this age, for in my own experience that has been extremely difficult. I offer only one example:

My time in the army represented two years of my life, and not merely life lived but life reported on through a newsman's eye—reporting on the army, on Germany, on the Cold War getting hot, on an innocent abroad, on fraternization with *Fräuleins*, on the black market, on army skullduggery, on leftover Nazism, and much more. I had and still have some of that world at my fingertips; also I've gone back twice to Germany to rekindle my memory.

Why? Well, I wanted to write about it all and did write about it—in short stories over a decade—and all those stories died. I also wrote about two hundred pages of a novel about it, and that died too. Obviously, in my case, it is not the material that makes a work of fiction come to life. It is, in fact, almost impossible to say what it is that does that. Material can begin a piece of work, emotion and ideas can keep it going, but in order for the work not to self-destruct along the way something else must happen. The writer must find himself in a strange place full of unknowns, populated by characters who are not quite strangers but about whom little is certain, and everything is to be discovered. There must be a transformation of the material, of the characters, of the age, into something that is intriguingly new to the writer. "Art," wrote Boris Pasternak, "concerns itself with life as the ray of power *passes through it*" (71).

The writer, when he is functioning as an artist, understands when this power is at hand, and he knows that it does not rise up from his notepad but up from the deepest part of his unconscious, which knows everything everywhere and always: that secret archive stored in the soul at birth, enhanced by every waking moment of life, and which is the source of the power and the vision that allow the writer to create something never before heard or seen.

This creation of the new is what a good reader seeks and will recognize. Listen to E. M. Forster trying to define *Moby-Dick*. He calls the book a yarn about whaling interspersed with snatches of poetry, also a battle against evil conducted too long or in the wrong way, also a contest between two unreconciled evils, and then he throws up his hands. "These are words," says Forster, "a symbol for the book if we want one. . . . The essential in *Moby-Dick*, its prophetic song, flows athwart the action and the surface morality like an undercurrent. It lies outside words" (200).

Almost, but not quite, just by the nature of Melville's effort, one might conclude he was striving for that "prophetic song" from the outset. But to think that is to believe in creation as nothing more than conception, that the song, the achievement, was already present in the embryo. If this is true, what then can we say of Melville's years of gestation among whales, his months of research ("I have swam through libraries," his narrator says in *Moby-Dick*, and so had Melville in his preparation for it), and his year and a half of writing and rewriting the text? One of his biographers has pointed out that although seventeen months seems a short time for the composition of such a book, it would have been an unusually long period given the manic pace at which Melville was writing.

Writers (and their songs) grow like plants, like trees, like children, like disease, like love. They go through stages of fragility, woodenness, pubescence, death, and passion. You'll note that I have put death before passion. This corresponds to the crucifixion, burial, descent into hell, and resurrection that befalls all literary careerists who keep the faith. F. Scott Fitzgerald's noted line, "There are no second acts in American lives," was cockeyed and trivializing. He was talking about stardom. Resurrection has come to many American writers: Melville (the most egregiously belated case), Henry James, Kate Chopin, Willa Cather, Edith Wharton, and Fitzgerald himself; and it is now happening with Hemingway. It even happened to Faulkner when he was still alive, the problem being that no one knew he was alive as his books were all out of print. Then suddenly they were in print and still are, along with those of the other writers in this group.

Not all of these writers wrote of their own age, though most did. Most of them were realists, but not Melville and not always James, who wrote romances and made excursions into the world of ghosts. In the words of Maupassant, they each made themselves "an illusion of a world," each according to his or her sex, knowledge, style, talent, joyful or melancholy disposition, mythic or mordant mind.

So whose realism is this, anyway?

And what of dreams? Are they part of realism?

And what of the surrealistic episodes that all of us have gone through but try not to accept as real? Kafka and Borges and Gabriel García Márquez have made them real, without doubt, just as they were supposed to, because they found it necessary. "The great artists," said Maupassant, "are those who impose their personal illusion on humanity" (27–28).

I am delighted to report that pursuing my own particular illusion, I have just finished a section of a new novel in which I use—at long last—that army experience I had in Germany so many years ago. I am also pleased to report that I have transformed it to such a degree that it no longer resembles anything I lived through. The character who inhabits this transformed experience is forever doing things that are wild and illegal and outrageous—not at all like me, which may be the reason I could never before write about the place. Yes. Absolutely. That last possibility is so clearly accurate that I hereby aver its truth: that I couldn't write it because I had lived it, because I knew it too well, because I knew how it would come out: boringly, as it always had.

Back in the late 1950s, when I was trying to read the complete shelf of William Faulkner, I kept coming across speeches or interviews in which he talked of uplifting man's heart. In his Nobel Prize acceptance speech he said it was the writer's "privilege to help man endure by lifting his heart" (120). In a literature class at the University of Virginia he said, "The artist believes what he's doing is valid in that it may do something to uplift man's heart, not to make man any more successful, but to temporarily make him feel better than he felt before, to uplift his heart for a moment" (*Faulkner in the University* 67).

This uplift business baffled me. I was reading and rereading *The Sound and the Fury*, *Sanctuary*, *Light in August*, *The Wild Palms*, and *Absalom, Absalom!*—tales of incest and whoring, and rape and dying love, and madness and murder, and racial hate and miscegenational tragedy and idiocy—and saying to myself, "This is uplift?"

But I kept reading and found I couldn't get enough; I had to reread to satisfy the craving, and came to answer the question in a word: yes. I felt exalted by the man's work, not by reveling in all the disasters, but by learning from his language and his insights and his storytelling genius how certain other people lived and thought. I was privileged to enter into the most private domains of their lives and they became friends or people I'd keep at least at arm's length, or people I pitied, feared, or loved. This was truly an uplifting experience, something akin to real friendship, and I began to understand the process by which writing reaches into another person's heart.

I received two letters from a man who had read my novel *Ironweed*. In the first, about four years ago, he wrote that he had been moved by the book and had to write and tell me. Two years later came the second letter, in which he hinted he might have known the street life, the drinking life of a bum, just as the book's hero, Francis Phelan, knew it. The letter writer was now living with his sister, doing handyman's work for her, and staying out of trouble. His sister didn't like drunks and would even cross the street to get away from a wino. Then her brother pressed *Ironweed* on her and got her to read the book. At the end she found herself crying, and she said of Francis, "You know, he wasn't such a bad guy."

That would be quite enough for me, but the story has a coda. The sister no longer fears winos, no longer crosses the street to get away from them. She now gives them her loose change. And at Christmas she passes out to them, one and all, half-pints of muscatel.

This is a true story. It is a realistic story of our age. It has been transformed somewhat by the writer, who is very glad to have written it.

REFERENCES

Faulkner, William. "Address upon Receiving the Nobel Prize for Literature." In *Essays, Speeches & Public Letters by William Faulkner*, ed. James B. Meriwether. New York: Random House, 1965.

Forster, E. M. *Aspects of the Novel.* New York: Harcourt, Brace & World, 1954.

Gwynn, Frederick L., and Joseph L. Blotner, eds. *Faulkner in the University: Class Conferences at the University of Virginia 1957–1958.* New York: Vintage Books, 1959.

Maupassant, Guy de. *Pierre and Jean*, trans. Leonard Tancock. London: Penguin, 1979.

Pasternak, Boris. *Safe Conduct: An Autobiography and Other Writings.* New York: New Directions, 1958.

The essay was first presented as the Hopwood Lecture at the University of Michigan in April 1990 and appeared in the *Michigan Quarterly Review* 29, 3 (1990): 393–405, and *The Writing Life*, edited by Nicholas Delbanco (Ann Arbor: University of Michigan Press, 2000) under the title "Writers and Their Songs."

Reinventing Albany in Fiction

Notes from a Native Son

> One of my deepest beliefs about fiction is that unless you understand the environment in which the human soul grows, flourishes, wanes and dies, then you have very little to work with.
>
> —William Kennedy

Before we proceed any further I must pause, for I am compelled to set the record straight about what has happened here during this past week or so. First, there is no such place as Albany, and second, there is no such person as William Kennedy. Not in the way we used to know them, anyway. They have both been reinvented—by one another—a rather improbable development. Then consider all the formalized attention and incredible publicity given to the work of one writer during these spectacular days. Let's face it. People are not usually nice to writers. And they are never *this* nice unless the writer is at least certifiably dead, and, preferably, lost at sea or eaten by tigers.

For purposes of maintaining sanity, I am going to consider this whole week and weekend a work of fiction, or perhaps the stuff of a movie; for the happy ending is a major element in most movies, and we certainly have here today a happy ending of a kind: a rite of passage for this city, away from public opprobrium and sarcasm—at least for the time being—and into the realm of idealized life. We all want to dwell in the ideal city, a city of the imagination, a city that befits us, a city like no other. And that is what Albany now seems to have become in the minds of many. This transformation was even certified two weeks ago in *The New York Times* when Albany was described as a "quiet, sleepy place" . . . once a symbol of "provincialism and arcane politics" . . . but which has now become an "integral part of the literary world."*

---

* Editors' Note: See the essay by Margaret Croyden, "The Sudden Fame of William Kennedy," in part 1 of this volume.

What the *Times* was saying, I like to think, was that in terms of abstract value, we have all moved up from mundane sociology onto the plane where legend or even myth is generated. Joseph Campbell, the great scholar of mythology and religion, once defined myth as "society's dream." I take that to mean that if we cannot inhabit the ideal city, then we invent it in our dreams. We create unlikely heroes and heroines, ogres, and sirens. We redefine morality, punish or perhaps reward evil, crown our protagonists with justice and glory, or possibly betrayal, death, and resurrection. We even recast the gods in our own images, and then, in the center of all this creation and recreation, we try to place ourselves.

This is what I also try to do when I write novels.

I have reinvented Albany to suit my own functional designs, social priorities, historical necessities, quixotic preferences, and profound psychological desires. When I say that there is no such place as Albany I mean that its ancient reality has been lost. But I also mean that there never was such a definable place, that it was always a continuing city—first the wilderness, into the days of Maquaas, the Mohawk Indians, then Fort Orange, then Rensselaerswyck, then Beverswyck, and then Willemstadt—which are all names of communities that no longer exist.

History pretends there is a continuity in them all that is now called Albany, but that is only a continuity of fragile and marginal time, of immutable space. Almost all of what existed within that space has been transformed, or has been cavalierly destroyed, or has disintegrated and is being forgotten—as usual.

Does anybody remember Joel Munsell? Librarians and history buffs do, I'm sure, but the extent of his contribution to the city's history is insufficiently known and appreciated today. He was a printer of excellence, who between 1849 and 1871 published ten volumes of invaluable history called the *Annals of Albany*, and four volumes called *Collections on the History of Albany*. He was a founder, in 1791, of the Albany Institute of History and Art, one of the oldest museums in the United States, and of him it was said, almost an epitaph: "He scarcely ever refused to put in print a valuable manuscript because it wouldn't pay."

Does anybody remember Thurlow Weed? He was an ally of John Quincy Adams, an enemy of Martin Van Buren. He was a founder of the Anti-Masonic Party, the Whig Party, and the Republican Party, and he was a president-maker. He also founded and ran the *Albany Evening Journal*, a most influential newspaper during his tenure and beyond. Horace Greeley was afraid of him. Weed tried, but failed, to dominate even Lincoln, who came to Albany to see him. It was said of him: "He affords decisive evidence of being by nature a great man," and he lived on Beaver Street.

Does anybody remember Beaver Street, when even into our own day it was Newspaper Row? Along its few blocks or around the corner stood the *Press Knickerbocker*, the *Atlas* and *Argus*, the *Morning Express*, the *Daily Press and Knickerbocker,* the *Evening Union*, the *Evening Journal* and, in my memory, the *Knickerbocker News* and *Times Union*. What a repository of American culture and history was there!

I've been reading about Munsell and Weed and about the Erie Canal and cholera epidemics and natural disasters in some of these worthy old papers and I'm transported into a strange world—one I barely recognize when I first enter it.

There, for instance, in the mid-nineteenth century, goes Piggy Parker, rounding up one of the four thousand pigs roaming at large in the town. An epidemic of cholera had put the fear into the people and they began to get the idea that cleanliness was good for you. So they started rounding up the pigs, and Piggy Parker, a champ at this, was paid for every pig he rounded up. Yet there was no end to the pigs still on the loose, and then one day Albanians figured out why. Piggy would round the pigs up during the day and let them out again at night. So Piggy was paid maybe three or four times for his work; which is precisely how it was done when we built the South Mall, a ninety-eight-acre state government complex officially known as the Governor Nelson A. Rockefeller Empire State Plaza, here above us for two billion dollars and paid for everything four times over. Piggy Parker lives.

Piggy and the Mall are true and actual parts of our history. They are facts. I've written about many of the facts of our history in *O Albany!* and I'm fond of most them, as I think a journalist should be toward the material he or she willfully accumulates. I think the current fondness for history in this city should be made permanent, should be translated into an ongoing re-creation of our singular odyssey in this nation. In two years we will celebrate the tricentennial of our being chartered as a city, the second oldest in America; and our history as a settlement even precedes that date by almost a century.

It is not my place to tell the editors of the local newspapers how to run their businesses, especially since they have been doing it so splendidly all week long. Nevertheless, I offer this suggestion: that they hire a historian or a history buff—in either case a lively writer and accurate reporter—to carry us back into the greater and lesser moments of our past on a regular basis. Columnists did that daily when I was a young newspaperman, and they introduced me to this town. Munsell did the same when I had the luxury of spending time with his books in the city's libraries.

I do believe in the facts, and in the preservation of them, as should we all. But I also know that facts take us only so far. To go the rest of the way we must ride the ultimate trolley car with the fiction writer.

I offer here a few simple examples of how I've at times juggled Albany's facts to suit fictional needs. In *Billy Phelan's Greatest Game* I moved the kidnapping of a politician's nephew from 1933, when it actually happened to Dan O'Connell's nephew, Johnny O'Connell, up to 1938, because for plot purposes I wanted it to happen during a gubernatorial election year.

In *The Ink Truck* I transformed a mild-mannered, three-week newspaper strike, in which I was involved, into a surrealistic nightmare that lasts a year; and I imported gypsies, scabs, hippies, pigs, and other unwashed intruders by way of populating the strikers' world; for this was not a report on the reality of a very forgettable moment in labor history, but a statement about the life we were living and imagining in the 1960s, and so more than the quotidian reality was called for.

Transformation of the city's facts in my novels goes well beyond these few examples. The change is pervasive, really, for fiction and myth have needs that are not always as tidy and portable as the facts. Those needs are sometimes mystical or surreal or full of news not fit to print in the daily papers: malignant, libelous, impossibly raunchy, perhaps sacred or beatific. In short, very like the real life of the body and the mind as most of us know it.

There are few if any objective truths about our lives, our deeds, our motives, such complex creatures are we. My aim in these remarks is to speak of the intersection of history with the creative imagination, and to track myself to the moment when they first came together most significantly. I haven't quite been able to pinpoint any single moment. What I have come up with are some moments in the novels when memory and motives are reconstitutable for such analysis.

In *Billy Phelan's Greatest Game* there comes the moment when Billy, this small-time gambler and pool hustler, is matched against a good pool shooter named Doc Fay. Billy is better than the Doc, but Billy decides to throw the match, rather than take money from the gambler man who is backing him, Morrie Berman. Berman is the man on whom Billy may be about to inform concerning a kidnapping. Just as Billy has very skillfully made the shot a scratch—that will make him lose the match—the lights go out all over town. Men go out of the pool room and stand on the street in darkness. Here's how that moment reads, with the story's center of consciousness being one of the novel's two principal characters, newspaperman Martin Daugherty:

> Martin gulped his drink and went outside. People were clustered under the canopy at the station, all cabs were gone, and a West Albany trolley was stalled between Maiden Lane and Steuben Street. Martin could see it in the headlights of cars. The night was a deep, moonless black, with only a few stars

> visible. It was as if rural darkness had descended upon the city. Faces were unrecognizable three feet away. Albany had never been so dark in Martin's memory. There were gas lamps in his boyhood, then the first few electric lights, now the power poles everywhere. But tonight was the lightless time in which highwaymen had performed, the dark night of the century gone, his father's childhood darkness on new streets cut out of the raw hills and grassy flats. A woman with a bundle came by, half running toward Clinton Avenue, pursued by the night. Alongside Martin, a match flared and he turned to see Morrie Berman lighting a cigar. (182)

I've seen Albany in darkness like that. I was working for the *Times Union* the night of our great blackout in 1965 and I wrote the story by candlelight. I saw that darkness outside the city from the newsroom's window on Sheridan Avenue. I understand rural darkness also, for I have lived in the country for twenty years. But this was rural darkness on a moonless night, imposed upon people who were used to the bright lights.

In Billy Phelan's story, it turns out that the McCall brothers, the men who control the city politically, are directly responsible for the power blackout, for they chose to silence a radio speech being made by their principal political enemy, the aspirant to the governorship in 1938, Thomas E. Dewey. My understanding is that the O'Connell machine actually did this to Dewey after he was governor; but that wasn't in 1938. It was more like 1942 or 1943.

Beyond that, the blackout also has metaphorical portent. The darkness of mystery and maybe death has descended upon the kidnapping victim. Further, Billy has decided to transgress darkly against his own moral code by informing on a friend. But he doesn't *quite* transgress; and because he doesn't the McCalls "mark him lousy," in the street vernacular, and he is cast into outer darkness.

There is another, more literary reason. I remember John Cheever saying once that he didn't think much of a fiction writer who didn't describe the sky. I was already a big fan of the sky when I read that, but I paid even closer attention thereafter, for I knew Cheever was right. Leaving out the sky is as bad as leaving out the fact that your protagonist is not really Chinese, and has only one leg. The reader is shortchanged by such incomplete storytelling.

There is a different use of history in the ending of the novel *Legs*. It has more to do with the fact that I grew up reading about him in the local newspapers. I also grew up as a young newspaperman listening to all the stories, all the memories of the reporters who had covered his nefarious doings in the Catskills and in Albany. On top of that I began to hear all the silliness, the exaggerations and the shameless lies told about him by people who, after the fact, wanted to place themselves somewhere in his infamous history. Still later I discovered that William Wellman's wonderful film, *The Public Enemy*, was advertised in Albany as Jack Diamond's story, which in a certain way it was. I saw Diamond portrayed as a nemesis of Eliot Ness on *The Untouchables*, I saw him as the subject of a dreadful film called *The Rise and Fall of Legs Diamond*; the subject also of a silly, skinny paperback biography. Then I took on his story myself, for by this time I was fascinated by the legend—how it grew, why it grew. And so what I began to see was the process by which we create legends in this country, and in the world. Jack Diamond had become as legendary as Wild Bill Hickok, and Doc Holliday, and Billy the Kid, and Jesse James. Before I could translate this idea into the reality of a novel, along came Arthur Penn's remarkable film, *Bonnie and Clyde*, further proving my case that the criminals of the 1920s and 1930s had replaced the legendary criminals of the Old West as raw material for mythic villains.

Not every legend becomes a myth, and it remains to be seen whether Jack Diamond makes the grade. I suspect he has a better shot at it than most because of the contradictory elements of his personality. I remember an editor of mine once very sagely remarking with a snarl, "I knew a lot of people who really used to think he was a nice guy."

Well he wasn't, and yet . . . but we won't go into that. That's what the *novel* is all about. What I want to read now is a bit of the ending of that novel, the short finale I called "Jacked Up," a phrase which means the same as "Katie bar the door," "too wet to plow," and "that's all she wrote."

Jack is dead in this section, shot three times in the head. But his specter—clad in underwear, flat out in bed, is still thinking things out. And Jack the specter sits up in bed and looks into the mirror at the bullet holes in his skull. Jack had been shot four times previously but never died.

"Those simple bastards," he said, "they finally did it right."

And then:

> He moved without being able to move, thought out of his dead brain, smiled with an immobile mouth, his face intact but the back of his head blown away. Already aware he was moving outside time, he saw the yellow fluid coming to his eyes, trickling out his nose, his ears, down the corners of his mouth. He felt tricklings from his rectum, his penis, old friend, and knew those too were the yellow. He turned his head and saw the yellow coming out his wounds, on top of his congealing blood. He had known the yellow would come, for he had been at the

> edge before. But he always failed to understand the why of it. The wisdom of equality, the Book of the Dead said, but that made no sense. Death did make sense. It was a gift. The dead thanked you with stupid eyes.
>
> "Do you think I worry because I'm dead?" Jack asked aloud.
>
> The yellow oozed its curious answer. (*Legs* 315)

Well the room begins to fill up with figures from Jack's life. His lawyer, Marcus Gorman is beside him providing legal counsel on how to behave in the next world. Damon Runyon drops by with some wisdom—"All life is nine to five against." Arnold Rothstein turns up, the master criminal for whom Diamond once worked. Jack, in homage, says Rothstein's prayer: "O Lord, God of Abraham, keep me alive and smart. The rest I'll figure out for myself." "Dummy," Marcus says to him, "you're dead. What kind of a thing is it, asking to stay alive?" Marcus eases Jack along, pressing on his nerve of eternal sleep, and suddenly Jack is totally out of his body, in front of the mirror: no more blood, no more yellow.

> "Am I completely dead?" he asked, and knew then his last human feeling: his body being blown to atoms, the feeling of fire sinking into air. . . . He felt his absent pupils dilate to receive the light, which was his own light as well as everyone else's. When the light came, it was not the brilliant whiteness Jack expected, but a yellowish, grayish light that made no one blink. The motion of the light was perceptible. It swirled around Jack's neck . . . like a tornado in crescendo, spun round his entire head with what was obviously a potentially dazzling ferocity, reduced in effect now by the horrendous life-tone of Jack Diamond . . .
>
> As Jack's awareness of the light peaked, he was already falling backward. Though he had no arms, he waved them frantically to right himself, and as he fell, twisting and flailing against this ignominious new development, he delivered up one, final, well-modulated sentence before he disappeared into the void, into the darkness where the white was still elusive.
>
> "Honest to God, Marcus," he said going away, "I really don't think I'm dead." (*Legs* 317)

I don't think it's my province to explain all the things I mean to say in that section. But one thing seems clear enough, Jack isn't merging with the whiteness of the next world. The final peace of Nirvana has eluded him, and he is to be reborn. In what way remains to be defined. Possibly as a character in an Albany novel.

What I want to do now is show you three slides and try to focus on the way it was for me when I was writing a novel about Albany and living in Puerto Rico; when all I had to transport me back here, or back in time—something I've always wanted to do—was Morris Gerber's first *Old Albany* picture book. These two photos do not appear in any of his books as far as I know. I came across them only recently, and it's because of the new memories they generate that I use them here now. It's not quite a *tabula rasa* but it's close. It's the story that might not have come without the suggestion that the details in the photographs offer to the imagination.

What we have here is a tennis court in winter in North Albany. It's a year in World War II, three days before Christmas, 1943. The date is on the negative. I am fifteen, a junior in high school and some of my friends have gone off, or are getting ready to go off, to war. My childhood is over and the fence along the upper edge of the tennis court is gone. I used to climb that fence as a

A tennis court in winter in North Albany in 1943.
City of Albany Engineering Division.

child and helped to wreck its wire mesh. Most of my childhood was centered around this open space and the space to the left that you can't see, which was the baseball field of Public School 20.

One of the houses my family lived in on this block (we lived in three from about 1932 to 1970) was 607 North Pearl Street, a one-family house (at far right) built by North End contractor Eddie Carey, as indeed were just about all the houses visible in this photo, plus a few dozen more. I am living in that house in 1943. I could even be looking out the upper window to the right, just above the porch roof.

We are looking northeast in the photo and in the center is the intersection of North Pearl and North Third Streets. The two peaks that you can see faintly in the background, are part of the Albany Felt Company, a firm long associated with the Corning family. Young Erastus Corning 2nd has been mayor of the city since 1941, and is in the European Theater with the U.S. Army, a private first class, but still mayor. I think the smokestack to the right of the tower may belong to the Bond Bakery. My uncle used to keep his car in one of the garages at the back of the vacant lot at dead center of the picture.

The house in front of the garages belongs to Doctor James (Jay) McDonald, a very important fellow. He treated me for a dog bite after I tried and failed to outrun a fox terrier. Six of my friends carried me to the doctor's, my bleeding leg wrapped in a red bandana. My mother saw us coming and thought I was dead. I was about seven years old.

The tennis court was in constant use on summer nights. Charlie Begley and his father were the best players. Charlie went into the Marines and died during the first wave of landings on Saipan in the Pacific. Gordon Jalet was also a pretty good player but he will be remembered less for his prowess than for his unique serve. He would stand in the extreme left corner of the photo to serve, and with an underhand stroke whack the ball half a mile into the air. He was quite good at this and when the ball came down it would land in the receiver's court. But before the receiver could return it, the ball would bounce half as high again, at least, and land on the other side of the fence, making it impossible to return. What ingenuity came out of North Albany!

Everybody on the block came out to watch one afternoon when the police raided 607 North Pearl Street. That was before I lived in it. The story went around that the men inside were bank robbers and for years after we moved in I looked for money they might have hidden in the attic and cellar. I found none, for they weren't bank robbers at all. I learned later they were merely dope fiends.

My grandmother had her purse almost snatched around the corner on North Third Street one night as she came home from the movies. She came into the house with her hat askew and told us what happened and her brother, Johnny Carroll, went out and tried to collar the lowly cur, but he'd gotten away. My grandmother refused to give the thief her purse, and hit him with it instead.

A policeman who lived behind us was kicked off the force in disgrace for consorting with gamblers, an incomprehensible crime in Albany, for everybody in town consorted with gamblers. But that's the story that went around. Another man on the block hanged himself in the cellar one morning while his family went to church. And a couple who kept company with one another for forty years finally decided to marry, but the groom-to-be expired before the wedding and I wonder, is that a sad story or was it the groom's way of staying single?

All the elm trees that lined the street grew blighted and died, as did so many of the people I've been talking about. You can't preserve a neighborhood or a tree or a family against death, but sometimes you snatch a few elements and write about them and extend their lives a few years. And so I ask you to keep an eye on that street light under my window in front of 607, and on the upper windows. One more point. They figure in the section I will read now.

This is from *Billy Phelan's Greatest Game*, a moment near the end after Billy has been marked lousy and has been feeling very dismal. But he goes down to the river, communes with the river spirits, and comes out on the other side of his predicament. He is in trouble and knows it, but he isn't giving in. He spruces himself up at Union Station and comes home to North Albany.

> He went out of the station and climbed into a parked Yellow cab. He rode it to North Albany, to Jack Foy's Blackout on Erie Street and Broadway, and told the cabbie to wait. Jack hadn't heard the news about Billy yet and so Billy hit him for a deuce and paid the cabbie and then hoisted two cold beers to cool his throat. He knew Jack Foy all his life and liked him. When the word came down from Pop O'Rourke, Jack would not let him inside the joint . . . .
>
> Billy drank up and walked across Broadway and up through Sacred Heart Park to North Pearl Street, which was deserted, silent at four in the morning . . . .
>
> He was in front of his house when he heard what he heard. First came the quiet snap, then almost simultaneously the streetlight exploded behind him like a cherry bomb, and he ran like a goddamn antelope for the porch.
>
> He crouched behind the solid railing of the porch and listened for new shooting, but the street was already reenveloped by silence. Still crouching, he leaped for the door to the

vestibule and, with key at the ready, he opened the inside door and crawled into the living room. He locked the door and peered over the radio, out a front window, then out a dining room and a kitchen window, without moving any curtains, but he saw nothing. He heard movement upstairs and went toward it.

The door to the attic stairway was ajar. . . .

Billy went back to the attic door and climbed the stairs. The upper door to the attic was also ajar. He opened it all the way.

"Hello," he said. Who the hell to? . . .

The front window was open. Two inches. . . . on the floor, Billy found an empty BB package.

He put the light out and went downstairs and met Peg coming out of her bedroom, pushing her arm into her bathrobe.

"What's going on? I heard walking upstairs."

"Is that all you heard?"

"What is it?"

"Somebody shot out the street light out in front."

"Shot it out?"

Billy showed her the BB package. . . .

They went into the room of Daniel Quinn, and Billy snapped on the wall switch, lighting two yellow bulbs in the ceiling fixture. The boy pulled the covers off his face and looked at them. Billy held up the BB package.

"Did you shoot out the streetlight?" Peg asked.

The boy nodded.

"Why?"

"I wanted it dark so when Billy came home the police wouldn't see him. I didn't know it was you, Billy. I thought you'd have your hat on." . . .

Billy went to Danny's bedside and poked a finger in his ear.

"Thanks for the protection, kid, but you scared the bejesus out of me. I thought I was bushwhacked."

Daniel Quinn reciprocated the remark with a smile.

"You got a hell of an aim with that pistol. That's gotta be twenty-five yards, anyway."

"I had to hit it thirty-two times before it busted."

"An eye like that, you'll make a hell of a dart shooter."

Daniel Quinn reciprocated that remark with another smile. (260–263)

A view along North Broadway, the Troy Road, ca. 1900.
Unidentified photographer, ca. 1915, gelatin silver print, Albany Institute of History & Art Library, Main Photo Collection, DI 1214.

Now I'd like to give you a look at two more North End photographs.

The first is a view north along Broadway, the Troy road, on a day whose date I don't know. There are no motor vehicles in the picture and so it could be the turn of the century or even earlier. It's probably after 1891, and the electric trolleys are running on those tracks. The camera is one block due east from where another camera photographed the tennis court and 607.

The second view shows the corner of Broadway and Main Street, a couple blocks south of the scene along Broadway. Just to the right, out of view, is Main Street's one-block span, sloping down toward the Erie Canal, the railroad tracks, the lumber district, and the river. Francis Phelan and his family lived on Main Street after he was married to Annie and started raising a family.

The corner of Broadway and Main, which slopes down toward the Erie Canal. Unidentified photographer, ca. 1915, gelatin silver print, Albany Institute of History & Art Library, Main Photo Collection, DI 1215.

For me the magical element in these photos is that I walked Broadway all the days of my young life but never saw it looking like this. It is my neighborhood before it was occupied by the people of my life, before the factories moved in, before the diner arrived, before the gas station went up on the corner, before there was such a thing as a gas station.

It becomes almost eerie to dwell on the future that you know is going to happen. Joe Girzone will live in a house at left and grow up to become a priest and write novels. Jack Dugan will live next door and become a mailman and a band leader. The Kileys and Pat Selley, a schoolmate of mine, will live in the white house beyond the fire hydrant. Knockout Lawlor, a buddy of my uncle, will live across the street, and King Brady's saloon will rise on the corner of North Street, beyond that big tree in the far right of the photo. The house in the right foreground is where Betty Phelan will live. She and I will look like brother and sister, both auburn redheads. I will have a date with her the night before she goes off to become a nun. I like to think our date did not have anything to do with her departure.

Every building begets memories, and taken together they shape, for me, a way of life, not only of what was and what is still to be, but also what never was and what might have been. One of my deepest beliefs about fiction is that unless you understand the environment in which the human soul flourishes, wanes and dies, then you have very little to work with.

I suppose in emphasizing the importance of place for my people that I oppose myself to the style of a writer like Samuel Beckett, who furnishes his world with two ashcans, a spindly tree, a single window, a mound of dirt, a river of mud. But Beckett is a genius, his work is invaluable and like none other, and it needs nothing beyond what he chooses to give it. He chronicles the final twitches of the body and the soul, and sometimes I struggle to do the same. But I need more than Beckett needs to make my people real on the page.

I want to read now from *Ironweed* to illustrate what I mean. This is the climax of the scene in which Francis Phelan walks from Downtown to North Albany without really understanding why he's doing what he's doing. The gravitational pull is beyond his conscious control; and he moves inexorably toward the family he fled twenty-two years earlier. He has just escorted his woman, Helen Archer, to a dead automobile where she will have to sleep with two drunken bums as a way of getting her in out of the weather; for Francis knows that if she doesn't have shelter tonight she will perish. And when she is *in* the car, he leaves her and walks alone up Broadway to Main Street.

> He walked with an empty soul toward the north star, magnetized by an impulse to redirect his destiny. He had slept in the weeds of a South End vacant lot too many times. He would do it no more. . . .
>
> Francis walked half an hour due north from downtown, right into North Albany. At Main Street he turned east toward the river, down Main Street's little incline past the McGraw house, then past the Greenes', the only coloreds in all North Albany in the old days, past the Daugherty house, where Martin still lived, no lights on, and past the old Wheelbarrow, Iron Joe Farrell's old saloon, all boarded up now, where Francis learned how to drink, where he watched cockfights in the back room, and where he first spoke to Annie Farrell.

He walked toward the flats, where the canal used to be, long gone and the ditch filled in. The lock was gone and the lock-house too, and the towpath all grown over. Yet incredibly, as he neared North Street, he saw a structure he recognized. Son of a bitch. Welt the Tin's barn, still standing. Who'd believe it? Could Welt the Tin be livin'? Not likely. . . . Was it in use? Still a barn? Looks like a barn. But who keeps horses now?

The barn was a shell, with a vast hole in the far end of the roof where moonlight poured cold fire onto the ancient splintered floor. Bats flew in balletic arcs around the streetlamp outside, the last lamp on North Street; and the ghosts of mules and horses snorted and stomped for Francis. He scuffed at the floorboards himself and found them solid. He touched them and found them dry. One barn door canted on one hinge, and Francis calculated that if he could move the door a few feet to sleep in its lee, he would be protected from the wind on three sides. No moonlight leaked through the roof above this corner, the same corner where Welt the Tin had hung his rakes and pitchforks, all in a row between spaced nails.

Francis would reclaim this corner, restore all rakes and pitchforks, return for the night the face of Welt the Tin as it had been, reinvest himself with serendipitous memories of a lost age. On a far shelf in the moonlight he saw a pile of papers and a cardboard box. He spread the papers in his chosen corner, ripped the box at its seams, and lay down on the flattened pile.

He had lived not seventy-five feet from where he now lay.

Seventy-five feet from this spot, Gerald Phelan died on the 26th of April, 1916. . . .

Maybe I won't survive tonight after all, Francis thought as he folded his hands between his thighs. He drew his knees up toward his chest, not quite so high as Foxy Phil Tooker's, and considered the death he had caused in this life, and was perhaps causing still. Helen is dying and Francis is perhaps the principal agent of hastening her death, even as his whole being tonight has been directed to keeping her from freezing. . . .

The new and frigid air of November lay on Francis like a blanket of glass. Its weight rendered him motionless and brought peace to his body, and the stillness brought a cessation of anguish to his brain. In a dream he was only just beginning to enter, horns and mountains rose up out of the earth, the

> horns—ethereal, trumpets—sounding with a virtuosity equal to the perilousness of the crags and cornices of the mountainous pathways. Francis recognized the song the trumpets played and he floated with its melody. Then, yielding not without trepidation to its coded urgency, he ascended bodily into the exalted reaches of the world where the song had been composed so long ago. And he slept. (87–90)

References

Kennedy, William. *Billy Phelan's Greatest Game*. New York: Penguin, 1983.

———. *Ironweed*, paperback edition. New York: Penguin, 1984.

———. *Legs*. New York: Penguin, 1983.

This essay was delivered as a speech on September 8, 1984, as part of the "William Kennedy's Albany Weekend," a celebration of Kennedy's work that included lectures, panel discussions, historical exhibits, guided walking and bus tours, and a citywide festival. Printed by permission of William Kennedy.

Learning from Faulkner

The Obituary of Fear

> Everything I've written is about today, about the moment that I write it, no matter how far back in time the story is set. The past becomes the vehicle simply because it seems—though it never is—complete; and I can at least begin to cope with it.
>
> —William Kennedy

When William Faulkner died, I wrote his obituary for my newspaper, the *San Juan Star,* in Puerto Rico. I had been a founder of that paper but, after two years as managing editor, I quit to become weekend editor only; for I'd begun a novel and discovered I could do justice to neither the editing nor the novel while trying to do both; and I knew, with certainty, that I would be a novelist.

My novel was about a family, the Phelans. I was also giving prolonged attention to another family novel, *The Sound and the Fury*. I'd been reading Faulkner for a dozen years and was mesmerized in assorted ways. Not surprisingly, Faulknerian syntax had crept into some of my sentences, and I even found myself cheering when I wrote a sentence that went on for a page and a half with only two commas. I knew this was a mistake and eventually I got rid of all such baggage, just as I had earlier banished my imitations of eight-word Hemingway sentences. But I was a young writer in search of a voice, and Faulkner and Hemingway were the most distinctive and unwitting literary ventriloquists in this country.

There was another aspect of Faulkner from which I felt no need to distance myself: the way his characters moved from one story to another, one novel to another; and Malcolm Cowley's explanation of the Yoknapatawpha saga made this intertwining of lives in a single place the most ambitious fictional device I could imagine. I was just beginning to discover Albany, my hometown, through the writing of that Phelan family novel, but I knew so little about Albany back then that I'm sure I never consciously thought of creating my own fictional cosmos. Writing just one novel was an immensity, never mind a saga.

And yet my fascination with recurring characters continued, fueled not only by Faulkner's work but by the prismatic lives of Nick Adams in the stories of Hemingway, of J. D. Salinger's Glass family, of Stephen Dedalus in Joyce's books. The creation of interlocking works is as old as Aeschylus and Sophocles, and probably reaches the height of human possibilities in the novels of Balzac. Faulkner, said his biographer Frederick Karl, was "the closest figure to a Balzac that America has produced" (4).

As quoted by Karl, Faulkner made the unlikely comparison of Balzac with Sherwood Anderson, who was Faulkner's early mentor; but the comparison was mainly on the basis of the difficulties both men experienced by being a writer in a culture hostile to artists. Faulkner recognized that Anderson "probably didn't have a concept of a cosmos in miniature which Balzac . . . had" (197), but he acknowledged that Anderson had taught him how to enter that cosmos: "I learned," Faulkner wrote, "that, to be a writer, one has first got to be what he is, what he was born; that to be an American and a writer, one does not necessarily have to pay lip-service to any conventional American image such as [Anderson's] and Dreiser's own aching Indiana or Ohio or Iowa corn or Sandburg's stockyards or Mark Twain's frog." And Faulkner then quoted what Anderson said to him on this subject: " 'You *have* to have somewhere to start from: then you begin to learn. . . . It dont matter where it was, just so you remember it and aint ashamed of it. Because one place to start from is just as important as any other' " ("A Note on Sherwood Anderson" 8; emphasis added).

I started using Albany in Puerto Rico, although I didn't know I had started until maybe a dozen years had passed. I finished that Phelan novel, which went nowhere; and I then wrote a dozen short stories that went to the same place. But in time I published a novel, then published another one, and by 1975 was beginning my third novel, about a young pool hustler. I went back to that old Phelan novel and took it out of its nowhere box and imposed the Phelan family on my pool hustler, whose book I called *Billy Phelan's Greatest Game*. I made the wino character, Francis Phelan, Billy's absentee father, and next I gave Francis his own book, *Ironweed*. In time I turned that whole dead Phelan book into a living story, *Very Old Bones*. And now I have six novels and a play, *Grand View,* and more works to come—a new novel just begun, a second play in its fourth draft—and all—and maybe more if I continue drawing breath—will be intertwined with recurring events and characters.

Some critics called Faulkner the Balzac of Mississippi; some book reviewers now call me the William Faulkner of Albany; and a Philadelphia book critic recently told me of two young writers who have been called the William Kennedy of Glasgow and the William Kennedy of Miami.

Any comparison of my work with Faulkner's on the basis of writing styles, or subject matter, or execution of the books is presumptuous. My turf, my people, my language, and my limitations are my own, and Faulkner should not have to bear any onerous linkage; and neither should I. Like unhappy families, writers are also unhappy in their own way. I noted in a history of Albany that I published in 1983, called *O Albany!*, that my city has been associated with any number of writers in its long life:

> Bret Harte was born here and left almost immediately, came back as a mature celebrity but was snubbed by the press, left in a terminal huff and died in England trying to forget the place. Harold Frederic worked here as an editor of the *Albany Evening Journal,* Dickens read from *A Christmas Carol* at Tweddle Hall, Mark Twain defended osteopathy at the Capitol, Robert Louis Stevenson passed through on his way to the Adirondacks, Edith Wharton's great friend Walter Van Rensselaer Berry grew up here, Joyce may have referred to the place secretly in *Finnegans Wake*, Hemingway married Martha Gellhorn, who used to work on the *Times Union*, and William Faulkner died unaware that Albany existed. (6–7)

Faulkner's birthplace *was* New Albany, Mississippi, but I had in mind the *old* Albany of New York, the oldest chartered city in the nation, where I was born. And yet Faulkner does now have a posthumous link to old Albany through what I learned from him about literary geography: my creation of Albany is the abstract image of Yoknapatawpha County; which is to say that I have tried to make my city real in ways that it actually was, and fictional in ways it never was; that I've imagined generations of the several families and assorted characters who inhabit the place, and that I control their destinies absolutely. My world, my people.

Because I work this way there have been indictments of me as a regional writer, an ethnic writer obsessed with social history; plus an odd begrudgery at my staying in one place, and writing exclusively about the past. It's true that the closest I've come to time-present in any novel in the Albany Cycle has been *Very Old Bones*, set in 1958, which I consider yesterday afternoon. I've gone as far back as the 1840s in *Quinn's Book*. My new novel, *The Flaming Corsage*, makes time leaps from 1884 to 1912. And the other three novels are set in the 1920s and 1930s.*

Faulkner often talked of time in his work, and once said, "There isn't any time . . . only the present moment, in which I include both the past and the future, and that is eternity" (*Lion in the Garden* 70).

Everything I've written is about today, about the moment that I write it, no matter how far back in time the story is set. The past becomes the vehicle simply because it seems—though it never is—complete; and I can at least begin to cope with it.

The social forces, the political, religious, and ethnic heritages that influence the lives of the people of my fictional city, are vastly different from, say, San Juan or Mississippi. I began discovering this singularity of place when I was a young newspaperman covering Albany crime and politics, and, more deeply years later, when I was assigned to write a series of articles on the origins of Albany's neighborhoods. I almost smothered myself then with the riches of history: an endless uncovering of the events, and the social groupings, and the peculiar lives of individuals who made the American nation, and often made it first in Albany.

Albany's history is fabulous—its life is as long before the Revolutionary War as it has been since then. I began exploring it by marking out the turf, then digging like the archeologist I once wanted to be; and I have been unearthing what I consider treasure ever since.

It would take me decades to understand anyplace else in an equivalent way. I knew this, decisively, forty-five years ago when I first started writing about Albany; for I found in that work a strength I'd never had in any writing I'd done about Puerto Rico. Even in these early writing days I knew infinitely more about the city than I thought I did.

It is very easy to become a victim of your own love of place, and of research. History is addictive, and can overload the imagination. It never was the reason I wrote fiction and never will be. I distort history whenever it's necessary for the story. My ethnic heritage is Irish American but my characters are ethnic mongrels, no matter what their names are. Fellini, Buñuel, and Bergman, Camus, Kafka, and Nathanael West have had more influence on me creatively than any Irish American writer or historian ever did. I am, and always have been, just a writer—a writer whose subject is not Albany or its locals—a writer whose overarching concern in fiction has been the continual asking of one question: What does it mean to be alive, and how is this meaning made manifest?

---

* Editors' Note: Kennedy's Albany Cycle extends into the 1950s and 1960s in his novel *Changó's Beads and Two-Tone Shoes*, published in 2011.

Faulkner responded to regional pigeonholing in a letter to Malcolm Cowley: "I'm inclined to think that my material, the South, is not very important to me" (14). And, to a group of law school wives at the University of Virginia, he elaborated: "People are the same . . . the milieu, the background, the environment will change the *terms* of their behavior not the act itself, and so the writer simply uses the background he knows . . ." (*Faulkner in the University* 168).

To some critics the most flawed of Faulkner's ambition novels is *A Fable*, and this is seen as the consequence of his leaving the background he knew in Yoknapatawpha. Robert Penn Warren saw *A Fable* as "abstractly conceived; it is an idea deductively worked out—and at critical moments, blurred out. . . . Faulkner, like Antaeus, could fight only with his feet on the ground—on home ground; . . . only in that world could he find the seminal images that would focus his deepest feelings into vision" (17).

I'm inclined to think that if I left Albany and undertook a novel set in Acapulco, or Havana, I might bring off a contemporary tale of romance, intrigue, double-dealing, mortal error, and so on. But I fear it might be romance and mortal error in a vacuum that I'd probably relapse into journalistic fiction; that my novel would lack what went most profoundly into that romance or that mortal error. It would lack time and the enduring influence of continuity and place. It would lack what I believe essential to any story: the palpable life that *was* at the moment it becomes *is*.

The mother of a good friend of mine, in her early eighties, had outlived all her close friends and family; and near the end she said she was glad of her long life because, "I got to see how everybody turned out."

That attitude is central to my attention to the past and to a single place. The primary motive is to follow the ongoing lives of my characters, who rarely die a permanent death. They recur in antecedent stories, or in the subsequent memory of other characters. They are with me forever, whenever I need them, whenever they demand to be heard: the inhabitants of my own eternal city, six hundred characters in search of their author.

In *The Flaming Corsage*, for example, I focused on a woman and man I've been tracking for twenty years: Katrina Taylor and her husband, Edward Daugherty. I invented them and their tragic marriage in *Billy Phelan's Greatest Game,* a novel set in 1938. Later I put Katrina into *Ironweed* in the year 1897, but only part of her. In *The Flaming Corsage*, I went back to her youth in the 1880s and gave her life, as much of its due as my story could tolerate. But I'm still not sure I'm done with her. I also have unfinished business with Daniel Quinn, protagonist of *Quinn's Book*, and likewise with Patsy McCall, Albany's Irish American political boss who's been in two novels and a play; but about Patsy I have only just begun to write. And the Phelans, having gone through three novels, emerged into their unpredictable present tense only at the end of their last novel, *Very Old Bones*, when the hidden past transformed them utterly from all that I, and they, thought they had been. And so it continues.

That obituary of Faulkner—I wrote it because I felt the wire stories about his career were insufficient. The next day I wrote an essay on him for the newspaper because my obituary was insufficient. The essay was weak and I never published it; but one line of it is still valid: "He gave us something heroic to try to be equal to."

I was then so new as a writer that I was only intuiting what was heroic in Faulkner: the scope of his literary ambition, very visible of course; his language, like nothing else in literature; and maybe his combative attitude toward fear. I remember being impressed by that.

The writer, Faulkner said, "must teach himself that the basest of all things is to be afraid" ("Address" 120). And he said elsewhere that you combatted fear through work: ". . . .if you have something to get up to tomorrow morning, you're too busy to pay much attention to fear" (*Faulkner in the University* 67).

I don't know what I was fearful of in those old days. The world seemed to be opening up before me; I had no serious enemies, no malaise of spirit, plenty of ambition, and a fair amount of faith that if I didn't own any talent I'd soon figure out how to get some.

Then the curtain rose on the real world.

I had a wife and two children and almost no money. I had an agent who could sell nothing I'd written. Foreclosure was relentlessly imminent. And I was writing in a critical void. I'd had some, but very little, valuing of my work. I had my own faith in what I was doing, but that faith was being eroded by a shapeless fear: "You are the problem," wrote Kafka. "No scholar to be found far and wide" (166).

Time passed and I somehow kept writing and published three novels. They made some money, but not much, and so in desperation—like Faulkner when he was financially desperate—I turned to the movies and paid the mortgage writing film scripts for a few years.

By the time I finished my fourth novel, *Ironweed*, which I judged my best work to that point, more Faulknerian darkness had descended; all my books were out of print, as were his in the years just before Cowley's *Portable Faulkner* effected his renaissance. Also *Ironweed*, like *The Sound and the Fury*, was about to be rejected thirteen times. My kinship with Faulkner seemed akin to a death wish. Yet if it was that, it proved also to be a prescription for how you elude all assassins: you refuse to die from trouble.

I am struck by how many people tell me they are buoyed, even inspired that, in spite of rejection, and no money, I continued to write novels. I did not think it so unusual. What I possessed was a simple truth: that I wanted to write more than I wanted to pay the mortgage. Time and again I put the work aside to do temporary hack work; I borrowed and begged, and my wife became remarkable in her ability to earn and find money through assorted business ventures and her natural acuity. And always I got back to work. I suppose I was tougher and more ruthless than I knew, for I would've done anything to finish that novel, and get to the next one.

I also discovered that I not only wanted to write, I loved to write; that creation was everything, and if its consequences were impoverishing, they were also sublime. Platoons of dunning creditors could not diminish the exaltation I felt at one o'clock in the morning, having written a seventeen-page scene in *Ironweed* during the previous seventeen hours, this exaltation followed by the giddy contemplation that I was probably mad to think this was a serious way to live, and concluding, as the night waned and I waited in euphoria for the sun to come up, that no other way would do.

Faulkner wrote of such a feeling, which he had when he knew he was ready to write *The Sound and the Fury*. "One day I seemed to shut a door between me and all publishers' addresses and book lists. I said to myself, Now I can write. Now I can make myself a vase like that which the old Roman kept at his bedside and wore the rim slowly away with kissing it" (*Faulkner: A Biography* 212).

Without knowing the first word of Faulkner's plan, or his desire, or his creative ecstasy, I confronted *The Sound and the Fury* as a young writer and loved its mystifying structure, its characters, its language. And for years to come I would offer my gratitude to whatever it was that created William Faulkner, the man who adversity could not prevent from writing a great book.

I'm sorry I never met him. I'm sorry he never came to Albany. But I'm very glad I've been able to come to Yoknapatawpha County.

References

Blotner, Joseph. *Faulkner: A Biography*. One-volume edition. New York: Random House, 1974–1984.

Cowley, Malcom. *The Faulkner-Cowley File: Letters and Memories, 1944–1962*. New York: Viking Press, 1966.

Faulkner, William. "A Note on Sherwood Anderson." In *Essays, Speeches & Public Letters, ed. James B. Meriwether. New York: Random House, 1965.*

———. "Address Upon Receiving the Nobel Prize for Literature." In *Essays, Speeches & Public Letters by William Faulkner*, ed. James B. Meriwether. New York: Random House, 1965.

Gwynn, Frederick L., and Joseph L. Blotner, eds. *Faulkner in the University: Class Conferences at the University of Virginia 1957–1958.* New York: Vintage Books, 1959.

Kafka, Franz. "Reflections on Sin, Pain, Hope, and the True Way." In *The Great Wall of China and Other Pieces.* New York: Schocken Books, 1970.

Karl, Frederick R. *William Faulkner: American Writer*. New York: Weidenfeld & Nicolson, 1989.

Kennedy, William. *O Albany! Improbable City of Political Wizards, Fearless Ethnics, Spectacular Aristocrats, Splendid Nobodies, and Underrated Scoundrels.* New York: Penguin, 1985.

Meriwether, James B., and Michael Millgate, eds. *Lion in the Garden: Interviews with William Faulkner 1929–1962.* New York: Random House, 1968.

Warren, Robert Penn, ed. *Faulkner: A Collection of Critical Essays*. New Jersey: Prentice-Hall, 1966.

This essay was originally delivered as a speech at the William Faulkner Conference in Oxford, Mississippi, on August 1, 1996, and was published as "Learning from Faulkner: The Obituary of Fear," by William Kennedy, from *Faulkner and the Natural World*, edited by Donald M. Kartiganer and Ann J. Abadie. Reprinted by permission of the University Press of Mississippi.

Gifts from Joyce

> The answer to why I liked the Albany novel better than my Puerto Rican stories is that I was doing what Joyce had done without knowing I was doing it: reconstructing a city that was long gone, and surprising myself every day with what was in my unconscious, what suddenly would make the leap into my imagination.
>
> —William Kennedy

The first gift James Joyce gave me arrived about forty years ago when I was ill with some now forgotten ailment and spent my three days of recovery reading *Ulysses* from cover to cover. The gift was twofold: it made me doubt my intelligence, and made me think English was not my native tongue. The book seemed like an artifact from an alien culture, about which I knew little; and it also seemed the product of another language, as impenetrable as a Sanskrit crossword puzzle. And yet the reading was a thrilling experience.

Of course it was ridiculous to think I had read the book in three days. I had grasped fragments, I had found that I liked Bloom and Molly enormously, thought Stephen a difficult and not-very-likable intellectual. I had ferreted out some of the book's scandalous passages, including the *Nausicaa* episode, in which Bloom and the young Gerty MacDowell achieve simultaneous orgasms-at-a-distance, a section I thought I understood; but I'd missed totally the mockery of the sentimental clichés of the narrator that so ebulliently define Gerty's world.

I remember James Agee's reaction to this sort of confrontation with Joyce. He wrote in one of his letters that he'd been reading *A Portrait of the Artist as a Young Man* and added, it

> makes me ashamed ever to have thought I'd read it before, and exceedingly suspicious on the whole question of when, or how, or how soon to read what: unless there is certain to be rereading; and suspicious even then; and suspicious for that

> matter of my illusion that I am reading it now. . . . I am sick in myself and others of the illusion of reading, which comes of somewhat intelligently skimming a great work, being somewhat excited by it, and thinking from that that you 'know' or 'understand' it. (117)

I never thought I 'understood' all of *Ulysses* and still don't. But if I was overwhelmed by my early encounter, I was not daunted. I carried it with me whenever I moved anywhere, and I have the same copy still, yellowing and dog-eared, the dust jacket gone, the pages marked, the text full of underlines; and while I understand it better now, it remains as strange a creation to me today as it was then. Much of *Ulysses* was a mystery I felt I would never fully solve, yet I loved its wit and wordplay, and valued it for the improbable ambition it presented to the youth I was. At some point it helped inspire me to begin thinking of an impossible enterprise: the creation of a book that would leap over my own conventional ambitions, a book that would be greater than what I knew I could do.

About twelve years after that first reading of *Ulysses*, I was on the phone with my father, who was then seventy-seven years old, and he was remembering Van Woert Street, the long Irish block with an old Dutch name where he had been raised; also he was remembering his friends, the O'Connell brothers, a quartet of Irish Catholic Democrats who successfully entered Albany politics in 1921, took the city away from the Republican Protestants, and never gave it back; and he was also telling some of his World War I stories that I knew almost by heart. His memories coalesced in me with such significance that I wrote down what I called "Idea for an Albany fantasy," a page and a half of pencil notes that would reconstitute the city's past—which is as old as the country itself, in terms of European colonization. The fantasy would begin with such characters as the great Revolutionary War general Philip Schuyler; the political wizard Aaron Burr; one of America's founding fathers, Alexander Hamilton; the British General John Burgoyne, all erstwhile denizens of eighteenth-century Albany; then move along to Herman Melville and Henry James, our nineteenth-century literary giants with an Albany connection, to Martin H. Glynn, a twentieth-century Irish newspaper editor from Albany, who became governor of New York State, and who played a small role in the development of the Irish Free State; also those political O'Connell brothers and a vast crowd of priests, nuns, gamblers, gangsters, mothers, whores, and laboring men, including my father; and central to it all, by way of the pleasure principle, a stunningly beautiful and sensual girl I knew extremely well. All these Albanians would be contemporaries in my novel, all eternally living out their destinies, over and over again, as they discovered one another's present and past.

I added at the end of the notes: "Commit a decade to the creation of this book."

Alas, I did not create the monster, for it was beyond my ability not only to execute but even to imagine beyond the broad outline. I wrote instead a novel of average size, then another, and another. But, as it turns out, I have been creating some sort of oversized creature after all: for out of the novels I have written, and others I hope to write, has emerged a schema of interlocking stories that I call the Albany Cycle, and which seems to be not just a series of books, but an effort to invent and populate an entire world; and the writing of it will probably occupy the rest of my life.

I recall the eminent critic Edmund Wilson writing about *Ulysses*, and the unknown future of its characters. We know Bloom has brought Stephen home after a day's and night's wandering, and that the sensual Molly immediately envisions an affair with Stephen, getting Italian lessons from him, giving him singing lessons in exchange; also we see Bloom asserting his absent manhood by demanding breakfast in bed from Molly, and one critic has suggested Bloom may even be ready to accept cuckoldry by Stephen in order to gain a son—letting Stephen father a child with Molly.

Of course we do not know what the Blooms or Stephen did, for *Ulysses* has no sequel. But so vivid are the people that we are able to imagine them in assorted future roles; and this is how it seems to be with me and my own characters—one novel begetting another, a secondary character demanding his or her own book, a story insisting on being continued. I believe this is partly a product of discovering my own excitement at meeting characters a second or third time, in the short stories of Sherwood Anderson, Hemingway, and J. D. Salinger, of seeing Stephen move from the *Portrait* to *Ulysses*, of being mesmerized by the work of William Faulkner, whose thirty interlocking volumes of novels and stories—the Yoknapatawpha saga—stand as perhaps the most ambitious undertaking in twentieth-century American literature.

Faulkner was a student of Balzac, another maestro of interconnectedness. The American novelist James Gould Cozzens, also a Balzacian, wrote about the phenomenon of related stories in a preface to a volume of ten novels by Balzac. "The point on which we (Balzacians) agree," wrote Cozzens, "is that there comes an indefinable pleasure in meeting, in a Balzac novel, a character with whom we have had dealings before; an old acquaintance, who seems sometimes closer to us than a brother" (x). Faulkner was a student of Joyce as well as Balzac, his most overt homage being visible in two of his greatest novels, *The Sound and the Fury* and *Light in August*, in which he uses, to great effectiveness, the stream-of-consciousness technique and, with lesser success, the Joycean portmanteau wordplay. Faulkner's copy editor on *Light in August* conscientiously separated the words that Faulkner had willfully run together, and Faulkner restored the fusion and noted in the margin: "O.K. as set, goddam it." And as the editing persisted he fumed anew and further noted: "O.K. as set and written. Jesus Christ. . . . I want it to stand as it is" (309). Some critics in their reviews of these Faulkner novels noted the influence of Joyce, but Faulkner's retort was that he had never read *Ulysses*, had never even seen a copy until after his two novels were published.

"You know," he told an interviewer, "sometimes I think there must be a sort of pollen of ideas floating in the air, which fertilizes similarly minds here and there which have not had direct contact" ("Interview with Henry Nash Smith" 30–31). He admitted being told *about* Joyce and conceded he might have been influenced by what he had heard.

Writers frequently deny any influence from the writers who have gone before them, out of fear that their own work will seem derivative. But unless that fear is well grounded, and their work truly owes its existence to grand larceny, such a denial in the name of originality is the silliest sort of posturing. You might call it the immaculate conception theory of literature—the work created whole, its creator undiddled by any literary ancestor. But even Joyce owed, and acknowledged, a debt to Ibsen, Flaubert, Goethe, Dante, Shakespeare, among others, and, not least, Homer, whom he reinvented as himself, a Dubliner.

In his late years someone asked Faulkner what he thought of Joyce and he replied ungrudgingly: "James Joyce was one of the great men of my time. He was electrocuted by the divine fire. He [and] Thomas Mann, were the great writers of my time. [Joyce] . . . might have been the greatest, but he was electrocuted. He had more talent than he could control" (*Faulkner in the University* 280).

T. S. Eliot, an admirer and booster of Joyce and *Ulysses*, wrote about this matter of literary inheritance: "No poet, no artist of any art, has his complete meaning alone. His significance, his appreciation is the appreciation of his relation to the dead poets and artists. You cannot value him alone; you must set him, for contrast and comparison, among the dead" (28).

I freely admit that I took heart and some direction from the ambition of the dead Joyce. I'm indebted also for his gift of courage in the face of the rejection, the opposition, and the censorship he encountered—in Ireland, France, the United States. I have never had to struggle against censorship, at least not yet. Joyce, Henry Miller, Norman Mailer, and others cleared the way for all of my generation to say whatever we wanted to say in whatever way we wanted to say it. But I did have a few go-rounds with rejection of my early work, and then, surprising to me, *Ironweed*, my fourth novel, which I thought was my best book up to that time, had thirteen rejections before being published with considerable success in the United States, and, since then, in many languages around the world.

The arrogance with which Joyce confronted his detractors, censors, and obstructers was admirable and inspirational, as was that cunning of which he has Stephen speak at the end of *Portrait*. But I was never much for cunning myself, never really knew how to get out of my own way, how to be anything less than the vulnerable witness, very like Bailey, the hero of my first novel, *The Ink Truck*, who when asked why, during a strike, he ran toward the company goons he knew would club him, responded, " 'That's all there really is.' . . . Run to the glory of the club" (160). Having been instructed by such gauntlet-runners as Joyce, and also Kafka, whose caveat was: "You are the problem. No scholar to be found far and wide" (166), I found myself clubbed and bloodied, taking the goon squad's worst, then found myself also getting up, having breakfast, and moving forward, making the goons irrelevant. This isn't much fun, but it certainly is Joycean.

I was in Dublin, in University College, twenty years ago, chasing after things Joycean, covering for an American magazine the doings of the 176 visiting scholars at the fourth annual James Joyce Symposium. I sat in on discussions of *Ulysses*, *Finnegans Wake*, and Joyce in general, and then went into the streets of Dublin tracking the man and his places—pubs and erstwhile homes, including the one in Bray where he set the Christmas dinner scene in *Portrait*, also The Gresham Hotel, which he used in *The Dead*, the Martello Tower, which was the opening setting of *Ulysses*, and Number Seven Eccles Street, the house where the Blooms lived and which I happened upon by happy accident when driving past it. All this attention to the real world had about it the feel of archeology, not literature; and yet there is a fine fascination about tracking the *world* in which Joyce actually lived, and discovering something palpable of the man who became the writer.

But the chief discovery for me was how the writer had *used* his world, how, when he left Dublin for exile in Paris and elsewhere, he took Dublin with him, venerating its memory by reconstituting it on the pages of his fiction. One of the Joyce symposiasts spoke of how Joyce "canonized the obsession with being Irish—the whole love of place, of knowing a particular street in Dublin and talking all night about it."

That is how it has been for me and Albany for many years. When I was in Puerto Rico I started to write stories about the expatriate life I'd chosen for myself. Puerto Rico was an exotic and romantic setting, a Spanish-language community full of hostility and reverence for the United States, with all sorts of volatile politics and left- and right-wing beach bums to write about. I loved the place and yet I came to see that I really couldn't use it as a basis for my fiction because I wasn't Puerto Rican. I couldn't identify with, or even begin to read, the Puerto Rican mind, even though I'd married one. I didn't know the Spanish language as well as I wanted, and so could never possess the literature, or the complex world of Hispanic and Latin scholars and political theorists, who abounded in the Puerto Rican reality.

I had written short stories and had started a novel set in Puerto Rico, but I finally rejected all that and started a novel about Albany. I suddenly found myself ranging through sixty years in the history of an Albany family—the Phelans, whose lives have preoccupied me ever since.

Making that transition from Puerto Rico to Albany had enormous consequences for me. To begin with I liked my own writing better, understood the people better. I found I understood the psychology of almost anybody in Albany—whether it was a baseball player or a politician or an artist or a drunk or a spinster or a clandestinely married woman—far better than I knew anybody in Puerto Rico. I called this novel *The Angels and the Sparrows*, and although it was never published, it did, in time, turn into the basis for my most recent novel, *Very Old Bones*. The *Bones* novel is much more complex than the early book, but the same people are present in both narratives. And so is the place.

The answer to why I liked the Albany novel better than my Puerto Rican stories is that I was doing what Joyce had done without knowing I was doing it: reconstituting a city that was long gone, and surprising myself every day with what was in my unconscious, what suddenly would make the leap into my imagination. I knew Albany far more intimately than I realized; and it would have taken me half a lifetime to know Puerto Rico in an equivalent way.

How can you possibly write about a place if you don't understand what the street names mean, or why the mayor is the mayor, or what political power means to your father, or how God is manifested in your neighborhood? I was little more than a tourist in Puerto Rico, and even when I began writing about Albany I discovered I didn't really understand the city's principal social force—the Irish Catholic Democratic bossism that held absolute power over the lives of almost everyone in the city. I hadn't paid sufficient attention to politics when I was working as an Albany newspaperman before going to Puerto Rico, hadn't observed my father and my uncles closely enough to know that they were truly political creatures.

I also disdained covering politics as a young newsman; and as a novelist I've always avoided political partisanship; for time very quickly changes political allegiances, and the novels premised on such allegiances blow away with the first winds of change. Yet if politics is missing from a novel about Albany then it would not be the Albany in which I grew up; for politics was a principal moral code of my city.

As a child and young man I heard very little condemnation of city politics on moral grounds, even from the church; especially from the church. For if you were Irish, which about forty percent of the city's population was, by derivation—back in 1875 one in six Albany residents had been born in Ireland—then you probably also belonged to the Democratic Party; and if you were a Democrat, you stood a very good chance of also being a Roman Catholic. And if you were Roman Catholic you gave allegiance not only to the church on the corner, but also to the political boss, Daniel Peter O'Connell—namesake of a great Irish patriot—and Dan was, himself, a pillar of the church, inseparably linked to the Albany bishop and the local priests, who revered him and prayed for him, and whose prayers were answered regularly by his benevolence. Saint Daniel, one maverick Democrat called him.

But Saint Daniel was also running gambling parlors, profiting handsomely from the all-night saloons, the baseball pools, the illegal card games, and the whorehouses. He was in collusion with the grafters and bankers, getting rich with the paving contractors, not entirely for his own sake, for he lived frugally, but for the sake of perpetuating his political power.

Wherever you could make a holy vow or an illegal dollar, that's where the Irish were, that's where Dan and his politics were. I don't mean to imply that the church was in league with the whorehouses, but it was common knowledge that the madams all kicked in to Dan's coffers. And the bagmen who made the collections were often city detectives. The clergy, with bountiful self-interest, chose to look the other way when this knowledge surfaced, which it did regularly.

I remember vividly in the middle 1960s when a radical Franciscan priest, who was working with slum people to upgrade their neighborhood, took a list of addresses of South End whorehouses to one of the monsignors who was then a figure of authority in the Catholic Diocese. The monsignor looked at the list and told the young priest, "I don't believe this. Dan O'Connell wouldn't let these places exist in the city." But the South End, for forty years, had been notorious for its red-light district. From the 1920s into the 1960s, Green Street, a very old thoroughfare, was the code name of Albany's bluest corridor of sin. It was as notorious and as widely known as Storyville in New Orleans, or the old Kips in Dublin that Joyce used for his Nighttown in *Ulysses*.

Within this peculiar prevailing morality, Albany families were interlocked in saintliness and chicanery; and chicanery was, sometimes, only another way of getting on in the world; and objective morality didn't interest the Albany Irish. They were more imaginative than that. They understood that they had been deprived, that in a previous era they had been social outcasts, unable to get jobs. Families were hungry, and hunger was immoral. Now the Irish were no longer hungry; they had jobs; they had power. Once Dan O'Connell became the political boss, he was as respected as the bishop. Dan was the man who would save your soul by putting you to work. Of course he was also a rascal; and through the use of loyalty, ruthlessness, generosity, and fear, he controlled Albany from 1921 until he died in 1977—a span of fifty-six years, unprecedented in the history of American machine politics.

Dan's last mayor, Erastus Corning 2nd, a wealthy patrician Protestant from an old Albany family, who had become Irish by osmosis, served as mayor from 1941 to 1983—eleven consecutive terms, another longevity record in American politics. Erastus continued controlling the city after Dan's death for another six years until he, too, died. This was how you removed a Democrat from power in Albany. You called the undertaker. Until this year.

Some months ago our then incumbent mayor, an Irish Catholic Democrat by the name of Tom Whalen, announced that after ten years in City Hall he'd had enough. He was resigning, and it looked to some—and rightly so, it turned out—as if he might have a federal judgeship somewhere in his future. This is unprecedented. Giving up city hall for the bench? The man must be daft. But no. He is of the new breed. Dan is dead, Erastus is dead. The machine is not dead but it is shrunken and arthritic. Albany is new, vigorous, even respectable. And can you believe it, our erstwhile metropolis of sin has been chosen as an All-American City. Dan O'Connell's bones must be dancing a scornful jig in their grave—dancing to that time-tested political theme of his bygone machine: *Honesty Is No Substitute for Experience*.

I am proud of my Irish heritage and yet I don't consider myself an Irish writer, or even an Irish American writer (just American, is my own perception). But I cannot escape the Irish connection, and neither do I try to avoid it. A writer like John O'Hara tried to bury his Irishness and came on as an Anglo-Saxon Protestant clubman; Scott Fitzgerald had a gift of Irish poetry in his soul, but he rarely identified it as such. A writer with whom I share the Irish American political burden is Edwin O'Connor, whose novel *The Last Hurrah* was a marvelous piece of work that convulsed me with laughter through its very witty treatment of urban and ecclesiastical politics in Boston. Mr. O'Connor understood the social topography of Boston down to the last pew of the church, the last illegal vote. And yet I felt his politics were too hygienic, too bereft of the darker side of the comparable Irish political life in Albany.

Arthur Power, a friend of Joyce's who kept notes from their conversations, eventually publishing them in a small book, once asked Joyce, ". . . .how do you feel about being Irish?" And Joyce responded, "I regret it for the temperament it has given me" (*James Joyce* 505). If anyone had asked me the same question I would have responded, "I am fond of it for the temperament it has given me." I am Irish all the way back on both sides of the family, and perhaps I have grown into the temperament, or resigned myself to it, but I would give no thought to exchanging it for something else. As one of my fallen-away Catholic characters says to a minister about what she now was instead of a Catholic, "Well, I'm certainly not a Methodist."

The element of darkness in the personality that seems to go with being Irish has become increasingly important to me in understanding anybody's life. I copied out a few paragraphs of what Joyce said to Arthur Power, something I already agreed with and had already put into practice in my novels, yet had never understood quite so clearly until I read Joyce's words. He said:

> When we are living a normal life we are living a conventional one, following a pattern which has been laid out by other people in another generation, an objective pattern imposed on us by the church and state. But a writer must maintain a continual struggle against the objective: that is his function. The eternal qualities are the imagination and the sexual instinct, and the formal life tries to suppress both. Out of this present conflict arise the phenomena of modern life. . . . Idealism is a pleasant bauble, but in these days of overwhelming reality it no longer interests us, or even amuses. We regard it as a sort of theatrical drop-scene. Most lives are made up like the modern painter's themes, of jugs, and pots and plates, backstreets and blowsy living-rooms inhabited by blowsy women, and of a thousand daily sordid incidents which seep into our minds no matter how we strive to keep them out. These are the furniture of our life. (74–75)

When I wrote my novels on matters akin to what Edwin O'Connor had written, I felt I had to bring in that furniture that Joyce speaks of—the violence and the gambling and the sexuality, along with the shenanigans of the political thieves and the haughty clerics of the church. O'Connor's comic ward heelers in Boston, and O'Hara's country club social climbers, didn't have anything to do with what was going on down on Albany's Broadway among those raffish people I knew—the Irish, German, Jewish, Dutch, and Italians—tough, dirty-minded, foul-mouthed hustlers, and gamblers, and bigots, and whoremongers, and, at the same time, wonderful, generous, funny, loyal, curiously honest, and very complex people. I felt that this way of life had to be penetrated at all levels; and I felt it also required the surreal dimension that is part of any society in which religion plays such a powerful role.

Even before my family and I moved from San Juan to Albany in 1963, I had started doing long interviews with my parents and uncles and neighbors, and I began to see the political and religious ramifications in everything. I was learning what lay beneath the surface of the worlds that I thought I knew—city hall, the church, the newspapers, jazz music, nightclubs, sports, family life in North Albany. I discovered the gangsterish life lived in Albany during Prohibition, the 1920s and early 1930s. I learned what it was like to make a living cutting ice on the river in the nineteenth century, what it meant to work in the Lumber District when Albany was known as the White Pine Center of the World.

And so gangsters populated my first Albany novel, *Legs*, and the writing took six years of my life, immersing me in not only Albany's history, but the history of the nation in those vicious years that were called the Jazz Age. That book propelled me into a novel called *Billy Phelan's Greatest Game*, which concerned the night world that my father and my favorite uncle had inhabited. In that book I wanted to dramatize the power of Irish American politics in the city: how the bosses—Dan O'Connell and his associates—could impose their will on everybody in town. They controlled the flow of beer in the city both during and after Prohibition. Dan owned a brewery, and if you didn't take his beer, called Hedrick's, the police would suspend your privilege of staying open after the legal closing hour, or they'd close your saloon down as a firetrap. And so Hedrick's beer was sold on tap in 200 of the city's 259 saloons. The bosses could raise the taxes on your house or your grocery store if you disagreed with them. Merely by spreading the word they could force a small-time gambler like Billy Phelan to be "marked lousy"—a phrase I still have never heard used outside of Albany, which meant if the pols wanted to isolate you, they could; and you wouldn't even be able to buy a glass of beer in your own neighborhood saloon.

That was real power, and the individual was subordinate to it. Billy didn't understand the way his own world functioned, although he thought he did, and so my novel became a study of his imagination, his extraordinary moral code, his misreading of the ways of power. And in order to show all this, I had to reconstruct the city-that-was—the Albany of 1938—the *place* that was at the heart of the communal behavior that shaped my story.

In my most recent novel, *Very Old Bones*, politics is not a dominant issue, though I know it is everywhere unseen in the life of the family. What is visible is the peculiar behavior of certain people in the family, who force their inherited morality, or their religious or sexual madness, on their wives, husbands, children, siblings, often with disastrous results. In *Very Old Bones* the story concerns the Phelans, an Irish and Irish American family; but I have been struck by a broad reaction to the book by critics, friends, even strangers, who say that the novel tells the true story of *their* own families. It is hardly news that once a story is developed with the specifics of a single place, it can then transcend that place and take on meanings that were neither intended nor even suspected by the writer. But I do believe that the key word here is specifics, which is how any provincial fictional world becomes transcendent.

Without those specifics the place remains unrealized; and you do not have fiction as I value it. The writer can do all the navel-gazing, all the private psychological analysis, that the novel can bear, but until it's centered on a place, then it's a vagrant pursuit, a discursive soap opera, a Sunday afternoon in the park counting leaves on a generic tree. It is disembodied life, lacking the dynamics that create the movement that defines the imaginations of the people who make the story. And they're very different people in Mississippi, or Puerto Rico, or Dublin, or even Boston, from the people in Albany.

Joyce was insistent on the essentiality of place. In one of his talks with Arthur Power he spoke of Turgenev's *A Sportsman's Notebook*, and he said, "You remember . . . how local it was—and yet out of that germ [Turgenev] became a great international writer. For myself, I always write about Dublin, because if I can get to the heart of Dublin I can get to the heart of all the cities of the world. In the particular is contained the universal" (*James Joyce* 505). My literary ancestors of place have been Irish in part, but many and various really, and I owe equivalent debts to Kafka, and Hemingway, and Nathanael West, and John Cheever, and Isaac Babel, and Saul Bellow, and so many more in whose work the sense of place is central. Even an abstractionist like Samuel Beckett is secure in his place—that cellar, that ash heap, that desolate room, that sterile plain—where his characters suffer the terminal torments of their cancerous souls.

There are cancerous souls everywhere, and pure souls, and lost souls; and Joyce put his in Dublin, and Hemingway put his in Paris, and Babel put his in Odessa, and Beckett put his in garbage cans. I put mine in a house on Colonie

Street in Albany. Souls are where you find them, I say, and one place to find them is as good as another. But it's never the same place. And because it isn't, it's never the same souls.

The last gift from Joyce is probably the greatest, and also the most unusable—his language. Whether it's the exquisite ending to *The Dead*, or Molly's exultation as she yields to Bloom for the first time, or any given passage of *Finnegans Wake* that affects the mind like a Bach suite, it is always the recurrence of proof that literature can exist without plot but not without language.

Faulkner was once asked whether an author has the prerogative to create his own language, and he answered, "He has the right to do that provided he don't insist on anyone understanding it" (*Faulkner in the University* 52). He added that a writer assumes an obligation with his vocation to write in a way that people can understand.

> He doesn't have to write it in the way that every . . . imbecile in the third grade can understand it, but he's got to use a language which is accepted and in which the words have specific meanings that everybody agrees on. I think that *Finnegans Wake* and *Ulysses* were justified, but then it's hard to say on what terms they were justified. That was a case of a genius who was electrocuted by the divine fire. (*Faulkner in the University* 53)

I wonder why Faulkner kept electrocuting Joyce. But maybe I don't wonder.

Hugh Kenner wrote of the coherent specificity of Joyce's language. In his essay on the occasion of Joyce's one-hundredth birthday in 1982, Kenner wrote of the secret of *Ulysses* being "utter cohesion, thousands of details quietly supporting one another." And he mentions how Joyce thought it was "stupid" of George Moore to "make a character look up the time of a train that stopped in his suburb at the same minute every day: rather like looking up the time of eleven o'clock mass." Such inattention was un-Joycean.

"Joyce," wrote Kenner,

> worked with tireless attention to what had previously been inadvertent. He knows how much change a character is carrying, and in which pocket (Bloom set out on that famous morning with four shillings ninepence). He knows the brand of Bloom's hat, Plasto's. He knows that 'wrote' for 'write' is a plausible error in Martha Clifford's typed letter, because *i* and *o* are adjacent on the keyboard. ("On the Centenary" n.p.)

Joyce waged war, Kenner wrote, "against nescience, against inadvertence, against the supposition that anything is anything else. Insofar as he could change the world of the mind, he changed it toward order" ("On the Centenary" n.p.).

But Joyce's order is of a particular kind, and is in many respects unusable by anyone else, a form of sudden death to imitators. Eliot said that the price of having a Dante or a Shakespeare (and he could have added Joyce) is that literature can have only one, and those who come later must find something else to do.

Any person who aspires to serious writing knows this. I constantly purge my work of anything that seems to be even slightly Joycean, though that word now has such a broad context that I would have to stop writing and take up mathematics to be rid of its implications entirely. Joyce's gifts to the art of writing are so abundant, so pervasive, that some things have ceased to be his. The interior monologue that he didn't create but popularized is only Joycean if it is used to excess; otherwise it is just another tool in the writer's kitbag.

That said, I must also say that I used Joyce overtly in my last novel, *Very Old Bones*, an interlude of homage to *Finnegans Wake* that was the fictionalizing of a true event in my life. That event took place at a closed-down Catholic summer camp on Lake Luzerne in the Adirondack Mountains, not far from Saratoga. I stayed there by myself for two weeks in 1971 when I was working on my novel *Legs*, trying to write enough text so my publisher would send money to avert foreclosure on my home and allow me to continue living at the genteel poverty level to which I had become accustomed. I was staying in a one-room cottage heated by kerosene.

It was October, when the temperatures fluctuate between the radiant heat of an Indian Summer day, and the sub-freezing mountain temperatures of the impending winter night. I had worked all day and, as usual, after cooking a very late supper, I settled in for some reading, which this night was *Finnegans Wake*. I was drinking Old Crow whiskey and smoking small Tiparillo cigars. I was up to about thirty cigars a day as a way of cutting down on cigarettes. Slowly I felt the chill in the room, and I put on my overcoat, checked the heater, found it cold, kept reading, smoking, drinking, put on my muffler, put on my hat and one glove, leaving the right hand free to turn the page, and in that condition, warmed by the whiskey and the language of the *Wake*, I defeated the weather utterly.

As usual, I read the *Wake's* pages without knowing very much about what I was reading, loving the jokes and the wordsmithery, thinking perhaps I had a grip on a meaning only to lose it, pushing onward into evermore mysterious and meaningless word games, continuing with the belief that surely something would come clear, ever so slowly getting the rhythm of the pages and feeling the onset of a response that was akin to the subliminal suggestions music creates in me—free-floating, then captivated by the growth of sensation first, then in the grip of a confounding emotion; for I found myself moved, almost to weeping, by the beauty of the meaning I could not put into words of my own, and from knowing I was being as genuinely touched in the unconscious as Finn himself is touched by his river of sleeping thought and memory, and I read through to the final pages, experiencing the sublimity of Ana Livia's monologue, as the River Liffey that she is flows into the Irish Sea, and into Finn's mind, and my own, and I decided when I closed the book that this was probably the premier reading experience of my life, for never had I been moved to tears and beyond by something that was fundamentally incomprehensible, a supreme lesson in the power of language alone to touch what is deepest in our memory, our imagination. I decided in a much later year to pass this experience on through the medium of my narrator in *Very Old Bones*, Orson Purcell, who undergoes the same experience I did, but in a summer hotel on the shore of Saratoga Lake. He lifts from that glorious monologue of Ana Livia this fragment and quotes it to make a point in his story of his life among the women who were all the world to him.

> 'Why I'm all these years within years in soffran, allbeleaved. To hide away the tear, the parted. It's thinking of all. The brave that gave their. The fair that wore. All them that's gunne. I'll begin again in a jiffey. The nik of a nad. How glad you'll be I waked you! My! How well you'll feel! For ever after.' (216)

Orson finds abundant allusions to his own life and love in this and other segments, as anyone must in Joyce's singular book. And then Orson, this young man who has been so put-upon by life, quotes again in conclusion: " '*I done me best when I was let. Thinking always if I go all goes. A hundred cares, a tithe of troubles and is there one who understands me?*' " (222).

That last question was what Joyce had asked his wife Nora in Dublin three and a half decades before he wrote that page of the *Wake*. And I think it's safe to say, even *nine* decades after he asked it, that the answer is no, no one. But we are trying.

Brian O'Nolan* wrote this about Joyce: "Perhaps the true fascination of Joyce lies in his secretiveness, his ambiguity (his polyguity, perhaps?) . . . His works are a garden in which some of us may play. [All that we can claim to know is] merely a small bit of that garden" (208).

But even that small bit of Joyce's garden: what a splendid gift it has been to us all.

---

* Editors' Note: Also known as Flann O'Brien.

References

Agee, James. *Letters of James Agee to Father Flye*. New York: George Braziller, 1962.

Balzac, Honoré de. *Balzac's Masterpieces: Ten Novels*. Introduction by James Gould Cozzens. Philadelphia: David McKay Company, 1931.

Blotner, Joseph. *Faulkner: A Biography. One-volume edition*. New York: Random House, 1974–1984.

Eliot, T. S. "Tradition and the Individual Talent." In *The Sacred Wood and Major Early Essays*. Mineola, NY: Dover, 1998.

Ellmann, Richard. *James Joyce: New and Revised Edition*. Oxford: Oxford University Press, 1982.

Gwynn, Frederick L., and Joseph L. Blotner, eds. *Faulkner in the University: Class Conferences at the University of Virginia, 1957–1958*. New York: Vintage Books, 1959.

Joyce, James. *A Portrait of the Artist as a Young Man*. New York: Penguin, 1993.

Kafka, Franz. "Reflections on Sin, Pain, Hope, and the True Way." In *The Great Wall of China and Other Pieces*. New York: Schocken Books, 1970.

Kennedy, William. *Very Old Bones*. New York: Viking, 1992.

Kenner, Hugh. "On the Centenary of James Joyce." *The New York Times*, January 31, 1982.

Meriwether, James B., and Michael Millgate, eds. "Interview with Henry Nash Smith." In *Lion in the Garden: Interviews with William Faulkner 1926–1962*. New York: Random House, 1968.

O'Brien, Flann. *Stories and Plays*. New York: Viking Press, 1976.

Power, Arthur. *Conversations with James Joyce*. London: Millington, 1974; Chicago: University of Chicago Press, 1974.

This essay was presented as a speech for the James Joyce Lecture at University College Dublin, on June 15, 1993. It appeared in *Salmagundi* 103 (Summer 1994). Reprinted by permission of *Salmagundi* magazine.

Saul Bellow In Memoriam (1915–2005)

A Great Insistent Gift

> Writers are sometimes persons of no character, socially speaking, but they should always be persons of character on the page; which is to say, they should have something strikingly original to say and they should have a marked idiosyncrasy that is noteworthy.
>
> —Saul Bellow

I met Saul forty-five years ago in Puerto Rico when I was the managing editor of a new daily newspaper, the *San Juan Star,* and I was also writing a novel in my spare time, of which I had none. Saul was in the middle of *Herzog* and also teaching fiction writing for a semester at the University of Puerto Rico. I applied and was accepted. He later told me this was the last writing course he ever taught; and it was the only writing course I ever thought of taking. Saul dealt with students individually, half an hour or more of conversation at the Faculty Club every other week, about six in all. I showed him two chapters of a novel in progress and he thought it was fatty, clotty, imprecise, and verbose. Otherwise he liked it. I wrote the fat, clot, imprecision, and verbosity out of it and a month later he liked it so much he thought it was publishable. He was wrong, but I invited him to dinner anyway and told him my beautiful wife, Dana, would cook. He became competitive and said he too would bring a beautiful woman, and he did and later married her, which is another story. My wife did cook, but she decided I should charcoal-broil the steak. I could not get the charcoal to ignite, for it was fatty and clotty, and Saul, who was hungry, became restive and snarly. When the steak, a great steak, finally arrived on his plate, his demeanor again became civilized and we got to be friends.

I moved my journalistic life and my novel writing from San Juan to Albany and in 1964, when Saul was to publish *Herzog,* I interviewed him at home in Tivoli in the Hudson Valley in the old, Dutch mansion he used as a setting for *Herzog*. I remember one prophetic line of conversation I didn't use—about the Nobel Prize for literature, and how some people were bad-mouthing it. Saul agreed that some worthy writers never won it and some not-so-worthy did, and then he said to me, "But we'd accept it if they gave it to us, wouldn't we, Bill?" I, who had yet to publish any fiction, said of course we would. And of course *he* did in 1976, explaining at a later moment that it was "one of those greatest-show-on-earth things, and why should I be too good to take part? So I clowned a bit and turned a few somersaults" (*Riding* 153).

At Tivoli, we also talked about realism in literature, and about departing from it—a prime example of such departure was his novel *Henderson the Rain King,* which at the time I was reading over and over. He cited Beckett's *Waiting for Godot* as another. He added what would be a recurring theme in later conversations: "I think we must trust the intuition of the artist when he departs from realism, and we must remember that the business of the artist is to illuminate and not to inform—so much realism has become just so much information" (Conversation with Bellow).

Herzog went on to win the National Book Award in 1965, and in a conversation I had with Saul in Vermont in a much later year, he recalled his encounter with Louis Fischer, who also won the National Book Award that year for his biography, *The Life of Lenin.* The two writers exchanged inscribed books and Fischer wrote in his: "To Saul Bellow, for deeper thought." Saul remembered thinking: "What's deeper about this?" and then he answered his own question:

> Fischer meant his book had bigger status than mine, that he was writing about the great disasters of the twentieth century . . . but I was only writing about private life. . . . The intellectuals say that true events are the public events. . . . Let's think big. Let's not think about these schnook professors (like Moses Herzog) with their cuckoldries and broken hearts. Let's think about Lenin who didn't want *any* heart in the revolution . . . (Interview with Bellow)

Saul moved back to Chicago after *Herzog* and I didn't see him again until 1981 when I went to Vermont to interview him for a national magazine. He was sixty-six, had just finished a draft of his ninth novel, *The Dean's December,* and was with a new wife. He greeted Dana and me in front of his old farm house wearing a polo shirt, cardigan, baggy trousers, and jogging shoes in which he didn't jog, but which he elevated when he stood on his head, his covert way of getting perspective on the world.

The plan was for us to talk through the afternoon and then for the four of us to go to dinner with novelist Bernard Malamud and his wife. We did talk for hours, far too much to summarize, but one theme surfaced from our old conversation about *Herzog*: the tension between fictionist and nonfictionist. Saul had just abandoned a journalistic book about Chicago. He had been writing of criminal detention, judges, conditions that breed crime—and all of that, he said, was "a subject for some kind of poetry, not a factual account. . . . You'd have to do it with a show of objectivity, and in the end it would all be dead" (*Riding* 147). He mentioned Rilke, "who wouldn't discuss the Great War with anybody . . . because [it] could only be held in newspaper language, and he felt this gave him a foulness in the mouth, and you could only betray experience this way" (*Riding* 146).

As the dinner hour approached, he said he didn't want to be late for the Malamuds. The destination was a month-old restaurant, Le Petit Chef near Wilmington. Saul brought a manuscript of *The Dean's December* for Malamud, who said he'd read it soon, but he was into a third draft of *his* new novel, *God's Grace,* so, "Don't push me on it," he said.

"It's okay," said Saul, "As Mae West said, 'I like a man who takes his time.'" The owner of the restaurant, Betty Hillman, stopped cooking when she heard Saul was on the premises and came to say hello. She shook hands with Malamud, thinking he was Saul; but Malamud said that was all right. Once, when Saul won a literary prize, the Albany *Times Union* ran Malamud's photo with the story.

In 1987, Betty Hillman came to our table again to greet another celebrated diner, Jack Nicholson, who was in Albany shooting the film from my novel *Ironweed.* Jack had told me he held the option on *Henderson the Rain King,* to write and direct it, with maybe Lee Marvin or George C. Scott playing Henderson. He said he'd never talked to Saul but would like to. So, I called Saul and he said sure, and Jack showed up in my driveway in a white stretch limo and he, Dana, and I rode, Beverly Hills style, into the woodsy back roads of Vermont. Saul later wrote:

> His white stretch limousine could not make the narrow turn between my gateposts. Silent neighbors watched from a distance as the chauffeur maneuvered the long car. . . . Then Nicholson came out, observed by many. He said, "Gee, behind the tinted glass I couldn't tell it was so green out here." He lit a mysterious-looking cigarette and brought out a small pocket ashtray, a golden object resembling a pillbox. Perhaps his butt ends had become relics or collectibles. I should have asked him to explain this, for everything he did was noted and I had to answer the questions of my neighborhood friends, for whom Nicholson's appearance here was something like the consecration of a whole stretch of road. (*It All Adds Up* 250)

Jack and Saul got on well and Jack now remembers it as one of the great days of his life. They talked about filming *Henderson,* but no script was ever developed and Jack said Saul's agent dropped the option.

The visit resonated as local gossip for years. At Saul's surprise seventy-fifth birthday party that his wife Janis gave at Le Petit Chef, Betty Hillman took the floor to celebrate her honored guest, and then she added: "You should've been here a few years ago when we had Jack Nicholson, a real celebrity." In a later year, I stopped at the restaurant but the waiter said there were no tables. "Look," I said, "are you sure? Remember Jack Nicholson having dinner here with Saul Bellow? I arranged that." The waiter nodded and said, "Bring Nicholson back and we'll find a table."

Because Saul supported my work, on one occasion in a way that changed my life, people sometimes asked him to react to what I wrote, and in my old files I found a quote he gave to a reporter who was writing about me. I don't think these remarks were ever published.

"Writers," he said, "are sometimes persons of no character, socially speaking"—you can see he had me in mind—but he carried on, as usual, into a larger dimension. Let me repeat the sentence:

> Writers are sometimes persons of no character, socially speaking, but they should always be persons of character on the page; which is to say, they should have something strikingly original to say and they should have a marked idiosyncrasy that is noteworthy. They must persist, and they shouldn't give up readily. They must want to make themselves known and go on record. The world has to be outwitted, and they should know how to impose themselves; yet their insistence should not be merely cranky or psychopathic. They should have something real to insist upon.

Saul really wasn't talking about me at all, but about his own homegrown strategy for being a writer. I never outwitted the world. But if I did *insist* upon anything, I suppose it was the life of the family. Saul also remarked on this; he wrote me about one of my novels:

> I'm glad you turned again to the family theme. I'm tempted to speculate that our family-less, out-of-the-void colleagues are anti-family on grounds of ideology (some from the Marx, some from the Existential side). That's okay for people who *really* come out of the void (South Bronx, or the slums of Rio) but for the majority it's an affectation—a put-on.

> For the likes of us, with powerful early connections—well, we *can* say no to those connections—but whether it's yes or no we have to live with them openly. Joyce, who was so cold to his Dublin family (perhaps to his Paris family as well) has Bloom pining for his dead little boy, his suicide father. Cruel and kinky-real, but not without curious feelings. If Joyce had been born in the fields, under a cabbage leaf—as Samuel Butler would have preferred to enter life—there would have been no *Ulysses*. (Letter from Bellow to Kennedy)

And if Saul Bellow had been born under such a leaf we might not have *The Adventures of Augie March* or *Herzog* and the rest. But he wasn't, and we do have those books, a great insistent gift. Nobody insisted like Saul. He lived at the pinnacle of insistence, all by himself.

References

Bellow, Saul. *It All Adds Up: From the Dim Past to the Uncertain Future*. New York: Viking Penguin, 1994.

Conversation with Bellow. At his home in Tivoli, New York, 1964.

Interview with Bellow. Vermont 1981.

Kennedy, William. *Riding the Yellow Trolley Car*. New York: Viking, 1993.

Letter from Saul Bellow to William Kennedy. May 6, 1992. William Kennedy Papers in the M. E. Grenander Department of Special Collections and Archives, University at Albany.

This essay was delivered as a speech at the American Academy of Arts and Letters Members' Meeting on November 10, 2005, and was published in the Academy's 2005 *Proceedings* and later in *Salmagundi* 153–154 (Winter/Spring 2007), 42–46. Reprinted by permission.

A Nonpareil Force Field

A Tribute to Norman Mailer

> He was the ubiquitous radical moralist, historian, and public scourge, his readers were legion, as were his enemies, and he was a singular mind, the literary phenomenon of his generation.
>
> —William Kennedy

When Norman Mailer was serially publishing his novel *An American Dream* in *Esquire* in 1964, a friend of mine said that he wished Norman would die. My friend was a jingoistic, sex-crazed novelist who revered Faulkner, wrote a hot bodice-ripper and then nothing else that was publishable; and was dead from drink eight years later. Norman lived four more decades as a nonpareil force field in America's literature, intellectual life, and popular culture; and his power to seriously oppress writers like my shameless friend was crystallized by Seymour Krim in a 1969 essay, "Norman Mailer, Get Out of My Head!"

Norman in 1969 was everywhere—in all the media, all the art forms, winning the big prizes, living out Krim's dream of literary activism, and gobbling up, with his "imperialistic personality," territory Krim wanted for himself. "I DON'T WANT to walk around the city constantly being Mailerized," he wrote (129, 128).

Even Krim's sister, who didn't read Mailer, came to visit full of questions: Was Norman as intense in person as on TV? And her husband, who stood for all that Mailer did not, raved about Norman's brilliance. Then came the unkindest cut: "I had a good chance of getting planked one night," Krim wrote. "The girl was darkeyed, salty, and keen"—but then she started to rave about *Barbary Shore*—Norman's second novel, which Krim hadn't liked; and "this Mailer-infected preacherette" kept thrusting *Barbary Shore* at him "like the sacrament." And Krim concluded grimly: "I lost my trick of the evening because of the stone I turned [in]to" (125, 126).

Barbary Shore had not been a great moment for Norman either. *The Naked and the Dead* showered him with literary success, money, and fame, which he loved and came to depend upon, and the critical ambush of *Barbary Shore* was an attack on his nervous system. "My status dropped immediately," he wrote. "I went through tiring years of subtle social defeats because I did not know that I was no longer as large to others as I had been. I was always overmatching myself. To put it crudely, I would think I was dropping people when they were dropping me" (*Spooky Art* 40).

This kind of physical and psychic confessionalism became part of the ongoing text of the true-life novel that Norman would write—and live—for the next forty years. His life was an open book, opened and written by himself—ego-driven, psychoanalytical, truculent, self-flagellating, coruscating, sometimes fictional, routinely brilliant. He discoursed on all the political, literary, gender, sexual, and racial fevers, the poisons and idiocies of our social fabric, its underbelly and its black holes. He was the ubiquitous radical moralist, historian, and public scourge, his readers were legion, as were his enemies, and he was a singular mind, the literary phenomenon of his generation. He also directed, wrote, and acted in films, wrote plays, became a raucous partygoer, a combative TV presence, ran the PEN club, ran the Actors Studio, ran for mayor of New York.

"I had some instinctive sense—right or wrong," he told *Playboy* in 1967, "that the best way to grow was not to write one novel after another but to move from activity to activity, a notion that began with Renaissance man; it's not my idea, after all" ("Crazy One" n.p.).

Part of this was his discovery of journalism when he became discouraged by the difficulty of writing his second and third novels in the early 1960s. Journalism was easier. But—and "this was the horror of it," he said of his discovery—audiences liked it better than fiction. They wanted real events. But Norman also saw that they wanted interpretation of the events, and he was ready.

"We perceive the truth of a novel by way of the personality of the writer," he wrote. "We tend to know, in our unconscious at least, whether the author is to be trusted, and where we suspect he is more ignorant than ourselves. That is the flavor of fiction. We observe the observer. Maybe that is why there is less dead air in fiction, and usually more light" (*The Time of Our Time* ix–x).

But now Norman was also applying this conclusion to his journalism, and what he found was that "the personality of the narrator was probably as important as the event. Not that the narrator would be important in his own person" (*Spooky Art* 187). But the narrator did reveal his prejudices to the reader, and the reader gained a point of view that was absent in so much journalism.

Norman's coverage of such events as the Democratic convention of 1960, and the march on Washington in 1967, gave new dimension to political reporting, and he became the high priest of a newly elevated and fervent American journalism. This wasn't necessarily a blessing for him, as he noted in *Armies of the Night* in a conversation with poet Robert Lowell—when both were going to speak at a party in Washington.

> "I suppose you're going to speak, Norman," Lowell said.
>
> "Well, I will," Norman said.
>
> "Yes, you're awfully good at that."
>
> "Not really."
>
> "I'm no good at all at public speaking," said Lowell.
>
> They lapsed into silence, though Norman kept thinking about Lowell. Then Lowell spoke up "You know, Norman, Elizabeth [Bishop] and I really think you're the finest journalist in America."
>
> Norman didn't react publicly but privately he was seething. Then Lowell said it again.
>
> "Yes, Norman, I really think you are the best journalist in America."
>
> "Well, Cal," said Mailer, using Lowell's nickname for the first time, "there are days when I think of myself as being the best *writer* in America."
>
> "Oh, Norman, oh, certainly. I didn't mean to imply, heavens no, it's just I have such *respect* for good journalism."
>
> "Well, I don't know that *I* do," Norman said. "It's much harder to write . . . a good poem."
>
> "Yes, of course," said Lowell. (*Armies* 19–22)

But in spite of his reservations Norman kept writing journalistic books—on the astronauts, sex, Marilyn Monroe, boxing, Henry Miller, and then *The Executioner's Song*, a work of vast reporting, but Norman called it a novel.

In remembering his apprenticeship as a writer Norman placed *Studs Lonigan* and *Captain Blood* among his shaping forces.* He graduated into Dos Passos and Hemingway, escalated to Proust, Joyce, Tolstoy, and Melville, the masters who fired his ambition to write the great novel. He was further persuaded by Thomas Mann's line that only the exhaustive was truly interesting, and so Norman wrote novels exhaustively.

---

* Editors' Note: James T. Farrell is the author of *Studs Lonigan*, and Rafael Sabatini is the author of *Captain Blood*.

Ancient Evenings took eleven years and had 700 pages; *Harlot's Ghost* seven years and 1,300 pages. He published forty-five books, a total of 16,871 pages. *The Executioner's Song* had a thousand; the lifetime collection of his work, *The Time of Our Time*, was 1,300 pages and binding it was troublesome; *Oswald's Tale: An American Mystery* took two years of research, 800 pages.

The Oswald book was presented as nonfiction, but you open randomly to Jack Ruby killing Oswald, and here comes Ruby's rationale, delivered not by Norman the speculative journalist-historian, but Norman the novelist looping in and out of Jack Ruby's head as Ruby castigates himself. "'You Jew, you do not have the guts to be a hit man—only Italians are that good.' So he wanted to give the Mafia a real signature, his own—three shots—wanted to show the world that a Mob-style execution was not out of reach for him, a Jew" (*Oswald's Tale* 757).

As early as 1967 Norman was saying he had been working on one book all his life. "Everything I write is a card out of the same deck. You can reshuffle them" (*Playboy* interview 1968). Forty years later, May Day, 2007, Norman came to Albany and convinced me that his "one book" was a novel. He was in Albany on his fourth visit to the New York State Writers Institute—which I started in 1983—this time to read from his new novel, *The Castle in the Forest*, about Adolf Hitler—from devilish conception through adolescence.

Russell Banks and I talked to him for an hour on video; and there he sat—the venerable atheist, knowing time was getting short, justifying his latter-day belief in God, reincarnation, and the devil, who is his narrator for the Hitler story. God and Satan, Hitler and Jesus—four more characters in Norman's one big book.

The Castle in the Forest had taken four years of research and writing, but it wasn't enough. "If I were fifty years old," he said, "I'd think, well maybe I should spend the next thirty years . . . writing a 10,000-page novel . . . maybe fifteen novels, one every two years."

Our conversation turned, as usual, to the warring forms in his work—fiction vs. nonfiction—and he was now unequivocal: "It's all fiction," he said. "I think one of the greatest swindles that civilization has been pulling on itself is that there are two literary forms. . . . Nonfiction is fiction because you never get it right."

His argument was that written history built entirely on fact will be full of error, and only the mind of the writer can synthesize facts into a reality that might have been. In *The Executioner's Song*, he said, "I wanted to prove a point, which was that fiction is a style that's employed to approach reality."

Norman was on the wane physically in Albany. He had admitted publicly he was failing. He'd been walking for years with two canes because of the punishment his arthritic knees gave him, and he'd recently had asthma, and a heart bypass. But when I asked how things were, he said, "It's only the extremities." His mind was very sharp.

He read for, and talked with, a crowd of six hundred, and it buoyed him. We had an interlude at a private home before the reading where he drank a couple of rums with orange juice—he would have a swallow of this same combination on his death bed. A late supper followed his reading and carried on till a late hour. Norman was very talkative and in great form. As we left the restaurant someone asked would he come back to Albany, and he said, "Oh yes, indeed," and then, invoking one of the characters in his novel, he gave a bit of a wink and added, "God willing."

Four months later, in September, I was at Cape Cod with my son and his family, and my wife Dana and I drove to Provincetown for a reunion with Norman and his ebullient and beautiful wife Norris. Norman got out of bed and came down with his canes to greet us, much frailer than in May. He had since suffered a collapsed lung and congestive heart failure, and the multiple assaults on his body had further crooked his back, shrunken his face, and wasted him into a ninety-pound specter of the old electric Norman. He speculated he had a secret cancer the doctors couldn't find.

But his spirit and wit were on full display, and with our wives and an old Mailer family friend, we lunched on lobster and wine, hashed over my novel in progress and the play he'd talked me into writing. The friend, Christine Pabst, a photographer, had a story that both Norman and I had forgotten. The night France gave him the Legion of Honor at the French embassy in New York, we were all at an after-gathering, talking about how Houdini died from an unexpected and brutal punch to the stomach. Norman was insisting I punch him comparably. I was inquiring whether I should punch the upper or lower abdomen when Christine interrupted to say how much she liked my work and pulled Norman away. She thought I'd damage him, or that it'd turn into a fight. Norman thought the story was hilarious. I thought I'd probably have splintered one of my arthritic knuckles on his undoubtedly case-hardened gut.

Anyway, the lunch progressed with talk about Texas Hold'em, and Brando, and movies, and Fidel, and Cuban politics, and how Norman might telescope his colossally ambitious Hitler trilogy into one sequel. He knew any sequel was beyond him, but *there*—to the very end—was that one big novel, driving the creative juices still in him.

The conversation had been unpredictable and funny, as usual, but after two hours Norman slapped the table with the palms of both hands and said, "Gotta go up. I'm really tired." We agreed that, without a doubt, this had been one of the great lunches, and he pushed himself back from the table.

We shook hands.
And we said so long.
Then he picked up his two canes and went slowly upstairs to lie down.

References

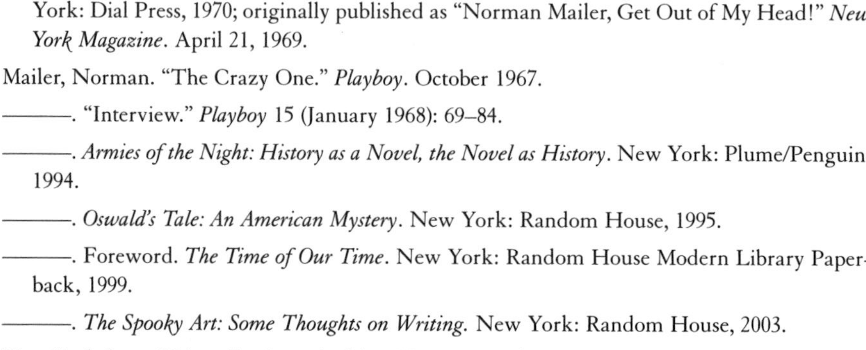

Krim, Seymour. "Ubiquitous Mailer vs. Monolithic Me." In *shake it for the world, smartass.* New York: Dial Press, 1970; originally published as "Norman Mailer, Get Out of My Head!" *New York Magazine*. April 21, 1969.

Mailer, Norman. "The Crazy One." *Playboy*. October 1967.

———. "Interview." *Playboy* 15 (January 1968): 69–84.

———. *Armies of the Night: History as a Novel, the Novel as History*. New York: Plume/Penguin, 1994.

———. *Oswald's Tale: An American Mystery*. New York: Random House, 1995.

———. Foreword. *The Time of Our Time*. New York: Random House Modern Library Paperback, 1999.

———. *The Spooky Art: Some Thoughts on Writing.* New York: Random House, 2003.

New York State Writers Institute Archive. Norman Mailer Interview. 05.01.07.

This essay was delivered as a speech at the Academy of Arts and Letters Members' Meeting on November 5, 2008. Printed by permission. A portion of the speech was delivered at the Memorial Service for Norman Mailer on April 9, 2008, at Carnegie Hall. That version appeared in the *Mailer Review* 2, 1 (Fall 2008). Reprinted by permission of the Norman Mailer Society.

A Box of Books

An Exchange, on Matters Literary and Postal, with Hunter S. Thompson

> Send all books at once to Louisville. . . . You've had time to read every goddam one of them. My novel has gone to pieces and I need a job. How about yours?
>
> —Hunter S. Thompson

As is well known among modern Caribbean historians, Hunter S. Thompson fled Puerto Rico in June 1960, a fugitive from prosecution on charges of public drunkenness and disorderly conduct in a fight at a beachfront bar over a check he refused to pay. He was facing a year in jail so he, his wife-to-be, Sandy Conklin, and their old friend Paul Semonin hired on as crew on a forty-seven-foot sloop, heading eventually for Spain, and were dumped in Bermuda with no money. Money was an ongoing problem with Hunter, who chose to live as a freelance journalist and would-be novelist but couldn't find a compatible employer or publisher. If 1960 wasn't the low point of his financial life, it was close. When he left San Juan, in a clandestine hurry, he left behind assorted debts, some of which I was aware of: a bill for a car rental; a bill for phone calls he denied charging to the *San Juan Star,* of which I was the managing editor; and he was jumping bail, something like $300, perhaps $1,000, on some bail bondsman or lawyer I barely remember putting him in touch with. In his sudden departure from San Juan, he also left his duffel bag, a box of books, and other items at my home in Isla Verde, with a note:

"Had no way of getting the duffel & the box to P.O.—so had to leave them here. If it's not too much trouble, could you mail the duffel bag, C.O.D., to [Florida address] & the box to me C.O.D. to [address in Spain] . . . .We'll drop you a line from somewhere in the islands and let you know what's happening." He left me a list of the books in his box:

Hardcover
Modern Spanish Course (two books)
Basic Elements of Spanish
Ulysses
Faulkner Reader [this was not in the box]
Lecturas Escogidas
Fitzgerald Reader
A Death in the Family
Ginger Man
Dylan Thomas Poems
Advertisements for Myself
Reynard the Fox
Last Tales
U.S.A.
Doctor Zhivago
The Plague
Proust, *Remembrance,* etc. (two books)
Don Quixote
Leaves of Grass
Child's Christmas in Wales

Paperback
War with the Newts
Heart of Darkness/Secret Sharer
My First 2,000 Years
Grapes of Wrath
Fear & Trembling/Sickness Unto Death
Green Mansions
Huck Finn
Portable D. H. Lawrence
Sound & *Fury*
Decameron
Heart Is a Lonely Hunter
Dante's Inferno
The Crack-up
Last Angry Man
Immoralist
Maggie Cassidy
Don Quixote
Naked & Dead
D. H. Lawrence collected poems

Word of Hunter's departure from San Juan got around, and so did word of his debt, which I probably commented on to someone, since it got back to him. He sent me a postcard from Bermuda in July of 1960: "What is this rot about me owing you money? I knew you'd try to cheat me as soon as my back was turned. If you keep fooling with my money I'll write the police and have you arrested. . . . Sandy says hello. Cheers, HST."

In early August he wrote from New York that his novel *Prince Jellyfish* had bounced for the third and last time, and he denied charging any phone calls to the *Star.* "I'm tired of being accused of things like that. My assaults are usually more frontal—or at least more damaging." He said that he had sold a tourism article on Puerto Rico to the *New York Herald Tribune*, which would square him on the debt for the car he rented to get the story. And he added:

"What is the status of my gear? Is everything still there? Don't worry about it not being paid for in Louisville. If it's cheaper send it all to [Florida]. But for God's sake send it C.O.D. I have my debts divided into 'general' and 'personal'—and I can't stand anymore in the personal column. I won $50 on a quiz show last week. Missed the $600 question."

I wrote him that I'd keep his belongings until he decided where I should send them. "So far I've received instructions to send all, sometimes part, to Spain, Florida, and Kentucky. If I had taken any or all of your advice they would belong to the world at large. Why don't I keep them until you light somewhere? Or, if you want, I'll send them to Kentucky. But please make up your goddam mind."

In September he was on his way to Seattle and San Francisco, and he wrote: "Hang onto bags & stuff until you get further word."

In October, Sandy sent us a blank check to cover the mailing of the duffel bag, by the cheapest possible method, to her in Florida. She longed to be back on the beach in San Juan. She said she was joining Hunter in San Francisco. She wondered what it would cost to send the books to Florida, as well as the "coconut set" that was in the book box. "I can't really say if Hunter's fine or not," she wrote. "I don't think he really knows. San Francisco is a good city, but I'm not sure just how long it can hold him."

Sandy sent us a card when the duffel arrived, and thanked us, and said that Hunter was wandering in the Big Sur area. I wrote Hunter about my adventure in sending the duffel to Sandy: "The goddam thing almost cost me a finger. The Post Office wouldn't accept it with a lock on it unless I attached the key. They didn't seem to care that I didn't have the key. So I had to buy a hacksaw blade, borrow a hacksaw handle, and saw the lock off, almost sawing off my thumb in the process. I mean, goddam, Thompson. If you get to Big Sur, give my regards to Henry Miller. Ask him if he ever tried it standing up in a hammock."

In 1961, Hunter wrote from Big Sur: "We have hot sulphur baths here, every day a long soak in a big roman tub—after the touch football. Just sit in that hot water with a beer and a cigarette, peering out at the surf, co-ed bathing—in all it's enough to give a man paws." He added: "Also—and this is vital—please send that cardboard box containing our coconut cups and my pipe rack. And—if they pack easily, and they should—my packet of books. As a matter of fact I think they were already packed. I would enclose a blank check for it, but oddly enough, we are temporarily out of checks—instead of money. If you feel like trusting us (me) for the blank check, send the stuff on. If not, get it ready for mailing and send it when the check arrives."

I wrote and told him that despite having to run a newspaper and write a novel and keep a wife and two small children happy, despite knowing what a goddamn martyr I was to conformity, I understood his condition out there in the freedom of the Big Sur sea spray, and I added: "I know how it is to be sitting there immersed in a hot sulphur bath engaged in co-educational nooky watching, Roman style, but . . . alas . . . with no pipe rack. You must be frantic, wondering what to do with your pipe." I said I'd try to figure out where I put the box of books. "Did the dogs get it? Did I let the kids play with it? Did the rust get it like it gets everything else?"

I received a postcard: "Dear Mr. Kennedy: Mr. Thompson is currently away on pleasure . . . he has asked me to write you and say that, because of your last letter, he will soon be on his way to Puerto Rico to destroy your teeth with a huge bamboo splint, and ram eight coconut cups far into your small intestine. I'm sure you're aware that Mr. Thompson is a vicious, brutal ass. As far as I'm concerned, your story is a touching one. I would advise you to take up writing as a form of therapy; they say it takes your mind off your problems. (signed) Annie Jo Feen, secretary to Mr. Thompson."

Then another postcard: "Still here, you pompous jap. Just returned from SF and a week of god-awful drinking. . . . Send my gear. I have got in a fight here & am barred from the baths. Drink is dangerous. Eros giveth and Eros taketh away."

I wrote and told him I was ready to go through the postal tortures to get his gear to him, but that I wouldn't do it at a financial loss to myself. I said I wouldn't let his inability to pay me back "annihilate a perfectly good friendship." I said I never doubted his honesty and integrity, but debts without urgency can go unattended and erode all goodwill. To forestall this, I said I would consider taking a few of his books in payment for my cost of sending them. I also mentioned that Paul Semonin had sent three dollars to the *Star* for a debt he owed, but no one could find such a debt and I was in possession of the three dollars. I said I was considering sending it back to Paul or maybe buying a bottle of rum with it. "Probably I'll buy the rum," I said.

Hunter wrote from Big Sur about me taking books as payment and asked for a list of my choices: "If you want the cream of my book crop I will say no and send money. If, however, you constrain yourself, selecting only those tomes I have no use for, we can settle the thing without resorting to cash." Either way, he said, "I will see to it that our friendship is kept solvent." He said he would tell Paul Semonin about my theft of his three dollars.

In May he wrote again asking for a map of San Juan and copies of the *San Juan Star,* saying that he was closing in on his novel *The Rum Diary.* Later he asked, "What about my gear? Have you ignored all my proposals?"

I replied that I had been away for two weeks and had sent my unfinished novel off to New York and had heard that an editor seemed to like it, but no word. I told him: "I have your pipe rack, coconut cups (no books yet) wrapped and tied for shipment. You must admit I am making headway. . . . I promise shipment before the year is out." But as to keeping any of his books as payment: "There aren't many of your books that I don't have or would care to have . . . the *Fitzgerald Reader*, D. H. Lawrence paperback, Dylan Thomas poems, and one or two others wouldn't be a bad swap. . . . I expect the postal tariffs will be somewhere under ten dollars. But I'm not sure."

In July he wrote with thanks for the map and the *San Juan Stars* I had sent, and added: "The pipe rack is hung, the cups are in use. . . . now, if you can just send those damn books, I won't have to write you anymore." He said he could pay cost of shipment, having sold a story and photos on Big Sur: "I have just whacked *Rogue* magazine for $350." He was finishing *The Rum Diary*, wondered about my novel, concluded: "If you want to keep some books, do—and if you want to send them all & let me pay, do that. Us rich writers don't give a damn. Noisily, HST."

I wrote him in early August that I had quit my job as managing editor of the *Star* to write full time and work only weekends, about a two hundred percent pay cut. People thought I was fired. "They can't conceive of a man leaving gainful employment to take the plunge," I wrote him. "Take the case of Hemingway, I tell them all. Consider Sherwood Anderson. . . . I have a friend on the coast who sits in a sulphur bath all afternoon, drinking whiskey and shooting out the window at his neighbors. Consider him. I don't expect to be understood. To be great is to be misunderstood, said Emerson. Take the case of Pythagoras and Luther and Galileo."

A few months later, he replied from Big Sur: "They're trying to arrest me here. Also trying to evict me. But I'm rolling in money now and they're awed. After months of insane poverty I have made $630 in the past six weeks. I am so used to poverty that I can waste most of it and not know the difference." He had bought a pistol, a rifle, and a dog. He didn't believe I'd really quit the editor's job: "I admire your plunge, if that it is, and hope you can muster the balls and the decent pages . . . to make it over the hump. . . . When you write send $2½ million. I need a few acres and some dogs and some guns and some whiskey and a few cars and a boat and a donation to CORE and god knows what else. It's hell to be needy."

In October I got a card: "Send no books until further word."

Then came a note: "Send all books at once to Louisville. . . . You've had time to read every goddam one of them. My novel has gone to pieces and I need a job. How about yours?"

I wrote back and told him about the two rejections of my book and my growing pessimism about ever selling it. It was viewed as too grim, too gloomy. I advised him to write an upbeat novel, but he didn't, and neither did I. I told him that if he was serious I'd send the books to Louisville, "but you've been serious before. California, Spain, New York, etc. Are you sure you're sure?"

In February of 1962, I wrote him again: "As for your books, your rotten goddam books, they are crated. . . . They have caused me no end of grief. First the kids spilled chocolate syrup over them. Then the mold set in. Then when the rain came in that time I protected them as best I could. Finally I got the sonsabitches packaged. . . . Then, fully prepared mentally to face the Postal Tortures, I lugged the box to the car, drove halfway to the Post Office only to recall that I had no money, neither with me nor at home. So I came back and they have been sitting . . . awaiting new mental preparations, availability of lucre, and the propitious moment, astrologically, for shipping books over the seas."

In January of 1964, after I had moved to Albany to live and work, I had a word from him that he had been hired by the *National Observer* to cover the West Coast on a regular basis, in his own style. His novel, he said, was stagnant, and *Cavalier* had rejected one of his old stories. He was going to be living north of San Francisco, he said, and I should come out and have a look at the coast. We hadn't communicated in some months, and he said he felt he was losing track of my whereabouts. He added: "I think you still have my copies of: 1) *The Hemingway Reader* 2) *The Fitzgerald Reader* 3) *The Ginger Man*. . . . please send them at once. . . . Repeat, send at once, collect or any other way that is quick. Send them first-class and I'll send you a cheque for the postage."

It's been more than forty-two years since then, and I have looked on all my shelves for those books. They are not here. I feel certain that I sent them.

The Secrets of Creative Love

A Short Story

> Quinn remained a writer, obsessed still with the past and its mysteries, and had reaped a few of the rewards and ironies such a life offers.
>
> —William Kennedy

In these months Daniel Quinn was reconstituting his youth out of restlessness with a maturity that would not hold. Twenty-five years earlier, when he read what Hemingway wrote about giving up the vanity of clothing (under the influence of Ecclesiastes?) and with the money saved having bought Picassos and Braques, Quinn left off buying clothes for their own sake. He accumulated no Picassos and could not say where the money went that did not go to the clothiers. Perhaps he bought more Hemingway or saw more films or drank more Jameson's. Certainly he rid himself of the unseemly wardrobe. He wore out the chocolate brown gabardine, the tan Palm Beach, the gray sharkskin with the one-button roll. And when the trousers of his blue serge double-breasted thinned at the seat, he converted the jacket to a blazer, adding buttons the color of burnished bronze, and wore it sparingly for the next twenty-five years, its splendid resistance to death by time or moths proving to be a symbol of his own enduring youthfulness.

Not even carnival sharpers had correctly guessed Quinn's age for at least fifteen years, though he made no secret of it. His hair had not gone gray, his face had developed no lines or furrows that revealed a ravaged spirit. Yet he moved through these days with a growing sense of drift and dejection that contravened the rewards due those who successfully fend off the pillaging of years. Without knowing why, but sensing that his decision of a quarter century ago had been misguided, he once again gave willful attention to clothing as a way of restructuring that mood of certainty, that pleasure in being well-dressed to meet life that had existed so vitally before the Hemingway-Ecclesiastes axis cleaned out his closet. He now read the men's fashion section of the Sunday *Times* magazine, questing for an image that transcended that of rumpled slug but halted this side of fop. He browsed in the shirt and suit departments of Brooks Brothers on a trip to the city and came away depressed at the irrational price of traditionalism. He bought a Yugoslavian suit the color of camel's hair, with pleated patch pockets, but was two months accumulating the money to take it out of the store. Then at the yearling sales in Saratoga with Maud and the Penningtons he found himself fixating on the compelling attire of a man of affluent girth who was oh-so-quietly bidding on a bay filly whose worth had rapidly ascended to six figures and was now moving toward seven.

"Who's bidding?" Sissy Pennington asked. "Do you see anyone?"

"I don't," said Quinn as he tried to scan the crowd face by face but found in it only the qualities that made so many of the people similar. There were more men with short blond hair, pulled away from the temples but falling from the crown with a soft flourish, and more men with blazers, half-glasses, and neckties (all the men, all of them, wore neckties), than is numerically normal for any gathering of humans under a single roof, this roof being part of the Finney Pavilion, a hemisphere of money across Union Avenue from the racetrack. The similarities Quinn saw in the spectators, all of them here because they belonged here, impeccable credit their common bond, seemed now to be comparable to racial characteristics. They were as alike as a roomful of Japanese technocrats or Portuguese fishermen. The more they stalked singularity the more they resembled the common image that lurked in every one of their chiffoniers.

"I hope they don't catch me raising a finger at the wrong time and bill me for three hundred thousand," said Fred Pennington, who had worn his blazer for the occasion, unaware how properly he was dressed. Quinn wore a pale blue seersucker jacket with a wine stain on the lapel that the cleaners could not eradicate, a white dress shirt whose collar was (still unnoticeably) beginning to fray, and a pair of classy six-dollar Italian shoes Maud had found in a sale on Fourteenth Street.

"You could wave like a cheerleader," Quinn told Fred. "You could wave a flag or a Boy Scout and they wouldn't look at you unless you'd established your credit with them."

"How do you know that?" Maud asked him.

"I know about credit."

"You know about not having any," said Maud.

"Negative knowledge is also knowledge," said Quinn.

They had known the Penningtons since before they all married. Quinn and Fred made the first connection, comrades in the city room after college for a year of reporting and after-hours carousing that was quick-drying cement for a lifetime friendship. Quinn remained a writer, obsessed still with the past and its mysteries, and had reaped a few of the rewards and ironies such a life offers. Fred had aspired to poetry before he met Sissy and it nagged his spirit after marriage. In the grip of a psychic fit he quit his job when the MacDowell Colony offered him two months of summer literary retreat in rural New Hampshire. He decided he would need no more purified time than that to compose one unarguably sanctified poem and thus confirm the worth of his muse. But when September came and the muse had finked out, he took a job with *International Currents*, an electronics magazine, and without poetic distractions he rose like an astronaut into a cosmic editorship, which in time allowed him to buy the former Saratoga residence of the VanCleeve-Batesons (aluminum), and never mind the price.

The auctioneer in the Finney Pavilion sat with his assistant in the middle of the arena on a high perch around which the grooms walked the yearlings. The floor of the promenade area was covered with green sawdust and policed by a scoliotic little black man with a Douglas Fairbanks mustache, a shovel, and a rake, working the racist end of the horses, rushing their regal droppings out beyond the glass doors where they sent up a thoroughbred reek into the starry August sky.

Four spotters stood anxious watch for the understated signals of the bidders as the auction proceeded, but Quinn watched only the spotter a few feet in front of him, a portly man whose head was bobbing with spastic professionalism.

"Yuh," he said, and again, "yuh," clearly in response to the bidder Quinn could not find.

"Will you give me seven hundred thousand," the auctioneer was saying in his machine-gun lingo, "gimmaree gimmaree gimmaree seven hundred thousand now seven hundred thousand I've got yes gimmaree gimmaree gimmaree yes seven hundred and twenty gimmaree . . ."

"Yuh."

"I see him," said Maud. "Third row, fat."

The bidder sat next to a dark-haired woman in a white dress and pearls, who sat beside a blonde with hair pulled away from temples in a soft flourish. The man, in blazer and necktie, was fifty-five, indisputably fifty-five, golden half-glasses riding low on his nose. He nodded, ever so imperceptibly, but a nod, and Maud giggled, and the spotter said, "Yuh," and the auctioneer said, "Seven hundred and seventy-five will you gimmaree eight hundred, gimmaree gimmaree . . ."

The bidding man wore a handsome shirt with dark blue stripes and gold cuff links in French cuffs, the left cuff extending three inches beyond the blazer sleeve. He also wore a blue and white polka-dot tie, which Quinn took to be a standard variation of the uniform of the day, though he had never seen the combination before. The combination should not have succeeded. It was an arrogant combination, absurd. In his most aggressive time Quinn would not have put polka dots with stripes. Quinn felt distanced from taste. He would be an also-ran on any best-dressed list. One needed imagination to keep up, to defy the taboos, to override the cluckings of critics and fuse polka dots with stripes stylishly, heroically.

"I've got nine hundred and forty, will you give me a million?" said the auctioneer. "Another sixty is all it needs and this horse has a better record than Genuine Risk had at the same age, how about just a little more . . ."

The bidding man gave the spotter a negative move of his left hand and the spotter's head paused in the silence.

"Yuh," said another spotter on the opposite side of the pavilion.

"I've now got nine hundred and fifty, will anyone say a million? Gimmaree gimmaree . . ."

The bidding man nodded, the least perceptible nod of the night, for Quinn almost missed it.

"Yuh," said the proximate spotter.

"Well bless my soul," said the auctioneer.

The Penningtons chose to sleep late and so Quinn and Maud went alone to the morning workouts at the track. They sat across from one another in the clubhouse watching Eddie Maple ride up the track and back again on Genuine Risk, and though neither of them would have recognized jockey or mount had the announcer not identified the noted presences, they felt satisfied that the morning had brought them into the realm of such high achievers.

"I had a vivid dream last night," Maud said when the waiter took away their plates.

"Do you want it analyzed?"

"No, I just want to tell it."

"It's after breakfast. It won't come true now."

"I should hope it wouldn't."

"Was I in it?"

"Would I leave you out? I was at the foot of a mountain and up the slope this glorious music was playing. You have no idea. I can't ever remember any music in a dream before. I went up a long path, though I knew I shouldn't. I needed permission but I couldn't find anyone to ask, and the music was so glorious. I wish I could tell you what it was like. And then in this high place I could see them making the music."

"What were they making it with?"

"I don't know that."

"Who was making it?"

"I couldn't see their faces. It was on another mountain. You couldn't get there from where I was. Then I was in a restaurant showing you how I could hold an abstract piece of cake in front of my face without touching it. It just hung there in the air until I was ready to eat it. You asked me how I did it and I said it had to be windy."

"I like the abstract cake," Quinn said. "The wind's not bad, but easy."

"Then we were in the Bronx, someplace very poor, and people had iron gates on their windows. I said to you, 'Isn't it amazing what crime has done for the iron gate industry?'"

"Was I amazed?"

"I think so, and I saw a woman in the window who was so shabby, so very, very shabby, and I told you how glad I was we didn't live here. We started to leave and you were sitting on the curbstone reading the newspaper and you said, 'Don't forget the turtle.' We had a turtle in a dishpan and I put it inside a globe so the water wouldn't spill, and you said, 'Let's turn the globe into a basketball so it won't break on the way home.' Then I saw Fred. He was in high school, very young, and he was playing marbles in the living room."

"What living room?"

"Where we first lived, over the garage."

"Did you play marbles too?"

"No," said Maud.

"Why not?"

"It's not my game."

That evening, when the Penningtons gave a party on the porch and lawn of their summer place on the shore of Saratoga Lake, Maud disappeared. Quinn walked down to the lake to look for her and saw that the Pennington boat was gone. He looked along the shore and in the distance saw the silhouette of a man and a woman holding one another at the waist, their faces close but not touching. Was it Maud? From the tilt of the head it seemed not. Quinn looked back toward the splendid Pennington house, built near the site of an old landmark restaurant where Henry James once had memorable tea, and he saw that the long, sloping, and dramatically lighted lawn, light fading into shadow, curled in upon itself in an unnatural but graceful way, and he could not say whether this was déjà vu or the work of a frangible imagination.

He saw Sissy Pennington standing alone by the outdoor bar and he remembered what James had said of the Saratoga ladies: that they adorned themselves elegantly, but to so little purpose. Sissy was never less than regal in her attire and her carriage, but she was too bright to take her regality seriously. Quinn walked to her and mixed himself a small scotch and water.

"I see you're having a swell time," he said.

"I'm resting between conversations about horses. I often wonder what it would have been like if Fred had kept on with the poetry."

"You'd be talking about horses as symbols."

A cluster of guests sat on lawn chairs in deep shadows beneath three grand trees. The others were on the porch, all of them growing dim with the drink and the darkness. The voices from the porch carried outward with acute clarity, Cesar Monteflores's above all. He was a sinewy Dominican horse breeder, a sleek-haired and handsome man with a silver incisor that gave a metallic glint to his remarks. Quinn had met him and his fetching young wife at the yearling sales the night before. He was now inquiring resonantly: Has anyone seen Carmen? Has anyone seen my wife? And it brought quiet to the porch. Cesar bounced down the steps, peered into the cluster of faces in the shadows, and elicited shakes of the head and nos to this question. Then he saw Sissy and came toward her.

"I haven't seen her," Sissy volunteered.

"Where is your husband?" asked Cesar.

"Where indeed?"

"Are they together? *Juntos?"*

"I suppose it's possible."

"If he is with her, that *maricón,* I will cut out his heart."

"He no longer has a heart," said Sissy. "And if he's such a *maricón,* as you suggest, then you have nothing to worry about."

Cesar walked down toward the shore calling his wife's name: "Caaaarme n . . . Caaaaaaaaaaaarmen . . . Caaarmenciiiiiita," the mournful cry of a hound in unassuageable grief. Quinn and Sissy said nothing, nor did they move. They watched Cesar dart in and out of the shadows of the shoreline trees, and then they watched him come back toward them, the machismo in his stride now at full brim.

"I know they are together," he said to Sissy. "I saw how he was whispering to her. He is having her and I demand my honor be preserved. I demand you give me the same satisfaction. *Igual,* you understand? And give it to me now, *ahora mismo!*

"That's not how we do things up here, Señor Monteflores," Sissy said. "We have different customs. If Fred really carries it off I could make you a baked Alaska. Do you like baked Alaska? Or I could let you have our orchestra seats for the symphony."

"I think that this is no joke," Cesar said, inhaling his outrage. "I am dishonored in your home."

"Our hostess has nothing to do with your dishonor, if such it be, Mr. Monteflores," Quinn said. "Her husband isn't with your wife. He's with my wife."

"How do you know this fact?"

"I understand the customs."

"He is with your wife and it gives you no import?"

"They're first cousins," said Quinn. "It's like royalty and thoroughbreds. You keep it in the family whenever possible."

Cesar Monteflores snorted and walked back into the house and past the silent guests. The talk then resumed on the porch and in the shadows beneath the trees, a grove of honey locusts.

"My hero," Sissy said to Quinn.

"I'm all for facing the reality," said Quinn, "even when I don't know what it is."

"Do you really think he's with Maud?"

"I believe in the possibility of the unlikely."

"But you don't feel dishonored."

"On the contrary. I demand satisfaction."

"When?"

"Now. We'll go for a swim."

"Why didn't I think of that?" Sissy said, and together they walked toward the lake. They walked along the shore to the small sandy cove where the four Pennington children swam with their friends in daylight hours, a safe, shallow harbor without algae or neighbors. Quinn and Sissy hung their clothes on the low branches of a birch tree and walked into the water together, Sissy wearing a bikiniesque transparency.

"How do you expect me to banish my dishonor if you don't take that thing off?" Quinn said.

"Do you really want to start this?" Sissy said. "It's been years."

"I like to keep my options open," said Quinn.

And so Sissy stepped out of the garment, hung it on a limb, and together they swam out into the warm, black water until it was over their heads. They splashed around on their backs, swam in circles, and then swam to where they could stand up. They held one another then, almost in the same way, Quinn noted, that the couple on the shore had embraced earlier.

"I remembered your breasts quite accurately," Quinn said. "In this light I can't be sure of the color, but I was right about the shape."

"The color is still white, but they're no longer the shape you remember, unless your memory has also sagged."

"They're quite beautiful."

"Do you really, really, really want to do this, Quinn?"

"I haven't decided."

"I'm not sure I want to."

"It's better not to be sure. When you're sure of everything you turn out like Cesar Monteflores. Be grateful for your uncertainties."

"I think you're starting to get personal."

"I think so too."

"Let's go sit down and talk about this."

They sat together underneath their clothing and looked at the moon and the summer stars and the scattered lights along the far shore. Quinn stared at Sissy and then stroked one of her breasts, testing his tactile memory against the real thing. He decided she had grown softer with age. They had loved intensely but briefly during the summer Fred courted his muse in New Hampshire.

"I think Fred plays with women now and then just to prove he hasn't died and gone to the vault of the Chase Manhattan," Sissy said.

"I don't want to talk about Fred," said Quinn.

"I suppose I don't either," Sissy said. Then she kissed Quinn lightly, a deft but soft-lipped kiss that slowly grew fervent. They then reconstituted the ritual in the style that neither of them had chosen to forget.

"I'm being a terrible hostess," Sissy said when they began to dress.

"You won't hear me complaining," said Quinn.

"They'll miss us," she said. "They'll say we've gone off together. They'll see our soppy hair and say we've been swimming. They'll ask if we wore our bathing suits."

"We can say we didn't go all the way in, that we only wet our heads."

Quinn did not want to return to the party yet. He stood holding Sissy's hand, staring out at the lake, and realized he was watching the Pennington speedboat returning, its light gliding slowly along the surface of the water, moving toward the dock. They heard the motor die, saw the light go out, heard a rustle of voices. Quinn felt he could present Sissy with any question whatever and it would yield its mysteries. Sissy was brilliant of mind, body, and soul and he would not make love to her again for twenty more years. He sat beside her on the rock and told her of Maud's dream about the glorious music and the abstract cake and the iron gates and him sitting in the gutter and the turtle and the basketball and Fred playing marbles over their garage and he ascribed meaning to most of the elements.

"Maud wishes we were rich like you," he said. "It's not reducible to greed. She just wants that abstract cake. I think it's brilliant how she invented that."

"What about the iron gates?"

"They keep people out. And in."

"And the basketball?"

"The basketball I don't have yet. I don't think it's terribly important. It's the turtle that's the key. We saw this story about turtles on Charles Kuralt last Sunday. This great, monstrous sea turtle, this incredibly aged and mythic creature, venerable really, lays her eggs on the beach and then sheds a giant tear as she goes back into the ocean. The people on CBS didn't know whether the tear was from her joy at the birthing or her pain at having to leave the kids behind. I suppose physical pain is a possibility, but I prefer not to credit that."

"As you prefer not to credit the basketball. Don't you really know what the basketball means?"

"I really don't," said Quinn.

"Well, I'll never tell."

"Did you have a nice swim?" Maud asked when Quinn and Sissy came into the kitchen. Her voice was full of champagne bubbles and rainbows. She was incomparably beautiful. "We had a lovely ride all over the lake, Fred took Carmen and Walter and me on the grand tour. We saw where Riley's was and Cary Moon's, which was all the rage a century ago, and we saw where the Whitneys swim and where Arnold Rothstein used to go wading in rolled-up trousers in the late afternoon. We saw where Victor Herbert almost drowned and . . ."

"It's dark out there."

"It was still light when we left. And there's a bright moon."

"Where is Carmen now?" Quinn asked.

"She's out on the porch, with Cesar. They're quite a pair of lovebirds, those two."

"Quite a pair," said Quinn, and in a voice that would not carry he said, "She didn't go with you. I saw her with a friend down by the lake."

"Shhh," said Maud, and in an equally conspiratorial whisper she said, "They came over to the boat when we docked and begged us to say they'd been with us."

"Who is us?"

"Who do you suppose?"

Quinn looked from Maud to Fred, who was smiling and stroking Sissy's wet and stringy hair, then to Walter, who was standing in the doorway to the living room, talking to Grover Milburn, a Mercedes-Benz dealer. Walter was an engineer, a partner in a titanium mining company that was headquartered in Montreal. He was perhaps thirty-five and his face had the raw power of the young John Garfield.

Maud raised herself an inch and kissed Quinn with her lips open, a meaningful statement. It resurrected his memory of their first kiss, the night when they met at a party in Frankfurt. Someone told Quinn she was German and that her name was Gisela; and Maud spoke both languages so well that she convinced him it was true. In his usual way of validating the unreal, Quinn fell in with her game and rhapsodized over her name, finding in it echoes of Galatea and Gaea, Giselle and Gelsomina, Gioconda, Guinevere, and even the Gleipnir, which, he explained to her alone, meant that chain of wondrous things that once fettered an enemy of the Norse gods. The chain, Quinn said with an eloquence that stunned the young Maud and made her his that night and ever after, was made of a Siamese cat's footsteps, the soft beards of yellow-haired women, the roots of round stones, the breath of small, golden fish, the nerves of female polar bears, and the spittle of hummingbirds in springtime.

Maud kissed him again with lips open and when he realized what she was now doing he knew he was again aboard a trolley, departing for the place from which he had just departed. But the trolley metamorphosed into a horsecar, and the horsecar into a stagecoach. And as people boarded, Quinn saw they were all dressed for their worst moments, ready for the road, flaunting their flaws, reveling in everything that made them freakish. When Maud boarded the coach, Quinn told her: "We're going back," and he meant to the age of his ancestral namesake who was shot in a love duel. The coach rolled past Maud's city of iron gates and out into the new country where love was as sweet and soft as Maud's small primeval bosom. The coach rolled smoothly along the dirt road behind a matched pair, and then curved upward toward a festive mansion, whose manicured lawn suddenly curled in upon itself in an unnatural way that made the horses shy. But there was grace in the inward curve and Quinn understood that the keeper of this lawn was an artist of the perverse.

Later, in an upstairs room, after Quinn had sponged himself and was wrapped in his yellow robe, he stood by a window and stared down at a woman of the age, sitting with two men. He recognized one of the men as himself. The three sat beneath a trellis designed as a Romanesque arch, upon which grew the blue roses of longing. One inhaled these roses and understood the secrets of creative love. The woman under the arch, whose back was to Quinn, stood and disrobed, her arms and shoulders suddenly bare. The second man was helping her out of her only garment by holding a sleeve, while the seated Quinn imperiously studied what was being revealed directly to him.

Quinn, accumulating meanings for the basketball in Maud's dream, turned away from the window to confront her totality as she stood before him, her long hair flowing over her shoulders. She opened his robe, and held him with exquisite nonchalance. Wrapped around her throat was an antique choker of wide, dark ribbon, its long, uneven ends falling the length of her torso to obscure part of her private hair. The visible hair was the color of caramel, the ribbon a deeper brown, the color of moist, fertile earth. Before Quinn's eyes had made the gesture, Maud rolled backward onto the simple iron bed, her legs rising, the ribbon falling naturally between her open thighs, leaving her gift mostly secret. In her mouth Quinn encountered the taste of abstract cake.

In the System

A Technology Play

Scene:	An office
Characters:	Two young men: ACE and DEUCE
	Young woman: DAPHNE
	MAN in car
	911 OPERATOR
	TV ANNOUNCER
	TV REPORTER

Ace is at his computer and Deuce is watching horse races on very large TV, a telephone on each of their desks. Overhead are six large computer screens.

DEUCE
They said it couldn't be done.

ACE
That's what they said.

DEUCE
Do you remember how much you got the first time?

ACE
To the penny. Nine thousand seven hundred forty dollars—and eighty cents.

DEUCE
What did you do with it?

ACE
Jumped in the car and went to Saratoga. You can't beat Saratoga in August. That empty blue canoe floating on the pond, the deep green of the turf, those stately elms . . .

DEUCE
The canoe is yellow and the elms died.

ACE
. . . the old wooden clubhouse, the Bloody Marys . . . those lonely women horseplayers.

DEUCE
The maître d' who expects thirty bucks to get you a table . . .

ACE
Fifty, if there's a crowd.

DEUCE
Going to breakfast to meet girls and watch the horses do an exercise run.

ACE
I liked the girls but I never cared for horses.

DEUCE
You shouldn't admit it.

ACE
I never liked dogs either.

DEUCE
They could get you for that.

ACE
They could get you for anything.

DEUCE
The replay is on. Shall we listen?

ACE
I know how it comes out.

Deuce turns up TV volume, and we see and hear the race.

TV ANNOUNCER (V.O.)
. . . top of the stretch and coming on the outside is Old Amigo . . . and it's Old Amigo by five lengths . . . and it's Old *Amigo*!

DEUCE *(lowers volume)*
Wanna hear what he paid?

ACE
I know what he paid.

As results appear on screen Deuce turns up volume.

TV ANNOUNCER (V.O.)
In the third race Old Amigo paid $62.50, $38.80, and $23.40.

Deuce turns off volume, TV screen fades.

DEUCE
A long shot. Nobody bets long shots in the Pick Six.

ACE
Doesn't your system find long shots? That's why we had you call in the bet.

DEUCE
My system? Hey, Old Amigo was my original pick. He's a four-year-old, which is a must. You divide the number of times a horse is in the money into the number of times he's run—no less than twenty races—and you play the horse with the lowest score, unless he's the favorite, and then you play the next lowest score with a price, unless he's got a bad post position. If the horse scores enough lower than his rivals, I mean a score of two or less, he can be played from the outside, but if not, then you go with a horse with a slightly higher score who's in the middle of the track, by middle I mean post positions three to seven. But some with a score of two and a half or three or even three and a half, are good, if the score is lower than the other horses. Sometimes a horse scores one and a half, but you don't bet it because he's only got sixteen races, and you gotta have twenty. You add his races from January first to April first to his previous year's races, then divide to get the score. If the horse with the low score is going up in the money class in today's race, you shouldn't let that worry you. I prefer that to going down in class, because if the owner isn't proud enough to keep the horse where it is, or up, why should I be? Proud.

ACE
But you weren't proud enough to play Old Amigo.

DEUCE
I didn't like the jockey.

ACE
I don't worry about jockeys, or post position, or past performances.

DEUCE
You just switch numbers.

ACE
I replace losers with winners. You haven't had a winner in three races. Don't you feel betrayed by your system?

DEUCE
I can lose a few.

ACE
I win them all.

DEUCE
They're going to the post for the fourth. I bet Dream Freak.

ACE
It doesn't matter who you bet. You'll have the winner.

Telephone rings.

ACE
Don't answer it.

DEUCE
It might be my lawyer.

ACE
You don't need a lawyer yet.

Deuce answers phone, listens in silence for ten seconds, hangs up.

ACE
Who was that?

DEUCE
Nine-eleven. Somebody being attacked by a dog. You don't like dogs.

Phone rings again, Deuce answers, listens, puts it on speaker phone.

Man, holding portable fire extinguisher, enters upstage right, talking on cell phone.

911 Operator enters from upstage left wearing a headset.

MAN *(mid-sentence)*
. . . I told you, I'm in my goddamn car.

911 OPERATOR
I need a location.

MAN
I'm in front of Walmart. I'm driving along and a goddamn deer jumps halfway into my back seat. I hit a concrete divider and ruin my front wheel and the car can't move. Then the goddamn deer bites my neck.

911 OPERATOR
Which Walmart?

MAN
Then this big goddamn dog comes running outta nowhere and attacks the deer, who's halfway out the window.

911 OPERATOR
This is 911, the emergency line. Can you give me a location?

MAN
Walmart, the goddamn Walmart. I get out and the deer kicks the dog with a hind leg and knocks him down, but he gets right up and comes at *me*. Why me? Because he can't get at the deer?

Man barks, emulating the attacking dog. Man will do all barking for the dog.

911 OPERATOR
I'm told we have four Walmarts locally. Can you identify a cross street?

MAN
I jump in the car, so the dog goes back to biting the deer, who still wants my neck. I grab my fire extinguisher and get out and go for the dog. I spray the fucker twice but he gets goddamn up so I get back in the car. He's jumping at the window right now, fuckin' nuts.

Dog (Man) barks and barks.

Phone connection clicks off, lights down on man and operator. We hear Frankie Laine singing "That Lucky Old Sun," then dial tone.

Deuce punches off speaker button.

Silence.

ACE
Was that your lawyer?

Deuce turns up TV volume.

TV ANNOUNCER (V.O.)
And they're off . . .

Deuce turns off volume, but we see the race.

DEUCE
I know which Walmart he's at. The other three Walmarts don't have deer.

Silence.

ACE *(watching the race)*
Your Dream Freak is fading.

DEUCE
They put blinders on him.

Deuce turns up TV volume.

TV ANNOUNCER (V.O.)
. . . and at the far turn it's . . .

COMPUTER VOICE
You've got mail.

Ace hits computer keys, screen of Monitor 2 brightens with large letters: WANDA WANTS A WAND. We see a bosomy woman, naked except for skimpy panties, holding phallic element. A cell phone on stylish chain dangles between her breasts.

As she appears on monitor she also appears upstage center, sitting on chair, with element.

DEUCE
I know that girl.

ACE
Lucky you.

Deuce rolls his chair for better angle of vision on Monitor 2.

DEUCE
That's Daphne.

Daphne is now trying to sit on the phallic element.

That is positively Daphne. Why the hell is she doing that?

Daphne opens cell phone with one hand, then dials as she performs.

Deuce rolls chair back to TV without getting up, turns up sound.

Daphne fades and TV brightens.

TV ANNOUNCER (V.O.)
At the Clubhouse turn it's Gallant Fool on the inside, Dream Freak second, and here comes Aromatic . . . As they go to the wire Aromatic takes the lead, Gallant Fool second . . . and it's *Aromatic*!

Deuce turns off sound.

Silence.

ACE
Your Dream Freak ran out of the money.

DEUCE
Yes, and Aromatic went off at forty-four-to-one. Two long-shot winners in four races. That's serious money. Who bets long shots in the Pick Six?

ACE
We do, today.

DEUCE
When do you do the switch?

ACE
Immediately after it's official for the first four races.

DEUCE
You have to go to the main computer?

ACE
I can get in from here. I send the encryption data on the tunnel link protocol and the server validates me.

DEUCE
You realize we got two long-shot winners? Do you realize that? Man's gotta be insane to bet two long shots. Would you bet two long shots in a Pick Six?

ACE
I don't play the horses. I go with reality.

DEUCE
I think we're going to jail.

ACE
They can't trace a thing.

DEUCE
You can't trust computers.

ACE
They're the only thing you can trust. People are what you can't trust.

DEUCE
But they know you've got access, and you've got the password.

ACE
And they'll know you're the one who phoned in the bet. Don't worry about it. All I do is log on to the OTB computer files, find the serial number of your bets, pull them up, and make you a winner in the first four races because you haven't even got winner one with your system. I don't have to change the fifth

and sixth races because you've got every horse in both races. If we got the first four races we got all six.

DEUCE
They'll know you've been in there screwing the numbers. What about those fingerprints they talk about?

ACE
I won't leave any.

DEUCE
How do you know?

ACE
All right, there is an audit trail when I log in. I do leave a digital signature that's time-stamped and can't be spoofed. But we're talking here about their ten-year-old, pre-hacker protocols, encrypted, secure, oh yeah, those linear, validation block hash codes, as if they mattered. They don't know that revealing the hash codes, even if you scramble them, opens the system to attack. You don't reveal the hash codes. You know what I mean?

Deuce is silent.

Think of it this way. Do salesmen roll back odometers on used cars? Do burglars leave front doors open while they're cracking a safe? What we're talking about is Boolean value, logical one and we're in, logical zero and we ain't. (*Pause*) No. Let me make it even easier. When I go in there's a log daemon running on the system that records my arrival. I flog the daemon with a few dash-nines. I thrash it long enough to start up a second connection while the daemon is busy restarting, and then I'm in the database through the default maintenance account that the idiots forgot to delete when they installed it. And then I run my little script—your bet—and I get out. On the way out I grep the log files and kill the telltale entries, and nobody can know I ever logged on. I've moved time backward. The poetry of the inside, you could call it.

Phone rings, Deuce puts speaker on. We hear a female voice as screen of Monitor 2 shows Daphne talking on cell phone.

DEUCE
Deuce here.

DAPHNE
Deuce, is that really you, love?

DEUCE
Daphne?

DAPHNE
Ace said you guys were watching me on the internet.

DEUCE
When did he say that?

DAPHNE
Last night.

DEUCE
Last night?

Deuce, incredulous, looks at his watch. He moves close to the monitor.

Daphne, busy with the phallic element, waves down from screen.

DAPHNE
We were here last night making a movie.

DEUCE
When did you start with these movies?

DAPHNE
Do you still want to take me to Paris? I'd love to go, I really would. Gotta go now. Call me, Deuce honey, you know I love you.

Monitor screen switches to WANDA WANTS A WAND website home page. We hear dial tone. Deuce disconnects from speaker phone.

DEUCE *(to Ace)*
I didn't know you knew Daphne.

All monitors go to black, lights down.

Silence.

Lights up on Ace, alone in the office.

Overhead the computer monitors become visible, one by one, Ace watching.

Sound comes up from one monitor at a time, then each sound fades so we can hear the next. No overlap. All dialogue must be audible, intelligible.

Monitor 1: Doberman is attacking rear end of deer hanging out of car window. Man gets out of car and sprays dog with fire extinguisher. Man barks as he sprays.

Monitor 2: Daphne, speaking on cell phone.

DAPHNE
Call me, Deuce honey, we'll go to Paris. Rue Montparnasse.

Daphne fades. Deuce and TV Reporter enter downstage left.

Monitor 3: Ace alone, watching Daphne on monitor.

Monitor 4: Deuce, in handcuffs, is speaking (no sound) to TV Reporter who holds video camera.

Monitor 5: Race results continuing.

TV ANNOUNCER (V.O.)
. . . Dream Freak second and here comes Aromatic . . .

Monitor 6: 911 operator.

911 OPERATOR
Is there a landmark near your Walmart?

Monitor 2: Daphne manipulating as she talks to herself.

DAPHNE
Deuce is the sweetest man in the world. I love him. Ace is the sweetest man in the world, too. I love him, too. But I really don't go for Deuce that much, and half the time Ace's brilliance is boring. Deuce has a beautiful soul, and Ace is adorable. *(Then, of her manipulation)* This is fun.

Monitor 5: TV announcer's face on screen, cut to full screen of Pick Six results.

TV ANNOUNCER (V.O.)
Unbelievable, folks, but the Pick Six had only six winning tickets, and they paid a total of 3.2 million dollars. All six were bought by one person.

Monitor 3: Ace picks up phone and dials.

Monitor 4: Deuce, handcuffs on, answers his cell phone.

DEUCE
This is Deuce.

ACE
Don't tell them anything, dummy up, loose lips sink ships, they won't know if you don't tell them, keep your trap shut, hold your tongue, shut up about it, keep the lid on, put a cork in it, mum's the word, muzzle it, sit on it. *(He hangs up, dial tone.)*

Monitor 1 and 6: Man and 911 Operator.

911 OPERATOR
Do you still think you're at a Walmart?

MAN
I sprayed the fucker twice but he gets goddamn up, so I get back in the car. He's jumping at the window right now, fuckin' nuts, this dog.

Dog (Man) barks.

911 OPERATOR
My supervisor says we have no Walmarts whatsoever in this city. You must be somewhere else.

Monitor 4: Deuce in handcuffs, holding phone, is being questioned by TV reporter.

TV REPORTER
And what about you and Ace?

DEUCE
Ace was always the explorer, took us places we'd never go by ourselves. He never gave a damn, smarter than everybody, a weird, intense geek who lived in his computer. I knew he was into movies but I didn't know he was into Daphne. In school they wanted me and Ace to fight. You think you can take him? Well, I say, I got the reach. Sure, they say, but are you as fast as he is? Fast? What fast? He's gotta reach me to hit me. Ace challenged me to fight once, but when I went outside to meet him he was gone.

TV REPORTER
What made you two think you could get away with it?

DEUCE
Ace thinks he'll die the same age his father died, which was twenty-nine. I got a ruptured stomach myself. We all got something. People will say that's why we did it. Fatalistic Ace and Ruptured Deuce.

Monitor 3: Ace dials telephone, Deuce answers.

DEUCE
Deuce here.

ACE
Tell them about my operation. *(hangs up)*

DEUCE *(to TV Reporter)*
Ace's great-grandfather and father were both born without a left testicle. Ace figured the malady skipped a generation and that his kid would be next, so Ace had an operation.

Ace's phone rings, he answers.

ACE
This is Ace.

DAPHNE
I'm very fond of Paris. The Left Bank, the foie gras.

ACE
After college I had a vasectomy.

DAPHNE *(waving her phallic element)*
Happy vasectomy, Ace! *(blows him a kiss)*

Monitor 5: Race continuing.

TV ANNOUNCER (V.O.)
And at the clubhouse turn it's Dream Freak leading the pack by four lengths . . .

Monitor 4: Deuce on TV

TV REPORTER
Would you say that fate was against you both?

DEUCE
The fact is, I did this thing for Daphne.

Deuce dials Daphne. Her phone rings between her breasts.

DAPHNE
Is that you Deuce?

DEUCE
The bet I made on the Pick Six paid $3.2 million.

Crowd roars. Deuce hangs up.

DEUCE
I think Daphne knew we were onto something.

Monitor 3: Ace on the phone.

ACE
It comes down to the Boolean value. Logical zero or logical one. It's simple. I'll say it again. Boolean value. Logical zero or logical one.

The following conversations overlap:

MAN
I sprayed the fucker twice.

DAPHNE
I love Deuce.

ANNOUNCER
At the club house turn it's Dream Freak leading the pack.

911 OPERATOR
Walmart closed fifteen minutes ago.

DAPHNE
I hated Deuce.

ANNOUNCER
. . . Dream Freak fades to second.

DEUCE
He's gotta reach me to hit me.

MAN
Twice I sprayed him.

DAPHNE
I'm very fond of Paris. Place Pigalle, Notre Dame.

911 OPERATOR
You are not at Walmart.

ACE
Doesn't matter who you bet, you'll have the winner.

DAPHNE
Foie gras.

MAN
The dog's nuts.

Dog (Man) barks.

911 OPERATOR
Could you be near Macy's?

TV ANNOUNCER (V.O.)
And it's Aromatic!

DAPHNE
This is fun!

End overlap.

DEUCE
For me Daphne was always a long shot.

Frankie Laine sings four bars of "That Lucky Old Sun."

Six seconds of dial tone.

Six seconds of silence.

ACE
Logical one and we're in.

He raises his fist, shakes it.

Dog (Man) barks twice.

Silence.

ACE
Logical zero and we ain't.

He cuts the air with a horizontal flat-handed stroke.

Six seconds of silence.

Dog (Man) barks and barks and barks.

Blackout.

END OF PLAY*

---

* Editors' Note: William Kennedy was commissioned to write *In the System* in 2003 for The Technology Plays, a bold interdisciplinary initiative sponsored by The Center for Humanities, Arts and TechnoScience as part of The College of Arts and Sciences at the University at Albany. The program promoted the exchange between the sciences and humanities and explored their profound impact on individuals and society.

In the System was produced in collaboration with Capital Repertory Theatre in Albany, New York, and Apple Computer. It was funded in part by the Woodrow Wilson National Fellowship Foundation's "Imagining America" Program. The project brought performers and diverse audiences together through a series of short, interactive plays that explored the complex relations between humans and machines. *The New York Times Magazine* included The Technology Plays in their annual roundup of the most innovative ideas of 2003.

In the System was previously published in the volume *TechKnowledgies: New Imaginaries in the Humanities, Arts, and TechnoSciences,* ed. Mary Valentis, with Tara P. Monastero and Paula Yablonsky (Newcastle, UK: Cambridge Scholars Publishing, 2007).

Reprinted with permission.

An earlier version of *In the System* was published in the *Paris Review* 168 (Winter 2003). Reprinted by permission of the *Paris Review* and The Wylie Agency LLC.

William Kennedy's Albany—The City and Inspiration

Buildings and landscapes of Albany appear throughout Kennedy's books, sometimes only mentioned in passing, but sometimes as major elements in the story. Here are some of the locales that sparked Kennedy's imagination. The photos are presented with historical information from Kennedy's nonfiction book *O Albany!* and brief excerpts from his novels for each location.

THE KENMORE HOTEL

The Kenmore Hotel, at Columbia and North Pearl Streets, was built in 1878 by Adam Blake, a hotelier who was the richest black man in Albany, and it became one of the city's premier hotels. About 1900 Robert Murphy bought it and ran it until he died in 1922, when his son, also Robert, turned it into a hot hotel with the flashiest nightclub between New York and Montreal. The great musicians of the age played there every week at the Rain-Bo Room—Tommy Dorsey, Frank Sinatra, Guy Lombardo, Rudy Vallee, Duke Ellington, Benny Goodman—and people came to dance at all hours, including lunchtime. The noted gangster Jack "Legs" Diamond, limelighter that he was, was a regular for a decade. He lived at the hotel in 1931 after Governor Franklin Roosevelt broke up the bootlegging empire Diamond had built in the Catskills, charging him with assault and kidnapping of a booze-truck driver.

—from *O Albany!*

Empire gone, exchequer sequestered, future wholly imperfect, it occurred to Jack that the remaining values of his life inhered chiefly in his women. Naturally, he decided to collect them, protect them, and install them in the current safe-deposit box of his life, which at the moment was a six-room second-floor suite in the Kenmore.

. . . .

[Sal, a Kenmore waiter who serves Jack in his suite:] I took a peek one day, the women got a room each, and Legs, he got a room all his own and the bodyguards got a room and they got other rooms for people in and out, transaction business.

. . . .

[Freddie Robin, the cop who guards Diamond, says,] Sal, you think they all wind up in bed together? Sal remembers his reply: I laugh like hell. Freddie, I say, how the hell anybody going to do anything with a woman when another woman alongside you?

—from *Legs*

The façade of the Kenmore Hotel on North Pearl Street.
Unidentified photographer, ca. 1900, gelatin silver print, Albany Institute of History & Art Library, Morris Gerber Collection, DI 1230.

The Rain-Bo Room, the nightclub in the Kenmore Hotel.
Photographed by Glen S. Cook, ca. 1936, gelatin silver print, 8½ x 11, Albany Institute of History & Art Library, Kenmore Hotel Papers, DI 1228.

THE TEN EYCK HOTEL

Original Ten Eyck Hotel.
Detroit Publishing Company photograph collection, Library of Congress Prints and Photographs Division, Washington, DC.

The original nine-story Ten Eyck Hotel opened on May 5, 1899, at the corner of State and Chapel Streets and took the elite trade away from the Kenmore.

Peacock Alley in the Ten Eyck Hotel.
Unidentified photographer, n.d., gelatin silver print, Albany Institute of History & Art, Main Photo Collection, DI 1224.

Roscoe Owen Conway, the main character in Kennedy's novel *Roscoe*, lived at the hotel and often did business for Albany's Democratic political machine in the dining room and lobby. In the novel he meets Patsy McCall, the machine boss, to tell him he wants to retire from Albany politics.

> "Patsy called. He'll be in the Ten Eyck lobby in fifteen minutes." . . . [Roscoe] went into the State Street entrance . . . and up the stairs to the lobby, which was cool and busy with people checking in. . . . Patsy sat here often, but he was out of place amid the gilded rococo furniture and Oriental rugs . . . and looked as if he'd be more at ease at a clambake.
>
> —from *Roscoe*

The seventeen-story Ten Eyck Hotel Annex at State and Pearl Streets opened in 1918.

Unidentified photographer, 1936, gelatin silver print, Albany Institute of History & Art Library, Main Photo Collection, DI 1218.

THE DELAVAN HOUSE

The Delavan House occupied the block between Steuben and Columbia Streets on the east side of Broadway.
Unidentified photographer, 1890, albumen print, Albany Institute of History & Art Library, Main Photo Collection, DI 108.

> The Delavan House, built in 1850, became a temperance house and was host to such notables as P. T. Barnum and Charles Dickens, later turning into an intemperate palace of political wheeling, where Boss Tweed held forth when he came to town to buy the legislature, and where swinish swells drank champagne from the slippers of scarlet actresses.
>
> —from *O Albany!*

The Delavan House after the 1894 fire. The hotel was razed and Union Station was built on the site.
Unidentified photographer, December 30, 1894, gelatin silver print from copy negative, Albany Institute of History & Art Library, Main Photo Collection, DI 1219.

The Delavan was mostly destroyed by fire in 1894. The fire becomes a major character in Kennedy's novel *The Flaming Corsage*.

> Edward had reserved this table at the Delavan's second-floor dining room, which was decorated with sketches and photographs of the luminaries whose visits gave credence to the Delavan's boast that it was one of the nation's greatest hotels. . . . On this penultimate night of 1894 the hotel was in its political but not yet swinish mode, abuzz with the noise, money, and power of the politicians who had come to Albany for the legislative session. . . . "Ladies and gentlemen," the maître d' announced in a loud but thoroughly courteous voice, "I suggest that everyone leave with all swiftness. The hotel is on fire."
>
> —from *The Flaming Corsage*

KEELER'S HOTEL AND RESTAURANT

Keeler's Restaurant on State Street *(right)*, ca. 1940.
Unidentified photographer, ca. 1940, gelatin silver print, Albany Institute of History & Art Library, Main Photo Collection, DI 701.

Keeler's Restaurant was established in 1864 at 85 Green Street by the brothers William and John Keeler. In 1884 the brothers opened, at 56 State, the upscale restaurant that served 1,500 meals daily and would become world famous.

—from *O Albany!*

Keeler's Hotel.
Detroit Publishing Company photograph collection, Library of Congress Prints and Photographs Division, Washington, DC.

The partnership between the two brothers didn't last, and Bill, in 1886 opened his own restaurant at 26 Maiden Lane. His business grew, took over eight buildings, in time occupying half the block as Keeler's Hotel, For Men Only, with entrances on Maiden Lane and Broadway.

—from *O Albany!*

Broadway during the Albany flood of 1913.
Unidentified photographer, 1913, gelatin silver print, Albany Institute of History & Art Library, Main Photo Collection, DI 494.

In *Ironweed*, Francis Phelan walks north on Broadway, past the location of Keeler's Hotel, and remembers an adventure he had with his son Billy during the flood of 1913.

> He walked up to Maiden Lane and Broadway, where Keeler's Hotel used to be, and where his brother Peter sometimes spent the night when he was on the outs with Mama. But Keeler's burned the year after Francis ran away and now it was a bunch of stores. Francis had rowed down Broadway to the hotel, Billy in the rowboat with him, in 1913 when the river rose away the hell and gone up and flooded half of downtown. The kid loved it. Said he liked it better'n sleigh ridin'. Gone. What the hell ain't gone? Well, me. Yeah, me.
>
> —from *Ironweed*

SCHLITZ'S HOTEL

Schlitz's Hotel, located on the west side of Broadway between Steuben and Columbia, catered to the city's German population. Kennedy explains in *O Albany!* that the two World Wars had a heavily negative impact on the Germans in Albany.

> . . . the antipathy generated by two wars . . . brought on a repression of Germanic life. At Schlitz's Tavern, sauerkraut was suddenly called Liberty Cabbage, and eventually the name of the establishment itself was changed to the American Hotel.
>
> —from *O Albany!*

In *Billy Phelan's Greatest Game*, Billy, the book's hero, hangs out at Becker's Bar, an annex of the American Hotel, which is a principal gathering place for the crowd that inhabits Albany's Nighttown. In a scene in the book, Billy walks down Broadway noticing the lights on the street and how they frame the unique German Fachwerk architecture of the hotel: "There was Albany's river of bright white lights, the lights on in the Famous Lunch, still open, and the dark, smoky reds of Brockley's and Becker's neon tubes, and the tubes also shaping the point over the door of the American Hotel."

—from *Billy Phelan's Greatest Game*

Schlitz's Hotel, aka American Hotel.
Unidentified photographer, William C. Schade, architect, n.d., gelatin silver print, Albany Institute of History & Art Library, Main Photo Collection, DI 1223.

THE LUMBER DISTRICT

The Lumber District in Albany's North End.
Unidentified photographer, ca. 1875, albumen print, Albany Institute of History & Art Library, Lumber District Photograph Album Collection, DI 378.

The Lumber District in the North End occupied space between the river and the Erie Canal. In 1854 the District had forty-six firms, seven doing more than half a million dollars in business annually. The logs came down the Erie Canal, were turned into lumber in the District's sawmills, and put on riverboats waiting at the slips that connected the Canal to the Hudson.

—from *O Albany!*

Kennedy provides some history of the Lumber District in *Billy Phelan's Greatest Game* and mentions it in *The Flaming Corsage*, as Katrina Daugherty's father was an Albany lumber baron.

> . . . the famous Lumber District . . . started at the Basin and ran northward two and a half miles between the river and the canal. Processing Adirondack logs into lumber was Albany's biggest business at mid-century, and the city fathers proclaimed that Albany was now the white pine distribution center of the world.
>
> —from *Billy Phelan's Greatest Game*

BOWLING ALLEY ON STATE STREET

The "bowling" sign on the right side of the photo marks the location on State Street where in 1938, in *Billy Phelan's Greatest Game*, Billy bowled a 299, one pin short of a perfect game.

> Scotty lived with his bowling ball . . . and when he found Billy and Martin playing eight ball at the pool table in the Downtown Health and Amusement Club, the city's only twenty-four-hour gamester's palace, no women, no mixed leagues, please, beer on tap till 4:00 a.m., maybe 5:00, but no whiskey on the premises, why then Scotty's question was: Wanna bowl some jackpots, Billy? Sure, with a twenty-pin spot, Billy said.
>
> —from *Billy Phelan's Greatest Game*

Bowling alley on State Street.
Unidentified photographer, gelatin silver print, Albany Institute of History & Art Library, Morris Gerber Collection, 1993.010.4535.4P, DI 317.

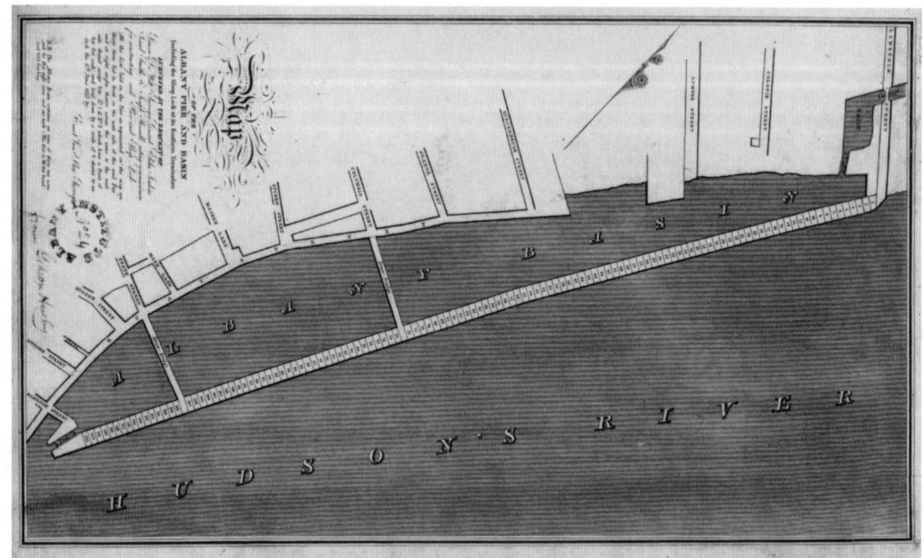

BASIN AND GREAT PIER

Map of Albany Pier and Basin.
Evert Van Alen (1772–1884), 1825, engraving on paper, Albany Institute of History & Art Library, MAP43, DI 504.

> The Albany Basin was a sheltered harbor that began at the mouth of the Erie Canal and ran south to Hamilton Street. The city, in 1823, began building the Basin, creating a pier that paralleled the shoreline for four fifths of a mile, with bridges from the pier to Columbia and State Streets. The pier was eighty-five feet wide and covered eight acres. The Basin had harbor space for a thousand canal boats.
>
> —from *O Albany!*

Albany Waterfront.

Unidentified photographer, n.d., gelatin silver print, Albany Institute of History & Art Library, Main Photo Collection, DI 1221.

The Basin and Great Pier area factors prominently in the opening chapter of *Quinn's Book*. Crowds gather to watch the great courtesan, Magdalena Colón, cross the turbulent, icy Hudson in a small skiff to get from Albany to Greenbush and then Troy, where she will again perform her scandalous Spider Dance. The skiff capsizes and the pier collapses.

Maiden Lane Pier. Basin area and Great Pier.
Unidentified photographer, 1917, gelatin silver print, Albany Institute of History & Art, Main Photo Collection, DI 1222.

The crowd had grown ever larger on the bridge . . . when suddenly, with a flagitious roar and an agonized whine, the old wooden span collapsed in twain, plunging a hundred or more of our citizens onto and through the fragile ice and into the deadly bath, while another hundred saved themselves with desperation leaps and wild clutchings to the fractured boards and railings. . . . A giant wall of ice that had formed in the middle of the river . . . exploded . . . into a Vesuvius of crystal . . . wounding an unsuspecting half-dozen people, killing two horses and a pregnant cat on the quay, and loosing a tidal wave that swept every object storehoused on the Great Pier . . . (and slaking the lime in a kiln on shore) would set fire to a block of stores along the quay frontage: fire rising out of flood—the gods gone mad.

—from *Quinn's Book*

67 DOVE STREET

Rooming house of Jack "Legs" Diamond, 67 Dove Street, Albany *(far left)*. Unidentified photographer, ca. 1930, gelatin silver print, Albany Institute of History & Art Library, Morris Gerber Collection, DI 314.

Jack "Legs" Diamond stayed here for a week while he was on trial in Troy for kidnapping a trucker over some barrels of hard cider, and where he was killed the morning after he was acquitted of the charge.

The rooming house was at 67 Dove and Mrs. Laura Woods was the landlady. . . . At five-thirty in the morning of December 18, 1931, Mrs. Woods heard two visitors arrive, heard them talking. [She] heard Jack pleading for his life. . . . Then, as is historically known, she heard several shots, of which three went into Jack's head, the rest into the walls. The assassins moved to the doorway, paused to reconsider. One of them said, . . . "Oh hell, that was enough."

—from *O Albany!*

Dove Street runs north and south in Albany through what for years was the rooming house district on the fringe of downtown. Number 67 sits on the west side of the street between Hudson Avenue and Jay Street, a two-story brick building with a six-step wooden stoop. . . . at 4:15 a.m. on Friday, December 18, 1931 . . . Jack pulled up in front of 67 Dove in his hired cab, Frankie Teller at the wheel.

—from *Legs*

PART THREE

Scholarly Perspectives

Critical Views of Kennedy's Novels

Introduction to Part Three

As part of the Association of Writers & Writing Programs' (AWP) annual conference that was held in Albany, New York, in April 1999, the New York State Writers Institute organized a mini-symposium and celebration of William Kennedy's work. The Kennedy symposium included papers presented by five scholars on various aspects of his novels; a talk by historian Douglas Brinkley on Kennedy's early career as a journalist; a panel discussion, "Talking About William Kennedy," with Irish American writers Frank McCourt, Peter Quinn, and Dennis Smith; and a reading by Kennedy followed by tributes from fellow writers E. L. Doctorow, Peter Matthiessen, and James Salter, all of whom had received the Edith Wharton Citation of Merit as New York State Author.

The Kennedy symposium began with Douglas Brinkley's presentation on Kennedy, the journalist. He recounts an improbable first conversation he had with Kennedy—a cold telephone call to him, encouraged by Hunter S. Thompson. Brinkley asked to visit Kennedy at his home the next day with a busload of college students who had read *Ironweed* and had some questions for him. "Bill and his wife Dana could not have been a more generous host and hostess for taking in a bunch of people that they didn't know," Brinkley recalls. "After that introduction . . . I started to read more about Kennedy and his work."

Brinkley goes on to explore how Kennedy's early experience as a journalist provided a springboard to his fiction writing. Journalism, says Brinkley, "forced him to become a keen observer . . . and nurtured in him a reverence for the historian's fact. It taught him style that would mold his entire Albany Cycle."

The remaining five selections are the papers presented by the academic scholars at the AWP conference. Together, they provide a critical analysis of Kennedy's work and a context for understanding the cultural worlds and collective histories of his characters' fictional realms.

Vivian Valvano Lynch focuses on the characteristics of Edward and

Katrina Daugherty in *The Flaming Corsage* to explore Kennedy's "warriors." In her essay "Edward and Katrina Daugherty: A Match Made in Albany, Not in Heaven," she defines warriors as characters who are always struggling to achieve something valuable in life. Lynch adds the attribution of "artist" to Kennedy's warriors. "Some are identifiable artists or would-be artists in practice," while others who don't define themselves as working artists still exhibit the "creative gifts and imaginative power" of true artists. These warrior-artists, Lynch argues, "actually do make or create something as they struggle," and their creative imagination helps them "fight their battles of survival."

Benedict Giamo addresses the representation of homelessness in *Ironweed* in his essay, "The Snows of Reduction." He points to the opening scene in the novel when Francis visits Saint Agnes Cemetery. Francis observes that the location and adornments of the graves in death mimic the economic and social status of the dead in their life. The homeless experience a "social descent," that separates them from their friends and families. They are treated as outsiders, thus dying a social death. Being identified as a "*bum* or better yet, *good for nothing bum*," results in a "total reduction of social status," and "a lasting condition of estrangement." The homeless live outside of the accepted spheres of organized social experience and are identified as worthless by the broader society. Giamo provides examples of how Kennedy's characters are constantly confronted with the dichotomies of worth and worthlessness, "a valued life paired with the growing menace of social death." Kennedy, says Giamo, "raises all of these relations into the imaginary light of fiction for our own vicarious involvement, immediate circumspection, and sustained contemplation."

Scholars and reviewers often compare Kennedy's Albany Cycle of novels to the magical realism of Gabriel García Márquez, where "women ascend into heaven, paper turns into a butterfly and flies, and men with enormous wings descend from the skies," remarks Christian Michener in his essay "A Magical Time in Albany." Instead of approaching a magical perspective "through an emphasis on a magical geography or action," Michener approaches the magical realism in Kennedy's fiction from the standpoint of time, "a time that is fluid and reversible and that offers—though it cannot promise—the opportunity for the redemption and forgiveness of its characters." Michener explores the novels in Kennedy's Albany Cycle "squarely within the continuum of Albany history," a history that refuses to "abide in progressive, linear narrative." For Michener, "each book serves as an epilogue and a prelude to another: their plots and characters refer back and forth to other books, prefiguring what is to come or revealing what follows."

In his essay "The Cyclical Impulse of *The Flaming Corsage*," Michael Patrick Gillespie takes an in-depth look at Kennedy's seventh novel. *The*

Flaming Corsage elaborates on events and characters "introduced in the recollections of Martin Daugherty in *Billy Phelan's Greatest Game* and on those of Francis Phelan in *Ironweed.*" Gillespie notes that *The Flaming Corsage* therefore "takes on an important role for all of the novels in the Albany Cycle, continuing the accretive pattern of narrative development . . ." As Gillespie chronicles the fluctuations and conflicted personalities of Katrina and Edward Daugherty, he also explores the narrative style of *The Flaming Corsage*. He says that the dramatic shifts from one time period to another "represent an impressive expansion to the disrupted chronology employed on a more limited basis in *Very Old Bones,*" attesting to the "author's technical polish."

Neila Seshachari examines Kennedy's treatment of his female characters in "Courtesans, Stars, Wives, and Vixens: The Many Faces of Female Power in Kennedy's Novels." Seshachari confesses that she came to Kennedy's novels fairly late in her professional career, but she was drawn to his work because of "his extraordinary voice, ubiquitous humor, versatile style, his bold and imaginative use of history and myth that weave throughout his narrative." She was also intrigued by the way "he fleshed out all his female characters as 'subjects' who voiced their own thoughts rather than those of their male creator. . . . Courtesans, homeless bums, mistresses, or wives, every one of these characters seemed to radiate her own unique power that precluded each from being pitied as victim or object." Seshachari elucidates her view by examining the lives and motivations of Katrina Taylor Daugherty, Maud Fallon, Magdalena Colón, Helen Archer, and Annie Phelan, among others, and how they exercise their power. "All of these women," she says, "lead their lives, albeit in a male-defined world, on their own terms."

The final event of the symposium included a reading by Kennedy, followed by brief tributes from James Salter, Peter Matthiessen, and E. L. Doctorow. Their comments provide a slightly different perspective from the critical analyses of the academic scholars that are worth noting.

Salter remarked on the simplicity of Kennedy's language, "its unadorned quality, and the fact that its poetry and power are in scenes and lines of dialogue. In his work there is humanity, and humility, and that unerring choice of incident, utterly true—or if not true, should be true—that one finds in the pages of great writers."

Matthiessen confessed that he received "a wonderful review from Kennedy . . . on a very problematical novel of mine called *Far Tortuga.* And my shame is I had no idea who he was, nor did I even know, except from the footnote, that he was a fiction writer." He emphasized that what was important to him about Kennedy's books, was that they each have "a mystery about them. . . . There is always something behind looming out, . . . and it gives these books a resonance that they might not have otherwise. The mystery in Bill's work is organic. It comes up from within and this is where mystery should come from."

Doctorow, who while editor-in-chief of Dial Press published Kennedy's first book, *The Ink Truck*, noted, "Kennedy was, while I may not have realized it at the time, one of the last of a breed of newspapermen turned novelist." Doctorow also said, "Every writer has two homes, there's the physical home, the biological, and then there is the home of the imagination. Kennedy's one of the lucky writers whose physical home *is* the home of his imagination."

—Suzanne Lance

William Kennedy as Journalist

Springboard to Novelist

Douglas Brinkley

> It is the work of daily journalism that gave him, early on, the self-discipline and the fundamental skills to write quality fiction.
>
> —Douglas Brinkley

William Kennedy is one of the finest novelists that America has ever produced, and he is certainly one of the most important postwar American novelists. I can promise you all one thing: fifty years from now there will be endless PhD dissertations and master's theses, and books dealing with all of the various aspects of his novels. You will see books about Kennedy in the way that people write about William Faulkner, Ernest Hemingway, F. Scott Fitzgerald, Toni Morrison, or some of the other great writers of the twentieth century. William Kennedy is certainly one of those.

My reason for being here is to honor Bill Kennedy, and I might begin by just saying how I first met Bill and his wife, Dana. I do a program yearly in which I lead a lot of high school students on civil rights tours through the South. We go to Birmingham and Atlanta and Selma and talk to activists who were part of the movement. We not only talk to well-known figures like Rosa Parks, Andrew Young, and Julian Bond, but we also talk to the everyday people who participated in the bus boycott of 1955–1956 to let the young people see what a community-based social revolution the civil rights movement was. When I do this program with college students, we travel across the country on my "Majic Bus," spelled M-A-J-I-C. We spend a semester on the road studying American history and literature. It's like an all-purpose, 3-D American history class. Students read some of the seminal works in American literature and history like Walt Whitman's *Leaves of Grass* and John Steinbeck's *The Grapes of Wrath*, and a dozen others. We go to historic sites that we read about, and we also bring in living writers.

I assigned in 1994 the book *Ironweed* to my traveling students. It's one of my favorite novels and a book I think every American should grow up reading. It is almost a mandatory novel, in the same way you grow up reading Harper Lee's *To Kill a Mockingbird* or Jack Kerouac's *On the Road* when you're young. I think everyone should read *Ironweed,* so I've included it in that Majic Bus course. We spent the evening sleeping at Val-Kill, Eleanor Roosevelt's home near Hyde Park, New York.

Let me digress just a bit. I had twenty students with me on a bus for a semester going across the country. And every year we visit Hunter Thompson out at Woody Creek in Colorado. Instead of autographing *Fear and Loathing in Las Vegas,* he shoots a copy of the book for the students with his gun. One year, I was talking to Hunter on the phone from the Hudson River Valley, and he said to me, "Brinkley, you're reading *Ironweed* and you're going up toward Albany and you're not going to see William Kennedy?" I said, "Hunter, I don't know William Kennedy and I don't have his phone number and I haven't written him and I have zero acquaintance with him." He said, "Here is his home phone number, call him right now, and tell him you are coming up right now and that I tell him that he should see you." I said, "Are you sure that you know William Kennedy that well?" At that point I did not know of their friendship. He said, "Oh yeah, he's one of my oldest friends."

Now, Hunter tends to exaggerate a lot, and I was also afraid that he was setting me up. Also, the thought of calling someone and saying, "Well, hi, I'm great friends with Hunter Thompson, and I want to come to your house with twenty college students in a bus traveling across America," seemed a little bit unreasonable. Hunter started to explain their history in San Juan and their friendship.

I remember very distinctly putting the change into the pay phone at the Ramada Inn just up the Hudson River not far from Val-Kill where the class was staying for the night—this was around 8 p.m.—and sort of asking Bill if we could visit tomorrow, "'cause we're all reading *Ironweed* and we'd like to talk to you about it." He said, "Absolutely." He asked how Hunter was; we had a nice conversation.

So the next afternoon we pulled into the driveway of the Kennedys' house, and Bill and his wife Dana couldn't have been a more generous host and hostess for taking in a bunch of people that they didn't know. We all talked about *Ironweed,* we spent time there, we had food there. We saw the faux grave, procured from the movie set, in the backyard. It was a thrill for some of the students to take a picture of that. The Kennedys were just wide open to talk about anything, and it is that hospitality that I remember. I've met a lot of writers who don't really like to give a lot. It does not necessarily come with great fiction writing that the writer is also a warm personality. I think that Bill Kennedy and his wife Dana certainly are. After that introduction, really, and their warm hospitality, I started to read more about Kennedy and his work.

Then, to my great surprise, when I was editing Hunter Thompson's letters in his volume called *The Proud Highway,* a lot of the stories I'd heard turned out to be true regarding their long friendship. The reason why it is relevant to my talk today on William Kennedy as a journalist is because they were two young journalists in Puerto Rico in the same era trying to make it as novelists. They had many interesting debates on fiction versus nonfiction; on Hemingway versus Fitzgerald; on, How did Faulkner write *The Sound and the Fury?* It's a funny relationship, which began with William Kennedy being an editor and Hunter Thompson being a kind of ne'er-do-well drifter. They developed a friendship, at any rate. If you want to find out how that occurred, I encourage you to read the book of Thompson's letters *The Proud Highway*, for which Kennedy wrote a foreword.

I work for National Public Radio giving weekly poetry commentaries so I'm putting together a presentation and I'm going to read a few ideas that I'm sketching out and then drift off my text to make some basic observations and perhaps do some storytelling. I have to say one thing that I was shocked to learn about William Kennedy: he was born when Calvin Coolidge was president. That put it into perspective for me. He is a seventy-one-year-old American literary colossus whose ongoing Albany Cycle of novels represents one of the true high-water marks in post–World War II fiction. Some people say that with his auburn hair, inquisitive eyes, paradoxical good nature, sense of wonder and doom, William Kennedy resembles an Irish American poet in search of a mythical past, a gifted wordsmith short on blarney but always ready with an apropos phrase. And although critics always try to label Kennedy and put him into some school of thought or philosophy, he really belongs to no school of writing. He absorbs so much of so many writers that you can't possibly point out one that had more influence than others.

I'm going to mention a few writers here and some of the things critics say, and then I'm going to say that a better way to look at William Kennedy is through journalism. For example, when early reviews of *The Ink Truck* came out, he was dubbed a manic, 1960s surrealist, blessed with a wicked sense of humor. When *Ironweed* (which won the National Book Critics Circle Award and the Pulitzer Prize for fiction) came out, he became identified as a magical realist by some critics, with comparisons often to Gabriel García Márquez. In fact, I was surprised to see how many times Kennedy's Albany in certain critical scholarly essays is compared to García Márquez's mythical South American town of Macondo.

Literature teachers often claim that his book *Legs,* which is a novel about the flamboyant Albany gangster Jack "Legs" Diamond, goes back to some detective fiction, like James M. Cain, only with an upstate New York Celtic twist to it. The entire Albany Cycle, I've read some say, is Kennedy's version of Thornton Wilder's *Our Town,* where ghosts take center stage to retell the trials and triumphs of their all-too-brief lives.

Of course, the most frequent comment made about Kennedy's work is that it somehow emulates William Faulkner, turning his hometown of Albany on the Hudson into a northern Oxford, Mississippi. There are also, of course, people who talk about the influence of James Joyce's work, and that what Joyce did for Dublin, Kennedy is doing for Albany. Then there are those who put William Kennedy in the Irish American tradition and lump him in along with Eugene O'Neill, James T. Farrell, Flannery O'Connor, John O'Hara, and F. Scott Fitzgerald. Those writers were certainly Irish, but they didn't really share enough of a similarity to group them together in the same Irish American category, which is sometimes done.

All these literary characteristics touch crucial elements of William Kennedy's fiction. I really believe, after reading and thinking about it, that there are two main currents that can be felt throughout all of his work. One is Albany, as a place, and the second is journalism as a springboard. As Kennedy once said about being a reporter, "It's a great training ground. I was served enormously well by it. No bail bondsman, no lawyer, no politician, no bartender, no actor can enter into the variety of worlds that journalism can." It was Kennedy's earlier apprenticeship in journalism that exposed him to a vast range of experiences that would ultimately form the core of *Ironweed* and *Legs.* It has forced him to become a keen observer and a tireless interviewer. It nurtured in him a reverence for the historian's fact. It taught him lessons in style that would mold his entire Albany Cycle. It also, I think, taught him about the importance of a strong lead.

One of the things I was talking about last evening at dinner was what an incredible opening *Ironweed* has. It is like a dream. It is the first thing you learn in journalism, how to get the lead, and it's probably one of the greatest leads ever. You read the first page and you are drawn right into the book. Journalism teaches you that. History, which I'm in, unfortunately doesn't.

I would also say that journalism has taught William Kennedy to be dubious of secondhand accounts, and to insist on doing his own reportorial digging.

As Emerson once put it, "the habit of fronting the fact, and not dealing with it at second hand, through the perceptions of somebody else." And of course, daily assignments at the Albany *Times Union* and *San Juan Star* allowed him to engage with a real world of real street people and discover the "soullessness of lonesome inhabitants" that populate a lot of his fiction.

Feature stories allowed him to conjecture about the meaning of observations and to experiment with style. "All I wanted to do and be was Damon Runyon," Kennedy has noted about his early love of newspapers and about his burning boyhood desire to turn a catchy phrase. And in a 1985 interview with Peter Quinn—which is really marvelous, and it's called "Tap Dancing into Reality" in *Riding the Yellow Trolley Car*—Kennedy notes that he writes fiction "for people like me who used to appreciate Damon Runyon sentences" (55).

When you think about the most frequent questions that come up in all these interviews that people have done with William Kennedy, they have always asked about the question of journalism versus novel writing, and fiction versus nonfiction, probably more than any other writer. Maybe someone like Tom Wolfe gets those questions as often as William Kennedy does. I will also say that even now, even though he is now a full-time novelist, his day isn't complete until he reads the morning newspaper. And he is still known to carry around a memo pad and jot down the details of everyday life in Albany.

Now, Kennedy of course isn't the first novelist to hone his literary skills as a newspaperman. Walt Whitman spent twenty-five years as a journalist and editor before the first edition of *Leaves of Grass* was published. During the 1840s in Brooklyn, Whitman was considered, in fact, the master of the penny press. I love a line in *Song of Myself* where Whitman reflects on his journalism career and sums it up in this line, "You shall no longer take things at second or third hand. . . .You shall listen to all sides and filter them from yourself." Mark Twain was a journalist for twenty years before he even wrote his first novel. Much of the material he used in his fiction was gathered while reporting. Ernest Hemingway spent his apprenticeship years working for the *Kansas City Star* and writing nonfiction stories in Europe in the 1920s and 1930s. But of course with Hemingway you get that famous break. He eventually said that he found newspaper work boring and unsatisfying. In a letter to Gertrude Stein, after he spent some time with her, Hemingway wrote, "I'm going to chuck journalism. You wounded me as a journalist last winter, and have been no good ever since." Hemingway serves as a point of discussion because he abandoned journalism and had some harsh things to say about it in typical Hemingway style. He becomes a lightning rod in this debate of the value of a journalism career as a springboard to becoming a fiction writer. I think Hemingway was full of some bluster and trying to get journalism out of his system so that he could write fiction, because if you look at the number of pre–William Kennedy American journalists who became novelists or poets, it is absolutely staggering.

In fact, Alexis de Tocqueville, traveling to America in the 1830s, commented on the influential role of journalists in the new country. De Tocqueville said, "The inhabitants of the United States have then at present, properly speaking, no literature. The only authors that I acknowledge as American are the journalists. They indeed are not great writers but they speak the language of their countrymen and they make themselves heard." And Professor Shelley Fisher Fishkin points out in her fine study, *From Fact to Fiction,* that the pattern of going from journalism into fiction is not necessarily unique to America. She goes on to talk about Dickens's career in journalism, Orwell's, and many others. These were men of journalism before they were men of fiction.

Journalism isn't the only important influence on these writers' development. I would be misstating things if I made it seem like journalism was *it.* When one considers William Kennedy, for example, one naturally has to reflect on his mother and father; on his time as an altar boy at Sacred Heart Church; his teachers at Christian Brothers Academy; his time spent in the U.S. Army; the James Cagney movies he watched growing up; the ghosts encountered in Shakespeare's *Hamlet* or Dickens's *A Christmas Carol;* the girls he dated; the saloons he drank in. One can go on and on for hours about the influences on people.

But it is the work of daily journalism that gave him, early on, the self-discipline and the fundamental skills to write quality fiction. I've always believed in Sinclair Lewis's maxim that the first rule of writing is to put the seat of your pants to the seat of the chair, and I think journalism provides that sense of discipline. In other words, the newsroom at the Albany *Times Union*, if you like, was William Kennedy's Iowa Writers' Workshop and the *San Juan Star* was his Bread Loaf. Put more starkly, journalism was how Kennedy made a living while trying to learn the skills necessary to write first-rate fiction. You do have to earn a living. William Kennedy worked on the San Juan newspaper until eleven at night, ate dinner, and came home to work on his novel until two in the morning. He needed journalism to give him the money so that he and his family could survive.

So what I wanted to take a look at was Kennedy's apprenticeship in serious journalism from 1949 until 1975, and contemplate how that helps to explain the roots of his fictional subjects, styles, and themes. I think the issue is to answer the questions: What was the impetus that got Kennedy interested in journalism? Was he any good at his trade? Can one find traces of his newspaper career in his novels?

Now, it would be foolish to say that journalism taught him how to experiment with linguistic constructs and inspired William Kennedy's surrealistic sweeps, because I don't think it did. I think reading fiction brought that into his work. Journalism did provide the foundation on which he developed the courage to find his own voice. Newspaper reporting is, as Kennedy once noted, the least boring profession in history. Journalism also taught Kennedy to put experience into action, if you like, ahead of philosophy in his fiction. In a time when life was ripe with dilution, hypocrisy, fraud and forgetfulness, according to Kennedy, journalism also taught him the value of vulnerability.

I had never heard that before or thought of that before. I had thought of some of those other things I mentioned about journalism before, but not that. So I just wanted to read you something about William Kennedy from his book *Riding the Yellow Trolley Car,* an excellent collection of essays and book reviews and the like. This is a very interesting point, I think, how journalism teaches one the need to be vulnerable, and again I think this is a unique observation on his part here. This is from an interview with Peter Quinn, and I'm going to skip a little part of it. Kennedy is talking about why he needed to leave:

> Exile came because I couldn't stay in Albany any longer and still function effectively. I had to go elsewhere. I went to Puerto Rico, which is exile under the American flag. It's as far away as you could get, and still be in the U.S.A. But cunning was not in my kit bag. I never felt that that was necessary. I was always aboveboard. I always put out my work for stomping, whatever I did. And I usually got stomped. But I never felt that it was necessary to retreat and stay home and nurse my wounds and never try again until I had a masterpiece. That was never my understanding of how to write, or how to live as a writer. Somewhere along the line I came across the phrase about "renewing your vulnerability." And that seemed to me a most important thing for a writer. You renew your vulnerability. Constantly. You start out feeling so vulnerable that you're afraid the criticism will kill you. But if you're not afraid of being vulnerable, if you say, "Go ahead, hit me again, I can take it," you get a thick skin.
>
> You get that as a journalist. Letters to the editor demanding "Throw this guy in the river." Or "Why did you hire him to begin with?" . . . You get to live with that. I remember I wrote a series of articles on the slums of Albany back in the sixties. The mail attacking me came in like you couldn't believe. I got

> hate calls and hate mail from grand bigots, wonderful bigots, really *creative* bigots. It didn't faze me, because I realized early on that when you get into the business of putting yourself out on the public chopping block, you have to figure you're going to get chopped at. (44)

That is a great lesson, I think, for the importance of journalism to becoming a writer. Getting your byline out there, reading it, taking hard hits, but being forced to do it again the next day. You might even make an error in a column, a factual error, but the next day you've got to go out there and write another story. I think that had an immense influence in bringing out, if you like, the invincibility of William Kennedy, the sense of always persevering. This is not somebody who ever threw in the towel. He kept at it, and it wasn't until 1983 when *Ironweed* became a big hit that he got the recognition that he long deserved. He struggled for a long time without a lot of money because he believed in what he was doing.

I thought I'd give a quick biographical sketch of William Kennedy as journalist and, no big surprise, the story begins in Albany. He was born in Albany on January 16, 1928, and first began writing at the Christian Brothers Academy. I asked Bill Kennedy about the clippings there, if there are any. He may or may not have any in his files, but I would think that if someone were doing work here that it would be fun to go to the Academy and find old issues, and see if you can find anything.

I'm writing a book on Jack Kerouac, and I'm finding that he used to go to a Catholic church where they had a big book log, and Kerouac used to write confessionals in this church book. I went to the church and asked the priest for these books, and he dug them out, and here were these books with fourteen-year-old Kerouac writing prose in this church book. So I think that kind of investigation into William Kennedy's career needs to go forward. Someday his archives are going to be a vast treasure trove for anybody who wants to study the second half of the twentieth century and beyond, due to the interviews he has done with all sorts of writers from around the world, due to the correspondence he's had with major writers, due to the drafts he's saved from his great novels.

He went on to work as the editor of the *Siena News* and associate editor of *Beverwyck Magazine,* both at Siena College here in upstate New York. He graduated in 1949 with a bachelor's degree in English and immediately became a sports writer and columnist for the *Post-Star* in Glens Falls, New York. For him to become immediately a sports writer and columnist shows that he had great direction, in the sense that he knew just what he wanted to do: to leave college and go to a newspaper. And then he had the gumption to continue writing for that paper even after he was drafted into the armed forces, which he soon was. He was drafted into the army in 1950 and was in Germany for two years. He never broke off that relationship with the paper, but as a man in uniform he sent columns back to the hometown paper to let them know what was going on over there. I think that shows his extra-burning desire to be a journalist.

Even at this early stage it is clear not only that he wants to take his journalism seriously, but also that he has a hankering to write fiction. Someday we might get to see the unpublished short stories of William Kennedy from this period. There is great debate going on whether people should be exposed to this sort of thing. With Ernest Hemingway—maybe you read the story in *The New York Times*—they are bringing out a new Hemingway novel. Some people think this shouldn't happen, that it was never meant to be published, and it will hurt his reputation.

William Kennedy was discharged from the army in 1952, and he learned many lessons during the time he served as the sports editor for the Fourth Infantry Division's weekly newspaper, *Ivy Leaves.* I think what he really learned—and again journalism provided this for him—he learned a lot from the opportunity that he had to travel. He got the opportunity to see Scandinavia, to report on the 1952 Olympics in Helsinki. He got to go and talk to different people from around the world—what an education for a young person, as you know. Getting to ride in a Jeep all over the place and talk to so many different people is just about the grandest education one can get for becoming a writer. He also, I might mention, did some work with the *Army Times* during this period. That gets left out of some of the material I've read. As a sports journalist, you see the influence of Grantland Rice or Red Smith on his writing. I would say that was the mark he was striving for, to be as good as those guys. I think pretty soon that mark went up and up.

Something else very important also happened in Europe, and again in Puerto Rico: Kennedy was reading a great deal of literature, such as *The Sound and the Fury,* which he told me was like a Chinese puzzle to figure out. It introduced him to a new kind of literary complexity. You strive to learn more when you start reading that kind of literature.

In 1952, at the age of twenty-five, he was discharged and hired here in Albany as a reporter for the *Times Union.* He worked at the newspaper from 1952 to 1956, when he was hired as a reporter and columnist for the *Puerto Rico World Journal,* an English-language newspaper in San Juan. He became an assistant managing editor, and it folded six months later. Now, the reporting job he had left behind in Albany was really not a bad post. Imagine coming back from the Korean War and getting to work at a major paper like the Albany *Times Union* in your hometown and getting to see your byline. It doesn't matter if you are writing obituaries or covering a sewage pipe breaking. The fact that you are in print in the hometown newspaper is a huge high, as any writer would understand.

But Kennedy comments frequently in both interviews and in essays that he got bored with Albany and started disliking certain aspects of his town, as young people tend to do. He had just spent time in Europe, and after a number of years here, still unmarried, working in his hometown of Albany, dealing with his family and friends, he wanted adventure and to get "out there." Puerto Rico provided that. As I said before, it was as far as one could go in exile and still be in the United States, in a way.

It was there that he met Dana Sosa, the Broadway dancer. She was born in Puerto Rico but lived in New York City. If you think William Kennedy is moving quickly in his professional life, take a look at his personal life. He met Dana on December 27 and they were married on January 31. There was a story I read that, when he first met Dana, he was sort of in a Hemingway phase of his life, and the first comment he made to her—in Hemingway fashion—was "good hair!"

At that juncture Bill Kennedy took a job reporting for the Miami *Herald* in Florida. He did some reporting on Cuban revolutionaries. He also got to have the Caribbean and South America as his beat. I think he still retains a large interest in those regions today. But imagine writing for the Miami *Herald* about Cuban revolutionaries at the time of Fidel Castro coming to power. That's heady journalism; that's not second-tier journalism. The Miami *Herald,* even today, does some of the best work on the hemisphere, and here he is writing on Castro and the changes taking place, Nixon's famous visit to Latin America where he's stoned and spat on, and the various transformations from the end of the Eisenhower years to the beginning of Kennedy's "Alliance for Progress." It was an interesting moment to be thinking about and contemplating Latin American history in this century. William Kennedy was getting the experience at that time of writing big stories for a big newspaper.

Kennedy worked for the *Herald* less than a year before returning to Puerto Rico, where he freelanced for *Time-Life*, the Miami *Herald*, and *The New York Times* tourism section. In the summer of 1959 he was offered a job as the managing editor of the *San Juan Star*, a new English-language daily, for which noted journalist William Dorvillier was the founder, editor, and publisher. During that time, Dana performed on television and was a model, and she was also on the cover of *Look* magazine. With regard to Kennedy's career,

1960 is the first time that you can see these two burning desires emerge simultaneously: to be a first-rate, serious journalist; and to be a novelist.

Now, at this time, Kennedy happened to meet and take a course with Saul Bellow. If somebody would ask me where in the world you might meet Saul Bellow, I would not pick Puerto Rico, but Bellow came to teach a writing course at the University of Puerto Rico and Kennedy, who was editing the *Star,* had a novel in progress, and applied for it. Bellow accepted him, which created a lasting friendship and a support mechanism. If Saul Bellow tells you that you are doing well and your writing is great, that is enough fuel to keep you going for a decade. So I think that was a very important intersection in his life, as he had that proverbial novel in his desk, like most journalists. It was not by accident that he dedicated his book *Riding the Yellow Trolley Car* "to all journalists with a novel in the desk drawer."

What is interesting is that in San Juan Kennedy made the acquaintance of Hunter S. Thompson. In the summer of 1959 Thompson applied to be the sports editor at the *San Juan Star* but was rejected by Kennedy, the managing editor, who, after a lively exchange of letters, offered to publish an essay on journalism by Thompson in the *Star's* first edition. Thompson wrote the essay, but Kennedy also rejected that. Thompson came to Puerto Rico soon after this, in 1960, and the two struck up a friendship that lasted forty-five years.*

Recently, Hunter brought out the first novel he was working on during this period, which is called *The Rum Diary,* and in it he tries to capture some of the spirit of the times. But, as is typical with Hunter's writing, it is really about Hunter, not so much about Puerto Rico, which was Hunter's strength and also his weakness.

In 1961, William Kennedy resigned his full-time position at the *San Juan Star* to work part-time so he would have more time to work in earnest writing his novel *The Angels and the Sparrows.* Parts of it later made it in different ways into some of his other books, including *Ironweed.* In 1963, when Kennedy came back to Albany to take care of his father, who was ill, he began again to report for the *Times Union.* But boy, was there a difference, a difference that the Puerto Rico–Bellow–Dana interlude made on his life.

When he came back in 1963, he began to write a series about different Albany neighborhoods. In these pieces, I think you can see a different William Kennedy. These stories eventually became the raw material for *O Albany!*, which wasn't published until 1983. In his reporting on Albany in this period, he is immersing himself in the neighborhoods, into issues of race and religion,

* Editors' Note: This story is told in Kennedy's foreword to, and their exchange of letters in, Thompson's first collection, *The Proud Highway*.

politics, corruption, gangsters. Those early essays were titled "The Changing Face of Albany." It was really Albany's urban side that was undergoing a change. Hundreds of houses were being demolished. We now, hopefully, in this country know better than to rip down our great old buildings, and how sadly we miss them.

I live in New Orleans and Interstate 10, the great interstate, is very important. It connects Jacksonville, Florida, to Santa Monica, California, and it gives us the transportation link that delivers our food. But it unfortunately destroyed Storyville, the great jazz neighborhood. It went smack through it because it was a black neighborhood, so if you want to go to Storyville, you can't find it.

The demolition of Albany's urban neighborhoods angered William Kennedy, and it comes across in these articles. The pieces also reveal a renewed affection for Kennedy's old hometown. He went back to the neighborhoods and talked to the old-timers, and if I had one photograph of William Kennedy it would be of him in a saloon, talking to some old-timers about what life in Albany used to be like. As a historian, I admire that interest he has in what it was like before him, in understanding ancestors and the cycles of change.

O Albany! is a marvelous book, an extraordinary work. Everybody in Albany should have a copy of it, and any parent who doesn't give a copy to his or her child isn't doing that child justice. It is a fundamental discussion of what this town is about and what it means. There is a lot of humor in it, a lot of history in it, and there is a lot of good journalism in it. It doesn't really fit any set genre category.

It is now becoming very popular, this notion of writing biographies of cities, in my field of history. Instead of doing a biography on Thomas Jefferson, you do a biography of Kansas City, a biography of San Antonio. I think William Kennedy's is the most sophisticated version of that kind of study that we have in this country. So beyond being an incredible novelist, take a look at his skills as a nonfiction writer.

One of the other things I like about William Kennedy, in particular in *O Albany!*, is the credit he always gives people. I'm a jazz fan. A lot of jazz musician friends always say thank you to the ancestors, the people they've learned from. *O Albany!* is full of thank-yous. Even at the end he says, I'm done with this long book and I still haven't thanked so-and-so, and I didn't tell you the story about this guy, and I didn't tell you about that. There is an essay, incidentally, about doing that ancestor-thanking by Susanne Dumbleton. It's called "William Kennedy: Telling the Truth the Best Way I Can," and she writes about this very well, and I'd suggest reading it.*

* Editors' Note: Bill Knight and Deckle McLean, eds., *The Eye of the Reporter* (Macomb: Western Illinois University Press, 1996).

Another thing Kennedy writes, and it's a thing all of us who write history or do research I think should admit, is, "I've pillaged hundreds of books to create this work." I like that statement. My mentor and colleague Stephen Ambrose always says the job of the historian is to read other people's mail. You do feel you are a snoop in people's lives in some ways when you do that kind of work.

William Kennedy ended up revising the articles in *O Albany!,* and one of the interesting points I make is that if you look at the articles as they are written, say, in 1963, and then you look at the revision that was done on them in the 1980s, you can see how the novelist is influencing the journalist. It is a pretty fascinating thing to trace.

I think that after that experience of writing serious journalism about the wrecking of Albany, by 1965 William Kennedy turned his attention to one of the two most volatile issues in the country: not Vietnam, but race in America. His reporting on the racial slums of Albany was just fabulous. It was nominated for a Pulitzer Prize, and it won awards from the NAACP, the Newspaper Guild, and the New York News Publishers Association. Kennedy writes about the "War on Poverty" waged by Lyndon Johnson, and about Bobby Kennedy grabbing on to that notion. He writes with such detailed interest about poverty that it brings to mind George Orwell's *Down and Out in Paris and London,* or the kind of approach that James Agee took in *Let Us Now Praise Famous Men,* when he was trying to understand the sharecroppers of the South. You can see that approach isn't just serious journalism, it has a great intent of purpose. He was going to tell this in a way that wasn't just newspaper reporting but transcended it.

What is so fascinating is from these experiences in journalism you really get, in many ways, as I've said early on, the springboard for William Kennedy's fiction. It would be hard to imagine *Ironweed* or *Legs* without the journalism. You really had to be a kind of historian or investigative reporter to do that groundwork on *Legs.* William Kennedy told me last night at dinner that he read the entire New York *Daily News* from the Legs Diamond period, and he had used a lot of clippings and profiles, boxes of them, which helped him to figure out who the real Legs Diamond was. So you can see his career in journalism having a profound influence, and helping him enlarge the possibilities of fiction.

Another benefit of journalism, and having a Latin American beat, was that Kennedy had a hold on Latin American culture, right at the time when interest in Latin American novelists was increasing. William Kennedy was on top of them before anyone else in the United States. He understood García Márquez and Jorge Luis Borges, read them. At that time there was that dreamlike quality to their works, and his work has this gritty realism. All the top-tier writers in Latin America have a great deal of admiration for William Kennedy. Recently, Carlos Fuentes told me he considered Kennedy one of the finest, if not *the* finest American novelist alive today.

In closing, I would simply say that one of the lessons from William Kennedy is, if you want to be a journalist, read great fiction. All good journalists have to read all of Faulkner, Hemingway, Roth, and Joyce. If you want to be good, it isn't enough to just go out there and record what happened. You really need to understand motives, intents, history, religion, and philosophy. I think that's what made William Kennedy such an outstanding journalist and why *O Albany!* is one of the really important books of journalism and history that has been written since World War II.

Reference

Kennedy, William. *Riding the Yellow Trolley Car.* New York: Penguin, 1993.

This essay was presented at "William Kennedy: A Celebration . . . A Symposium on His Work" held at the Omni Albany Hotel (now Hilton Albany), Albany, New York, on April 15–17, 1999. It is a transcription of the original presentation. Printed by permission of Douglas Brinkley.

Edward and Katrina Daugherty

A Match Made in Albany, Not in Heaven

Vivian Valvano Lynch

> Here is the darkest of Kennedy's novels, a novel that for all its sentimental melodrama and puckish humor carries the author's most formidably disturbing suggestions about class consciousness, class conflict, romantic love, talent, betrayal, and the vulnerability of the human mind.
>
> —Vivian Valvano Lynch

I believe Edward and Katrina Daugherty are two of William Kennedy's warriors. Kennedy himself has repeatedly used the term "warrior" to distinguish certain of his characters who "are always working towards being something valuable in life. (They're trying) to sustain a serious attitude toward survival. It's always a war."[1] Naming Billy Phelan, Legs Diamond, and Daniel Quinn as warriors, Kennedy once asserted that "they all struggle and fight against themselves, if nothing else, against tides that are very strong against them, against wars in their own minds, and in their own societies. So, in a sense, they are a form of not heroes but extreme figures who are willing to go to the limit."[2] I have argued elsewhere that William Kennedy's warriors are artists. Some are identifiable artists or would-be artists in practice, for example, writers or painters; facets of their artistry are their arsenal. Others, while not fitting a conventional, denotative definition of artist—not actually and consciously working on something intended as art—still possess creative gifts and imaginative power and likewise merit the appellation. These characters actually do make or create something as they struggle; this facility distinguishes each from an everyman or everywoman, even if he or she might seem absolutely ordinary.

Creative imagination helps the Kennedy warriors fight their battles of survival. Not all Kennedy warrior-artists apply their gifts to admirable causes. But they all use their talents to wage their personal, individualistic wars. The results range from the brim to the dregs: from the sublimity of the attainment of the empyrean (the artificer Francis Phelan's successful construction of his own redemption in *Ironweed*) to the legally and morally stained curtain falling on the performance of a lifetime (the actor Jack Diamond convincing the world for a long time that he is not a bum but is the gangster Legs Diamond in *Legs*). The pages of Kennedy's novels to date abound in the journeys of his warrior-artists. In this essay I will concentrate on characterization of two of them, Edward and Katrina Daugherty, as they are revealed in the course of the earlier novels and culminate in *The Flaming Corsage*, in which they share center stage.

I have also contended elsewhere that the identification of some Kennedy characters as warrior-artists (a definition not always attributable solely to the protagonist of a novel) sometimes develops in a manner comparable to awareness of pentimento in painting. Pentimento refers to the gradual, eventual emergence of something that was originally painted beneath the top layer of the visible painting, something that a viewer of the top layer does not know, does not realize, was always there. The viewer only becomes aware of the original foundation art, or artistic effort, when the passage of time and certain physical conditions cause the original colors and shapes to begin to show. Even so, the viewer must necessarily observe very closely; a cursory look or a quick glance can miss pentimento even when its traces have begun to emerge. The painter, of course, knows that he or she has used a canvas that already held a painting, or he or she has painted over a self-made, all but hidden, foundation. The painter knows what is beneath the visible layer. Likewise, as Kennedy's oeuvre has grown, certain characters reappear in later texts, after an initial presentation. Occasionally, a glimpse of the warrior and a spark of creativity may surface in the original text, noteworthy but not affording concrete information by a close reading to permit definitive labeling of the character as a warrior-artist. More glimpses of the creative struggle germane to the thesis of warrior as creator may, however, surface in later texts. This becomes an intriguing part of the interwoven fictional milieu of the novels and applies significantly to Edward and Katrina Daugherty. By examining the pentimento of *Billy Phelan's Greatest Game* and *Ironweed*, then concentrating on the fuller portraiture of *The Flaming Corsage*, I hope to show what their idiosyncratic talents are, what ends those talents serve, and what levels of success they achieve. Edward and Katrina are fascinating individuals in their own rights and are an equally fascinating pair. Their union is a match made in William Kennedy's Albany, not in heaven.

In *Billy Phelan's Greatest Game*, one of whose central themes involves intricate father-son relationships, we are introduced to Edward Daugherty, father of one of the novel's seminal warriors, Martin Daugherty. Edward as presented in this novel is apparently a playwright with a social conscience. He may be a scandalous philanderer, but his early play, *The Car Barns*, is depicted as a work of proletarian literature, exposing the oppression of the worker and immortalizing the heroic figure of a scab killer modeled on the young Francis Phelan. Martin's difficult relationship with his aged father encompasses burdensome memories of Edward's extra-marital affair and his treatment of Katrina, but it also encompasses recognition that Edward, now spending his last days in mental confusion in a nursing home, was once a renowned, critically acclaimed author. He wrote of the struggles of Irish immigrants in an often-hostile America.

Martin, a journalist by profession, quickly disclaims to Francis Phelan any similarity between his own writing ability and his father's; clearly, Martin considers the elder Daugherty's work superior and more valuable. Edward's tantalizing characteristics prompt the reader to crave more information. It could be that a warrior-artist, now apparently senile, is living in that nursing home. There is just a glimpse here, but it is enough to cause one to wonder about Edward. His play *The Flaming Corsage*, unabashedly modeled on both his affair with an actress and the breakdown of his wife, reflects his independent nature.

Billy Phelan's Greatest Game insinuates that Edward is worth examining as he materializes in later Kennedy books. His deceased wife Katrina, as recalled in the same novel, obviously suffered some mental problems and apparently seduced the young boy Francis Phelan. Indeed, she walked out of her home stark naked before young Francis. But she has one unforgettable militant moment in Martin's memory, Martin's being one of the principal consciousnesses mediating the action in *Billy Phelan's Greatest Game*. Martin remembers the occasion when she strode into the local Catholic school and enacted vengeance for all the little boys whom she had watched, from her window, as Brother William hit them with a ruler. Katrina, Martin recollects, beat the Brother with his own ruler, slapped him with her bare hands, pursued him and drew blood, and sent a bunch of stunned but grateful boys home to report the day's activities to their parents. This is quite a theatrical undertaking. It would be wise to watch for Katrina in later novels. Mental instability notwithstanding, she has a distinctive flair for the bellicose dramatic gesture.

Francis Phelan's recollections of Katrina are, characteristically for this purgatorial protagonist's ruminations, complex. At a glance, she may seem like a wicked-willed woman who seduced a young boy, her evil intent perhaps tempered a bit by nuances of mental and/or emotional distress. There is no question that Francis's thoughts of her are as laden with affection as his thoughts of his mother, Kathryn, are laden with hatred. On closer inspection, Katrina, as in *Billy Phelan's Greatest Game*, displays traces of being something more than an unbalanced eccentric or a seductive temptress. In *Ironweed*, her patrician family's intense opposition to her marriage to the playwright Edward is clarified. Her elegant, sophisticated ways at first annoyed her Albany neighbors, but eventually she won over everyone except Kathryn, who despised her always, before and after Francis's involvement with her. Katrina's queenly carriage distinguishes her. Abundant, yellow, wild weeds grow on her grave out of season: realistically, this prompts curious visits to the gravesite; symbolically, this signals distinctiveness in the character of Katrina and a similarity to Francis, the ironweed. Apparently, she suffered in her past, felt trapped as an adult, and saw her life as a war and her marriage as something in which she had to fight to survive. Francis recalls her cryptic statements to him about an oppressive yet emotional relationship with Edward. Katrina seemingly justified her seduction of and her relationship with young Francis as a means of attempting survival in a problematic life. Francis's recollections of her, as he passes her old home site on All Saints' Day, do more than provide information about a woman who is important in his story. They also provide evidence that she had her own story, her own battles, and her own attempts at survival.

Katrina was nothing if not creative. She told Francis that she engineered her naked exit from her house as a deliberate enticement to him; her schooling of her young devotee was likewise planned. While her seduction of the young boy was immoral by conventional standards, it apparently had a defensive and shielding purpose in Katrina's mind. Again, and even more so than in *Billy Phelan's Greatest Game*, Katrina Daugherty seems to be a creative fighter. Her narrative is still not complete in *Ironweed*, so categorically naming her a warrior-artist would be unwise, but there are glimpses, once again in the text, and they seem to be getting clearer.

When Francis Phelan leaves his wife Annie's house after the family turkey dinner, he is still seeing ghosts, and he determines to stand up to them. He is also seeing images of the living. One face meshes into another: the three women he envisions working on the thread of his life, his Fates (his mother, Katrina, Helen Archer) all eventually become Annie. He determines to go on living, deciding that he has never hurt anybody. Fortunately for the soul of Francis, he does not stay with this simplistic notion for long. Soon, he vividly remembers two persons important to his young life. One is Emmett Daugherty, who taught him about the trials and hardships of the nineteenth-century immigrant Irish, taught him that Irish labor built American cities, railroads, and canals, and taught him that anti-Irish bigotry pervaded the time. Emmett's lessons went from the general to the specific as he repeatedly narrated for Francis his own story: his experience on a plague-ridden coffin ship from Ireland; his frustration in trying to meet his brother when the Albany officials refused the boat docking privileges for fear of disease; his years of hard labor; his years as a labor organizer. Francis ascribes to Emmett's tutelage the emergence of the young Francis Phelan who was present and angry at the 1901 trolley strike.

The other important person who Francis recalls is Edward Daugherty, Emmett's son, once again, the playwright who immortalized the scab-killer Francis via the protagonist of the play *The Car Barns*. However, Edward's protagonist, Francis now deciphers, was actually a fusion of characteristics of the young, strong Francis and the older, well-known labor crusader and agitator, Emmett. Edward's play, apparently a potent example of propagandistic proletarian writing in the vein of Clifford Odets's *Waiting for Lefty* (1935), had a tremendous effect on young Francis. (Of course, the Odets play is set in the Depression period rather than the earlier period of Francis's strikebreaking activity, but it concerns a strike and its theme is potently anticapitalism and prolabor, as is Daugherty's fictitious play.) Young Francis believed the play and envisioned himself as something he was not: a labor hero. Indeed, the Daughertys, father and son, as recalled by Francis, exhibit tendencies of warrior-artists. The entirety of their stories is not narrated, and, as with Katrina, there is not enough to label them definitively. However, Emmett, in his instruction of the young Francis, and Edward, in his utilization of the young Francis's story as well as the character traits of his father, exhibit creativity. Edward's case is particularly interesting; he uses facts in service of his art, creating a play catalyzed by the inspiration of history but fostered by the powers of his own imagination. He sounds not unlike a contemporary American author who used facts that he knew about Jack Diamond but imaginatively created a novel rather than write a biography.

Both Emmett and Edward obviously had causes and beliefs that they fought for. Again, as they reappear in Kennedy's cycle, they will merit attention. Their chief importance in *Ironweed*, though, is that Francis, having thought of them, reaches critical realizations. He cannot read Edward's play as an accurate rendition of his life and perceive himself as the firebrand radical striker created in the image of Emmett Daugherty. The reader can now readily see why the young Francis did not immediately understand that it was a baseball player, not a striker, who threw the stone at Harold Allen. He had been affected by a confusing illusion of himself as a labor crusader, an illusion initiated by the lessons he learned from Emmett and nurtured by the creative dramatization of his experiences by Edward. Francis, much more mature now, will mediate on his own real life, not Edward's script, and realize that his enemy has been not uncontrollable hands or uninvited ghosts, but himself. He can never undo the things about which he feels guilty. Perhaps, however, he who exhibited such a concern for honesty at the start can now face his past with unbridled honesty.

Later, with a group of bums, Francis is able to do publicly, in front of strangers, what he has never been able to do before: state the truth about Gerald's death and confess, unequivocally, that his inability to handle it caused him to apply an old pattern and embark on a long flight. Realistically, such a confession does nothing for the other bums. They all have their own lives and problems and purgatorios; they cannot be expected to learn a snap lesson from Francis's announcement. But Francis is now purged. He can never hope to understand everything completely, to come to definite conclusions. All he can be sure of is that he does carry guilt for his past actions and that he will not let that guilt defeat him. He can face it, live with it, and do the best he can in a world that demands constant struggle. Francis's resolve is quickly tested as Legionnaires invade and burn the hobo jungle where Francis and Rudy are spending the night with other bums and desperate, homeless families. I must leave further discussion of the ironweed for another day, but the point here is that awareness of the creative differences between Edward's play and his own real life had a strategic impact on Francis's redemptive journey. Now we can turn our attention to the novel in which Edward and Katrina are most fully delineated.

In the penultimate moments of *The Flaming Corsage*, Edward Daugherty ironically thinks of himself and his doppelganger Thomas Maginn as "comrades of the imagination."[3] Had Edward been more astute and less self-serving, he might be able to categorize himself and the other truly imaginative character in this novel, Katrina Taylor Daugherty, as bona fide "comrades of the imagination." However, by the time Edward draws his bitter comparison, Katrina, a damaged warrior, lies dead; Edward's by now fragile weapon, his imagination, is soon to undergo its most stringent test. Here is the darkest of Kennedy's novels, a novel that for all its sentimental melodrama and puckish humor carries the author's most formidably disturbing suggestions about class consciousness, class conflict, romantic love, talent, betrayal, and the vulnerability of the human mind.

The Flaming Corsage, a prequel to *Billy Phelan's Greatest Game* and *Ironweed*, ranges in plot between 1884 and 1912. Plunging the reader on the opening page into a brief, charged account of the "love nest" killings of 1908, no names provided for the murdered wife, the suicide husband, the second woman, or the wounded man, Kennedy then amasses concise narratives, without attention to sequential or chronological order, which gradually identify the persons in the Manhattan hotel room: Dr. Giles Fitzroy, the killer and suicide; Felicity, his murdered wife; Melissa Spencer, the survivor; and Edward Daugherty, the wounded man. More substantial than the identification of the individuals, and even as *The Flaming Corsage* acquires some features of a traditional murder mystery in its exposure of intrigue and motive, the novel probes the relationship between Edward and Katrina. Stubbornly resisting full disclosure, Kennedy fills in with strokes tantamount to brushstrokes his previous pictures of the two. He swiftly recovers ground already known to readers of the cycle but crucial to his neophyte audience: Edward, son of the Irish American and Catholic working class, has avoided much of its toil and hardship by virtue of an annuity granted to his heroic father for Edward's education by the grateful foundry owner whose life Emmett Daugherty saved; the foundry owner being Lyman Fitzgibbon, maternal grandfather of Katrina Taylor, puts Edward in an environment with this daughter of Dutch-Anglo and Episcopalian blueblood stock. Now Kennedy shows how the two fell in love, energetic children of promise in 1884 America: he a handsome, articulate, and ambitious writer, she a beautiful, elegant, bright, passionate, and stylish debutante. To democratic thoughts that in America, the great equalizer, the two can eradicate archaic notions of class superiority and privilege, Kennedy delivers a stunning defeat, a defeat all the more poignant when one realizes how much unrealized potential Kennedy has infused into his warrior-artists.

The situation at first looks hopeful as the well-schooled and eloquent Edward delivers a "manifesto" (30) to Katrina's disapproving parents. Using the books in the Taylor library as ammunition to embarrass them with details of British oppression of Ireland, he announces an inheritance of noble Irishness and a debt owed to him by the Taylors as children of Cromwell. Jaws drop in the face of Edward's virtuoso performance; the Taylors cannot dispute the potency of his brilliantly researched and fervid oratory.[4] Easily matching Edward's inventiveness, Katrina, whose tastes run to the scandalous poets Baudelaire and Verlaine rather than to more conventional writers recommended in her finishing school, blithely choreographs her loss of virginity to Edward at the Angel of the Sepulchre statue in the cemetery. She also wins over the crusty old Emmett, who is concerned about Edward's excommunication from the Catholic Church, with an instantaneous decision to leave her own church. The pair of lovers seems highly imaginative and may seem perfectly balanced; if one looks closely, however, it is clear that the match is uneven. Edward correctly recognizes the uniqueness of Katrina as superior to his own particularities as he reflects on her resourcefulness in his family's kitchen: "What Katrina had done was akin to her action at the cemetery, and Edward now knew she would have this effect on everyone, that the directness of her idiosyncratic behavior was a singular gift. He coveted it, felt the young man's ambition to conquer life with a stroke, as Katrina just had" (57).

The young Edward may love (or think he loves) Katrina, but he is a jealous suitor, his envy targeted not at mere physical rivals but at something intangible, Katrina's imagination, an imagination that he perceives as superior to his own. Once Kennedy posits this envy in the narrative account that veers into Edward's self-righteous and defensive interior monologue, a direct-address self-congratulation by a pouting Edward, the novel's die is cast. Katrina's skill, not Edward's bringing her to the Daugherty home, won the day's battle for the newly engaged couple; had Edward been able to admit that publicly, to commend Katrina's ingenuity publicly, an entirely different marriage might conceivably have unfolded. As it happens, Edward's jealousy and failure to communicate his thoughts to his intended bride herald a pattern of deceit and secrecy that will worsen markedly in the future.

Katrina is not blameless, however, in the area of early failed communication between the couple. Suffering recurrent headaches, all but obsessed with the death-laden imagery of her favorite poets, Katrina desires physical passion but fears the social consequences of her marriage to Edward. Partaking of a solitary late-night tea in the Taylor drawing room, she peruses her family's possessions. As she catalogues various decorative items, Katrina concentrates on a mirror and a portrait that connect her family to the historical background of Dutch Albany and even of America itself. Her reflection concludes:

> I do believe this house is paradise. . . . I believe it is a palace of brilliant crystal, softest velvet, golden light, pervasive elegance; and memory overflows with beauty and the holiness of history. I see a proud elevation of spirit and mind in the splendid people of my life. I will lose my birthright to these things if I marry Edward. (39)

Katrina sounds like she has been reading more Yeats than Baudelaire here. Her affection for the physical accoutrements of her family's house as well as her faith in the essential rightness and splendor of her family's ancestral history evoke Yeats's paeans to the Big Houses and, more importantly, to their inhabitants, the Anglo-Irish Ascendancy.[5] Marry Edward, of course, she does; as Kennedy's headnote from *The Mikado* intones, ultimately, "'tis death." Young Katrina, like Edward, is guilty of failing to share her feelings and fears with her intended spouse. However, a major difference between the two is her ability to recognize a serious truth without self-serving posturing or immature claiming of credit for another's skill.

Edward's problem is quite deeply rooted. It is doubtful that he can sustain the level of performance achieved in the Taylor library. The cold, hard fact is that Edward is not as talented as he wishes to be, or at least not talented in the way that he wishes to be. He aspires to compose plays that will make him feel he is an artist. Indeed, Kennedy has stated his desire to create in his character an artist of the period of American theater history that preceded the emergence of Eugene O'Neill.[6] Social statements, whether in fiction or in drama, do not fit Edward's authorial aspirations, although there are certainly counterparts to the efforts of Kennedy's fictional playwright in the American theater of 1890 to 1915. In particular, the socially conscious plays of Edward Sheldon, for example *Salvation Nell* (1908) and *The Boss* (1911), complement Edward Daugherty's social statements, however reluctant they may be.[7]

Edward's early novel, *The Mosquito Lovers*, about Irish convict laborers building the Erie Canal, satisfied not the young writer's ambition but a debt to his labor leader father. His best dramatic pieces, most notably *The Car Barns*, which made Francis Phelan a household name in Albany in its recreation of the throwing of a rock/killing of a scab by a striking worker who happened to be an excellent baseball player, have proletarian themes. Again, such work pleases Emmett Daugherty. However, Edward would rather please himself. To be fair, his desire reflects a none-too-surprising, if none-too-subtle, familiar Freudian wish and need to shed the father. He even articulates this to Emmett while discussing his courtship with his disappointed father, and surely one must commend his lack of hypocrisy. Edward credits his father with providing the necessary instruction for his composition of *The Mosquito Lovers*, but he implores his parent to realize that he now wishes to "celebrate the mind and the imagination" (52). Accordingly, the young playwright wants to write art plays. It takes his buddy in days of whoring to serve as his nemesis in critical commentary: shrewd Maginn, a capable but not brilliant writer himself, labels Edward's attempts at art plays, like his rendition of the Pyramus and Thisbe myth, as the inferior products that they are. Harkening back to *The Ink Truck* for a moment demonstrates the disturbing full circle that Kennedy has drawn. If *The Ink Truck's* striking journalist, Bailey, vivifies the question of what a talented writer can do when the vehicle of his art is suddenly removed, Edward vivifies the question of what happens to a talented writer when he fails to recognize the nature of his talent. Throughout much of *The Flaming Corsage*, the answer seems to be that he turns into a popular but not scholarly success, a marital infidel, a social juvenile, and a bit of a pompous ass. Fortunately for Edward, Kennedy allows him to redeem himself considerably via imaginative action as the novel draws to a close, but this will not bring back the dead Katrina.

Katrina is one of Kennedy's favorite characters. He remarked as early as 1989, "I love Katrina."[8] More recently, he reaffirmed being intrigued by her and having "great fondness for her eccentricities."[9] Her creator's fascination with her is unmistakable in the text. For all the information presented about Katrina, for all the astonishing moments revelatory of her whimsical behavior, for all the sudden dives into the center of her consciousness, Katrina remains a tantalizingly incomplete, somewhat impalpable character. It is highly doubtful that Kennedy has finished probing her, the most dynamic warrior-artist of this novel. The young Katrina is capable of conquering her young swain and even conquering his father, whom she tearfully and astutely toasts at his death scene in 1903 as a "soldier of the righteous wars" (94). Once again, as in the subtle recognition scenes delineated in *Very Old Bones*, a Kennedy warrior-artist recognizes true kin. Ironically, and underlying the strength of that kinship, Katrina recognizes Emmett's worth even as she is profoundly pained by her guilt at loving her father's old enemy. The text assumes direct address of its female protagonist for a few moments and queries, as she must be questioning herself:

> What does your poet say to you now, Katrina? He says that the world goes round by misunderstanding, the only way people can agree: for if they understood each other they would never agree on anything, such as marriage to the enemy: that man across the room whom you say you love, who woke you into a terrifying nightmare, who had you screaming for release before you even made the bond with him, who led you, docile woman, out of fire into salvation; that man who is the son of this virtuous man dying in front of you. What part of this dying father has passed into that living son, do you know? (93)

One fears here that the answer to this (thankfully) unanswered question is "Not much," but the novel is not over. More to the point at the moment is that Katrina, conqueror of swain and father-in-law, is not capable of conquering life.

Nine years after her marriage, in 1894, Katrina goes to the Delavan Hotel with her commercially, if not artistically, successful and flush husband; he has been busy writing social satires that strain no one's powers of perception, satires about bourgeois Irish social climbers and venal Anglo lumber barons. Her intensifying discomfort with her father's refusal to accept her marriage and religious conversion has been exacerbated by deepening nostalgia for the way of life of her girlhood. Edward hopes to alleviate the situation by buying his in-laws' approval through a collection of ostentatious gifts, one of which, the racehorse named "Gallant Warrior," serves as a subtle reminder of what is missing in the company.

The catastrophic fire at the Delavan, mentioned repeatedly in earlier Kennedy novels but now graphically described, brands Katrina's breast with an ember flying through her violet corsage, presaging the beginning of the end for her.[10] Apparently, the troublesome dreams and headaches of her youth augured a potential breakdown. Her inherent goodness is patent just after the fire in her concern for her family and for her former servant, the Irish Cora.[11] But her mind is becoming unhinged even as she makes daily visits to the ruins. Eventually, when both her father and sister die, she vacillates between self-guilt and blaming Edward, who in fact saved her from the fire, for the deaths. The hyacinth girl's lines in T. S. Eliot's *The Waste Land* follow the reproduction of Wagner's lines about the whereabouts of an Irish maid; Katrina, having stared for days into the Delavan rubble as the workers search for the remains of Cora, the Irish maid, is Kennedy's hyacinth girl. The flowers have been changed to violets, but the girl is equally lost, neither living nor dead. Hauntingly, she tells Maginn of her desire to bury the dead.[12] Her world, except for her passionate sexual affair with the teenager Francis Phelan in 1898 and whatever flirtations she may be a party to, becomes increasingly hidden and private. Her breast pierced by a literally flaming corsage, her very being traumatically damaged, her attachment to Baudelaire now resonates with funereal prescience: for her, there are indeed "les fleurs du mal." Nevertheless, Katrina's possibilities as a warrior cannot be simply dismissed even as one notes, and perhaps sympathizes with, her decline. In *The Flaming Corsage*, Katrina keeps a diary; this may be a weapon of the warrior, even if she eventually is labeled by many as a madwoman. The reader sees very little of Katrina's diary, which is reason in itself to pay close attention to the few entries extant. After the Delavan fire, after a sarcastic remark from Edward about her love of and need for death, Katrina writes of the problematic union between herself and her mate. The fire binds them, but the tie is extraordinarily complex and even abnormal. She compares their condition to Siamese twins sharing a solitary heart. Katrina avers intense but aberrant intimate bonding and anticipates inexorable destruction. Her acuity as a writer stuns the reader. Remembering her flair for the perfect setting at the Angel of the Sepulchre and her flair for the perfect response in Emmett's kitchen, one can certainly conclude: with talent like this, perhaps *she* should be writing plays. Doubtlessly, any subsequent diary entry should be carefully perused.

Edward's responses to Katrina's retreat into a private world (with occasional public flashes of the original and dazzling person that she once was) include affairs with women and hanging out with the boys. The former is highlighted by his affair with the actress Melissa Spencer, who is possibly also involved with Felicity Fitzroy as a lesbian lover; the latter is highlighted by the sophomoric fireman's wife sting[13] perpetrated upon the ever lusty Maginn, the joke whose repercussions resonate into the love nest killings of 1908. Edward eventually insists on public display of the affair and public commentary on the killings through his thinly veiled 1912 play *The Flaming Corsage*.[14] Knowing that Katrina is so mentally and emotionally fragile by this point makes Edward seem exceedingly cold, callous, and downright mean. A close examination of the events between 1910 and 1912, however, establishes that Edward, despite all his previous shortcomings, is ultimately a warrior-artist; it also establishes splendid moments of creativity for Katrina, who may yet hold secrets of her imaginative prowess.

Various versions of the incidents in the hotel in 1908 conflict and confuse. Was Felicity robbed and raped by Cully Watson? Was Felicity a willing sexual partner with Cully? Did Melissa have sex with Cully willingly, unwillingly, or not at all? Were Felicity and Melissa involved in an assignation? What was Felicity doing at the hotel with an elaborate mask and cloak? Not until Edward visits Melissa on her movie set in 1910 does a pattern of what the reader actually needs to know begin to surface.

Edward's old reporting experience serves him well; through investigation, he learns that Melissa herself bought the mask and cloak. His former mistress, when confronted, explains that she and Felicity had been setting up a treat for Edward, that Felicity in fact had long lusted for the playwright and that Melissa had no objection. As for the rape of Felicity, Melissa pleads ignorance and strongly implies that Felicity could have been Cully's willing partner, all the while insisting that she herself was never involved with the man. Edward leaves Melissa with a perceptive observation: her statement sounds believable, but he recognizes that her virtuosity lies in prefabrication. Virtuosity in lying is what Edward will need to defeat Maginn, and perhaps he realized that by recalling his appraisal of Melissa.

Soon after this meeting, Edward finds and reads parts of Katrina's diary, segments that are lying on his desk in plain sight, boldly marked and patently inviting him to snoop. Edward learns of the Taylors' financial jeopardy in 1894, of Geraldine's willingness to sell her own jewels, of Jacob's infidelities and Geraldine's pose as the loyal, silent wife. He learns of Katrina's view of him as a person dismissive of anything serious or courageous about her mother. He learns of Giles's attempts to seduce Katrina in 1894 and of Katrina's pointed conclusion: feeling no passion for Giles, she nevertheless began to entertain the possibility of having a lover. Marital infidelity would punish her husband for (paradoxically) succeeding in the very thing she had planned, the taking of her virginity, and would perhaps forestall the aging process of the soon-to-be-thirty-year-old woman. Katrina's mental confusion is hardly opaque in this entry; ravaged by insidious guilt, desperate to levy spousal punishment, and obsessed with intimations of fleeting beauty, she was a truly troubled woman on the cusp of her thirtieth birthday. Her leaving of the 1894 entry for Edward's discovery is a bold and creative strategic attempt at providing him with information and asking him for help. Her affair with Francis Phelan follows the entry by a few years, and she never admits to the affair to the suspicious Edward. However, through her diary, through her carefully crafted decision to let him see a few key passages more than a decade later, she tries to let him know how betrayed she felt, how vulnerable she was to a potential affair, and even how unfair he was in failing to consider Geraldine's worth as a person. Perhaps more importantly, she tries to let him know how dangerously confused she felt in 1894, a condition that has presumably worsened. If anyone has found an imaginative way to call for help, even from the depths of an aggrieved mind, it is the talented writer Katrina.

The second diary entry that she leaves in Edward's path is clearly meant to do several things. First, it assists him in his investigation about the love nest killings. Dated in 1908, the entry records Giles's almost hysterical arrival at the Daugherty home and his display of a crude cartoon and poem he recently received implying a ménage à trois among Edward, Melissa, and Felicity. Now Edward has the concrete motivation for Giles's murderous arrival at the hotel. Further, apart from solidifying for Edward that she has known about his affair with Melissa for some time, Katrina advises him of her feelings in 1908 despite their marital estrangement: as she informs Giles, she still deeply loves Edward. Finally, she reminds Edward of her flair for the theatrical and her original approach to problems in her unique method of momentarily calming Giles: a private disrobing. Again, the strategic choices made by Katrina are brilliant. One out of three has an immediate effect: Edward utilizes the new information in his investigation, interrogates Clubber at the slaughterhouse, and proves to his own satisfaction, if not to the degree that he can bring matters to a court of law, that Maginn egged on Cully Watson to deliver notice of cuckolding by way of the dead bull's head, the cartoon, and the poem to Giles Fitzroy. Edward is actually a good interrogator and a creditable news gatherer; this should not come as a surprise, since portrayal of social realism was his obvious bailiwick in *The Mosquito Lovers* and *The Car Barns*. Edward, however, is very poor at acknowledging gratitude. Nowhere is there evidence of his thanking Katrina for the tip that leads to a break in his investigation. Again, this should not come as a surprise, as the reader recalls Edward's refusal to attribute public credit to Katrina so many years ago in Emmett's kitchen.

Regarding Katrina's other aspirations in leaving the diary entry, informing Edward of her feelings and reminding him of her uniqueness, the effects are more difficult to determine and adjudge. Unable or unwilling to approach Katrina and discuss their relationship, Edward eventually writes the play that exposes their problems.

The last eight breathlessly short chapters of the novel flow through a few days in May 1912. They establish a pattern of comparison and contrast between Katrina and Edward. Both exercise their creativity for the last time in the text, and both spend their requisite Kennedy moments with their personal ghosts and memories. The respective outcomes are excruciatingly disparate.

In May 1912, the forty-seven-year-old Katrina visits with her dead father at the soon-to-be auctioned Taylor mansion and sees the men of her life as apparitions in her family's gilt-framed mirror. Apparently interpreting these appearances, especially her father's ghostly visit, as harbingers of impending disaster, Katrina packs precious possessions for inclusion into her safe deposit box. These include her seven-volume diary and what she determines as the remnants of the Taylor fortune. The latter comprise various pieces of jewelry (some of obviously considerable material value, some of questionable material value) as well as a piece of silver from a tea service traceable to Cromwell. The only diary section that Katrina pauses over before packing is the Francis section, "Francis of the excellent face" (152). Katrina's thoughts as she recognizes Francis's beauty eerily presage Peter Phelan's 1930s ruminations on his brother as recorded in *Very Old Bones*. Near a newspaper clipping of Francis about to throw a runner out at first lies Katrina's grief-stricken but ingenious 1898 statement of awareness that the love affair she so cleverly induced is now over:

> If you saw me plunge a knife into myself would it baffle you? Would you think it a miracle? Do you understand what I mean when I say I have no ability *to slide in and out of love*? Would you be tempted to pull the knife out of me and cut off my face? Would you kiss me while I bled through my eyes? (153, italics added)

Katrina's diary readily announces her talent here. Her entry reveals the intensity of her emotions and her desperation at losing her young lover; more meaningfully, it evidences the craft of the strategic writer who has found the perfect metaphor, a baseball metaphor, to yield the visual image of her comment on the depth of her love. If Edward ever finds this entry, his jealousy is all but certain to resurface.

One of Katrina's mirror apparitions is nightmarish: her recollection of Maginn trying to seduce her and claiming that Edward, Melissa, and Felicity were a ménage à trois in 1908. Smashing the mirror with an iron poker, dismissing ghosts and memories for the moment so she can deal with reality, Katrina marches off to war armed with her complete diary and her selected family mementos. First, she sits for a photographer's portrait for which she constructs the pose: open buttons and a scrupulously placed dried sunflower reveal just a hint of décolletage, enough to show the top of the breast scar from the Delavan fire. Katrina anticipates but effortlessly dismisses possible accusations of her impudence in exposing such a scar. The portrait will make the photographer famous, and Katrina will leave an unforgettable statement just as Femmitie Staats did in her portrait, a portrait cherished by Katrina for its ancestral relevance, with her coy smile. The soon-to-be dead Katrina has engineered her final image as a living woman; both the woman and the sunflower she wears, "two kindred blossoms of nature's intelligence" (160), will soon dissipate. Moments later, Katrina places the story of her life, all seven volumes of the diary, along with her judiciously selected family possessions, into the safe deposit box.[15] Due to lack of space, she removes old legal documents and some of Edward's plays, momentarily removing, but later replacing, her favorite, *Lunar Majesty*, the one that showed commiseration and understanding for her. Katrina's choices mark her strategy. Clearly, she wants her own version of her life to be safely intact. Quite naturally, in the face of the impending Taylor auction, she has chosen to preserve mementos that primarily reflect old wealth, pride in heritage, and familial affection, but she also honestly includes a questionable collection of bracelets that might be evidence of the Taylors' eventual financial debt.

Presumably, given the clarity of the few diary entries the reader has been privy to, the diary can guide an observer or investigator through the choice of possessions, and one can detail a history of Katrina's ancestry through the artifacts. There is simply not enough room for all the old papers, so Katrina must choose. Copies of plays that Edward has by now published certainly no longer need safe depositing, birth certificates can be replaced, and while it is usually wiser to leave legal documents in the confines of a vault, Katrina's removal of Lyman Fitzgibbon's old annuity agreement for Edward and the deeds to the Daughertys' two houses (Emmett's old house on Main Street, Edward and Katrina's house on Colonie Street) will probably cause no serious legal problems. However, the house deeds and annuity agreement are tangible items that connect both to Edward's heritage and to his move into the sphere of the Fitzgibbon-Taylor social world. Katrina has decided to preserve items resonant only of her own connections to her past. This is not petty revenge on her part. She has decided on her priorities, and it is more crucial to store in safety the one play in which Edward, whom she believes actually wrote about her in all his works, really understood her. There is nothing in the text to indicate that *Lunar Majesty* has ever been published; should something disastrous occur, a fire at the Daugherty house, for example, Katrina's hidden copy may well be the only one to survive. Otherwise, what Katrina sees as Edward's "overstated" but correct appraisal of his wife (Katrina is not only an astute writer but an astute literary critic) may disappear forever: "I'm convinced she's walled in behind the energy of her derangement, sane as anyone alive, mad as the queen of Bedlam—the stigmata, the sickness, the lesions visible in her eyes and the clutch of her hand. Such a marvel of womanhood, as pure and as fated as Eve before the serpent" (163). Unquestionably, Katrina senses her imminent death; her account to Archie of her visit with her father makes this abundantly clear. Unbeknownst to Edward, she has also assumed all the guilt for the estrangement with her father and the deaths in her family; one can only wonder whether his brother-in-law will eventually tell Edward of Katrina's statements. It remains for Katrina to view act 4, scene 1 of *The Flaming Corsage* in rehearsal and thus to learn what her husband, who has apparently lost any and all ability to communicate directly with her, believes.[16]

Reflecting on what she has watched, Katrina wonders how Edward knew that Maginn did in fact approach her and wonders doubtfully about Maginn's claim of bedding Felicity. Seeming rather amused at Edward's conclusions about herself and Francis, she notes that he will eventually know some of her hidden life but can never know it all. Katrina's perspicacious appraisal of *The Flaming Corsage* is: "He is giving a shape to the chaos that overtook us. What he said at dinner—when the matter is ready the form will come" (171). Indeed, Katrina has accurately labeled Edward's attempt at artistry in his play. In trying to give a shape to the chaos, he has created a scene between his dramatic renditions of Katrina and Melissa and has devised answers that in real life, he does not actually have.[17] Edward's dramatic version admits to his adultery but assuages his guilt, praises his artistic powers, and announces Katrina's infidelity. Katrina, admiring exactly one line of her playwright husband's theatrical effort, concludes that it is time for an attempt at complete honesty. Knowing where her talent lies, she resolves to write Edward a letter explaining why she never told him about Giles's seduction or Maginn's poem and revealing some secret information about Felicity.[18]

Making a brave start by questioning her fate, the exhausted woman falls asleep at her husband's desk only to awaken to the smell of smoke. Recognizing her old nemesis, fire, this time at the Christian Brothers school next door, she acquiesces to its power without a fight and dies moments later on the sidewalk in Edward's arms. After all, she had interpreted the previous day's warning of her ghostly father correctly. She had protected her diary and her precious belongings. Unfortunately, she ran out of time before the reader, not to mention Edward, could read her letter. In the absence of Katrina's proposed but not executed final work of art, the reader is bereft. One can only remember and savor the few brilliant passages of the diary, perhaps hoping that the rest of it may someday be removed, via a future Kennedy text, from the vault at the State National Bank. Who can say what riches might then unfold? At Katrina's funeral, Edward gets it right as he differentiates for his grieving son between Katrina's originality and madness.

Katrina's death places the novel's final spotlight on Edward. As responsive playwright, he alters the concluding scene of his play. As the son of Emmett Daugherty, the son who has so utterly botched so many things, he briefly considers using Emmett's old .32-caliber revolver; however, that is not the appropriate weapon for this Kennedy warrior-artist. Edward fights Maginn, the instigator of the love nest killings, using words as his weaponry. He crisply tells Maginn that through Cully's confession, Maginn has been exposed as the instigator of Giles's decision to commit murder. He calmly adds that his own investigator found the detective who questioned Cully, and he is willing to testify, not from memory, but from accurate notes. Finally, he smoothly states that the investigator has found a man who claims that Cully's murderers were hired hands, and the description of the hirer matches Maginn. Edward is bloodied and bruised after a dirty brawl with Maginn and his whores, but his words do their work. Maginn is sufficiently frightened to leave town. The words are products of Edward's fertile imagination: neither confession nor investigator nor witness exists. Edward can use his talent to fight after all, and "[h]is mood improved as he thought of Maginn, with fewer teeth, and fettered with whores, forced into midnight exile by the power of fiction" (204).

Edward's instantaneous and effective utilization of his authorial gifts merits noteworthy credit for him. This is much more suitable to the articulate man that we heard so many years ago delivering an excoriating diatribe in the Taylor library than so many of our ensuing observations of him. However, it is a pyrrhic victory that cannot bring Katrina back. Further, Edward would still like to leave his mark as a talented playwright, not just a talented architect of words, so he returns once more to *The Flaming Corsage*, even if it may never be performed again.[19] Using real names, he creates two new scenes. The first demonstrates that he has apparently learned something from his experience: in touching contrast to the relationship of the real Daughertys, player Edward and player Katrina discuss her obsession with death, implying at least a possibility of their reconciliation and mutual understanding. Ironically, to return to the wording that so intrigued Katrina in her final hours, the matter is finally ready and the form finally comes, but form comes to a constructed piece of writing, to a play, to a work of art, not to a living, human relationship. Kennedy's attribution of warrior-artist credentials to Edward is frustrating even as it is dauntingly realistic: words that could have been so effectual had they been rendered in real life can be effectual here in the artist's work, a play. The artist's gift is fine-tuned too late to foster happiness for himself and Katrina, but it does improve his play. Kennedy suggests a heart-breaking emotional and intellectual paradox in Edward's failure cum success: perhaps, even probably, the artist's gift cannot legitimately enter the realm of the real after all.

Bleak as the situation is, it is not hopeless. It remains for Edward to meet his ghostly father and be cryptically prodded and encouraged to go on. Returning once more to his play, Edward writes Katrina's death scene, naturalistic in setting, passionate in action, and obscure in meaning. Player Katrina dies quoting Verlaine in uncertainty of her love for player Edward, even as player Edward seems able to recall their earlier ardor:

EDWARD:
You won't die, Katrina. It's wrong to die now. You won't die, Katrina. You won't die.

KATRINA:
Life is something that should not have been.

EDWARD:
I loved life when you loved me.

KATRINA:
I loved you?

(Pause.)

Quite likely. I forget.

(Katrina dies in his arms.) (208)

Kennedy leaves appropriately unanswered the question of whether the dialogue of the death scene is an accurate memory, a fabrication of Edward's recently inspired imagination, or some mysterious combination of the two. Edward may have had his moments as a jealous lover and a poor husband, but he has ultimately proved that he is an artist. He is entitled, as are all artists, to his secrets. We last see him on the novel's final page determined to prepare bacon in Emmett's old kitchen. Recalling the ephemeral Francis Phelan at the close of *Ironweed* and Annie's offer of light, refreshing Jell-O, we are struck with the heaviness and greasiness suggested by Edward's chosen repast.[20] Actually it is a perfect selection. Bacon is hearty fare redolent of Edward's

Irish American childhood home. Capable of satiating his very empty stomach after the violence with Maginn, it is, however, thick and fatty and hard to digest. Perhaps Edward will never really rid himself of its taste or its effects. It is an apt metaphor to close this novel of histories that carried burdens of plans that went awry. "A pig is turned into bacon," thinks Edward, "bacon becomes food that gives unity and purpose to the imagination. . . . he went to the icebox for the bacon, which will always be with us" (209). Edward as artist must create from the raw material he is given, regardless of how mean some of that material may be. From that raw material, from the past, from experience is an imagination like Edward's nourished and vitalized.

Edward has finally realized just how strategically fire transforms. For anyone, fire destroys; it kills the cloddish and abusive Brother William, turning him into a cinder. For anyone, fire provides edible food; it transforms even a homely pig into succulent bacon. For the gifted few, fire is the imagination, the imagination that must be nursed (and is nursed quite adequately) by the provender and comestibles of everyday life, by what Kennedy has previously referred to as the quotidian. Joyce's Stephen, ruminating on the name of the artificer Daedalus and envisioning him flying above the waves, questions whether he is "a symbol of the artist forging anew in his workshop out of the sluggish matter of the earth a new soaring impalpable imperishable being."[21] Stephen's thoughts are more elegantly and more poetically rendered than Edward's, but they amount to the same thing: the epiphanic realization that the impetus of the real spurs the gifted imagination to creation.

Did novelist William Kennedy's Katrina Taylor Daugherty, who died in the arms of Kennedy's Edward Daugherty, die quoting Verlaine, as playwright Edward Daugherty's Katrina did? Quite unlikely.

Notes

1. Susan Agrest, "Tough Guy with a Golden Touch," *Hudson Valley Magazine*, July 1987, 45.
2. Melissa E. Biggs, "William Kennedy: The Singularity of Fiction," in *In the Vernacular: Interviews at Yale with Sculptors of Culture*, ed. Melissa E. Biggs (Jefferson: McFarland, 1991), 117.
3. William Kennedy, *The Flaming Corsage* (New York: Viking, 1996), 195. Subsequent references to *The Flaming Corsage* appear parenthetically in the text and refer to this edition.
4. Kennedy credited a 1973 trip to Ireland as the personal source of his interest in relaying the information of Edward's manifesto. He noted: "I wrote some pieces then, but one I never wrote was a piece on Connacht. I saw that situation over there, saw how people had to live, had to take endless rocks out of the land, to exist on small patches of soil. It was a horrifying thing, like a lunar landscape. It still exists; it's a monument to desolation. I always wanted to use that some place. I tracked it down historically for the manifesto." Kennedy's research sources included Cromwell's letters and histories written by both British and Irish historians. William Kennedy, telephone interview by author, March 3, 1997.

5. The most cursory look at Yeats's poems of homage to the Big House and its inhabitants will display Katrina's affinity for the poet's perspective. See, for example, "Upon a House Shaken by the Land Agitation" and "Meditation in Times of Civil War: Ancestral Houses" in W. B. Yeats, *The Collected Poems of W. B. Yeats*, ed. Richard J. Finneran (New York: Collier, 1989), 95, 200. Yeats's verse play *Purgatory* (1939) chillingly portrays the poet's nightmare vision, the destruction of the Big House via the unsuitable marriage between the daughter of the house and a loutish peasant; for Yeats, the literal destruction and violence attendant to the marriage initiate a cycle of recurrent and ever-worsening destructive proportions. See William Butler Yeats, *Purgatory*, in *Eleven Plays of William Butler Yeats,* ed. A. Norman Jeffares (New York: Collier, 1966), 199–206. Notwithstanding the concerns of the young Katrina, given that Martin Daugherty, issue of her marriage to Edward, eventually reaches a comfortable if not perfect life and, more importantly, the dimensions of a successful warrior as recorded in *Billy Phelan's Greatest Game*, Kennedy's vision does not replicate the nightmare of Yeats.

6. William Kennedy, telephone interview by author, March 3, 1997.

7. The period between 1890 and 1915 in American theater is generally discussed in criticism as a period of transition, moving in slow steps away from melodrama and presaging the genius of O'Neill. Brenda Murphy, *American Realism and American Drama, 1880–1940* (Cambridge: Cambridge University Press, 1987), cogently describes the time: "the commercial theater (sought) to absorb the new realistic principles and put them to use in commercially successful plays. . . . During these twenty-five years, the typical notion of setting for playwrights whose conscious aim was realism went from mere window dressing to the representation of a regional way of life, a character-determining milieu, or an interior expressive of its inhabitants, through carefully chosen detail. The dialogue went from stilted stage English or broad dialect to dialogue that captured the rhythms of normal speech and was appropriate to the class, personality, experience, and social perspective of the character who spoke it" (110). Of work of the period's many playwrights, Edward Sheldon's offers the closest points of comparison to the young Edward Daugherty's. Decades before the more direct statements of Clifford Odets, Sheldon presented a heroine who fought the intimidation of urban squalor via work with the Salvation Army in *Salvation Nell*. In *The Boss*, he focused on an Irish municipal boss, Michael Regan, who marries the Anglo-Saxon, upper-class Emily Griswold. An exposé of the graft and corruption of municipal political machinery is intertwined with the story of the marriage whose partners come from opposite sides of the tracks. See Murphy's chapter, "The Transition: American Realistic Drama in the Commercial Theater, 1890–1915," in *American Realism and American Drama,* 86–111. Additional sources for background on the pre-O'Neill American theater are: Gerald M. Berkowitz, *American Drama of the Twentieth Century* (London: Longman, 1992); Gary A. Richardson, *American Drama from the Colonial Period through World War I: A Critical History* (New York: Twayne, 1993).

8. Edward C. Reilly, "On an Averill Park Afternoon with William Kennedy," *South Carolina Review* 21, no. 2 (Spring 1989): 20.

9. In my telephone interview of March 3, 1997, Kennedy's appraisal included: "(Katrina's) probably the most complicated woman I've created. As an achievement of creating character, I think she stands alongside Helen Archer in *Ironweed*. They're so different, but they are equally complex."

10. The Delavan House was built in 1850. For a time, it was a temperance house, but it eventually earned a reputation as a venue for intemperate political meetings and deal-making sessions, especially in the graft-ridden days of Boss Tweed. Most of the Delavan was destroyed by the 1894 fire on which Kennedy bases his event; one part of the hotel survived, but it was razed for the building of Union Station in 1900. See William Kennedy, *O Albany!* (New York: Penguin, 1987), 182.

11. Cora, a seldom seen character in the novel, prompts thoughts about Irish servant women at the end of the nineteenth and beginning of the twentieth centuries. Three sources that provide valuable information are: Hasia R. Diner, *Erin's Daughters in America: Irish Immigrant Women in the Nineteenth Century* (Baltimore: Johns Hopkins University Press, 1983); Janet A. Nolan, *Ourselves Alone: Women's Emigration from Ireland 1885–1920* (Lexington: University Press of Kentucky, 1989); and Kerby A. Miller, with David N. Doyle and Patricia Kelleher, " 'For love and liberty': Irish Women, Migration and Domesticity in Ireland and America, 1815–1920," in *Irish Women and Irish Migration,* vol. 4, ed. Patrick O'Sullivan (London: Leicester University Press, 1995), 41–65.

12. The pertinent lines from *The Waste Land* are:

Frisch wehr der Wind
Der Heimat zu
Mein Irisch Kind,
Wo weilest du?
"You gave me hyacinths first a year ago;
They called me the hyacinth girl."
—Yet when we came back, late from the Hyacinth garden,
Your arms full, and your hair wet, I could not
Speak, and my eyes failed, I was neither
Living nor dead, and I knew nothing,
Looking into the heart of light, the silence.

See T. S. Eliot, *The Waste Land*, in *The Complete Poems and Plays: 1909–1950* (New York: Harcourt, 1971), 38. The section of *The Waste Land* in which these lines appear, "The Burial of the Dead," also includes allusions to the doomed lovers Tristan and Isolde as well as lines from Baudelaire, most notably from the preface of *Les Fleurs du Mal*, "You! hypocrite lecteur!—mon semblable—mon frère!" (39).

13. For a complete description of the fireman's wife joke, see the chapter "Courting the Fireman's Wife" in *The Flaming Corsage*, 110–113.

14. Marriage, divorce, and the double standard of morality judgments as applied to men versus women were frequent topics of humorous, satiric plays at the turn of the century. Bronson Howard's 1906 play *Kate* is credited with shifting the tone, at least occasionally, from the lightness of social satire to a more serious level. *Kate* begins in satiric mode and has a dizzying plot line of lovers and would-be lovers who eventually wind up in the right places only after much ado about many things. However, Howard allows his characters to discourse on their respective views about marriage, infidelity, morality, and sexual attraction. Murphy, in *American Realism and American Drama*, emphasizes the distinction between *Kate* and typical marriage-based comedies; Howard's audience perceives psychological conflict within the characters, even watching and listening as the characters struggle with that conflict (103–104). The same can be said for Edward Daugherty's audience, particularly as they listen to the dialogue between the vying women.

15. Katrina's construction of the portrait setting and preservation of memorabilia are reminiscent of Helen Archer's determination to initialize her death scene in *Ironweed*.

16. Examining the dialogue of Edward's play alongside Katrina's diary entries is rather amusing and leaves me in no doubt as to which of the two is the more creative writer in the family. Edward can write the most preposterous dialogue, including a line sure to make a serious actress shudder, "Mangan is unhumiliatible" (168).

17. The stubborn unwillingness of the plot line of Kennedy's novel to fall into complete cohesion is discussed by Lisa Meyer in a perceptive review. Meyer notes that "the novel also

suggests that art is an 'ism.' Edward writes plays in a futile effort to give meaning to his life. His play *The Flaming Corsage* is a neat version of his chaotic relationship with Katrina, and Kennedy's novel portrays this chaos. At the end, however, we don't know just how the murder-suicide came about. Lies mix with truths to create a murky reality." See Lisa Meyer, "A Rough and Ready Romeo and Juliet," review of *The Flaming Corsage, Los Angeles Times Book Review*, July 14, 1996, 9.

18. In 1907, at the Daugherty's Fourth of July dinner, the text registers Edward's careful observations, again verifying the good investigative reporter that he is. He notes that Katrina realizes that Giles and Felicity are both mesmerized by Melissa, that Melissa knows Edward is observing her, and that Melissa is pointedly staring at Katrina. Whether Katrina, while planning her 1912 letter, does not realize that Edward noticed Felicity's fascination with Melissa, or whether she has information more concrete and factual about Felicity to reveal to her husband, remains unresolved in the novel. Perhaps there is something in the diary, but we cannot get to it.

19. The revival of the play in Albany in 1938 is treated in *Billy Phelan's Greatest Game.*

20. Edward's ability to recognize something special in Francis should be mentioned. At the June 1906 picnic, Edward observes to a humble Francis, who disclaims his status as a hero, that he is eloquent and people notice it. Francis's riposte credits Emmett as his guide and labels Emmett a " 'gift' " (102). Kennedy warrior-artists habitually recognize kinship.

21. James Joyce, *A Portrait of the Artist as a Young Man* (New York: Penguin, 1993), 183.

This essay was presented at "William Kennedy: A Celebration . . . A Symposium on His Work" that was held at the Omni Hotel (now Hilton Albany), Albany, New York, on April 15–17, 1999. Portions of it also appear in Vivian Valvano Lynch's book *Portraits of Artists: Warriors in the Novels of William Kennedy* (Lanham, MD: International Scholars Publications, 1999), 229–249. Reprinted by permission of Vivian Valvano Lynch.

The Snows of Reduction

Representing Homelessness in *Ironweed*

Benedict Giamo

> The intimate relationship between the dead and the living dead is enriched symbolically by virtue of both time and place. As a homeless outcast, dead to his social world, Francis cuts a ghostly figure and appears as good a haunt as any to be in the cemetery on Halloween, the time "when grace is always in short supply, and the old and new dead walk abroad in this land."
>
> —Benedict Giamo

The snow is general all over Albany, "the snows of reduction," dissolving in time, time dwindling: first go the seasons, then the solidity of forms, shapes, the peculiar angle of memory, and, finally, the very rondure of life. "Things is like they are" (103), Francis Phelan remarks offhandedly at his mother's wake in *Very Old Bones*. Who could dispute that, for "one by one they were all becoming shades."[1]

But the Francis of *Ironweed* is not dead—not yet, and so the snows descend upon the living and the dead, weaving both into inescapable webs of significance and insignificance. The snow was general all over Albany when Francis recalled grieving over his father's open grave: "He . . . realized then that one of these days there would be nobody alive to remember that he cried that morning . . . No trace of grief is left, abstractions taken first by the snows of reduction" (16).[2] Even the eminent dead of old Albany—the Banions, Skinners, and Whipples—would all succumb in time, their names eroded from the etched-in limestone grave markers. Their heirs would also succumb, first to the memory of their ancestors—the initial descent—then to the impermanence of their own being-in-time, and finally, through their posterity, to the collective erasure of all traces of existence. Or, in the elegiac mood of "the poet of order":

It is an illusion that we were ever alive,
Lived in the houses of mothers, arranged ourselves
By our own motions in a freedom of air.

Even our shadows, their shadows, no longer remain.
The lives these lived in the mind are at an end.[2]

It would take a figure like Francis, someone to sleep in the weeds and drink under the moon, to resurrect for better and for worse that which was dead and gone. This "tidy, sensitive" bum, as Rosskam the ragman calls him in *Ironweed*, is nothing less than the carrier of the dead, the voice and vision of his deceased family, forsaken loved ones, antagonizing haunts, and vanished hometown, all restored in memory, enhanced by reverie. Though the snows of reduction continue to descend, Francis struggles vigorously to sweep the drifts from his chilled shoulders, scraping his worn boots clean for the farther tramp.

Heavy, heavy, what hangs over . . . True to the epigraph from Dante's *Purgatorio, Ironweed* opens within the neighborhood of the dead. On the bum for twenty-two years, Francis Phelan takes on some day labor at Saint Agnes Cemetery. It is 1938, All Hallows' Eve, and Francis is working to pay off a debt to Marcus Gorman, an Albany lawyer who got him off on a technicality for registering twenty-one times to vote. More important than this pretext for being back in his hometown is the real and symbolic landscape of the dead that confronts him.

In the cemetery, death is at once physical and social, mimicking the hierarchical organization of humankind. The grandeur of Arthur T. Grogan's simulated Parthenon—built as if to ward off those mounting snows of reduction—depicts the prestigious dead, while monuments and cenotaphs mark off the next level of privileged ones. Francis, glancing over such finery, eventually locates his kith and kin among the undistinguished masses whose modest headstones and crosses define their backgrounds.

From underground, we glimpse the dead at various stages of rest and unrest. In fact, in the opening chapter their point of view is comically juxtaposed to the vaudevillian banter and gallows humor of Fran and his sidekick, Rudy. As Francis fills in the hollow graves of the recently deceased, the dust of his father and mother, and of the dead, both ancient and new, come to mind and narrative consciousness. Daddy Big Dugan, one-time Albany pool hustler, now among the freshly dead, advises him to avoid that which sent him down under: "Never inhale your own vomit" (5). Two brothers, both canallers killed and dumped into the Erie Canal in 1884, comment sympathetically on Francis's alcoholic desolation and outcast status: "The brothers looked at Francis's clothes, his ragged brown twill suit jacket, black baggy pants, and filthy fireman's blue shirt, and felt a kinship with him that owed nothing to blood ties" (3). The "tenement grave" of Strawberry Bill, once a fellow traveler, contrasts with the rich and powerful Grogan and reminds Francis of his own plight.

Although alive, Francis seems as good as dead. Marked for life by his experience with violent death and homelessness, he bears the death taint: ". . . he knew . . . that he would be this decayed self he had been so long in becoming, through all the endless years of his death" (99). One could call it stigmata, those befitting of his namesake, though drastically transvalued. But a special relationship to the past and to the otherworldly accompanies these stigmata, for it is through Francis, fallen and lowly mortal, that the dead—and old Albany, unreal city of the dead—rise to vibrant life again.

From the very beginning of the novel we face the naught of reduction, the new pits yawning underneath Francis and Rudy, the old pits rumbling for some measure of narrative space. Mr. Kennedy obliges, closing and opening those subterranean rooms of being and nothingness willy-nilly. In the process, certainly thought, memory, and influence have not perished from the earth. Rather, they remain; and they remain to taunt, jest, chastise, remember, sympathize, and provoke. The dead, in this flight of literary fancy, commune with the living—those transient products of America (to borrow a phrase from William Carlos Williams) gone crazy, but crazy on their own terms, the terms of the homeless—outsiders and outcasts to all that is and ever was, virtual cuckoos, loons, and bedbugs, in Francis's own benign slang toward his brethren. This affinity between the transient products gone and the transient homeless lingering, between physical death and social death, gives Francis an edge on death and its mysteries of being and nonbeing. In this sense, one could consider him among the eerie elect; for his life—what's left of it—adds up to a momentary stay against the rank forces of reduction.

The intimate relationship between the dead and the living dead (i.e., between literal and social death) is enriched symbolically by virtue of both time and place. As a homeless outcast, dead to his social world, Francis cuts a ghostly figure and appears as good a haunt as any to be in the cemetery on Halloween, the time "when grace is always in short supply, and the old and new dead walk abroad in this land" (29). This affinity between literal and social death is certified and mutually reinforced by virtue of Francis's membership in the "brotherhood of the desolate." As the setting for the novel shifts from the cemetery to the skid row mission, we see that, although the forms have changed, the underlying structure remains the same: "Bodies in alleys, bodies in gutters, bodies anywhere, were part of his eternal landscape: a physical litany of the dead" (29). Try as he might, he cannot escape the encompassing landscape; he cannot break away and release himself from the depth of his attachment to it. It is all that he is and, perhaps, will ever be.

Like his homeless kith, Francis had "lived long . . . suffered much, and was inching toward death." Living up to the fullest potential of his social descent and alienation as a homeless outsider, Francis, fully propelled into this downward thrust, accommodates his very identity and being to the utmost limits of failure, humiliation, and filth; he internalizes the derogatory definition leveled at his kind by the broader society. As Kenneth Burke would say, in an apt rephrasing of Aristotle's entelechial principle, he has grown "rotten with perfection."[3] As such, Francis carries the death taint, representing the very societal notions of pollution and taboo that are commensurate with social death and the suggestion of its literal counterpart. At the end of the long day, and now in the clean cultural domain of the Mission of Holy Redemption,

> he smelled his own uncanceled stink again, aware that it had intensified since morning. The sweat of a workday, the sourness of dried earth on his hands and clothes, the putrid perfume of the cemetery air with its pretension to windblown purity, all this lay in foul encrustation atop the private pestilence of his being. When he threw himself onto Gerald's grave, the uprush of a polluted life all but asphyxiated him. (33)

This inextricable relationship between literal and social death illuminates the two senses of reduction that bear upon Francis's life in the novel. The first sense of reduction, as previously presented, is universal in nature: mortality, time's relentless erasure of human form and its traces in collective memory. No less devastating, though not as yet final, the second sense of reduction exists in the realm of society. It is embodied in the identity of *bum*, or better yet, *good for nothing bum, filthy bum*, as the popular phrases go. The peculiar achievement of being a homeless outsider requires this total reduction in social status, the result of a process of descent, redefinition, and accommodation to a lasting condition of estrangement.

The correspondence between these two senses of reduction is direct and immediate, a fusion of the universal and social conditions into a totality of absence and presence. For, though drifting into nothingness, "inching toward death," Francis, by virtue of his reduction in social being, both loses and gains in this version of the Faustian bargain. Strangely, his losses not only fund but compound his interest in attaining a synthesis of death, memory, and the supernatural. His penetrating insights into the seamless dimensions of both mortal and immortal existence are granted as if in compensation for his sacrificial derangement in society. Francis and his "brotherhood" become "martyrs to wrath, to booze, to failure, to loss, to hostile weather" (76). It is through this brand of martyrdom, perfectly amplified by All Saints' Day (which encompasses more than half of the novel's time period), that they rise in kindred spirit with the anonymous and martyred dead.

Do not be misled. The "brotherhood of the desolate" stands in ironic contrast to their more venerated counterparts; clearly, members of the former are martyrs of a different order. Perhaps it is fairer to say that they are martyrs of disorder, gaining in symbolic currency in direct proportion to their degradation. Nevertheless, the currency is real and its exchange value sky high. To the extent that the role of martyr mixes with that of homeless survivor, Francis (and the reader) will continue to reap the grisly profits.

As Robert Jay Lifton has so rightly asserted, "The profoundest insight is attainable only by the survivor: he who has touched death in some bodily or psychic way and has himself remained alive."[4] In general, for the homeless survivors among us, the insights that accrue from their daily rounds include the following: a heightened awareness of life's horrors and tragic ironies; a mastery of the strategies for survival; the wisdom and pride granted from living on the streets; a sharpened knack for gallows humor; a flood of unconscious logic and power; and the felt experience of distress wrought by loss, by distortion, and by silences so deep, so contagious, that the possibility of sound seems a miracle of creation.

In particular, for the fictionalized Francis, he has no doubt touched death physically and absorbed it psychically, and has remained alive, barely. Like all genuine survivors, he remains behind to reveal the trivial, the grotesque, the bizarre, and those more profound insights of his arcane knowledge, a comprehension given by his special status—one emerging from beneath the bottom of the social hierarchy. Although crushed in body and mind, and broken in spirit, Francis, empowered from below, fuses the disparate elements of people and places, gone but not utterly. They too survive through the *achievements* of this outcast and survivor. This special status unstiffens Francis's being, bringing him into frequent and close association with the specter, consciousness, and memory of the dead. It enables him to transform nothing into something, like no other insider to society—necessarily stiffened and indifferent—could manage. Through Francis, both experience and perception are intensified in order to maintain a continuity of community and meaning, thereby staving off the gathering snows of reduction, which threaten at every moment and at every turn to dissolve such continuity.

But for now, interested more in the dissolute, downside of that Faustian bargain, a further examination of social reduction is in order. Since social death rests in the lower regions of disorder, its link with pollution and taboo, and its necessary opposition to Order, enlarges both the cultural meaning and social significance of the issues at hand. The dividing line between Order and Disorder is paralleled by the division between home and homelessness. If we regard the conception and existence of home as something essential to American society, then the meaning of homelessness becomes apparent by means of a simple inversion: "less-than-home."[5] To say that to be homeless is to be "less-than-home" reflects simultaneously the social reduction of the Other and the basic assumptions of culture itself, that is, how it understands and organizes social experience.

As a fundamental unit of social order, *home* presupposes a commitment to the broader culture's guiding ethos: a belief in family, stability, income, prestige, cleanliness, and the materialistic and rationalistic emphases that go hand-in-hand with private ownership. The reigning ideology embraces the primary goods bound up with capitalism, technology, bureaucracy, utility, competition, and success. In short, home, made out of the brick and mortar of American ideology, and reiterated throughout society, builds the social order, which is necessary for living, working, and reproducing in time. Therefore, to be "less-than-home" is to be living outside of the established and accepted spheres of social idea, value, and construction.

As outsiders, the homeless disrupt this cultural ethos and practice of social order. In doing so, whether wittingly or unwittingly, they are regarded as dirt, the rot and "uncanceled stink" of the relatively uncontaminated social landscape. According to the cultural anthropologist Mary Douglas, "dirt is essentially disorder"; and if, as Douglas argues, "dirt offends against order," then the homeless outcasts must be seen as the flagging dissidents of good order, the very detritus of *homo hierarchus*.[6] Mining a similar vein as Douglas, though from a different angle, Kenneth Burke discovers an even more essential proposition, which can be used as a fundamental support for the connection between order and disorder. From Burke's perspective, "implicit in the idea of Order is the idea of disobedience." In urging us to recall the story of Genesis, the Creation of unity and the Fall into divisiveness, Burke reveals the motive of this principle:

> Both Satan (in his rebellion) and Adam (in his fall) have a particular role to play. Their role is to *represent the principle of disobedience implicit in the idea of Order*. In this role, they *necessarily* fail to persevere in virtue. *For how otherwise could they properly represent the principle of disobedience?* Is not their disobedience a narrative requirement of their role?[7]

In bringing the insights of both Douglas and Burke to the surface, they can be thus pressured into a new amalgam: As an embodiment of dirt and as an expression of disorder, homelessness represents one of the most dramatic forms of a falling away from the social order, away from the idea of unity. Moreover, in transgressing cherished cultural notions and values inherent in the construct of good order, the homeless violate inadvertently a social taboo. Like Douglas's definition of dirt, the homeless have become "matter out of place," threatening by the trajectory of their fall, menacing by *virtue* of their pollutants. But the process does not end here, for such matters, in turn, evoke the prevailing culture's deeply felt sense of fear, disgust, and uncertainty. For a society suffused with the "hierarchal psychosis," such sins of transgression are ever before it and must be continually rejected.[8]

Such a major transgression of Order, and the symbolic load of pollution and taboo that accompanies it, engenders a crisis of ambiguity in the larger society. By what means resolution? That old handy device of expulsion, taken from the certain Biblical hand of the One and placed into the shaking secular hands of the many, is bound to fail out of sheer mortal ineptitude. Though try we shall, fail we must. No, our narrative of order has been diminished, and so the reigning paradigm is fright, uncertainty, mystification, perhaps even victimization. No doubt, society becomes unsettled by the breach between valued American ideals (and principles of order) and the collective signs of disorder and failure in its midst. As witnessed in the novel with Reverend Chester and the Mission of Holy Redemption, this cultural ambiguity demands resolution of a different kind: terms for reordering the social design, and principles, rules, and practices to impose a sense of unity onto the fragmented social system. The program to settle the ambiguity wrought up over transgression demands atonement and conduct that conforms to the ideals of good citizen, humble servant: "No booze, no smoking upstairs (for drunks are fire hazards), carry your share of the work load, and then rise you must, rise you will, into the brilliant embrace of the just God" (43). In the absence of such corrective and purifying processes, society will relegate (not expel) the dirt to the appropriate zones of human discard: skid rows, flophouses, hobo jungles, railroads, and weeds. (These zones can be easily updated to fit our present situation.) By regulating disorder in this manner, that which is uncertain and threatening is either reassimilated into the good society, or resolved symbolically via the principle of unity through segregation. In both cases, however casuistically managed, the idea of order is reclaimed.[9]

In the novel, Reverend Chester is one traditional agent for the restoration of good order in the lives of the hard-core homeless. His setting for rescue and rehabilitation is, of course, the skid row Mission, a kind of halfway house where the dynamic forces of order and disorder collide. The agency of his mission is the evangelical Christ, whom Chester enlists to help put the wayward back on the right path: "'Who will save you from your sloth? Who will give you a ride on the turnpike to salvation? Jesus will! Jesus delivers!'" Chester, a recovered alcoholic, took the ride years ago himself and now, on the straight and narrow, resolves—with a little help from on high—to bring "the dipsos, the deadbeats, the wetbrains, and the loonies" back into the bound traffic and defined lanes of that one-way pike. As the Reverend surveys his lost flock from the lectern, his thoughts run both ways—toward the crossroads of rule and rabble:

> What they needed was a structured way, a mentor and guide through the hells and purgatories of their days. Bringing the word, the light, was a great struggle today, for the decline of belief was rampant and the anti-Christ was on the rise. It was prophesied in Matthew and in Revelation that there would be less and less reverence for the Bible, greater lawlessness, depravity, and self-indulgence. The world, the light, the song, they would all die soon, for without doubt we were witnessing the advent of end times. (34)

Despite the despair over the seeming predominance of "end times," Chester pulls out all the stops for salvation: ". . . .He breaks the power of canceled sin, He sets the prisoner free; His blood can make the foulest clean, His blood availed for me." But the men, and one woman (Helen), are not buying it. "Well not me, Francis said to his unavailed-for self" (33). The transgression cannot be so easily undone, nor the filth removed with a mere flick of the wrist. Chester's vision of good order, which combines Christian morality with the Protestant ethic and bourgeois individualism, is one that employs religious salvation and unity to legitimize the social order. But the rhetoric hollows, and, when the Reverend implores the brethren to come front and center for the obligatory nosedive, no one moves, no one seriously considers taking the Reverend up on his offering of a "structured way," though there is a great rush toward the daily bread and soup of the house upon the long awaited "amen."

At the very best, Chester and his program manage to put a roof over the disorder and arrest its development into a further chaos ever broadened and deepened by the Depression era. But the program, with its tidy insistence upon the necessary social qualities of accepted conduct (sober, clean, upright, productive, etc.) fails abysmally to prick the conscience of the homeless. They remain true to their oppositional form, and resist the imposition of evil, sin, atonement, and the principle of obedience that underlies their potential reintegration into the social order. They hold fast to the requirements of their role, ever subverting, ever frustrating the attempt by the agents of culture to resolve the ambiguity:

> They were . . . questing for the behavior that was proper to their station and their unutterable dreams. They . . . knew intimately the etiquette, the taboos, the protocol of bums. By their talk to each other they understood that they shared a belief in the brotherhood of the desolate; yet in the scars of their eyes they confirmed that no such fraternity had ever existed, that the only brotherhood they belonged to was the one that asked that enduring question: How do I get through the next twenty minutes? They feared drys, cops, jailers, bosses, moralists, crazies, truth-tellers, and one another. They loved storytellers, liars, whores, fighters, singers, collie dogs that wagged their tails, and generous bandits. Rudy, thought Francis: he's just a bum, but who ain't? (23–24)

That last line brings to mind a seasoned quip from a real homeless man who lived on the New York Bowery: "Remember, you can't spell bum without 'u' in it."[10] A fine statement to clinch that implicit connection between the realms of order and disorder. For Francis, the disorder manifested by the "bum" is projected outward and upward, counterbalancing the Reverend's projection of order to all those below.

But Francis and his ilk are outnumbered, and they are constantly put in their place—reduced—by the handy rhetoric of condemnation. "You're a bum," the good Reverend reminds them (43). Disorder is thus classified, made visible, and renounced in ritual fashion. Or, as Rosskam the ragman concludes after a day's work with Francis, reinforcing the deadening level of reduction: "A bum is a bum" (150). There is nothing to be derived from this identity other than its echo of nonexistence. The point is brought home in a luminous detail during the Mission scene when a young man, soon to be evicted from his residence there for being drunk (on two beers), enters: "He held the doorknob with one hand and stood directly under the inside ceiling light, casting no shadow" (42). Immediately sniffed out by the preacher, he is duly confronted and dismissed from the site. The Mission, as an outpost for a righteous society, is hell-bent on holding up order (and its sign of sobriety) as an ideal, and punishing disorder as defilement. Emblematic of "matter out of place," this homeless man is so dead to his society that he casts no shadow in the world of rescue and rehabilitation. Like the "brotherhood" to which he belongs, he is so thoroughly reduced in social standing that his claims to being are rendered naught. Thus evicted, he is made most conscious of his sin of transgression, his disobedience to the principles of social order. The Reverend admonishes: "Oh no. You're in the beyond. . . . You are a contumacious young man" (43–44). Once classified as a polluted Other, he is then given the bum's rush. If you will, contrast this figure with Dante who, even in the Christian underworld, has enough corporeal substance to cast a shadow, thus verifying his status as worldly being, much to the consternation of the shades around him.

For the homeless, cast out and diminished, to throw a shadow onto their delimited social world is no small achievement. It is the very sign of presence, and the challenge to Francis and his cohort throughout their trials in the novel will be to establish, however meager, a sense of dignity, worth, and merit to their lives. Although fighting a downhill battle against both the external forces of order and the internal implosion of disorder, the effort to meet such a challenge is all that they have left; it is a sign that they remain alive to the human need for meaning and purpose. At certain turns in the novel, the reader stumbles upon such attempts to turn nothing into something, however small the result. Francis's and Rudy's encounter with Sandra, "doing the dead man's float in the dust: face down, arms forward, legs spread" in the vacant lot next to the Mission (30), is one case in point. Filled with the "poison," she too is denied entry into the Mission. As Francis and Rudy see to her, providing soup and blankets, they not only try to fix her present predicament but manage to reach backward in time to that which is not this. Francis begins the dialogue:

> "She a bum or just on a heavy drunk?"
> "She's a bum."
> "She looks like a bum."
> "She's been a bum all her life."
> "No," said Francis. "Nobody's a bum all their life. She hada been somethin' once."
> "She was a whore before she was a bum."
> "And what about before she was a whore?"
> "I don't know," Rudy said. "She just talks about whorin' in Alaska. Before that I guess she was just a little kid."
> "Then that's somethin'. A little kid's somethin' that ain't a bum or a whore." (31)

Although Sandra is later found dead from the freezing cold, partially chewed away by the dogs, with no one who can recall her last name, at least something has been salvaged from her anonymous reduction. And yet, characteristic throughout the novel, such a trace of redeeming light is often held in contention with its opposite. Not knowing her surname doesn't make much difference now that she is dead, Francis concludes, but then again, as Pee Wee reminds him, it never made much difference anyway.

Other examples that reflect such contention between worth and worthlessness (the quiet affirmation of a valued life paired with the growing menace of social death) appear frequently throughout the story, confirming the dynamic interaction between order and disorder that moves the novel along. The resulting powerful torque reveals the driving force of Kennedy's novelistic vision, one marked by complexity, ambiguity, and by an interest in the relentless antinomies of the mind. Along for the ride, we are moved to meditate on the matters at hand, "matter out of place," and matter firmly fixed in place. It seems as though Kennedy's novelistic purpose realized in *Ironweed* works to fulfill Douglas's intellectual thesis: "Reflection on dirt involves reflection on the relation of order to disorder, being to non-being, form to formlessness, life to death."[11] Kennedy raises all of these relations into the imaginary light of fiction for our own vicarious involvement, immediate circumspection, and sustained contemplation. In the present light of the bum's classic duet, those gravelly voices that float both down and out of the matter, one is reminded of the one-two combination of inferiority and outsiderhood that brings on the snows of reduction, laying one's being flat out on the slab of social death. All the better then to appreciate the flight of Rudy's vagrant refrain: "Where the wind don't blow. . . . I wanna go where the wind don't blow, where there ain't no snow" (196).

Notes

1. The quoted phrase—"one by one they were all becoming shades"—is taken from James Joyce's short story "The Dead," in *Dubliners* (New York: Penguin, 1992), 224.

Since Joyce is one likely ancestor for Kennedy's own Irish American literary sensibility, the selection of the quote (and the source) is not arbitrary. In this story of reunion and celebration around the time of the Epiphany in Victorian Dublin, the image of snow and the feeling of impending mortality combine throughout the tale, blending together tone, texture, and theme. The resonant meaning of William Kennedy's phrase "snows of reduction" is discerned in Joyce's story, particularly at the very end when Joyce evokes the consciousness of death in his main character: "[Gabriel's] soul had approached that region where dwell the vast hosts of the dead. He was conscious of, but could not apprehend, their wayward and flickering existence. His own identity was fading out into a gray impalpable world" (222–225).

The phrase "the snow was general all over Ireland," which appears twice in Joyce's story, is an existential forecast for the human condition. It certifies the senses of reduction: the trajectory of our mortal lives and the very "general" dissolution of structure—of "the solid world itself" (225, 212).

2. In the conclusion to his novel *Very Old Bones*, Kennedy alludes to "the poet of order." This poet is none other than Wallace Stevens, and Kennedy invokes several lines from Stevens's poem "The Dwarf," weaving them into the main character's own thoughts on the mysteries of the universe. See William Kennedy, *Very Old Bones* (New York: Penguin, 1992), 292.

Similarly, I invoke Stevens here to strike an elegiac mood befitting my evocation of the "snows of reduction." The lines are from Stevens's poem "The Rock," from *The Collected Poems of Wallace Stevens* (New York: Knopf, 1954), 525.

3. For the ironic implications of perfection as a motivating principle of the "symbol-using animal," see Kenneth Burke, *Language as Symbolic Action* (Berkeley: University of California Press, 1966), 16–20.

Burke adapts Aristotle's entelechial principle, "the notion that each being aims at the perfection natural to its kind" (17), but limits his use of the principle to the domain of symbolic action. Burke also broadens the motive of perfection to include its ironic meaning, "as when we speak of a 'perfect fool' or a 'perfect villain' " (39).

Therefore, to speak of Francis and his ilk as being "rotten with perfection" registers the notion that social context shapes the direction (upward or downward) of the compelling teleological forces inherent in the motivating principle. In the case of the "brotherhood of the desolate," Burke would call the irresistible impulse toward the "irrational" counterpart of Order an example of a "transcendence downward." In keeping with his nature as social outcast, Francis adapts the sights of the "symbol-using animal" accordingly.

4. Quoted in Benedict Giamo and Jeffrey Grunberg, *Beyond Homelessness: Frames of Reference* (Iowa City: University of Iowa Press, 1992), 136. For further reading on Robert Jay Lifton's insights into the survivor, see the following: *History and Human Survival* (New York: Random House, 1970); *The Future of Immortality* (New York: Basic Books, 1987); and *Death in Life: Survivors of Hiroshima* (Chapel Hill: University of North Carolina Press, 1991, 1968), 479–541.

5. The phrase "less-than-home" was spoken by Jerzy Kosinski, interview with Giamo and Grunberg, *Beyond Homelessness*, 32. This expression served to sharpen Kosinski's "optics" on homelessness and clarify his overall perspective. For the full context of the phrase, see "Chance Beings," in *Beyond Homelessness*, 32–49.

6. Mary Douglas, *Purity and Danger: An Analysis of Concepts of Pollution and Taboo* (London: Routledge & Kegan Paul, 1966), 2. For further discussion on the relation of "dirt" to the symbolic systems of order and disorder, see chapters 2 and 10, "Secular Defilement" and "The System Shattered and Renewed," respectively.

7. Kenneth Burke, "Order, Action, and Victimage," in *The Concept of Order*, ed. Paul Kuntz (Seattle and London: University of Washington Press, 1968), 187, 189.

8. The phrase "hierarchal psychosis" was frequently used by Burke to encompass the social order-at-large. See, for instance, *Permanence and Change* (Los Altos, CA: Hermes, 1935, 1954), 292–294.

9. Such a symbolic resolution has been the one constant throughout the history of homelessness in America. From the almshouse to skid row to the shelter, the reclamation of unity through the segregation of disorder has appeared to be the primary motive behind the public response. Though the situation of disorder still exists, the root conflict (between the ideals of democratic liberalism and the facts that would assert otherwise) is eased through its concealment; therefore, the crisis of ambiguity that had widened is now settled. Because of its continued dispersion and visibility, the new conditions of homelessness make any facile resolution of the conflict difficult to sustain, and any final settling of the crisis a momentary stay against a larger breakdown in the social order.

10. Benedict Giamo, *On the Bowery: Confronting Homelessness in American Society* (Iowa City: University of Iowa Press, 1989), 214. To put the quip within the broader social context of the modern Bowery, and its homeless subculture, see 171–203.

11. Douglas, *Purity and Danger*, 5.

This essay was presented at "William Kennedy: A Celebration . . . A Symposium on His Work" held at the Omni Albany Hotel (now Hilton Albany), Albany, New York, on April 15–17, 1999. It also appears, in a slightly altered form, in Benedict Giamo's book *The Homeless of "Ironweed": Blossoms on the Crag* (Iowa City: University of Iowa Press, 1996), 1–18. Printed with permission © University of Iowa Press, and Benedict Giamo. Quotations from William Kennedy's *Ironweed* are from the paperback edition (New York: Penguin Books, 1984).

A Magical Time in Albany

Christian Michener

> At some point, of course, there will be no more Albany novels, but for now, of what we do have, each book serves as both an epilogue and a prelude to another: their plots and characters refer back and forth to other books, prefiguring what is to come or revealing what follows.
>
> —Christian Michener

Thanks to William Kennedy and his work, the city of Albany now appears starred on the map of American literature along with places such as Sherwood Anderson's Winesburg, Ohio, and William Faulkner's Yoknapatawpha County. But in this essay I would like to look not at "place" so much as at "time" in discussing the Albany of the Phelans, Daughertys, Quinns, and other important characters who people Kennedy's Albany Cycle. Ultimately this look at "time" will take us back to "place," to Albany, as I hope to show the novels in Kennedy's cycle all share a special conception of time, but one that is predicated on a sense of the active presence of the past, or of history. Of course, the history we are talking about is the history of Albany, whether the real American city or its imagined counterpart in Kennedy's fiction. What I would like to point out overall is what a magical time Albany offers.

The magical strain in Kennedy's work has already been noticed by critics, and Kennedy often finds his work being discussed as an example of contemporary magical realism.[1] I would like to refine this approach in several ways. First, while Kennedy's Albany Cycle does in fact often embrace a magical realist perspective on the world, it does so, as previously noted, not so much through an emphasis on a magical geography or action or character as through an emphasis on a magical kind of time, a time that is fluid and reversible and that offers—though it cannot promise—the opportunity for the redemption and forgiveness of its characters. Secondly, as already implied, Kennedy's brand of fictional magic differs from the common conception of magical realism in how it is located so emphatically within one specific and recognizable locale, that of Albany. Lastly, Kennedy differs from many of the magical realist writers to whom he is comparable in that his work both reduces and extends what is meant by "magical." This may sound paradoxical, but as we shall see, Kennedy's novels sometimes reduce the magical world by isolating it to a few specific incidents or characters, as happens in several of the early novels. But then, by the end of the cycle, the Albany novels extend the arena of the magical by embracing art—or its counterpart, the imagination—as the source of magic in the narrative. This focus on art and its power replaces the magical narratives of the earlier works but continues what they began, the implicit critique of the limits and confidence of empiricism and rationalism that survive so confidently in realistic texts.

In magical realist works, real events, those crafted through verisimilitude and adhering to expected laws of physics and to predictable behaviors of psychology, are without comment interwoven with magical and fantastic events. In the work of Gabriel García Márquez, the classic exemplar of magical realism, women ascend into heaven, paper turns into a butterfly and flies, and men with enormous wings descend from the skies. In William Kennedy's work, Francis Phelan walks onto a bus and confronts a man who has been dead for decades. One helpful way to understand magical realism is to note Scott Simpkins's schema (141) in which he lists characteristics which distinguish realism from magical realism (see table 1). By listing these characteristics side by side, Simpkins hopes to show the contrasts between realism and magical realism, although obviously one must approach this list holistically rather than as a catalogue of required characteristics or ones exclusive to one mode of representation or the other.

TABLE 1

REALISM	**MAGIC REALISM**
History	Myth/Legend
Mimetic	Fantastic/Supplementation
Familiarization	Defamiliarization
Empiricism/Logic	Mysticism/Magic
Narration	Meta-narration
Closure-ridden/Reductive	Open-ended/Expansive
Naturalism	Romanticism
Rationalization/Cause and Effect	Imagination/Negative Capability

In addition to the insights Simpkins provides, it is important to note also what simultaneously distinguishes magical realism from its two cousins, fantasy on the one hand and realism on the other. As Amaryll Beatrice Chanady reminds us, perhaps no characteristic is more important in this distinction than "authorial reticence"—namely, that the narrative voice in the magical realist work cannot pause or show surprise over a magical event. If the text does express surprise, then the magic does not seem "real" but "unreal" and unexpected. Such surprise invades and draws distinctions between worlds that are meant to be seamlessly combined in the magical realist universe.

However we distinguish these categories—the fantastic, the real, and the magically real—the distinction is more than an enjoyable literary game, for what constitutes something "magical" often involves potentially volatile discussions of cultural notions of belief or the dominance of Western rationalism in the modern world. As a literary development, magical realism has often, though not exclusively, been seen as an expression of rebellion by historically marginalized groups, as a way of challenging the cultural hegemony and historical monopoly of those in power. Some argue that is why the notion of magical realism is so closely associated, especially at its outset, with Latin American fiction, work that emerges from areas in which the Spanish European culture clashed so painfully with that of the indigenous people, and why the style of magical realism appears so eloquently in works from authors of historically marginalized groups—such as what we see in the novels of Louise Erdrich or Toni Morrison. These novels are often read as critiques not only of those who control power—the whites, the Europeans, the men—but also as a challenge to the Western reliance on such "un-magical" notions as empiricism and rationalism.

Obviously William Kennedy's work, situated so precisely and consistently in a northern industrialized city colonized by Europeans, is a far cry from those cultures found in García Márquez or Erdrich. But Kennedy does offer a similar vision and, implicitly, a similar critique. His interest in Albany affords him a historical glance at the once-marginalized Irish of the city, and if today we feel that this group has safely assimilated itself into American culture, we at least can recognize the critique of Western empiricism implicit in Kennedy's appreciation of living history, the presence of the past in our lives. In Kennedy's work, knowledge is never permanent or stable, time never absolute, history never only chronological. Recognizing these characteristics of history in Kennedy's fiction becomes particularly important in some of the later books of the Albany Cycle, for by then, most notably in *Very Old Bones* and *The Flaming Corsage*, we have left behind the more familiar examples of magical realism that we find, say, in *Ironweed*, and instead live in a world where magic is located in the imagination, the world of the artist: the magic is still there, but we have moved, as we shall see, from a familiar example of magical realism to a familiar example of postmodernism. We make the journey, though, without ever leaving Albany and while still residing in narratives dependent upon the fluidity of time and at ease with uncertainty, intuition, and possibility, all far cries from the confidence and certainty of Western empiricism and realism. Even Kennedy's *Roscoe*, in some ways Kennedy's most traditionally realistic work, relies on uncertainty in both its plot and in the surreal viewpoints of its interchapters.

Kennedy acknowledges the magical world of Albany, and, in fact, its magical control over time, in the opening essay in his collection *O Albany!* The essay appears not insignificantly in the section entitled "The Magical Places." In this introductory essay, Kennedy writes,

> [Albany] is centered squarely in the American and the human continuum, a magical place where the past becomes visible if one is willing to track the multiple incarnations of the city's soul. I confront even a single street corner and there emerges an archetypal as well as an historical context in which to view the mutations of its trees, its telephone poles.
>
> It is the task of this and other books I have written, and hope to write, to peer into the heart of this always-shifting past, to be there when it ceases to be what it was, when it becomes what it must become under scrutiny, when it turns so magically, so inevitably, from then into now. (7)

As this statement makes clear, Kennedy himself addresses the magical notion of time—the way it allows for the archetypal to emerge from the historical, the way it turns so "magically . . . from then into now"—and simultaneously reveals that this magic is firmly rooted in the experience of a particular place, the street corners and telephone poles that are part of the soul of the city of Albany.

Kennedy first came to explore this magical side of Albany in an anonymous way through his first novel, *The Ink Truck*. Like the novels we will discuss more fully later, *The Ink Truck* involves a magical journey through time, in this case in the trip that its protagonist takes one day into the past of the city as he attempts to struggle through a newspaper strike in which he is the most significant—and sometimes only—participant. But while Albany is recognizable in *The Ink Truck*,[2] it does not appear as a named locale until *Legs*, the novel that is most often cited as beginning the Albany Cycle. In *Legs*, friends and admirers of Jack "Legs" Diamond, a real-life 1920s gangster, assemble over drinks several decades after his death and begin to reminisce about him. They ascribe to him such magical powers as tying both his shoes at once or turning on a light by snapping his fingers, and then the novel turns back in time to explore Diamond's life. Although this reminiscing is only a metaphorical return to the past, Diamond's life does indeed seem "magical" in the way that it takes the shape of a perverted and dark storybook fairy tale as Diamond rises to the top of his own little illegal kingdom. At one point, the narrator Marcus Gorman describes Diamond's "mythic vehicle" as it tries to make its way up an "enchanted mountain" (78), and in one scene Diamond is described dancing with his wife and mistress simultaneously as they spin "up, up, and up into the ethereal sphere where people truly know how to be happy" (248). In addition, Diamond's continued ability to evade the law and repeated assassination attempts can only be described, as they will explicitly be, as miraculous.

All of these instances, however, could be hyperbole or metaphor. But in at least one instance we have what would be considered a classic example of magical realism. While Diamond is returning from a trip to Europe by ship, he descends into the hold and notices a shipment of canaries. For some reason, the birds all instantly stop singing as soon as Diamond enters, as if they had a magical awareness of the evil nature of the criminal who is watching them. And when Diamond puts his hand into one of the cages, a bird pecks at it and instantly falls dead. Later Diamond learns that the sailor who has been caring for the birds has feathers on his biceps and, so the sailor says, used to be a barn swallow (113).

Although instances of such magical moments appear in *Legs*, and will appear again in most of the other novels, it is only in *Ironweed* that the entire narrative moves along the obviously magical-realist plane. But what does appear consistently in each of the novels is the magical sense of time. In the closing chapters of *Legs*, this magical time appears at the moment of Jack Diamond's death. In this chapter, the mortally wounded—in fact, dead—Jack Diamond impossibly converses with the narrator, Marcus Gorman, as well as the newspaperman Damon Runyon, a favorite of Kennedy's, though neither Gorman nor Runyon could have been present at Diamond's death. This magical chapter begins with the "incipiently dead" Diamond realizing what has happened to him—he has been shot, gunned down by unknown killers (though Kennedy will create ones later in *Roscoe*)—and then thinks "out of his dead brain" (315). Diamond is moving, as Kennedy significantly writes, "outside time" (315) into a narrative moment free of the restricted linearity of realism. A mysterious vortex of gray and yellow light spins around Diamond's body and seems to be Diamond himself; soon it begins to fade away, taking Diamond with it, but Diamond gets in the last words of the book: " 'Honest to

God, Marcus,' he says to Gorman, 'I really don't think I'm dead' " (317). In this magical death scene, the narrative abandons without comment the believable linearity of normal chronology, as well as the notions of realistic character and space, and winds up the book in an eschatological moment of mystical becoming (or unbecoming).

The mystical moment "outside" of time at the end of *Legs* would be noteworthy on its own as a sign of the magical tendencies in Kennedy's fiction, but here we are seeing it in the context of its introducing the magical awareness of time itself that pervades Kennedy's Albany Cycle. Like *Legs*, *Billy Phelan's Greatest Game*, the second book of the Albany Cycle, is not without its own "magical moments" also; of these moments, in fact, one not only toys with the notion of time but also introduces the related theme of the retrieval of that time, of regaining the past in order to overcome the problems, the origins of which lie within that past. In this novel, Billy Phelan, the small-time hustler and son of the Francis Phelan hero of *Ironweed*, attempts to negotiate his way through the days of the kidnapping of Charlie Boy McCall, an acquaintance of Billy's and the son of the powerful political McCall family in Kennedy's fictional Albany. The problem for Billy is that the McCalls hope for his help in catching the kidnappers, while for Billy it goes against his personal code of ethics to rat on anyone. When Billy thus refuses to help the McCalls, they pull the plug on his gambling privileges, and it is only with the help of the older newspaperman, Martin Daugherty, that Billy is eventually restored to good graces. Part of this restoration, however, derives from Billy accidentally—and without even knowing it—having important information about where, in fact, the kidnappers end up hiding. In a realistic text, this information would be pure coincidence, and it might even come up for criticism as a violation of verisimilitude. But in Kennedy's world, and particularly in the world of Martin Daugherty, a self-labeled "mystical naturalist" (24), Billy's inadvertent help makes perfect sense, as it does to Kennedy himself, who calls Billy a "mystical catalyst."[3] Martin Daugherty writes that Billy's advice about the kidnappers is a sign of "insight as much touched with magic, or spiritual penetration of the future, as was any utterance of the biblical prophets which time has proved true" (272). Billy's accidental awareness is, thus, in its own way, an acknowledgment of the fluidity of time: we can know the future now, as in the future we can also know our past.

Despite the insistence here from Martin and from Kennedy himself on Billy's magic prescience, it is Martin Daugherty himself who, in fact, makes the journey through time that serves such an important thematic role in the novels of the Albany Cycle. Martin's particular journey, occurring as it does while the McCall kidnapping case unfolds, concerns the enormously complicated events surrounding the love nest scandal that will itself be the subject of *The Flaming Corsage*. This novel, and the play of the same name written by Martin's father, details the complex circumstances of an affair Martin's father purportedly had with a beautiful actress, Melissa Spencer, many years earlier. Part of this complicated story involves the fact that Martin himself had an affair with Melissa, in part to avenge himself on his father for cheating on his mother. In the time of the narrative in *Billy Phelan,* Melissa has returned to Albany to act in the very play about her, although, curiously, she takes the role of the "other woman," Martin's own mother. When Martin goes to see the play, he thus finds himself watching his own life, his own past, reenacted on stage.

After seeing the play, Martin rejoins Melissa in order for the two of them to have sex again, to reenact their earlier affair. As Martin and Melissa make love, Martin has a vision of a mysterious light and of a goat-like figure, seemingly representing lust,[4] that had also appeared to him earlier in the day. A huge scar, inspired in Martin's mind by the scar his mother bore from a fire, grows and floats behind him and Melissa. Into this white scar a "maternal flame" appears and burns up the goat-child (209–210). While it is true that Martin "saw to it" that the goat-figure was there, and thus that the whole scene might be his hallucination, the figure itself, as well as the light behind Martin, seems to take on a life of its own. The scene is neither realistic nor hallucinatory, and it becomes thus a magically real moment in Martin's metaphorical return to his past. This past is, of course, inextricably connected, as always, to Albany itself, where at the end of the novel the resurrected Billy enters "Louie's pool room, a place where even serious men sometimes go to seek the meaning of magical webs, mystical coin, golden birds, and other artifacts of the only cosmos in town" (282).

While this reading of *Billy Phelan* both limits and yet admits the magical notion of the world of the novel, there is yet another magic at work in the book that must be mentioned because it reveals a special twist to the notion of magical narrative as it appears in Kennedy's work. That twist is the magical nature of art. As we will see most notably in *Quinn's Book* and *Very Old Bones*, art in Kennedy's work offers the possibility of healing, a means of redemption for the artist or the subjects of their art. In *Billy Phelan*, the art is the reenactment of Edward Daugherty's play, *The Flaming Corsage*; its dramatization allows Martin to reenact his own "debauch" with Melissa Spencer and in the process admit to his "psychic mendacity" (214) concerning the affair. Through this process, he heals himself, a fact verified by what he does after he has sex with Melissa—he helps Charlie Boy McCall, reconciles himself with family members, and delivers an important letter to the *Times Union* that encourages the McCalls to forgive Billy Phelan. And all of this takes place because of the healing nature of art, the play Martin watched; and art is, of course, as Keats so ably noted in "Ode on a Grecian Urn," a timeless and eternal world, a world outside of history. It is also significantly the realm of the "imagination," one of the very characteristics of magical realism we saw proposed by Scott Simpkins.

While *Billy Phelan's Greatest Game* may serve as a limited introduction to the magical time of Albany, the same is not true of the next novel, *Ironweed*, a book that is often cited as the very example of what one means by magical realism itself. From the very beginning of the book, in which Francis Phelan journeys to a cemetery and various Albany shades, including relatives and friends of his, comment on his presence, we are clearly in a world in which the magical occurs unquestionably within the real and where the past will play an active, living role in the present. The traditional linear progression of time, ending as it does for all of us in death, does not describe the Albany of *Ironweed*, where around the feast of Halloween in 1938, the dead actually move among the living.

In *Ironweed*, the Francis of 1938 is about to begin a quest into all-time, into numerous times of his life, one that will be centered squarely within the continuum of Albany history. That quest is ordained, and the magical world of Albany affirmed, by one of the most significant dead who appear in the novel, Gerald Phelan, the two-week-old baby Francis accidentally killed in 1916. From his grave Gerald decides "through an act of silent will" to impose "on his father the pressing obligation to perform . . . final acts of expiation for abandoning the family" (19). Obviously such a charge from the long-dead son of Francis Phelan puts us into a magical world. Ghosts are, in fact, a familiar site in magical realist fiction, as readers of Toni Morrison and other writers are aware.[5] And in the course of Kennedy's novel, covering three days in which Francis Phelan wanders through the city of Albany, ghosts from his past appear to Francis and haunt him into returning to his wife and home. Because of the point of view of the opening section of the novel, we know that these ghosts are not Francis's hallucinations, and so when Harold Allen, a trolley scab Francis killed with a rock during a strike in 1901, appears on a bus, neither we nor the narrator pause or doubt. And as should be obvious too, the appearance of Allen and the other ghosts in the book is a manifestation of the fluid nature of time in this magical Albany: the past and the present have converged and created a magically new world. Ghosts, as Lois Parkinson Zamora emphasizes, serve an important role in magical realist texts. "Magical realist apparitions . . . ," writes Parkinson Zamora,

> unsettle modernity's (and the novel's) basis in progressive, linear history: they float free in time, not just here and now but then and there, eternal and everywhere. Ghosts embody the

> fundamental magical realist sense that reality always exceeds our capacities to describe or understand or prove and that the function of literature is to engage this excessive reality, to honor that which we may grasp intuitively but never fully or finally define. Magical realist texts ask us to look beyond the limits of the knowable, and ghosts are often our guides. (498)

As Parkinson Zamora implies, the ghosts in Kennedy's fiction can be both the magical side of Albany we have been noting as well as the representation of the fluid nature of that city's history, its refusal to abide in a progressive, linear narrative: the ghosts embody the essence of Kennedy's world, a magical past that lives on in the present.

In addition to representing the fluid nature of time, ghosts in magical realism, including that practiced by Kennedy, imply a critique of the modern confidence in Western epistemology. In being asked to believe, or suspend disbelief, in the existence of ghosts, even if just in fiction, authors implicitly challenge the scientifically verifiable notions of knowledge that define Western empiricism. Parkinson Zamora makes this connection herself: "Because ghosts make absence present," she writes,

> they foreground magical realism's most basic concern—the nature and limits of the knowable—and they facilitate magical realism's critique of modernity. Their presence in magical realist fiction is inherently oppositional because they represent an assault on the scientific and materialist assumptions of Western modernity: that reality is knowable, predictable, controllable. (498)

Kennedy certainly joins this critique, but what is interesting is that, in his later novels, he will abandon the use of ghosts (except, in a small way, in *Roscoe*) or other similarly "magical" notions for a reliance on art and the imagination. But while this reliance on art changes the nature of the novels and their magic, it does not change the implicit critique of certainty: whether describing ghosts in *Ironweed* or the artist in *Very Old Bones*, Kennedy's novels all celebrate the uncertain pleasures of intuition and mystery and the imagination.

Examples of this celebration of the magical nature of time pervade *Ironweed*, but two often-cited scenes will have to suffice here as evidence. The first is a vision Francis has while he is helping collect junk with Rosskam, an Albany junk collector. The journey on Rosskam's wagon takes Francis uncomfortably close to the area of Albany where he grew up. As he approaches the area, Francis envisions his mother and father simultaneously sharing their honeymoon bed and their grave, "a spatial duality as reasonable to Francis as the concurrence of this moment both in the immediate present of his fifty-eighth year of life and in the year before he was born" (98). The rest of this vision reinforces this notion of the mixture of past and present by comparing and interweaving the notions of life and death itself, and the vision culminates in a remarkable transcendence of time and chronology as Francis witnesses his own conception and maturation: he "watched [a] primal pool of his own soulish body squirm into burgeoning matter" until it "stood fully clad at last in the very clothes Francis was now wearing" (99).

The one other significant piece of evidence of the timeless nature of the Albany of *Ironweed* that we note here occurs when Francis finally returns to visit his devoted wife Annie. She has been waiting like her counterpart Penelope for over twenty years for her "hero" to return, and when Francis does, bearing a gift of a turkey, he ascends into his attic and opens up an old trunk of his belongings. When Francis opens the lid of this trunk, "the odor of lost time filled the attic air" and Francis first "felt drugged by the scent of the reconstituted past" (168). This feeling comes from what he discovers in the trunk, for inside it, "staring out from a photo, was his own face at age nineteen" (168). Once again the past is alive in the present moment, "reconstituted" now by the magic of the attic and the trunk, a transfiguration captured in the image of the youthful Francis gazing up at the old and ruined Francis of 1938.

This scene and the one on Rosskam's junk wagon are just two of numerous examples of this conflation of time in the novel. Readers of *Ironweed*, however, will probably know where we go after this attic scene, for after Francis's return to his past, literally in revisiting Annie and magically in reconstituting the past in his attic, Francis confronts a two-score collection of ghosts, suitors pushing him from his home. Out on the street again, unable to be comfortable at his old home, Francis eventually ends up fighting in a riot against legionnaires and killing a man. Afterward he hops a train, and in remarkably ambiguous language seems to return to the "holy Phelan eaves" of his old home.[6] However one interprets the ending, it is clear that Francis has regained, either literally or in a magically conditional eschatological world, a sense of assurance, a sense of who he is. The remarkable nature of magical realism, and of the Albany books' own peculiar brand of magic, is that it asks us to stand without deciding between at least two possibilities—a real and a magical one—and I can think of no better example of this request, and one no more eloquently written—than the ending of *Ironweed*.

If readers are disconcerted by the ambiguous ending of Francis Phelan's journey in *Ironweed*—a reaction I would argue is unfair in light of the magically ambiguous nature of the book—there can be little doubt about whether Daniel Quinn, the eponymous and sometime narrator of *Quinn's Book*, achieves his own quest, consummating his love for Maud Fallon. Quinn first meets Maud when the two, still adolescents, come together during a horrific ice flood—Quinn is a canal-boat apprentice on the Hudson—and he spends the next fifteen years trying to reconnect with and win over Maud. Although *Quinn's Book* differs from the previous novels in its wide-ranging view, emphasizing society over individual, history over character, the book still contains an Albany that is as open to magic as the Albanys of the other books. And nowhere is this magic more apparent than in the opening sections, where first we see a flood, wrought by a terrible ice jam that in turn ignites a huge fire, an amalgamation of actual historical events. What sets these events apart from historical description—realism, in other words—is their mythical quality, one of the characteristics of magical realism Simpkins identifies earlier. The "fire rising out of flood" sounds like an event from the apocalypse and is indicative, as the book says, of the "gods gone mad" and "cosmic, mythic rage" (11). This is no ordinary event, no realistic disaster; it is realism turned into myth, history into archetype.

Like *Legs* and *Billy Phelan's Greatest Game* before it, *Quinn's Book* does not share the wholesale character of magical realism found so eloquently in *Ironweed*. Much, though not all, of what appears in the novel after this cosmic flood remains decidedly realistic. And yet despite this qualification, the novel is hardly a predictable realistic tale. The mythic storm that opens the book sets in motion the entire plot of the novel; none of the book would have happened, in other words, if not for the mythic natural disaster, including the most outrageously fantastic event in the whole novel, the resurrection of Magdalena Colón, Maud's aunt who had been trying to cross the river when the ice flood struck. When Magdalena dies in the flood, Quinn's master, John the Brawn McGee, lifts her corpse from the water and helps carry it to a friend's house. On the way Maud warns Quinn not to look into the dead woman's open eyes or "you see your fate" (17). Despite this warning, Quinn looks and does indeed see scenes that will be part of his future, a movement forward in time with which we should be familiar in this magical Albany.

The magical nature of Magdalena's tragedy, however, does not culminate with these visions. Once Quinn and the others get Magdalena's corpse to her friend's house, John the Brawn mounts the dead woman and begins to have intercourse with her. The necrophilic sex so inspires Hillegond, Magdalena's friend, that she too requests to make love with John, and Maud and Quinn watch their coupling while, miraculously, Magdalena rises from the dead, "resurrected from wilt by the sunny friction of joy" (30), brought back from the world of eternal rest to the world of time and its passing.

While these opening pages include most of the "magic" of the book, the novel continues to explore two important related themes apparent throughout the Albany Cycle, the fluidity of time and the role of art in understanding the meaning of that time. The interpenetration of various moments of time, exemplified by Magdalena's visions and resurrection, resurfaces at novel's end when Magdalena, still alive, requests her own wake, a celebration of her death, in a sense reversing the beginning of the book when life was returned to her from her death. And when Daniel Quinn contemplates the mysterious family disk that he owns, with its curving lines that always seem to shift into a different picture, Quinn realizes that the "accumulating and organizing [of] facts and experience" (265) that he did as a journalist has failed to reveal the truth of history to him; instead, he now realizes, only in the "contemplation of mystery was revelation possible" (265–266). What he must depend on, he argues, is "intuitions culled from an anarchic faith in unlikely gods" (266), which he can foster only through using his imagination. No Western rationalism here, no logic or microscopic analysis. Instead, Quinn embraces the anarchic and mysterious, the gods of mythic uncertainty and the power of the artist's imagination, all in "an act of faith, not reason" (280).

This stress on the imagination in *Quinn's Book*, and in its role in the creation of the timeless world of art, is important to consider when we turn to look at Kennedy's next novel, *Very Old Bones*. Here the book not only tells about the construction of a work of art—a suite of paintings by Peter Phelan—but it is also a self-conscious work of art itself, a memoir written by its narrator, Orson Purcell. The narrative of this book all takes place on one day—July 26, 1958—as the ragtag remainder of the Phelan family assembles to hear the will of Peter Phelan read even though Peter is still alive, yet another example of the death-in-life motif that we saw in Magdalena's celebration of her own wake. The story proceeds in fits and starts, going back and forward in time, covering the lives of many Phelan characters from 1887 to the present year of 1958. It is a familiar structure in the Albany novels, embodying in shape what the books embrace in theme, the interpenetration of various moments in time.

In addition to this narrative structure, the book's attention to the past and its constant resurfacing in the present is embodied in the adult lives of several of the Phelan children, such as Sarah Phelan's attempt to live exactly as her dead mother did or the aborted baby Molly Phelan secretly buried in the Phelan basement. The most noteworthy return to the past takes the form of Peter Phelan's painting a suite of pictures dramatizing the most horrific (and once hidden) part of Phelan history, the murder in 1887 of Lizzie McIlhenny, Kathryn Phelan's sister-in-law, by Kathryn's brother Malachi.

None of these instances of the fluidity of time, of course, is anything but structural or symbolic. But in the case of the narration itself, we do have an instance of Kennedy's reliance on the inherently magical, though with an important twist for our understanding of the last few books of the cycle. This twist involves the narrative point of view, for the complicated plot of *Very Old Bones* is ostensibly narrated by Orson Purcell, the bastard son of Peter Phelan and Claire Purcell, though much of this supposed memoir could not be part of Orson's memory at all because it takes place where he is not or even before he was born. While such a feat might seem "unrealistic," Orson has a ready explanation and does not take lightly what he himself is doing. By way of defending his knowledge, Orson first writes that his father Peter could paint so successfully about the Phelan past because Peter "projected himself into the lives of the people who had lived and died so absurdly, so tragically, in the days before and after his own birth" (20). Orson explicitly equates Peter's power with the Keatsian notion of "negative capability" (20), one of the characteristics that Simpkins himself significantly cited as a defining characteristic of magical realism, and he says that Peter could "throw his soul into any person, or object, that he confronts, and then speak out of that person, or object" (20).

These descriptions of Peter are significant because they also describe what Orson himself does in the course of the novel. He invokes Keats, Orson says, in order "to project myself into realms of the family where I have no credentials for being, but am there even so" (21). This projection is told with a confidence—and ultimately with a self-effacement of ego—equal to the ontological status of fact. Immediately after his Keatsian defense, Orson says that he knows "what is going on in the Quinn house on North Pearl Street in North Albany" the morning of the reading of the will (21) even though he himself is not in the house. What follows then is an explicit description of the morning activities, including sex and the wanderings of the senile Annie Phelan, in the Quinn household.

The story that Orson goes on to tell, then, is that which can only be told through a magical narrative, one in which the limitations of human perception and awareness are transcended. It could be argued that in fact Orson is not an artist but a lunatic, for in the course of the story he suffers at least two serious nervous breakdowns and is prone to hallucination. But what saves *Very Old Bones* from becoming merely Orson's fantasy is both his claim toward the power of "negative capability" and the extensiveness of his imagination; as *Ironweed* set up its program of a universe peopled with ghosts from its outset, *Very Old Bones* in its entirety is the magical memoir of Phelan history Orson himself unfolds. The entire plot of the book, since Orson is our consciousness, depends upon our willing suspension of disbelief, our willingness to take Orson for his word as he tells about the daily activities of the Quinns now or the Phelans of the past. In fact, only two paragraphs after Orson makes his claim for negative capability, he as narrator has disappeared (for a while) and we are in direct third-person narration of events. The "subordination of the self" (20) that Orson says is required for negative capability is complete: Orson is gone, whether he is crazy or sane, and a disembodied and implicitly reticent narrative voice picks up where he left off.

The magic of art that affects the narrative point of view of *Very Old Bones* is also a crucial issue in the next Albany novel, *The Flaming Corsage*. In this story, Edward Daugherty, father of the Martin we met in *Billy Phelan's Greatest Game*, attempts to overcome his "ghetto" Irish heritage through the prestige, power, and money gained by his playwriting and through his marriage to Katrina Taylor, the upper-class daughter of one of the Albany-Anglo aristocracy. In *The Flaming Corsage*, arguably the most complicated book of the Albany series, Kennedy has come a long way from the simple magical realism of *Ironweed* into a text more akin to the postmodern experiments we find in much of American anti-realistic literature in recent decades. The book tells its tale of the famous love nest scandal—the tangle of indiscretion and adultery mentioned in *Billy Phelan*—through such tactics as direct narration, documentary reports, and play scripts. But never does the novel seem clearly to resolve what actually happened in the confused and dangerous game-playing between Edward, his wife Katrina, his mistress Melissa Spencer, and Edward's acquaintances, Felicity and Giles Fitzroy, and Thomas Maginn. This lack of clarity, however, is exactly the point: we know already from Daniel Quinn that truth resides not in fact but in imagination, and *The Flaming Corsage* is a story of the power—and the danger—inherent in that imagination.

As should come as no surprise, *The Flaming Corsage* is structured, like several of its predecessors, by winding forward and backward through dates and into documents that are outside of time altogether. But the journey through time that is such a hallmark of the Albany Cycle appears here more significantly in Edward's attempt to use the past, the history out of which he comes as an Irishman in New York, as a source for his art. He does this first in his novel *The Mosquito Lovers*, a tale of the Irish Erie Canal builders, and then in his plays. For a while this plan of Edward's seems to succeed, but eventually it begins to disintegrate. He draws the ire of his already displeased in-laws by being critical of the Anglo ascendancy of which the Taylors are a part in such works as *The Baron of Ten Broeck Street*, and he alienates his own Irish compatriots in such works as *The Stolen Cushion*, a play in which he hoped to show his fellow Irishmen "how to transcend the peasant caste into which they'd been born" (67). After a few years he begins to realize how difficult he has made things in writing his plays, especially in his marriage to Katrina, and in an attempt to smooth over his troubles with his in-laws, he inadvertently leads the family to a hotel at which a fire breaks out—a fire which eventually, sometime later, causes the death of Katrina's sister and father. Katrina not only blames Edward for these deaths, but she herself reverts into a life obsessed with death and dying. Complicating the situation with Katrina further is the love nest scandal itself, a kaleidoscopic, multileveled collection of intrigue and bad jokes and infidelities almost too complex to describe.

In an attempt to make sense of this adulterous scandal and his life, especially his unstable wife, Edward writes *The Flaming Corsage*, a play, the name of which derives from a burning flower that struck Katrina's chest during the hotel fire. As the playwright character within Edward's play says, he will write his own drama in order to "synthesize events, discover answers" (137). What these "answers" are, however, remains elusive throughout the book. For one thing, Edward so conflates the characters in his plays—even playing games with names by calling Katrina "Marina" and Melissa "Clarissa"—that the truth recedes with each step toward it. Though Katrina herself believes that Edward gave "shape to the chaos that overtook" (171) everyone, and though she sits down to write out her own version of the truth, we ourselves see little of that shape because Katrina dies just as she is about to divulge what she knows. She lets a fire that started in a school next door overtake her and embraces at last the death that so obsessed her in life.

By the time we arrive at *The Flaming Corsage*, we have come a long way from the magical world that characterized the first four novels of the Albany Cycle, especially that of *Ironweed*. Instead we have entered a new kind of magic, a new kind of faith, not so much in the city of Albany and its magical time, but in the magic of art outside of time altogether. But the realism that has always been kept at bay by the magic is kept in check in this novel in other ways. While there are no inexplicably magical scenes, the "meta-narrative" and "open-ended" character of the book resembles several descriptors from Simpkins's notion of magical realism. And the conflation of characters that Edward himself achieves in writing his plays reminds one of the confused identities in a work such as *One Hundred Years of Solitude*. Let's also recall Parkinson Zamora's discussion of ghosts in magical realism and how they "unsettle modernity's (and the novel's) basis in progressive, linear history" and "embody the . . . sense that reality always exceeds our capacities to describe or understand or prove. . . . Magical realist texts ask us to look beyond the limits of the knowable . . ." (498). While there are no ghosts in *The Flaming Corsage*, what Parkinson Zamora says they achieve elsewhere is decidedly similar to the character of *The Flaming Corsage* itself: the reality of the love nest scandal is too "excessive" to "describe or understand or prove." We must look beyond the "limits of the knowable" and engage instead the probable, the possible, the maybe that is at the heart of the mystery of this novel. If by the sixth book in the cycle the incipient magic of *Legs, Billy Phelan,* and *Ironweed,* their natural kind of folk magic, has disappeared, it has been replaced by the aesthetic magic of postmodernism, a sleight of hand that is closer to the magic of the stage than of the landscape.[7]

In *Roscoe*, the book immediately following *The Flaming Corsage*, Kennedy has in some ways moved even further from the Albany folk epic of *Ironweed* back toward an older model of social realism. The book concerns the efforts of Roscoe, the eponymous protagonist, as he tries to disentangle himself from a life of political manipulation and power brokering. With his two cronies in politics (including the Patsy McCall famous from *Billy Phelan*), Roscoe has for years directed the fate of Albany politics as a behind-the-scenes manipulator. As the book opens, Roscoe only wishes to retire, but fate and circumstance conspire against him: Elisha Fitzgibbon, the third member of the Albany power trio, commits suicide for unknown reasons, and Roscoe is forced through threats to the happiness of Elisha's wife and Roscoe's longtime love, Veronica, to engage even more deeply in the unseemly side of Albany politics. Not only are Roscoe's adventures in this novel told in a straightforward, believable narrative, but the book often completely gives over for several pages to a kind of narrative history of a fictionalized Albany. Though not the real history of the political machine of that city, it serves as a believable analogue, and the book at these moments is notably absent of any intervention of the supernatural or surreal.

But even so "realist" an endeavor as *Roscoe* is not free from the uncertainty and surprise as well as the magic of Kennedy's conception of fiction. Sections of the novel are broken off by interchapters in which Roscoe seems to move in a kind of dream world; were there any narrative explanation—and of course it's significant that there is not—we might even interpret these sections as Roscoe's dreams themselves, but "authorial reticence" justifies no such conclusion. Brief, surreal, and deeply enigmatic, the chapters include, among others, a story of Roscoe meeting "women who died of love" one day on the road ("Roscoe in a Courtly Mode," 73), a conversation between Roscoe and a "billygoat who resembled Elisha" ("Roscoe and the Fum," 111), and a visit by Roscoe to the Museum of Forgotten Sounds ("Roscoe and the Sounds," 261). In these and other instances, we leave behind the straightforward narrative of political history, and even the psychological development of character, for the uncertain fictions of a postmodernist universe.

In addition to these interchapters, the novel also includes examples of Kennedy's affection for myth (e.g., Veronica calls Roscoe a "mythic creature" [71]) as well as his interest in the teasing uncertainty of the postmodern cosmos in which his characters reside. This uncertainty is most obvious in the primary plot of the novel: in this thread of the novel, Roscoe attempts to discern and then act on the uncertain motivations behind his friend's suicide, ones he feels are connected to the machinations of Veronica's sister to try to regain custody of her biological son, whom she has allowed Veronica and Elisha to raise as their own. While serving as Veronica's lawyer, Roscoe speculates on what drove Elisha to his death and who the real father of Veronica's adopted child might be (Elisha himself? a Russian emigré? even Veronica's other son?), yet the book never allows a definitive answer, leaving us to ponder the clues without consolidating them into fictional fact. And framing this uncertain quest toward an uncertain answer are Roscoe's own occasional confrontations with those old Albany ghosts: when Roscoe is first called to the site of Elisha's suicide, the dead Elisha stands up and shaves while Roscoe yells at him for dying (28); and toward the end of the novel, after Roscoe has won the day for Veronica, he takes her and her son to a vacation home where two old ghosts seem to materialize in front of the hearth.

Do either of these confrontations with ghosts actually happen? Kennedy even here toys with us by titling one section of the book "Does Roscoe Really Believe in Ghosts?" As one might expect, we get an answer that isn't an answer: "Roscoe allows for all realities," Kennedy writes, "including those that do not exist" (275). Does this paradox bother us? It might in the world of straightforward empiricism or in narrative realism—the world of linear fact, of the knowable—but not in a magical world outside of the normal dimensions of time: in short, the world of Kennedy's Albany novels.

No attempt is intended here to define the corpus of Kennedy's work as magical realist. But it seems that the concept is a useful one, not only for appreciating those works of Kennedy's that fall comfortably within the concept of magical realism, but also to see the magical workings of all of the novels, no matter how differently that magic may appear. One's sense of the magic of the Albany books, specifically the magic of time—of history and the past—depends not only upon the readings of the novels but upon one's definition of what is magical. By the time we fall into the later works of Kennedy's cycle, the traditional folk magic has fallen away into a celebration of the mysteries, surprises, and uncertainties of the artistic vision—and then later, as in *Roscoe*, to the uncertainties of all reality, narrative or political, real or surreal. It is striking to consider Gabriel García Márquez's comment on realistic texts as a "premeditated literature that offers too static and exclusive a vision of reality. However good or bad they may be, they are books which finish on the last page."[8] This critique of realism may convince us of just how magical Kennedy's work is, not only in a pseudo-realistic text like *The Flaming Corsage* or *Roscoe* but in the Albany Cycle as a whole, for the books as a group do not seem to have a last page at all. At some point, of course, there will be no more Albany novels, but for now, of what we do have, each book serves as both an epilogue and a prelude to another: their plots and characters refer back and forth to other books, prefiguring what is to come or revealing what follows. Each book magically portrays the presence of the past or of history in the lives of its characters, but each book is part of a larger whole too, a suite of novels whose combined history, whose intertextual dialogue and nonlinear progression, embodies the very magical notion of time that the individual novels play out. And of course they all do this in the "magical place" of Albany where history becomes archetype, where the confident epistemology of Western empiricism is replaced with the celebratory intuition of the imagination, and where the real and the magical, the actual, and the imagined, are the same.

Notes

1. In an interview with Kennedy, for example, in "Beyond Realism: William Kennedy on the Surreal and the Unconscious, the Religious, the Sublime and the Gonzo," Philip Baruth says that, to him, Kennedy's work seems "to move from a moment or two of surrealism in *Legs*, to a more foundational use of magic realism in *Billy Phelan* in the sense of second sight, to a full-blown magic realism reminiscent of García Márquez in *Ironweed*" (121). Such a perception is the very thesis of Robert Gibb's 1986 dissertation, probably the first lengthy study of Kennedy's work. Though now dated by the publication of other Kennedy novels—Gibb's work ends with *Ironweed*—the study traces what Gibb sees (and what Baruth mentioned) as the growing tendency of Kennedy to become more of a magical realist in each of the first three Albany novels he wrote. Most attention on Kennedy's magical realist character, in fact, is focused on *Ironweed*, what Baruth and Gibb identify as the culmination of Kennedy's magical realism. Melissa Stewart, for example, studied this idea in "Roads of 'Exquisite Mysterious Muck': The Magical Journey through the City in William Kennedy's *Ironweed*, John Cheever's 'The Enormous Radio,' and Donald Barthelme's 'City Life,'" in *Magical Realism: Theory, History, Community*; and Lori Chamberlain has written about *Ironweed* in "Magicking the Real: Paradoxes of Postmodern Writing." Kennedy has himself acknowledged his interest in the works of such famous magical realists as Gabriel García Márquez, and in his interview with Baruth mentioned an early attraction to authors such as Franz Kafka and Thornton Wilder, writers who, like Kennedy, found room in their fiction for elements of the fantastic (122).

2. For a discussion of the makeup of the Albany Cycle, specifically in regard to *The Ink Truck*, see my *From Then Into Now: William Kennedy's Albany Novels* (Scranton: University of Scranton Press, 1998), 10–13.

3. Quoted in Baruth, "Beyond Realism," 123.

4. See Daniel M. Murtaugh, "Fathers and Their Sons: William Kennedy's Hero-Transgressors," *Commonweal*, May 19, 1989, 300, or *From Then Into Now*, 82–83, for the nature of this goat image.

5. See Wendy B. Faris, "Scheherazade's Children: Magical Realism and Postmodern Fiction," or Lois Parkinson Zamora, "Magical Romance/Magical Realism: Ghosts in U.S. and Latin American Fiction," both in *Magical Realism: Theory, History, Community*.

6. For a discussion of the ending of *Ironweed*, see, among other places, *From Then Into Now*, 148–153.

7. There have been numerous discussions of the relationship between postmodernism and magical realism. See especially Theo L. D'haen, "Magic Realism and Postmodernism: Decentering Privileged Centers," and Faris, "Scheherazade's Children."

8. Quoted in Scott Simpkins, "Magical Strategies: The Supplement of Realism," 143, and found in *The Fragrance of Guava*, 56.

References

Baruth, Philip. "Beyond Realism: William Kennedy on the Surreal and the Unconscious, the Religious, the Sublime and the Gonzo." Interview with Kennedy. *New England Review* 19 (1998): 116–126.

Chamberlain, Lori. "Magicking the Real: Paradoxes of Postmodern Writing." In *Postmodern Fiction: A Bio-Bibliographical Guide*, ed. Larry McCaffery, 5–22. Westport: Greenwood Press, 1986.

Chanady, Amaryll Beatrice. *Magical Realism and the Fantastic: Resolved versus Unresolved Antinomy*. New York and London: Garland, 1985.

Delbaere-Garant, Jeanne. "Psychic Realism, Mythic Realism, Grotesque Realism: Variations on Magic Realism in Contemporary Literature in English." In *Magical Realism: Theory, History, Community*, ed. Lois Parkinson Zamora and Wendy B. Faris, 249–263. Durham and London: Duke University Press, 1995.

D'haen, Theo L. "Magic Realism and Postmodernism: Decentering Privileged Centers." In *Magical Realism: Theory, History, Community*, ed. Lois Parkinson Zamora and Wendy B. Faris, 191–208. Durham and London: Duke University Press, 1995.

Faris, Wendy B. "Scheherazade's Children: Magical Realism and Postmodern Fiction." In *Magical Realism: Theory, History, Community*, ed. Lois Parkinson Zamora and Wendy B. Faris, 163–190. Durham and London: Duke University Press, 1995.

García Márquez, Gabriel, and Plinio Apuleyo Mendoza. *The Fragrance of Guava*. Trans. Ann Wright. London: Verso, 1983.

Gibb, Robert. "The Life of the Soul: William Kennedy, Magical Realist." Dissertation. Lehigh University, 1986.

Kennedy, William. *The Ink Truck*. New York: Dial, 1969 (Viking, 1984); London: Macdonald, 1970.

———. *Legs*. New York: Coward, McCann, 1975 (Penguin, 1983); London: Cape, 1977.

———. *Billy Phelan's Greatest Game*. New York: Viking, 1978 (Penguin, 1983); London: Penguin, 1984.

———. *Ironweed*. New York: Viking, 1983; Harmondsworth: Penguin, 1984.

———. *O Albany! Improbable City of Political Wizards, Fearless Ethnics, Spectacular Aristocrats, Splendid Nobodies, and Underrated Scoundrels*. New York: Viking, 1983; Albany: Washington Park Press, 1983.

———. *Quinn's Book*. New York: Viking, 1988. London: Cape, 1988.

———. *Very Old Bones*. New York: Penguin, 1992.

———. *The Flaming Corsage*. New York: Penguin, 1996.

———. *Roscoe*. New York: Penguin, 2002.

Michener, Christian. *From Then Into Now: William Kennedy's Albany Novels*. Scranton: University of Scranton Press, 1998.

Murtaugh, Daniel M. "Fathers and Their Sons: William Kennedy's Hero-Transgressors." *Commonweal*, May 19, 1989, 298–302.

Parkinson Zamora, Lois, and Wendy B. Faris. "Introduction: Daiquiri Birds and Flaubertian Parrot(ie)s." In *Magical Realism: Theory, History, Community*, ed. Lois Parkinson Zamora and Wendy B. Faris, 11–14. Durham and London: Duke University Press, 1995.

Parkinson Zamora, Lois. "Magical Romance/Magical Realism: Ghosts in U.S. and Latin American Fiction." In *Magical Realism: Theory, History, Community*, edited by Lois Parkinson Zamora and Wendy B. Faris, 497–550. Durham and London: Duke University Press, 1995.

Simpkins, Scott. "Magical Strategies: The Supplement of Realism." *Twentieth Century Literature* 34 (1988): 140–154.

Stewart, Melissa. "Roads of 'Exquisite Mysterious Muck': The Magical Journey through the City in William Kennedy's *Ironweed*, John Cheever's 'The Enormous Radio,' and Donald Barthelme's 'City Life.'" In *Magical Realism: Theory, History, Community*, edited by Lois Parkinson Zamora and Wendy B. Faris, 477–495. Durham and London: Duke University Press, 1995.

This essay was presented at "William Kennedy: A Celebration . . . A Symposium on His Work" held at the Omni Albany Hotel (now Hilton Albany), Albany, New York, on April 15–17, 1999. Printed by permission of Christian Michener and University of Scranton.

The Cyclical Impulse of *The Flaming Corsage*

Michael Patrick Gillespie

> Familiar features also punctuate the discourse of *The Flaming Corsage* as it takes on an important role for all of the novels in the Albany Cycle, continuing the accretive pattern of narrative development that has marked Kennedy's books since *Billy Phelan's Greatest Game*.
>
> —Michael Patrick Gillespie

Each successive novel attests to William Kennedy's growing virtuosity as a writer, and *The Flaming Corsage* in its turn provides ample evidence of the author's thematic diversity. In exploring the lives of the Daugherty clan, it asserts the potential of a family other than the Phelans to provide an alternative narrative axis for subsequent Albany stories. It offers revealing elaborations of the events introduced in the recollections of Martin Daugherty in *Billy Phelan's Greatest Game* and in those of Francis Phelan in *Ironweed*. *The Flaming Corsage* also shifts the topical perspective from that of previous novels by moving the emphasis to individuals from the *fin de siècle* generation. This gesture in turn gives a much stronger sense of the complex personalities and of the frustrated lives of its central characters: Edward and Katrina Daugherty.

Familiar features also punctuate the discourse of *The Flaming Corsage* as it takes on an important role for all of the novels in the Albany Cycle, continuing the accretive pattern of narrative development that has marked Kennedy's books since *Billy Phelan's Greatest Game*. Just as the conclusion of *Very Old Bones* provides information that can mitigate a reader's response to the repressive behavior of Kathryn and Sarah Phelan, the discourse of *The Flaming Corsage* greatly enhances our understanding of the forces motivating the conduct of Edward and Katrina Daugherty. By the end of the novel, one has a sense of their conflicted consciousnesses that extends far beyond the characterizations that have appeared in *Billy Phelan's Greatest Game* and *Ironweed*.

Although selfishness remains a prominent aspect of his identity, a measure of sensitivity emerges in Edward's nature. While a series of tragic events cannot fail to leave their mark on her consciousness, one sees from a very early age a willfulness bordering on mania acting as a compelling aspect of Katrina's personality. These revelations present a degree of complexity informing the motives of the characters participating in those incidents that makes them vastly more interesting than previously suggested.

Kennedy also expands upon a stylistic approach, introduced in *Very Old Bones,* which adopts a much more flexible chronologic scheme than any found in the previous novels. *Very Old Bones* breaks up the conventional, linear pattern of narrative development, and consequently succeeds in illuminating elements in the lives of individuals in the Phelan clan that show them as much deeper characters than one might initially assume. Though it opens on July 26, 1958, the narrative ranges in a rather leisurely and somewhat disjointed fashion back and forth across seventy-five years of family history. Nonetheless, *Very Old Bones* maintains its continuity by the familiarity (at least for those who have read his other Albany novels) of the topical references, which allow one to adjust fairly easily to the periodic oscillation.

The Flaming Corsage takes up another family—the Daughertys—and, through an even more striking formal approach, brings out a depth in their natures not evident in previous works. The intensity of individual portrayals comes in no small part through this striking evolution in Kennedy's narrative techniques. A progressive movement away from linear development gives an episodic quality to successive segments of the discourse, and throws into relief features delineating individual figures. One sees in the nonsequential episodes of *The Flaming Corsage* intense reflections of human identity. These passages operate without the framework that usually provides interpretive support to a reader's sense of a particular character. (Think, for example, of how the meticulous development of the idiosyncratic world of Dickens's Victorian London prepares us for the eccentricities of Mr. Micawber.) In consequence, as figures appear in chapter after chapter outside the conventional progression of narrative, readers focus all attention upon aspects of identity as the only means to form a unified impression of the discourse.

This decontextualization represents an impressive expansion of the disrupted chronology employed on a more limited basis in *Very Old Bones*. By way of contrast, *The Flaming Corsage* introduces briefer narrative segments with shifts from one period to another coming much more abruptly. This conveys the narrative's ability to introduce complex polymorphic development in compact descriptions. Such changes testify not only to the author's technical polish but to a confidence in his reader's capacity to respond to his multilayered discourse.

The book's epigraph—made up of two short passages taken from Gilbert and Sullivan's *The Mikado*—provides an early and useful example of a key creative feature, the inclination to play upon antinomies that enables Kennedy to pack so many interpretive possibilities into a relatively brief passage. In the selection quoted, first Yum-Yum laments the fact that she will be put to death as a consequence of marrying Nanki-Poo. Then Yum-Yum and Nanki-Poo elaborate upon the dilemma of being genuinely in love yet knowing, "'Tis death to marry you!" In *The Mikado*, of course, the gruesome fate that threatens the lovers loses much of its menace because the comic context of the Gilbert and Sullivan operetta offers the formulaic promise of a contrived happy ending. *The Flaming Corsage*, ostensibly a tragic love story, raises very different generic expectations. Consequently, the bathos and pathos juxtaposed in the epigraph introduce conflicting protocols for the narrative that follows. Specifically one wonders, despite the agonizing suffering of Edward and Katrina Daugherty and a number of other characters, should a reader assume that as often as not banality, rather than dignity, informs the catastrophes of the novel? This conjecture by no means undermines the force of the narrative but rather calls attention to its multiplicity.

Horrific events, like those detailed in its opening chapter, seem to invite one to give *The Flaming Corsage* the classification of tragedy, yet, as with the epigraph, context insistently generates resistance to conventional readings. The description of a brutal murder-suicide in a Manhattan hotel introduces the major themes—violence, promiscuity, deception, and misprision—that will dominate the subsequent action. More significantly, however, it presents the shaping incident of the novel in language that insinuates ambiguity into a putatively straightforward account. The conflicting reports of Giles Fitzroy's last words before killing his wife, Felicity, preview the way a range of often contradictory descriptions surround key events throughout *The Flaming Corsage*. Further, in the chapter's final lines, a play on words with a heavy-handed pun underscores the tawdriness and the ambiguity of what has transpired. It describes the naked, adulterous Felicity as Giles's "exposed wife" (2), and leaves the reader wondering what to make of the conflated representation of her physical disposition and public shame.[1]

Immediately after this episode, the narrative turns to a time twenty-three years previous to the hotel killings and establishes dual patterns of achronicity and venality that will figure so prominently in the discourse. It introduces Edward Daugherty and Thomas Maginn as two young men with complementary literary ambitions and a shared, coarse sensuality that dominates their immediate consciousnesses. They are visiting a bordello where Maginn is recognized as a well-known patron.[2] Familiarity, however, does not translate into acceptance, another theme reiterated throughout the novel.[3] The whores quite obviously prefer Edward's patronage, and Maginn immediately evinces a competitiveness that, periodically reinforced by Edward's dismissiveness, will stand as an undercurrent throughout the narrative.[4]

In the world of the novel, however, status and disapprobation stand as conflicting forces driving nearly every character, no matter what his or her position on the social scale. Thus, in the layered society of late nineteenth-century Albany, Edward finds himself as vulnerable to disdain as Maginn. When later that evening Edward encounters the beautiful and privileged Katrina Taylor dining with her mother and father at the Kenmore Hotel, Katrina's parents can barely conceal their contempt for him. The antipathy that they feel echoes, in a heightened form, Edward's condescension toward Maginn, an early sign of the pattern of narrative oscillation—familiar from other Kennedy writings—that permeates the novel: a tendency to link apparently antipathetic figures by tracing similarities that shape their lives.

Further chronologic fluctuation, however, disrupts easy generalizations about the social framework of the novel. A retrospective glance at events in 1840, for instance, recounts how Emmett Daugherty had saved the life of Lyman Fitzgibbon. The gratitude of Fitzgibbon shapes the lives of two generations of Daughertys, taking the form of underwriting the education of Emmett's son. This benevolence establishes a relationship that explains how the working-class Edward could come to know Lyman's granddaughter, Katrina Taylor, and feel the confidence to tell her of his plans "to pursue you with a fervid Irish passion, unlike anything you've ever imagined" (20). Edward's febrile diction expresses the same sort of lightning bolt passion that Francis Phelan recalls feeling for Annie Farrell in *Ironweed*, that Daniel Quinn undergoes for Maud Fallon in *Quinn's Book*, and that Molly Phelan experiences for Walter Mangan in *Very Old Bones*. The analogues are telling, for in each case the figure affected assumes that mere passion will prove sufficient to ensure happiness. Events in *The Flaming Corsage* instead demonstrate the catastrophic results of reliance on such a feeling alone.

Even as the narrative announces the commencement of Edward's intense courtship, it goes to great lengths to warn against a sentimental reading, reminding us how the disparities of class differences—features apparent throughout the Albany novels—enforce the hopelessness of affecting any accommodation between the world of the Taylors and that of the Daughertys. In a neat reversal of expectations, for example, the narrative traces Edward's abrupt realization that an alliance with the Taylor family means a break with lifelong friends, not because they feel that he is contemptuous of them. When Edward visits a saloon owned by Black Jack McCall to ask him to be the best man at his wedding, he is caught in the middle of a brawl between Maginn and a drunken lout named Matty Lookup, who has taken exception to a perceived ethnic slur. Edward ends the melee by throwing a pot of hot bean soup into Matty's face.[5] In thanking Edward for his help, Maginn drains his remarks of any real gratitude by gratuitously emphasizing class distinctions. "Quick thinking, old man. I myself might've reached for a bottle to club him with, but I'd've never gone for the soup. A genteel weapon. Your prospective in-laws would doubtless approve the choice" (28). The heavy-handed sarcasm of the remark not only reflects Maginn's envy, it makes Edward realize the class prejudices among his own people. "Edward could not now ask Jack to be his best man. A great fellow, Jack. A generous man if ever there was one. . . . But he doesn't approve of Katrina. Everybody's generosity ends somewhere" (29). Taken no further, the issue of social position would settle into a lampoon of sectarian snobbishness, but Kennedy explores the matter by deftly accentuating the ambiguities of Edward's own status: working-class ethnic by birth and upper-class nativist by education.

A subsequent visit to the Taylor household presents the obligatory view of Katrina's parents as stuffy and prejudiced, but it also foregrounds Edward as a young man with the subtle insecurities that come from finding himself between two cultures and unable to assimilate into either. As Edward waits in the library of the Taylors' home, every book in the room confirms his sense of their anti-Irish prejudices. This leads him to "conjuring his own seventeenth-century forebears," who through Cromwellian confiscations of their estates were "reduced to lowly cottiers tilling the land of others" (32–33). He then goes on to trace the Daugherty family's immigration to Albany and its subsequent economic and social recovery "to heights where you [he tells himself] can court the modern get of an ancient devil" (34). Though he subsequently chastises himself for "demonizing my love . . . to make her the equal of what her parents think I am" (34), Edward does not fully comprehend the direction of his own thoughts. Though clothed in references that seem to decry the English persecution of the Irish, on close inspection his grievance takes a very individualized form with Edward's concern focused not on Irish suffering in general but on the way events have shaped his own status in the community. Christian Michener has rightly summed up a driving force of the novel as "Edward's dream of becoming a representative upper-class Irishman."[6] What emerges as the tragic aspect of this desire is not so much his failure to achieve it in the end, but his failure to see how circumscribed such an ambition is.

When he finally does confront the Taylors, his rapid-fire announcement of his intention to marry their daughter—in a speech mired in shaky logic and delivered in an offensive tone—never rises above the facile and serves to corroborate the biases that these people hold. (Katrina later confirms this, telling

Edward that "her mother thought him 'a rude social climber' and was furious at his suggestion that her family had committed violence against the Irish; and her father, baffled by Edward's 'babbling about atrocity and slavery,' wondered, 'What world is that overeducated maniac living in?'" [50].) Indeed, the inherent flaws in Edward's speech, despite the time that he has had to prepare it, suggest to the reader that a rhetorical sleight of hand remains the only argument that Edward can offer for the acceptance of his proposal.[7] Although the couple does not yet realize it, the pronounced differences of their backgrounds in fact preclude any union between Katrina and Edward other than a physical one.

Along these lines, the next episode offers a glimpse of the amalgamation of calculation, sensuality, recklessness, and cruelty that make up Katrina's character. At the same time, it sets in motion a series of events that show the vulnerability of an individual who stands aloof from the prescriptive guidance of societal mores. In meeting Edward at the Albany Rural Cemetery, Katrina torments another suitor, Giles Fitzroy, who brings her to the assignation, offends the sensibilities of her ancestors by proposing intercourse in their graveyard, and takes control of the sensual life of their marriage by dictating where and when sexual activity will occur. "It's nineteen days since my time. I now have nine days when I cannot conceive. It's an ideal moment for the estrus to strike, and strike it has" (46). Both Edward and Katrina see this act as a pledge of their love. Nonetheless, as the narrative will later make clear, that act has contradictory implications that ultimately blight their marriage.

Even at this point in the novel, however, the attentive reader will begin to detect signs that, despite the commitment implicit in their intimacy, Edward and Katrina still do not understand the profound contradictions that plague their proposed union. The narrative demonstrates their continuing naïveté in an account of a meeting with Edward's parents analogous to his visit to the Taylor house. Just as Edward's tirade on social equanimity stunned the Taylors, Katrina's declaration of her intention to convert to Catholicism renders the Daughertys speechless. As with Edward's disquisition before the Taylors, the young couple seems to take silence for consent, but unperceived complications persist. Specifically, several issues arise out of this exchange that, because they remain unresolved and even unacknowledged, presage significant difficulties for their marriage. Some years previously, Edward's uncle, a union organizer, had been brutally beaten and left permanently injured by men employed by Jacob Taylor. This sets up a Montague and Capulet type of feud and suggests that any association with the Taylors shows a deficiency in Edward's family loyalty. It begs the question how, if he does not demonstrate a clear sense of his obligations to his own family, his own marriage will survive? Further, neither Katrina nor Edward seems to understand religion as anything other than a social institution. They see it as a public acknowledgment of adherence to certain rituals that distinguish but do not mark the individual. To their detriment, they do not grasp the need for ethical commitment to some structure of belief, whatever its basis, nor do they understand the broad communal repercussions set off by a public affirmation of a commitment to a particular religion. As evidenced by many of Kennedy's characters, one can survive quite well in the world of his novels without either an ethical commitment or a sense of communal affiliation, but whoever operates without both courts destruction.

Nonetheless, in the discourse of *The Flaming Corsage* this deficiency rarely results in an abrupt shift in fortune. Rather, the narrative builds with meticulous care the interrelated conditions that will precipitate disaster. This often occurs through the most ridiculously grotesque gestures like the report by Fintan (Clubber) Dooley of a practical joke in which he and Culbert (Cully) Watson put the head of a bull on the porch of Dr. Giles Fitzroy. At this point in the narrative, the matter seems to reflect merely the coarse humor of a certain level of society, with only its date, one day before the murder-suicide described in the opening chapter, hinting at its ominous implications. This account nonetheless serves to enforce the reader's sense that anarchy and violence continually lurk at the margins of this society, posing a constant threat to those who cannot avail themselves of communal protection.

The next episode shows how quickly the danger on the periphery of ordinary life can move into the center of the action. The understated irony of its title, "Dinner at the Delavan Is Interrupted, December 30, 1894," chillingly alludes to the impending tragedy of the hotel fire, and graphically underscores the omnipresent threat of chaos to overwhelm order.[8] While the violence of the blaze dominates the immediate action, an undercurrent of profound emotional discord counterpoints events. Edward has enraged the Taylors by writing a play, *The Baron of Ten Broeck Street*, with a central character based on Jacob Taylor. He has arranged a conciliatory supper with his in-laws to announce that he is withdrawing the play from production. He aims to placate Katrina, who has begun to show signs of regret over leaving behind her family home and the world of her childhood and resentment of Edward "for luring her away from her maidenly joys with his eloquent tongue, his hot love" (68). Edward has already attempted to address this by building "a scaled-down replica of the Taylors' Gothic Revival town house . . . to assuage her loss of the resplendencies she had left behind" (68). The irony of this description subtly insinuates itself through the architecture—a style, simultaneously derivative and pompous. Like "the candelabra . . . once owned by the Bonaparte family" (39) and now a Taylor family treasure, the house with its expensive and borrowed pedigree betrays its occupants as parvenu.

Edward's concern draws the reader's attention to an instability in the Daughertys' marriage and the growing influence of erratic elements within his wife's consciousness. The truly unbalanced behavior that emerges in Katrina's seduction of Francis Phelan will not take place for four more years. Nonetheless, one can already note that without the anchors of family and moral belief, her willful, ungoverned nature is dangerously adrift.

The calamitous events of the evening, however, interrupt a close examination of Katrina at this point. When a fire breaks out in the hotel, Edward keeps his head and saves his wife and father-in-law and another woman, abandoned by her husband. Unfortunately, the physical courage that he displays does not prevent his wife from blaming him for the suffering that the fire inflicts upon her family. Its traumatizing effect goes well beyond the physical injury that Katrina suffers when a blazing stick ignites her dress and the corsage she is wearing. In fact, the tragedy of the fire deals with the Taylors in a cruelly ironic fashion. Her sister Adelaide seemingly survives a jump from the top-floor window ledge of the hotel only to die seven days later from a ruptured spleen. Firemen rescue Adelaide's husband, Archie Van Slyke, but the shock of the event turns him into an ineffectual alcoholic. Jacob Taylor escapes the burning building, but two months later dies of a heart attack. Katrina takes an immoderate interest in all of the suffering, and like others in her family feels a need to fix blame. "Katrina was not the one to articulate the accusation, but she came to believe what her mother had said first: Edward killed Adelaide and Jacob" (81).

Just as the conflagration at the Delavan House underscores, among other things, Edward's isolation from the world in which Katrina's family exists, the death of Edward's father eight and a half years later shows his wife's tenuous understanding of the world from which he emerged. Further, it suggests how mania and bitterness have warped her. Katrina, feeling more compassion for Emmett than for her husband, comes to visit her dying father-in-law, but holds herself aloof from the Daughertys' working-class world.

This alienation becomes apparent from the moment that she sets foot in the house and meets Annie Phelan, the wife of Francis, who as a former neighbor has come to offer her condolences. Katrina finds herself unable to treat the woman as either a subordinate or an equal. "I can't call her Annie. Mrs. Phelan? No" (83). She solves the problem by speaking without using either name. This seemingly trivial exchange reminds readers of the impact of class distinctions upon concepts of identity. Katrina Daugherty does not face Annie Phelan as an equal, seeing before her the wife of a former lover. Rather, she relegates the woman to the position of nonentity, refusing to grant her any status whatever.

This conflicted view of Annie Phelan remains unvoiced and the dynamics of the struggle within Katrina are subtle enough to elude perception, but subsequent events throw her own dubious social position into relief. At Emmett's request she goes to find a priest to administer the last rites and to buy ale for a final drink. Her exchange with Father Loonan shows that Katrina does not have a clear sense of what liberties her position allows her. When she attempts to patronize him, Father Loonan refuses to grant her that privilege and delivers the sort of rebuke reserved for shallow creatures who require correction but no explanation: "Don't get flibbertigibbet on me" (86). When she enters a saloon to buy ale, her imperious manners cannot overcome prohibitions against serving unaccompanied women. She receives a dispensation only after invoking Emmett's name.

Near the conclusion of the episode, after Father Loonan has anointed Emmett, Katrina proposes that they drink a final toast to him. While her gesture seems to spring from genuine emotion, the tone and language prove more embarrassing than moving: "All praise to Emmett Daugherty. . . . All praise to a great man, I say. The truly great men are the poet, the priest, and the soldier, and Emmett Daugherty is a soldier of the righteous wars" (94). Katrina has dismissed her poet husband at the chapter's opening, she has tried unsuccessfully to patronize the parish priest in its middle, and in praising the "soldier of the righteous wars" she seems to forget that her father is responsible for crippling that soldier's brother. While these are not yet the ravings of a lunatic, even when striking a noble pose Katrina shows how profoundly self-delusion grips her.

In harsh succession to the scene of Emmett's death, the narrative recapitulates a newspaper story announcing the lynching of Cully Watson, a year and a half after he participated in the bull's head practical joke. Watson was being returned to New Orleans in the custody of two detectives when armed men kidnapped him. A short time later, police discovered Cully's body hanging from a telegraph pole in front of a Bourbon Street hotel where he had raped and tried to kill a woman ten days earlier. The details of Cully's New Orleans crime (95) proleptically mirror Edward's recollection of Felicity's account of Cully's assault on her (129). Nonetheless, when arrested, Cully had attempted to bargain with police by giving a lengthy account of his version of the events leading up to the killings at the Millerton House two years earlier. Both the violence and the achronicity may seem jarring here, but in flashing forward to Cully's death, the narrative alerts readers to the long-term significance of the description that immediately follows of the seemingly senseless mayhem that occurs at an annual outing on the Hudson River sponsored by a number of Albany social organizations.

Like the fire at the Delavan House, "A Picnic on the Barge, June 17, 1906" gives a graphic account of unexpected violence that starts a number of characters on courses of action that will lead to profound unhappiness. Unlike the Delavan fire, however, Katrina is not present, and her reasons, recounted by Edward, make it clear that she has given up any illusions about fitting into the world that her husband inhabits. "[S]he said she couldn't abide all that family sweetness, all those dowdy biddies, all the rowdiness. So she stayed home. Avoiding the class struggle" (98). Katrina's description of the scene is accurate on all counts, but that precision only heightens our awareness of her alienation. Giles Fitzroy, coming from the same background as Katrina, avoids such isolation by using practical jokes as a way to negotiate class differences. In a bitterly ironic twist, however, the fireman's wife joke that he initiates here,[9] which turns on the false promise of an adulterous liaison and a feigned murder, presages real adultery and the actual killings at the Millerton House.

Edward himself endures his own measure of alienation, using an aura of familiarity to mask his sense of inhabiting neither the world of his parents nor that of his in-laws. A chance encounter with Francis Phelan, paralleling the earlier meeting between Katrina and Annie Phelan, reflects this strained condition. Edward behaves in a cordial, if slightly distant, manner toward the young man. Nonetheless, his unvoiced response to Francis's good-intentioned comments contrasts his own bitter accommodation with events with the disarming naïveté of one still too young to realize that all acts have consequences.

> "If the Daughertys ever need anything. I'm there."
> Edward nodded and thought: I'll pass the word to Katrina. (103)

A further irony charges this already conflicted situation. Despite his bitterness over his wife's infidelity with Francis, Edward does not hesitate to form his art by drawing vicariously upon the working-class world of the young man's experiences. Edward has already used Francis's killing of a scab during the trolley strike of 1901 as the basis for the play *The Car Barns*, and he will weave the affair with Katrina into the play *The Flaming Corsage*, whose production concludes this novel.

Unvoiced animosity gives way to real violence when a gang of thugs, led by Cully Watson, starts a fight over beer. With a catastrophic rapidity that reminds readers of the tenuous hold on order exerted by even the most established social groups, they beat two policemen, take their guns, and escape during the ensuing brawl to the Rensselaer shore in a lifeboat rowed by Maginn. Unlike the battle twenty-one years earlier in Black Jack McCall's saloon, Maginn switches sides in search of a story and perhaps excitement. While the narrative seems to treat the matter as a momentary lapse, it in fact marks Maginn's shift to the fringes of society. It is a gesture that mimics Edward's effort to reposition himself among the social groups of Albany with only the direction, down instead of up, varying. In both cases, the move proves ultimately disastrous.

A seemingly ancillary episode immediately following the fight on the barge sets in motion the chain of events that will culminate tragically four years later in a New York City hotel room. Giles Fitzroy, Jimmy Cadden, and Edward Daugherty make a fool of Maginn, who is taken in by the fireman's wife joke. Like any false effort at conviviality, the hoax produces alienation rather than congeniality. The humiliation "generated a predictable withdrawal in Maginn, but also in Edward, whose guilt was such that he stopped work on his new play" (113). What the perpetrators fail to recognize, just as Francis Phelan has in his earlier conversation with Edward, is that any such action will provoke an equal and opposite reaction.

One year later, a Fourth of July gathering at the Daugherty house reveals the corrosive effect that life has had on a number of principal figures in the novel. All of the characters, with the exception of the ingenuous Giles, now operate under dissolute protocols very different from what their public personae suggest. Katrina presides in a drawing room filled with mementoes meant to evoke the hotel fire, "her chamber of venerated memory, her sumptuous crypt of exhausted life" (115). As she looks on with jaded indifference, Edward choreographs a dinner that will allow him to begin an affair with Melissa Spencer. The young actress in turn wishes to cultivate Edward because of his reputation as a playwright. Felicity Fitzroy has assumed the dual role of public prude and private coquette. And Maginn struggles through bravado to suppress a sense of sexual insecurity brought on by the fireman's wife joke.

When the narrative finally takes up the events surrounding the violent incident that opened the novel, the contrasting descriptions are now charged with the reader's evolving sense of the conflicted attitudes of the characters involved. In the first account, Edward transmits Felicity's description of Cully Watson robbing and raping her, and then dressing her in the cloak and mask that she was wearing when Giles shot her. Cully offers a radically different version, asserting that he had consensual sexual relations with Felicity and insinuating a lesbian relationship between Felicity and Melissa. Cully claims to have had no part in the murders. "When I heard about them I didn't blame the Doc. His wife was no good. But she was a pretty good fuck" (132). That bit of coarse bravado leaves the reader, like Edward, "sifting what happened."

Intertwined themes of sexual desire and emotional betrayal haunt Edward and compel him to seek the truth about the killings in New York. The wound from Giles's pistol penetrated his left chest but missed his heart, like the burning stick that injured Katrina, and, like Katrina's wound, it exerts significance as a psychological rather than as a physical scar. Clarification becomes a means of expiation, and toward that end Edward turns to Melissa, who offers yet another conflicted account, making it clear that she feels no impulse to reexamine those events.[10] While this attitude does not necessarily reflect guilt, it does underscore her genuine disinterest in anything but the moment, anything but physical gratification. Edward ends his interview by complimenting her ability as an actress and casting doubt on her story. "You make it quite credible. . . . I don't doubt any part of your story. But I'm absolutely certain you're a virtuoso liar" (142).

By this point in the novel, the narrative adopts an accelerated pace that mirrors the hectic, fragmented condition of the disintegrating lives of Edward and Katrina. When Edward returns home after speaking with Melissa, he finds that Katrina has left on his desk two volumes of the diary that she keeps, one for the year 1894 and one for 1908. In the essay that she has written for this volume, Vivian Valvano Lynch has commented very perceptively on Katrina's possible motivations for offering these intimate insights. While for my readings these motivations remain of subsidiary importance, her actions, nonetheless, enhance the interpretive complexity.

The 1894 diary has a passage for April 19 marked. It details a series of seemingly unconnected impressions: recollections of her mother's selling jewelry to cover her father's financial losses in the panic of 1893; mention of her father's mistress, Madame Baldwin; a description of an anti-suffrage meeting that her mother chaired; and an account of Giles Fitzroy's declaration of his love. Despite the episodic nature of these anecdotes, they offer evidence of the madness growing in Katrina's mind well before the hotel fire:

> I have no desire for Giles, but the idea of a lover is taking hold. It has everything to do with resisting my age, for I will be thirty soon. I know how vain and foolish this is, but it is no less real for that. Also I must punish Edward for despoiling me. I sought it, yes, but he did it, as he should have, or I would not have married him. But I cannot forgive him. He does not yet understand the craft of dying. I wonder, shall I be truly beautiful all my life? (145)

This irreconcilable condition that Katrina constructs underscores her mental and emotional turmoil, and mitigates any harsh attitude toward Edward's treatment of his wife that might have arisen solely from impressions gathered from the narrative of *Billy Phelan's Greatest Game* and *Ironweed.*

The second entry is dated October 17, 1908, the day that Giles murdered his wife and killed himself. It gives an account of a visit from Giles in which he shows Katrina a poem implicating Felicity, Edward, and Melissa in a ménage à trois and put in his mailbox at the same time that the bull's head appeared on his porch. Katrina's response is the sort of *non sequitur* that now characterizes her life. She disrobes for Giles, and tells him not to touch her. "He stared at me and we didn't speak, but I felt glorious, basking in the light of my dear friend's wan smile. . . . I had banished his frenzy" (146). The passage ends without further comment, leaving the reader to interpret how this stark solipsism offers a chilling glimpse of the disturbed features of Katrina's mind.

In counterpoint to these emotions, Edward very deliberately continues his efforts to reconstruct both the events and the causes of the tragedy at the Millerton House. He goes to see Clubber Dooley to pursue Maginn's connection in the matter. In the process he convinces Clubber that the bull's head joke in fact precipitated Giles's trip to New York and the murder of his wife. As a result of Edward's revelations, Clubber twice tries to kill himself, and is consequently committed to a mental institution. The narrative's dispassionate report of Clubber's end provides a relentless account of the ramifications of violence, even upon those ignorantly involved in its perpetration. This indirectly enforces the sense of the importance of community that has run as an undercurrent through the novel, for awareness of one's social group heightens one's sense of the repercussion of acts. Without this concern, one may not take into consideration the full consequences of one's behavior.

By this point in the novel, the narrative has focused upon Katrina to embody an individual's fragile grasp upon sanity and the vulnerability of anyone who moves through the world unsupported by community or individual belief. Though both she and Edward have prided themselves on having a knowledge of the world that produces a superior understanding of it, the discourse reiterates the unreliability of what each knows. As she prepares to leave her house on what will be the last day of her life, a disturbing exchange with Maginn seems to take place in Katrina's parlor. Maginn offers lurid new information about Edward, Melissa, and Felicity, and urges Katrina to commit adultery with him as an act of revenge. The conversation abruptly ceases, and later in the narrative (171) it becomes clear that Katrina has been remembering an exchange that took place sometime earlier. The incident's seamless insertion into the narrative, however, forces the reader to ask how Katrina herself perceived it and what if any distinction she now makes between the material and the imaginative world.

As the narrative continues to trace Katrina's movements, it shows that her actions do not simply underscore increasingly eccentric behavior. They reflect several of the dominant themes of *The Flaming Corsage*, specifically the unavoidable and far-reaching consequences that inevitably grow out of any deliberate act, and the inability of an individual to exist without communal support.

Seemingly on a whim, Katrina has her photograph taken. In the picture she assumes an idiosyncratic slightly flirtatious pose.

> The billowy V-neck of her dress was adjustable by hidden buttons, two of which she undid, allowing the neck to open to the edges of her shoulders. The separation of her breasts then became visible, but she concealed most of that with the sunflower, whose stem she snapped to shorten it, then tucked the stem inside her bodice. In her mirror image she had become different, new yet again. And, for the first time, the top of her white, oval scar from the Delavan was visible to the world, above the edge of her dress. (159)

This picture of a forty-seven-year-old coquette becomes Katrina's unwitting valediction and establishes her image as the paragon for female allure. "With the making of this picture [Pirie] MacDonald would elevate himself, for a time, to the status of master photographer of eastern American beauty" (160). The irony of this legacy, which would not have been lost upon her had she lived, is that it derives its charm from revealing so much in her nature that Katrina had spent a lifetime concealing.

During this day Katrina also visits her brother-in-law, Archie Van Slyke, at the State National Bank. Her errand ostensibly aims at tidying papers that have accumulated in a safety deposit box, but their inventory serves to adumbrate the decline of her family: jewelry, "what remained of the Taylor fortune"; birth certificates, endowments, deeds, all documents relating to wealth no longer held and individuals no longer alive; all seven volumes of her diary; and several of Edward's play manuscripts, one "Katrina cherished . . . for its compassion and insight—into her, of course—she the enduring heroine of all of Edward's works" (163). As Vivian Valvano Lynch has noted, Katrina here preserves her own version of her life. In the midst of this familial nostalgia, however, Katrina reinforces her sense of isolation from those around her. With an imperiousness that one has seen as early as her drive to the cemetery with Giles Fitzroy in 1885, and with a remarkable lack of connection with other people, she lectures Archie on his inability to cope with life.

> "Thank you so much, Archie. I must go up to the Hall now and see a bit of the dress rehearsal of Edward's play."
>
> "Yes, I saw a notice in the paper."
>
> "I believe he's written the tragedy of our lives. And do stop drinking, Archie. You're such a good man without it."
>
> "You should learn to mind your own business, Katrina."
>
> "Yes, I suppose I should. But I have so very little business to mind." (164–165)

The flippancy of those last lines enhances rather than diminishes their impact. Like her stunning last photograph, this final pronouncement on her life carries the full weight of an accurate representation strengthened by its heedless regard for audience. What Katrina does not acknowledge is that she has "so very little business to mind" because she has in a premeditated fashion cut herself off from the communities represented by the keepsakes so carefully preserved in her safety deposit box.

In the final and most revealing series of representations, Katrina makes good on her intention to visit Harmanus Bleecker Hall to watch a rehearsal of *The Flaming Corsage*. The scene that she views features an exchange between the two women who represent her and Melissa. Marina (Katrina) talks of how Mangan (Maginn) conceived the plot to expose her husband and his lover, Clarissa (Melissa). As the two women spar back and forth, readers of the novel have for the first time a delineation of Edward's own view of his infidelity.

> You linked yourself to my husband when he was a rising star, and now, after you've risen on his back, you want to destroy what remains of his life as a fallen star. . . . You began as a frivolous soubrette, full of intrigue, and in short order you've risen to become a sublime slut. Do your sluttish things, as you must, but don't speak to me of love. . . . Love is vertical. You are relentlessly horizontal. (170)

Katrina sums up her dispassionate judgment of the scene in a single line. "He makes me cleverer than I am" (171). While the solipsism of this remark attests to how little Katrina concerns herself with others, it also reiterates the impression generated by her photograph: the lasting impressions of Katrina derive from poses that she has initiated and that have been captured by others.

At the same time, whether an accurate view of his wife's intellectual ability or not, this portion of the drama gives readers additional insight into the dynamics surrounding Edward's adultery. Edward's decision to give his wife the most powerful lines in the play—despite her opinion that it subverts reality—demands our reconsideration of the impact of his promiscuity upon his consciousness. Further, the stunning condemnation of this dialogue underscores his view of how unreflective Melissa is even as it glosses her liaison with Martin, described in *Billy Phelan's Greatest Game*, as far more complex than it might initially have appeared.[11]

By the time Katrina returns home, the retrospective tone of the day has created a detached sense of herself. Questioning her life takes the form of a perspective already set in the past. "What, really, was my destiny?" (172). This suggestion of closure, of finality, has an important bearing then on how one interprets the final moments of Katrina's life. Her actions stand out clearly, but her motivations remain opaque. When she notices that the Christian Brothers school next door is on fire, the conscious decision she makes to remain in the house seems almost instinctual.

> She went to the window of the office and parted the curtains to see the Christian Brothers school next door in flames. It was clear to her that the fire would make the leap to this room in a matter of minutes. She went back to Edward's chair and put her head down on his desk. The smoke was familiar in her mouth. She had breathed fire before. (172-173)

For readers the most intriguing feature of this selection is not Katrina's decision to allow the flames to consume her but the question of how to judge that passive acceptance of death. On the one hand, one might see her as a victim of conflicting social forces that she could neither foresee nor control. Conversely, one could view her as a perverse manipulator, dying in a gesture of disdain for all who cared for her. The strength of this account lies in its willingness to allow readers to make that choice.

Edward's response is equally ambiguous. He has her funeral mass said in Sacred Heart Church, and then buries her privately in Albany Rural Cemetery. This alternating demonstration—public Catholicism and private Protestantism—neatly captures the ambivalence of their relationship. Edward knows that Katrina was never part of his society, yet a Catholic Mass allows him to thumb his nose once more at her side of the family (though only her mother remains alive). By interring her at the Albany Rural Cemetery, he denies her link to his family and returns her to the place where they consummated their relationship twenty-seven years earlier. A further twist to this behavior comes in the chapter's final lines when Edward makes clear his belief that she is a suicide by telling his son, "We will regret forever that she has willfully left us" (177). Again, it remains for readers to decide if conscience or callousness shapes his decision not to bury her in the hallowed ground of a Catholic cemetery. (Those inclined to a hasty judgment either way should recall the marvelous contrast of veneration and sacrilege in the scene at Saint Agnes Cemetery that opens *Ironweed*.)

Accounts of the completion, performance, and closing of Edward's play follow in rapid succession, inextricably linking that drama and Katrina's life (or at the very least her death). *The Flaming Corsage* folds after one performance, condemned by Thomas Maginn, not as immoral but simply as bad drama.[12] In a gesture that presages the novel's conclusion, Edward returns to his art to comprehend the experiences that have overwhelmed him. He composes a fragment of a play, set at Sing Sing and detailing the execution of Maginn for unspecified crimes, with Giles and a deceased Edward present as witnesses. The scene has the aura of magic realism that has hovered about Kennedy's writing since *The Ink Truck,* but putting such a slant in a play avoids the problems of continuity that arose from this approach in his earlier works.

The narrative now increasingly mirrors Edward's desultory search for meaning. It shifts to a description of Edward's reclusive life in his parent's home. As he strolls the streets he had known as a child, Edward thinks of his dead father, perhaps unconsciously comparing their lives. On his walk, he meets Cappy White, whom he and Katrina had encountered with his wife Mamie on the day that Edward brought Katrina to meet his parents. Mamie is long dead, and Cappy now leads the life of a hermit. The exchange between the two desolate men shows the stunning power of Kennedy's economic language.

> "Hi ya, Cappy," Edward said.
> "Who's that?"
> "Eddie Daugherty."
> "Eddie, yeah, you're back. I heard you lost everything."
> "That's right, Cappy."
> "So did I."
> "I know."
> "How you livin'?"
> "Best way I can."
> "You still got your son," Cappy said.
> "I guess you could say that."
> "I lost my son."
> "I know you did. I hate that, Cappy."
> "So do I."
> "You get out much, Cap?"
> "Nope. No reason to."
> "Maybe it'll get better."
> "No, it won't get no better. You oughta know that."
> "I keep wondering whether it's finished."
> "It's finished."
> "How do you know?"
> "They ain't nothin' worth doin'."
> "It seems like that, all right." (190–191)

Though both men find themselves in the same situation, their language in terse but eloquent phrases traces their diametrically opposed views: Edward's timid optimism and Cappy's exhausted nihilism. The scene represents the emotional conclusion of the novel, but the narrative continues in deference to Edward's perhaps unrealistic determination to impose meaning upon the events that have shaped his life.

As the novel moves toward its end, a more conventional narrative pattern struggles to impose a kind of closure. It leads Edward to confront Maginn in a whorehouse where the latter is now residing, with the seediness of the place serving as an ironic commentary on the consequences of living the life of venereal obsession that Maginn had always claimed he sought. As a locus of adult fantasies, the bordello serves as an apt backdrop for Edward's explanation of the complex scheme—involving the hotel shooting and the death of Cully Watson—that Maginn hatched to bring about Edward's destruction and to avenge himself for the humiliation that he suffered through the fireman's wife joke. Maginn counters with his own version of the story that adds another level of deceit to the actions of almost every character involved, and the only truth that emerges in the telling and retelling of the events surrounding the shooting at the Millerton House is the breadth of human venality—from the banal to the purely evil—of which characters are capable. Deceit has made the truth irrecoverable, and violence becomes the only way to bring this bitter disquisition to an abrupt halt. One of the whores knocks Edward unconscious with a lead pipe. When Edward comes to, Maginn's flight serves as a way of forcing an explanation of the ambiguities that muddled perceptions of events at the opening of the novel.

The final pages, however, revert to a form that undermines any inclination to draw a clear conclusion from the experiences of any of the characters. Returning home, Edward engages in two dramatic dialogues with Katrina that articulate Edward's view of what had undermined their marriage. The conversations will seem biased to any reader with sympathy for Katrina, for they highlight both her mania and her frigidity. In the end it is solipsism more than anything else that characterizes her. Edward's own failings do escape him, but they do not necessarily get past the reader. Near the close of the chapter Edward speaks rhetorically to his father: "Did you ever consider . . . that I never was the Irishman on horseback? It may be I was free of racial and social destinies, and that what I wanted was altogether different from what had gone before" (207). While all this may be quite true, Edward fails to grasp the significance of what he has said. Being "free of racial and social destinies" and wanting something "altogether different from what had gone before" mean simply being cut off from his community and living outside the structure afforded by its ethical system. Such an isolation may have no effect upon a character who moves from that community. (Arguably the life of Peter Phelan demonstrates that.) But no one who chooses to remain in Albany can sustain himself alone without becoming another Cappy White.

NOTES

1. All quotations are from William Kennedy's *The Flaming Corsage* (New York: Viking Press, 1996).

2. The bordello is made up of four tents located on the State Fairgrounds just past the Bull's Head Tavern, the scene of one of John the Brawn's boxing triumphs described in *Quinn's Book* and a name that here has a proleptic *double entendre*.

3. Given Maginn's disreputable behavior later in the novel, one might be tempted to see the polarities of their occupations and their characters as Kennedy's comment on the nature of literary critics. Being one myself I cannot help but hope this is an oversimplification of his motives.

4. Here the analogue between sex organs and cameras first adduced in *Very Old Bones* recurs again with the female-camera association replaced by the male-camera.

5. This may recall for some readers a similar incident in *Billy Phelan's Greatest Game* when Billy cowed a rowdy teenager with a hot cup of coffee.

6. Christian Michener, *From Then Into Now: William Kennedy's Albany Novels* (Scranton: University of Scranton Press, 1998), 247.

7. For a very different assessment of this exchange, one that gives a much kinder view of Edward's motivations, see Michener, *From Then Into Now*, 241–245.

8. The episode is based on an actual Albany hotel fire of the period. See R. Z. Sheppard, "Living with the Ashes," *Time,* May 13, 1996, 92–93.

9. For a complete description of the fireman's wife joke, see the chapter "Courting the Fireman's Wife" in *The Flaming Corsage* (110–113).

10. The narrative confirms that the affair between Edward and Melissa Spencer lasted no more than a year and was over when Giles burst in on them in the hotel. Though *Billy Phelan's Greatest Game* may leave the impression that Melissa and Edward have a prominent and long-running affair, it is really Martin who will have the more sustained relationship with her.

11. Needless to say, the entire chapter sheds new light on why in 1938 Melissa will have such a keen desire to play the Katrina character in a revival of the drama.

12. In *Very Old Bones* the narrative claims it lasted for two performances.

This essay was presented at "William Kennedy: A Celebration . . . A Symposium on His Work" held at the Omni Albany Hotel (now Hilton Albany), Albany, New York, on April 15–17, 1999. It also appears in Michael Patrick Gillespie's book *Reading William Kennedy* (Syracuse: Syracuse University Press, 2001), 146–166. Reprinted with permission of Michael Patrick Gillespie and Syracuse University Press.

Courtesans, Stars, Wives, and Vixens

The Many Faces of Female Power in Kennedy's Novels

Neila C. Seshachari

> Kennedy's singularity in treating women is that he portrays them all as they see themselves, as heroic women, who are not given to driveling self-pity, nor to self-deprecation and self-doubt.
>
> —Neila C. Seshachari

I must begin this essay with a confession. Sometime in the mid-1970s, just about the time I was appointed at Weber State University, my taste in reading literature underwent a subtle but cataclysmic change. I continued to appreciate well-written fiction and poetry, but the way writers portrayed their female characters shaped my decision of whether or not to complete reading their works. I became more sensitive to the treatment and development of female characters in any given work.

My introduction to William Kennedy's works came late. A few weeks before I saw the film *Ironweed* in the late 1980s, I read the book and was moved by its humanity, mysticism, and spirituality. In Saratoga Springs, New York, at the New York State Summer Writers Institute in 1991, I picked up a copy of *Quinn's Book* to get it autographed after Kennedy's scheduled reading. Bill Kennedy saw the hardback copy with interest and, as he turned the book to write an inscription, his eyes fell on the abominable thin blue line along its folded pages. "A remaindered book," he chuckled. I winced, but he was happily writing his inscription: "For Neila, in the midst of wine, horses, & literature at Saratoga (See p. 239 et seq.)." With a flourishing line that dived to the bottom of the page, he signed, William Kennedy, and after a split second he added impulsively, in parenthesis (see you in Utah).

Getting *Quinn's Book* autographed made a big difference in my professional life. Within the next few years, Kennedy visited Utah as a featured speaker at the Rocky Mountain MLA Conference that I organized at Weber State University, and he completed his one-act play, *Dinner at the Phelans*, to be published alongside Tom Smith's interview with him, both of which I had requested as editor of *Weber Studies: An Interdisciplinary Humanities Journal*. By the following year, I was working on *Conversations with William Kennedy* for the University Press of Mississippi, and for which I interviewed Kennedy at his home in Averill Park, New York, in December 1996.

Kennedy's works pleased me for a number of reasons: his extraordinary voice, ubiquitous humor, versatile style, his bold and imaginative use of history and myth that weave through his narratives, and his use of Albany as the one "magical place" where the "multiple incarnations" of human drama take place. But what intrigued and fascinated me most was the way he fleshed out all his female characters as "subjects" who voiced their own thoughts rather than those of their male creator. Courtesans, homeless bums, mistresses, or wives, every one of these characters seemed to radiate her own unique power that precluded each from being pitied as victim or object.

In the heyday of feminism, critics who were rethinking women's roles in terms of power were discouraged by the gloomy evidence they detected everywhere in literature of "woman as victim" or "woman as the oppressed Other." Critics like Nina Auerbach even pleaded that women's power must be "searched out and insisted upon" (7). Judith Lowder Newton, in *Women, Power, and Subversion*, noted that to survive the chronicle of a timeless and unchanging oppression, the women's movement needed to develop coping strategies in discovering covert power in women. *Signs: Journal of Women in Culture and Society* devoted its initial volumes in 1975 to theoretical analyses of "Power and Powerlessness" to identify the sources of female power.

One does not have to search for female power in the Albany Cycle of novels. Kennedy's women characters carry the aura of their power like bright halos around their heads. All of Kennedy's female characters are individualistic, some outstanding, all very different from one another. There is no stereotyping here of any kind. When I interviewed Kennedy, I asked him how he managed to portray them so differently in voice and point of view.

"It's the same as I depict the men," he said seriously, "discovering what is singular about them, in some way, extremism of behavior. The protagonists of my books are always *extremists*" (*Conversations* 259, italics mine). Herein lies the key to understanding Kennedy's creation of women characters.

Bernard Shaw, in explaining the powerful women in his plays, told *The New York Times Magazine* in 1927, "I always assumed that a woman was a person exactly like myself, and that is how the trick is done" ("As Bernard Shaw Sees Woman," June 19, 1927, 2; qtd. in Watson 114). Shaw's vision enabled him to imagine his women in nontraditional roles; Kennedy's imagination similarly enabled him to vitalize the women in his novels in nonstereotypic ways. Both writers make the shift from woman imagined as an object to woman treated as subject, a woman who is a sentient being. We might note here that the best writers imagine all characters as subjects.

Kennedy's female characters are not driven into behavioral extremism by external circumstances; they are self-directed into extremist behavior, which is their own choice and exercise of power. They derive their power through directing their own lives within the social confines of the historical times in which they find themselves. Katrina Taylor Daugherty, Maud Fallon, Magdalena Colón, Helen Archer, Giselle Marais Purcell readily come to mind. However, Annie Phelan in *Billy Phelan's Greatest Game*, Molly in *Very Old Bones,* Hillegond in *Quinn's Book,* Alice Diamond and Kiki Roberts in *Legs* are no less powerful as individuals, even though their roles in the respective novels are relatively minor. All these women lead their lives, albeit in a male-defined world, on their own terms.

Historically, our definitions of power, like our very conception of history itself, have systematically excluded consideration of women. In any discussion of female power, it is important to distinguish between power as control, which is a particularly masculine concept, versus power as agency or ability, which has been recognized as a resource more available to women. Elizabeth Janeway first noted that the *Oxford English Dictionary* gives two core definitions of the word "power": 1) the "ability" to do something or anything; 2) "dominance." "What is the relationship between these two?" Janeway asks, and she suggests, "The liberating power of capability may be power-as-seen from within, while the limiting power of domination is power-as-experienced by others." She goes on to suggest that "if one's power is felt by others as dominance and compulsion, then it is morally dubious, for it can be justified only if it does not impinge on the capability of others" (103). It is with these distinctions in mind that I explore the female power of Kennedy's women characters.

I was drawn into reading Kennedy through *Quinn's Book,* so I shall begin my inquiry into the power of William Kennedy's "female protagonists," as he calls them, with an examination of this book's major female characters—Maud and Magdalena Colón. It may be a misnomer to talk of "female protagonists" in Kennedy's Albany Cycle of novels because none of Kennedy's novels has a female protagonist in the traditional sense of the word. Yet novels like *Quinn's Book, Ironweed*, and *The Flaming Corsage* feature major female characters, who lay claim to sharing the title of protagonist. In every novel, whether they are major characters or not, Kennedy's female characters project themselves with such individuality that they draw attention to themselves.

Quinn's Book charts the career of the adolescent Daniel Quinn, an orphan, from the time he sets eyes on "Maud, the wondrous," who is then only twelve years old, until he is on the verge of consummating his love with her fifteen years later. In the interval between these two events, Daniel Quinn sets forth on his own adventures—into a career in journalism, which draws him into the historic Civil War, gives him opportunities to help slaves flee North, and develops his personality as a well-educated thinking individual, with his head and heart in the right places.

The first paragraph of the novel sets the tone, not only for the book and its events, but for the power and autonomy that Kennedy's female characters command:

> I, Daniel Quinn, neither the first nor the last of a line of such Quinns, set eyes on Maud the wondrous on a late December day in 1849 on the banks of the river of aristocrats and paupers, just as the great courtesan, Magdalena Colón, also known as La Última, a woman whose presence turned men into spittling, masturbating pigs, boarded a skiff to carry her across the river's icy water from Albany to Greenbush, her first stop en route to the city of Troy, a community of iron, where later that evening she was scheduled to enact, yet again, her role as the lascivious Lais, that fabled prostitute who spurned Demosthenes' gold and yielded without fee to Diogenes, the virtuous, impecunious tubdweller. (5)

This beginning fixes part of the reader's critical mind on the book's mythic dimension. Daniel is the mythic hero; Maud is the object of his affection. In mythic terms, as Joseph Campbell has noted, the quest of the hero, the sum total of all his bravery, gets equated with his ultimate goal of acquiring and possessing his love. The object of his affections becomes the end-all, and winning her love has echoes of a fairy-tale ending: "And they lived happily ever after." This "mythic power" of the woman, no matter how heartwarming to women, is male defined; it answers the psychic needs of males. The woman is the symbolic Anima that enhances, complements, or completes the Animus within the male hero. The roots of this search can be traced to chivalric ideals which, as Kate Millet shrewdly observes in *Sexual Politics* (1969), lead to the exploitation of women. Mythic power rarely comes to the aid of a woman in her daily life. But in *Quinn's Book,* the suggestion of this mythic power only heightens the book's aura of magical realism without in any way impinging on the freedom of either Maud or Magdalena Colón. While the opening paragraph voices the mythic dimension of Quinn's *personal* dreams, the actual events take off in their own directions. If we think of Quinn and Maud's love as a fairy-tale love, then we must recognize right away that this fairy tale develops along a new paradigm: Daniel and Maud each go their own way to seek their destinies after they find each other, after she asks him to kidnap her, and after Daniel falls in love with her.

Likewise, Magdalena Colón, Maud's widowed aunt and caregiver, might appear at first to be the mythic Crone. In mythic terms, the withered and aging woman, who is no longer defined in relation to a man, becomes a wise counselor and caregiver. She is rendered sexless. But not Magdalena. As a courtesan, Magdalena wields sexual power in whose presence men turn "into spittling, masturbating pigs." She has the attributes of Lais, "the lascivious and fabled prostitute who spurned Demosthenes' gold and yielded without fee to Diogenes, the virtuous, impecunious tubdweller." Traditionally, sexpots become "objects" of cheap love. Far from eliciting this stereotypical response, Magdalena actually turns out to be the power that commands men into doing her bidding.

Magdalena is a crafty businesswoman as well. Her recklessness in crossing the Hudson on a stormy day is a clever commercial to pack audiences for her performances. She flamboyantly advertises in the *Albany Chronicle* that she would pay one hundred dollars, "a bloody fortune," to any boatman who would take her from Albany to Greenbush, where she would board a carriage bound overland to Troy. She is the master of spectacle in show biz. At the Great Pier, with calculated craftiness, she speaks in her "fraudulent, Hispanicized English" and hands over a hundred-dollar bill to boatman Carrick with pomp and ceremony, after lifting his woolen hat and kissing him on his lumpy forehead. Magdalena demands admiration and gets it.

"One dead slut," says her macho rescuer, John the Brawn, as he heaves her and her floating trunk into his skiff after the boat capsizes, but his lecherous sex act with her corpse revives her literally from the world of the dead, and he ends up being her slave-lover, escorting her everywhere on her performance tour.

Magdalena is adored by her young niece as well. Twelve-and-a-half-year-old Maud tells Quinn that her aunt is vastly superior to her own mother as a human being. Lusted after by men and hated just as fiercely by women, Magdalena incites extreme reactions. A woman rose from beside her inert man and bit a chunk out of Magdalena's cheek and spat on her chest as she lies "dead," we are told.

Quinn and Maud witness Magdalena's corpse staring at them with one open eye. "Close her eye," pleads Maud. "If you look into their [corpses'] eyes you see your fate. And one must never know one's fate if one is to keep sane" (17). But Magdalena's closed eye opens again and Quinn sees disturbing visions that he must learn to interpret. Power accrues to Magdalena in every way. She expects to dominate all who come in contact with her and she succeeds. Her masterstroke in her power plays undoubtedly is the wake she holds for herself fifteen years later, a week before she actually dies.

But at this moment when Quinn sees visions of his fate in "dead" Magdalena's open eye, Maud takes charge of her own life and Quinn's future as well. She tells him she is never going to grow up to be like her hated mother, or even like her saintly whore of an aunt, and that he, Quinn, should steal her away from Hillegond Staat's house if Hillegond tries to take charge of her life. "Now kiss me," she commands Daniel (19).

Thus the wondrous Maud, literally the damsel in distress, turns out to be the arbiter of her own fate. The fairy-tale princess here is not passively asleep in a deadly pall, unaware that her entire future is in the hands of a Prince Charming who must kiss her to bring her to life and then "kidnap" her, as Walter Scott's young Lochinvar does, in order to share his romantic future with her. Quinn may be her future Prince Charming, but she tells him that she is never going to marry anyone. She is on her own personal quest.

Maud's personal search is quite singular—she forays into seances and the world of spirits, and she pursues a career as a performer and dancer of rare courage and artistry. Like a male hero, she too is initiated sexually in the way of the world. We are not told of Quinn's sexual experiences. We see him earning our respect as he aids the freeing of slaves, gets involved as a journalist in the Civil War, comes home and is booed when he portrays the reality of war. His achievements are not dependent on Maud's love or her faithfulness, as hers too are not dependent on his support. They are both individual achievers, both possessing "singularity of character," both exhibiting "extremism of behavior," whose lives intersect at the end, with the smitten Daniel poised to enter her life.

Book 1 of *Quinn's Book* begins with an inscription from Albert Camus, ". . . man's work is nothing but this slow trek to rediscover, through the detours of art, those two or three great and simple images in whose presence his heart first opened." I want to suggest that the image of a powerful woman with *varying representations,* an archetypal woman certainly, but also one who is nobody's minion, who gives herself the autonomy she yearns for and therefore blames no man for her destiny, seems to be one of the images that Kennedy's writerly heart opens up to. For what comes through in *Quinn's Book* is not just the magical realism of churning myth and history but also the strength and power of Kennedy's female characters who capture his imagination. These characters are no victims in any male-dominated situation; they are the agents of change in their own lives. They exude female power.

Maud is not a supporting character or the beloved who *helps* her man change the world. J. K. Van Dover, who thinks of Daniel Quinn's romantic interest in Maud as the central action of the novel, points out that Maud's independent life "that has no connections with the love plot"—her conversations with the spirit world, her career as a dancer, for instance—takes away the "coherent center" of the novel (110–111). But the center of the novel, in a real sense, comprises the trajectories of these two singular characters, whose lives weave a collage of activities that reflect not only the mythic magnitude of their historical times, but their own extremism of behavior and singularity as well.

Also, Maud, as well as Magdalena Colón, defies the female code of sexuality. Our culture has always been ambivalent about sexuality and the mysteries of Dionysian energy in women; in Kennedy's world, however, the female is not bound by the restrictive code of sexuality or even matrimony. Even more significantly these women recognize, as Maud knows, as does Katrina Daugherty, that with marriage, their lives are likely to be restricted. When they step into matrimony, they make the conscious decisions to do so.

If Maud and Magdalena are major characters who exercise their powers by making decisions that determine their life-paths, there are others, like Molly in *Very Old Bones,* who exercise their power heroically and quietly within their limited lives. Molly is not a "major character" by any means. She is one of many women in the Phelan family who engage our attention in this novel, which technically begins and ends on the same day, Saturday, July 26, 1958, when Peter Phelan brings all his family together, including his "bastard" son Orson Purcell, who becomes its narrator, to read them his will. The entire novel can be read as a novel of reconciliation and expiation, of making peace with oneself and within one's family for all the sins committed willfully or unwittingly. Structurally rich and complex, *Very Old Bones* weaves a tapestry of the Phelan family history, which includes a large number of women characters, mostly not lovable, but all noteworthy.

Molly stands out as perhaps the most powerful and lovable, inasmuch as she quietly appropriates power to herself and exercises it confidently and unobtrusively in both familial and social, as well as spiritual ways. The youngest daughter of the seven children born to Kathryn and Michael Phelan, Molly is also the most unfortunate in worldly terms. Molly gets pregnant when she and Walter Mangan are courting at Grand View Lake House on Saratoga Lake soon after her mother's death in 1934. She decides to abort her fetus secretly all by herself. Unsuccessful in her attempts, she gives birth prematurely after four months to a stillborn son, then buries the baby boy in the Phelan family cellar, safely tucked away "with boxes of horseshoes and jam jars on top of him" (221). Married subsequently to the child's unsuspecting father, she is widowed within two years, when Walter Mangan is killed in a car accident in 1937, and she returns "home" permanently to the Phelan household. In accepting the traditional lifestyle of middle-class women in the 1930s, Molly may appear to be passive, but she is in reality the silent powerhouse that sustains the dour Phelan family as its tired members eke out their lives.

In discussing Molly's female power, we may find it useful to keep in mind the views of two theorists on the subject. Berenice Carroll has pointed out that the definition of power primarily as "control, dominance, and influence" is of recent origin and that the primary meaning of power as late as 1933 was "ability, energy, and strength." Carroll sees "ability" as the capacity to assert "one's will over one's body, one's own organs and functions, and over the physical environment—a power which is seen as inherently satisfying and not merely as an instrument to other ends, as neither requiring nor leading to the power to command obedience in other persons" (585, 591). It is a form of self-definition and self-rule.

Barbara Bellow Watson persuasively argues that "[w]e must observe women as agents—*even secret agents*—as agonists though not always protagonists. . . . [T]hese are not visions of woman triumphant but of woman militant, the agonist who is active and perceptive and, if she loses, defeated by circumstances and overpowering forces not by masochism or *passivity*" (115, italics mine). Molly exemplifies most closely the type of woman both Carroll and Watson would have had in mind.

Molly's life is beset with unfortunate circumstances not of her making. Her personal life is punctuated with deaths of her loved ones. Christian Michener, for instance, observes that Molly's relationship with Walter is "defined by death" (208). Molly and Walter fall in love when they are both independently vacationing at the Grand View Lake House on Saratoga Lake. She picks up an injured waxwing that has fallen from a tree and he helps her revive it for a few days until it looks healed. On its first flight to freedom, it sits on the same tree for a while and falls dead. Their shared grief helps them cement their intimacy. During this courtship, Walter's hint of a forthcoming marriage proposal comes to her only in cryptic Kennedian grotesque: "How'd you like to be buried with my people?" (209). Molly, as events turn out, has Walter buried in the Phelan graveyard.

We see Molly's powers when Walter dies in the accident on his way to Virginia. As she tells Giselle in their "colloquy, September 1954," she comes to know of his death only when the abominable Mangan family informs her of the wake through their funeral services. She goes to the wake accompanied by her own undertaker, and she exercises her "widow's rights." She wants to take Walter's body with her for his final wake before burial in the Phelan family plot. She exhorts them sternly, "I hope none of you try to stop me, because I have a letter my lawyer got me from the courts . . . and if you raise one finger against me I'll have the police on you." She confides in Giselle, "I really didn't have a letter; I made that up" (210). In making that momentous decision, Molly exercises the kind of judgment or power that is normally assumed by males.

In all her dealings with her unwanted pregnancy, Molly shows not only her moral power in taking charge of her own body but religious and spiritual power as well. There is no shame or sin for a young Catholic greater than premarital pregnancy. Refusing to be marginalized by Church and society, and unable to share her anxiety with any of her sisters or brothers, or even her own lover, Walter, who has not yet proposed to her formally, she taps into her own inner strengths instead of giving way to spiritual disillusionment or depression. She refuses to implicate Walter in this "sin" for two reasons: Since he has not proposed to her formally, she does not want to put moral pressure on him to do so as a result of her pregnancy, as she tells Giselle; and she perhaps wants to protect Walter and herself from social embarrassment and spiritual shame that would surely be pronounced by the Church. She decides single-handedly that the "right action" to take is aborting the fetus. Florence Nightingale, in *Suggestions for Thought to Searchers After Religious Truth* (2:24), asks a searching question on morality that may enable us to understand Molly's plight and decision. Nightingale asks, "What is morality to be referred to? Is it not *to our sense of right?* But we have referred it to a book [the Bible], which book makes many contradictory assertions" (qtd. in Jenkins 41, italics mine). Seen in this light, we may recognize that in Molly's own eyes, her decision is a moral action, devoid of guilt.

The Church also has a history of marginalizing women of their spiritual powers. But Molly quietly claims this spiritual power to baptize her son "with water from the sink in a teacup" and name him Walter Phelan, not Walter Mangan. "We don't know how strong we are, do we?," she says to Orson as she takes him into confidence. "God was with the Phelans, don't you think? He took the baby but saved us from scandal and he let me have my love back" (221). The baby, who gets his name from both the father and the mother, remains buried in the Phelan cellar for almost two decades until Molly gets a chance to bury him properly when her sister Sarah dies in 1954. Molly exhumes baby Walter's remains with Orson Purcell's help and puts the swaddling cloth in its "burial packaging" of brown paper and a white linen napkin with the scrolled letter "P" on one corner, all tucked in a small purse. She asks Orson to place the purse under the pillow in sister Sarah's coffin.

Thus Molly appropriates to herself another spiritual birthright as well—the right to give her baby a Christian burial. The decision to abort one's baby is never easy on any woman, and the way Molly deals with her long ordeal is heart-wrenchingly admirable.

Molly exercises her spiritual power to legitimize her stillborn son's connections with his God and, in his burial, his biological bond with his rightful family, the Phelans. Molly's Church-patriarchs would have relegated her innocent baby to a life in Purgatory for eternity; Molly has the courage to circumvent, even subvert, their censure by reclaiming the God-given power of ritual to the believing. I find Molly to be the most courageous, generous, and most powerful of Kennedy's women characters.

Molly may appear to some as a victim in her circumstances, but she does not think of herself as one. She feels helpless, depressed, and guilty only when she cannot intercede on behalf of her siblings with the dour and masochistic Sarah, cannot prevent Sarah from beating up Tom into a literal cripple for misbehaving with an elderly woman à la Charlie Chaplin (197). But she is otherwise a sunny creature, who connects with everyone. "She was wonderful at human relationships and I loved her," says Orson (278).

Molly is a liberated woman, despite her sixty-four years, even in her sexuality. When she and Orson, twenty-five years her junior, feel attracted to each other, she goes to Grand View Lake House and relives her cherished moments of her courtship with Walter when she waltzes repeatedly with Orson to "When I Grow Too Old to Dream" by Ray Noble and his orchestra. This is a dance of celebration of life by two intimate people who have fallen "in love with each other's failed love" (223). Later, when they are sitting in the hotel parlor and watching the fire glow—the same in whose presence she tells him about herself and about aborting her baby—his hand wanders over her face and then comes down on her bosom. She tells him it is all right to fondle her. She too runs her fingers through his hair and reaches enough emotional intimacy to kiss him "with the fullness of her mouth." But she sets parameters on their relationship right away when she removes his hand gently and puts it back on his lap. "We must find a way not to be naughty" (220), she says. Molly's benevolent love is powerful. As Orson confides in us, his readers, "She [Giselle] says she envies me the family ties, and that she's come to understand she and I might be divorced now if it weren't for Molly" (249–250). As he recalls earlier, Molly was the one to oversee his reentry into the human race after his alcoholic depression and grave illness (215).

Women's friendships can often become sources of power. Through her friendship with bootlegger Cubby Conroy's dying widow, Charity, Molly gets a windfall of a total of twenty-seven thousand dollars in cash, which she astutely converts into gold coins and, through the years, distributes a gold coin of different denominations each to various family members on special occasions such as birthdays. To Orson she gives forty ten-dollar gold pieces when he first moves to the Lake House (in 1953) to recuperate from his mental breakdown. As Orson comments after she inherits another tidy sum, this time from her brother Peter Phelan, she is "the self-sufficient dowager, ready with the quick fix for family trouble" (279).

Molly possesses an abundance of self-worth and generosity. The notion of power encoded in public life is not available to her and therefore does not interest her. She has, however, tremendous "influence," which she exercises, albeit unconsciously, on various individuals who inhabit her personal world. In exercising her ability in taking charge of her own affairs, she exercises a form of resistance to dominant values. In foregrounding her own female ability and her subversive undercutting of family control, she exercises her power.

In evaluating William Kennedy's women characters, one has to consider connections between text and historical contexts, and to the changing ideological and material situations in which the evolution of all power—but particularly female power—takes place. One recognizes how "literature has more to say about power than might first appear" and how "literature teaches that power is relative and confused; that power is everywhere in a variety of forms and degrees; that all our [initial] formulations about power are [often] too simple" (Watson 113, 118).

A close reading of Kennedy's works reveals his dual representations of women: 1) women as they are seen by male characters (by macho men like Jack "Legs" Diamond or his outlaw buddies, depraved men like Maginn or Marcus Gorman, as well as by sensitive men like Daniel Quinn or Orson Purcell) and 2) women as they see themselves. Kennedy's singularity in treating women is that he portrays them all as they see themselves, as heroic women, who are not given to driveling self-pity, nor to self-deprecation and self-doubt. They are either capable of exercising their influence as arbiters of their own fates or they are social "victims" who deal with their fallen conditions with dignity. Helen Archer, for instance, is dignified in every way and singular enough to even choose the way she dies.

Other women characters who hold our admiration and deserve extensive attention in Kennedy's complex world are: Katrina Daugherty, who dominates two novels in which she is a relatively minor character—*Billy Phelan's Greatest Game* and *Ironweed*—and who shares the limelight in *The Flaming Corsage;* Giselle Marais Purcell in *Very Old Bones,* who is a photographer of global renown, "a pioneer feminist in a man's world" (284); Helen Archer and Annie Phelan in *Ironweed*. Helen and Giselle can take care of themselves in ways that have historically been seen as uniquely male. (Unfortunately, I have time only to mention all these powerful women here.)

One may legitimately ask how Kennedy's women characters are unique. They do not fall into the traditional mold of passive, submissive women—a concept we see propagated by some writers even in our own times. Even Annie, the most traditional of Kennedy's women characters, manages to rise in stature the day Francis Phelan visits her with a turkey after twenty-eight years. Annie welcomes him with dignity, leads him up to the attic to show him the trunk with all his baseball things in it, gives him back his self-relinquished power as a member of the family by telling him he could share the room with grandson Daniel Quinn if he decides to stay. But she lets him know obliquely that her spousal relationship with him is over. In the decades of the 1920s and 1930s, women whose husbands walked out on them may have felt discouraged and discarded, but not Annie. She creates no melodrama of an abandoned housewife when Francis comes home. She rises in stature not only in our own eyes for conducting herself with dignity, but in Francis's as well, as one who has never blamed him for dropping their infant son, Gerald, to his death.

Kennedy's uninhibited women free themselves of oppressive societal restrictions. This is not to say that Kennedy does not portray the downtrodden. Far from it. Kennedy's world is full of fallen characters who are also singular. *The Flaming Corsage* begins with a scene in which Maginn and Edward Daugherty visit a house of ill fame. But the prostitutes are highly individualistic. They come alive. Rose, the older woman who initiates Edward, is witty and lighthearted, without self-pity. In her memorable tête-à-tête with Edward, she elicits our admiration. In *Legs,* both Alice Diamond and Kiki Roberts, Jack's wife and mistress, display their feisty independence and conduct themselves with the dignity that is worthy of our respect.

Katrina is the fascinating, uninhibited, obstinate, true aristocrat who does not give a hoot about what other people think of her. In *Billy,* she is the seductress who initiates Francis. In *Ironweed* and *Bones,* she haunts as memory; and in *The Flaming Corsage,* she vies with Edward, her husband, to be treated as a protagonist, rather than a major but peripheral character. One detects in her independence a dialectic of power play that goes beyond the simple male/female realm. Not surprisingly, Kennedy thinks of her as his "most complex female creation" (*Conversations* 254). Katrina's death is neither a passive nor a desperate act. It is a conscious choice.

Kennedy's representations of women vary somewhat depending on the times they live in, especially in light of the shifting social mores of those times, but his women characters are always tough and powerful. In order to assess their female power, we must not look for their nonexistent declarations and manifestos, but for their unspoken convictions, their actions that subvert accepted values, the hidden meanings that emerge from their day-to-day living strategies. Kennedy uses toughness in complicated ways to break or bend gender stereotypes. His women characters, who come from all walks of life, owe their courage and power to their creator, who makes no distinction between the creation of his male or female characters, abundantly bestowing on each the gift of singularity and extremism of behavior.

References

Auerbach, Nina. *Communities of Women: An Idea in Fiction.* Cambridge: Harvard University Press, 1978.

Carroll, Berenice. "Peace Research: The Cult of Power." *Journal of Conflict Resolutions* 16 (December 1972): 585, 588, 589, 591.

Janeway, Elizabeth. "On the Power of the Weak." *Signs: Journal of Women in Culture and Society* 1, 1 (1975): 103–109.

Jenkins, Ruth Y. *Reclaiming Myths of Power: Women Writers and the Victorian Spiritual Crisis.* Lewisburg: Bucknell University Press, 1995.

Kennedy, William. *Quinn's Book.* New York: Viking Press, 1988.

———. *Very Old Bones.* New York: Viking Press, 1992.

Michener, Christian. *From Then Into Now: William Kennedy's Albany Novels.* Scranton: University of Scranton Press, 1998.

Newton, Judith Lowder. *Women, Power, and Subversion: Social Strategies in British Fiction, 1778–1860.* Athens: University of Georgia Press, 1981.

Seshachari, Neila C., ed. *Conversations with William Kennedy.* Jackson: University Press of Mississippi, 1997.

Van Dover, J. K. *Understanding William Kennedy.* Columbia: University of South Carolina Press, 1991.

Watson, Barbara Bellow. "On Power and the Literary Text." *Signs: Journal of Women in Culture and Society* 1, 1 (1975): 111–118.

This essay was presented at "William Kennedy: A Celebration . . . A Symposium on His Work" held at the Omni Albany Hotel (now Hilton Albany), Albany, New York, on April 15–17, 1999. Printed with permission of the author's estate.

Epilogue

This volume has endeavored to present the full measure of William Kennedy's literary career from a variety of perspectives, ranging from literary scholars to the author's own words. The portrait that has emerged shows a restless, relentlessly engaged creative imagination that has conjured a limitless literary universe from the compact blocks of North Albany, downtown, and the lower wards of New York's capital city, where Kennedy was born, raised, came of age, and returned after an expatriate's hiatus in Puerto Rico.

This volume has also clearly delineated his writerly progress from young journalist to journeyman newspaperman to freelance magazine writer to aspiring novelist trying out experimental fictional forms before discovering his own creative voice and writing style. These varied examinations of Kennedy's work and the author's own candid and revealing analysis during in-depth interviews underscore how he persevered despite years of penury and rejection. He steeled himself against doubt and disappointment by an unwavering belief in his own literary talents and his core conviction that he had important stories to tell about the human condition by reconstituting the history of Albany, both real and imagined.

At the heart of all Kennedy's writing in its myriad forms—especially his novels, but also in the speeches, essays, play, and short story collected here—is his journalistic training. He is never without pencil and notebook wherever he goes, and he approaches a new work of fiction much the way he approached a major work of journalism: immersing himself in the subject through background reading, archival research, interviews, and numerous drafts. He works at his craft with the intensity of a literary blast furnace, taking in tons of raw ore and extracting the precious metals of a narrative. His process of inventing a work of fiction yields piles of tailings, as it were, the by-product of his journalistic commitment to each subject.

The vast accumulation of Kennedy's raw material has been saved and preserved. It offers a treasure trove for future scholars of his work. During his prodigious career that has spanned seven decades, Kennedy and his research assistant, Suzanne Roberson, maintained an exceptional archival collection that illuminates not only Kennedy's writing but the long sweep of Albany's history as well.

In 2003, the University at Albany acquired the William Kennedy Papers, more than forty cubic yards of archival material now housed in the M. E. Grenander Department of Special Collections and Archives. The collection includes correspondence with acclaimed writers, research notebooks, drafts of his novels and screenplays, letters to editors and publishers, and other materials—conveniently arranged and catalogued for each book, readily accessible and easy to use for researchers. At the ceremony where Kennedy officially turned over his papers to the University at Albany, Mark Shechner, professor in the University at Buffalo's English Department, presented remarks on Kennedy's work and the importance of literary archives. He noted that there is "no simple way to sum up [Kennedy's writing] except to say of course that it seldom departs from Albany . . ." He went on to compare Kennedy's sensibility to that of his early mentor Saul Bellow.

> Both writers are profoundly rooted in city life: both are urban and urbane. . . . There is a great knowingness, a worldliness about both men. They embrace the cosmopolitan life of the city and the qualities of mind and spirit it fosters: the heightened sensuousness, the broad human tolerance, the quick attention, the nervous vivacity, the turbulence, surprise, competitiveness, curiosity, cunning, quick and easy humor, the awareness of life as struggle, the tenacity of determination of those who scrap to get ahead, or just stay afloat. . . . Like Bellow, Kennedy draws his characters from all rungs of the social ladder, from brothels to bowling alleys to barrooms to ballrooms . . . all of them fully human, all of them quick with the pulse of life, the grime and sweat of struggle.

As a James Joyce scholar, Shechner also remarked on how fortunate he was that the University at Buffalo houses the largest collection of James Joyce manuscripts anywhere in the world. Having studied the collection extensively, he provided a scholar's perspective on the importance of literary archives: "They have a life of their own [and] give a second life to an author's work. . . . It is the scholars, rediscovering literature from different angles: the angle of the author's life, the author's correspondence, the author's drafts, the author's backstage struggles, . . . who take up the work of memory that is so essential to the life of our literature."

It is a pleasant confluence that Kennedy's papers are located on the third floor of the University at Albany's Science Library, a mere fifty yards away from the offices of the New York State Writers Institute that he founded.

The Writers Institute also bears Kennedy's stamp and contains an extraordinary literary repository with inscribed books and signed posters from nearly all two thousand writers from around the world who have visited Albany since it was established in 1983. Another Suzanne, Writers Institute Associate Director Suzanne Lance, recently retired after twenty-nine years there. She is also an archivist at heart who nurtured and preserved an incomparable audiovisual archive of interviews, readings, and conversations with the writers, poets, filmmakers, and creative artists working in every genre who visited the Writers Institute over the past thirty-five years. Those archival materials are gradually being digitized, catalogued, and formatted in a searchable database that will enrich the study of world literature for generations to come. The Writers Institute is actively seeking grants and partners to advance and complete this labor-intensive digitization process.

There remains today a strong and abiding interest in Kennedy's work and a fascination with his Albany Cycle of novels that continues to express itself in a variety of new ways through various art forms. On April 20, 2007, the Albany Symphony Orchestra presented the world premiere of *Roscoe, Concerto for Violin and Orchestra*, composed by Kevin Beavers, who was inspired by Kennedy's novel. Kennedy read selections from *Roscoe* at the performance to introduce the movements of the work. Beavers had previously composed a tone poem, *Eyeball High*, based on Kennedy's novel *Legs*.

Kennedy's first full-length play, *Grand View* (1996), the story of a political war between the state governor and Albany's political boss, was staged in the spring of 1996 at Capital Repertory Theatre in Albany. A second play in progress, *The Light of the World*, which explores an ancestral legacy of the Phelan family of 1934, had a staged reading at the New York State Summer Writers Institute at Skidmore College in July 2012. He continues to work in 2018 on a dramatic play version of his novel *Ironweed*, which has had readings at the Atlantic Theater and the New York Theatre Workshop in New York City, with Mark Ruffalo and Jessica Hecht in the principal roles of Francis Phelan and Helen Archer.

In February 2017, after a thirty-three-year career as a reporter and columnist at the Albany *Times Union* (Kennedy is the paper's most famous alumnus), I was hired as the new director of the New York State Writers Institute. It is my dream job. Having written countless articles about the programs of the Writers Institute and having interviewed a host of its visiting writers over the years for the *Times Union*, I felt a strong connection to the Institute's distinguished history and mission. I am proud to join the Institute in its thirty-fifth anniversary year. I hope to bring new energy to the Institute as it is poised to expand and achieve a new level of excellence that continues to fulfill Kennedy's vision and assertion that "literary conversation is the best conversation in the world."

In an effort to ensure a financially stable future for the organization, in the fall of 2017, the Friends of Writing, an advisory group to the Writers Institute, assisted by the University at Albany Foundation's development team and the Institute's staff, established the William Kennedy Endowment Fund. It was the first such fundraising effort of its kind at the Institute. The group set a fundraising goal of $90,000 to celebrate Kennedy's ninetieth birthday on January 16, 2018. The fundraising drive has been an overwhelming success and has raised more than $125,000, a significant foundation for an endowment that we hope to grow manyfold in future years to help sustain the Institute's literary programming for decades to come.

For Kennedy's ninetieth birthday, the Friends of Writing, led by Kathryn Gibson, organized a festive dinner party spearheaded by member Mary Valentis as a way to thank endowment fund donors. It was held at Cafe Capriccio in Albany, and chef-owner Jim Rua, a longtime friend of Kennedy, created a memorable culinary feast. The night featured the hallmarks of a Kennedy gathering: great food, great friends, red wine, speeches, music, singing, merrymaking, and convivial energy that ran strong into the wee hours. Kennedy's writer pals Russell Banks and Colum McCann offered toasts, as did a range of longtime friends, associates, and family members. Kennedy's son Brendan screened a touching video tribute to his father that included heartfelt messages from Kennedy's friends and collaborators, including Francis Ford Coppola, Malachy McCourt, Peter Quinn, Gay Talese, Mark Ruffalo, Ed Burns, U.S. Senators for New York Kirsten Gillibrand and Chuck Schumer, Albany's Catholic Bishop Emeritus Howard Hubbard, and more.

A few nights later, the City of Albany and Mayor Kathy Sheehan hosted a citywide celebration in the City Hall Rotunda that drew a standing-room crowd of hundreds of community members who were entertained by performances from Albany Pro Musica, readings of *Roscoe* by members of the Hudson Valley Writers Guild, and tributes by local elected officials, including Lieutenant Governor Kathy Hochul.

At ninety, Kennedy is working as hard as ever. He is making revisions on *Ironweed* the play, tinkering with various screenplays of his novels, and beginning to research and make notes on what might become a new novel. He's also thinking about writing a short nonfiction book about Cuba, detailing his many meetings with Fidel Castro and his experiences on trips to the Caribbean island during the long decades of exile and embargo from the United States.

Moreover, Kennedy and his wife, Dana, are ever-present hosts at the dozens of literary events and visiting writer dinners organized by the Writers Institute each year. Kennedy remains engaged in planning the programs and in leveraging his enormous influence in the literary world to convince world-class writers to come to Albany.

Kennedy's remarkable personal journey and achievements as a writer were not foreshadowed by his upbringing in a small apartment without books in a working-class neighborhood of North Albany. What he possessed was grit and a resilience as tough as the weedy plant that gave its name to his Pulitzer Prize–winning novel. In the final analysis, Saul Bellow was right: He called Kennedy "just a pure writer." He writes because he has to write, because he has something he has to say, and surely he will continue to write until his last breath. That's what writers do.

Perhaps Kennedy himself said it best in a speech he gave in honor of his literary hero, William Faulkner. Kennedy delivered his remarks at the William Faulkner Conference in Oxford, Mississippi, on August 1, 1996, and the speech is included in this volume.

Here is part of what Kennedy said:

> I am struck by how many people tell me they are buoyed, even inspired that, in spite of rejection, and no money, I continued to write novels. I did not think it so unusual. What I possessed was a simple truth: that I wanted to write more than I wanted to pay the mortgage. Time and again I put the work aside to do temporary hack work; I borrowed and begged, and my wife became remarkable in her ability to earn and find money through assorted business ventures and her natural acuity. And always I got back to work. I suppose I was tougher and more ruthless than I knew, for I would've done anything to finish that novel, and get to the next one.

—Paul Grondahl
March 15, 2018
Guilderland, NY

Acknowledgments

This project had its genesis when the New York State Writers Institute hosted a symposium on the work of William Kennedy as part of the Association of Writers & Writing Programs' (AWP) annual conference held in Albany, New York, in April 1999. It was the Writers Institute's intention to collaborate with State University of New York Press to print the proceedings of the symposium, but the project unfortunately never came to fruition. We approached the press again eighteen years later to see if they might be interested in revisiting the book project. This time, we had something very special to celebrate: William Kennedy's ninetieth birthday and the thirty-fifth anniversary of the founding of the Writers Institute. In addition to the scholarly papers presented at the 1999 symposium, this revamped edition would also include a collection of reviews and interviews, selections of Kennedy's own writing, and two photo galleries.* We also asked if the press could expedite publication so that the book could be released in time for the kickoff of the inaugural Albany Book Festival, presented by the Writers Institute at the University at Albany on September 28, 2018, as a capstone to Kennedy's ninetieth-year celebration. We received an enthusiastic response from James Peltz and Donna Dixon, co-directors of State University of New York Press, who are extraordinarily patient as well as kind. We are most grateful for their support, encouragement, and expertise that finally carried this book across the finish line after an eighteen-year hiatus.

In addition to the consummate professionals at the press, including Aimee Harrison, Fran Keneston, Dana Foote, and Laurie Searl, many people and organizations have contributed in various ways in support of this publication.

* Bringing the work of many authors in multiple genres and across many decades between the covers of one book invites editorial intervention. In consideration of the reader, minor adjustments have been made to documentation of quoted sources in previously published articles, essays, and reviews. For instance, titles of texts are included in citations where the context does not provide this information, and references to editions of Kennedy's work are included.

We thank all the writers, editors, and publishers who gave us permission to print or reprint their essays and articles. We sincerely appreciate the cooperation of the following family members for granting us permission on behalf of their deceased relatives who wrote the pieces: Ronald Melk and Phyllis Dain, on behalf of Margaret Croyden; Nancy Edwards and Sarah Edwards-Schmidt, on behalf of Thomas R. Edwards; Caitlin Flanagan, on behalf of Thomas Flanagan; Priya Sanger, Ranjit Mavinkurve, and Roopa Hashimoto, on behalf of Neila C. Seshachari; and Patricia Towers, on behalf of Robert Towers.

Special thanks are due to Jennifer Kowalski, Program Assistant at the Writers Institute, for tracking down and obtaining all the required permissions. Suzanne Roberson, Research Assistant for William Kennedy, spent hours combing through Kennedy's files and the archives at the Albany Institute of History and Art, Albany Public Library, and Albany City Engineer's Office to locate and scan copies of articles and photos that appear in this volume. We thank her for her diligence. We also express our gratitude to the Albany Institute of History and Art for granting us permission to use the historic photos of Albany from their collection, all facilitated by Executive Director Tammis Groft and Alison Munsell-Napierski, Digitization Operations Manager for rights and reproductions. We are grateful for photo permissions from the Albany *Times Union*, Elaine Rosen for the use of Hy Rosen's cartoon, Tomas Sennett, for the Kennedy portrait that appears on the book cover, the University at Albany Office of Communications and Marketing, the M. E. Grenander Department of Special Collections and Archives, and the New York State Writers Institute's archive.

We are also extremely grateful for the time and energy of our proofreaders and researchers including Kathryn Gibson, Michael Huber, Jennifer Kowalski, Jessy Poole, and Elise Coombs.

Finally, we offer our most sincere thanks and appreciation for the contribution of William Kennedy himself. His remarkable literary legacy provided the inspiration for this entire project. He offered his hands-on participation in preparation of the manuscript, including eagle-eyed proofreading skills, and intense attention to every detail and every fact, qualities that he applies to every single piece of writing that he produces. As the author himself describes his character Roscoe Conway in his novel *Roscoe*, Kennedy is Albany's "bootlegger of the soul, a mythic creature made of words and wit and wild deeds and boundless memory."

Happy birthday, Bill.

Contributors

Stefan Beck is a fiction columnist for *New Criterion* and a freelance writer in Hudson, New York. His criticism and essays have appeared in the *Wall Street Journal, Barnes & Noble Review*, *The Daily Beast*, *New Republic*, *Poetry Foundation*, and *Columbia Journalism Review*.

Douglas Brinkley, a professor of history at Rice University, bestselling author, eminent scholar of American history, and CNN's official Presidential Historian, has written numerous biographies of American presidents, politicians, and other newsmakers. His latest *New York Times* bestseller is *Rightful Heritage* (2016), on the environmental legacy of Franklin Delano Roosevelt. Brinkley has also edited *The Proud Highway: The Fear and Loathing Letters, Volume 1* (1997), a collection of the private correspondence of Hunter S. Thompson, for which William Kennedy wrote the foreword.

Margaret Croyden (1922–2015) was a theater critic who contributed regularly to *The New York Times Magazine, Village Voice,* and *American Theater Magazine.* She wrote about theater, music, and opera in a long-running online column in *New York Theatre Wire,* titled "Croyden's Corner," from 1998 to the time of her death. She was one of the founders of the League of Professional Theater Women.

Thomas R. Edwards (1928–2005) was an English professor at Rutgers University and editor of *Raritan*, the quarterly journal published by the university. At Rutgers, he received the Warren I. Susman Award, the university's highest honor for teaching. Edwards also received a Guggenheim Fellowship, and his book *Imagination and Power* (1971) was a finalist for the National Book Award.

Thomas Flanagan (1923–2002) was a professor of English literature at the University of California, Berkeley, and the State University of New York at Stony Brook. Flanagan wrote a trilogy of Irish historical novels, *The Year of* *the French* (1979), which won the National Book Critics Circle Award, *The Tenants of Time* (1988), and *The End of the Hunt* (1994).

Benedict Giamo is an associate professor of American studies at the University of Notre Dame. With a scholarly focus on homelessness in the United States, Giamo has published works that examine the issue in both real life and fiction. His book *The Homeless of "Ironweed": Blossoms on the Crag* (1996), includes a literary and cultural analysis of motifs in William Kennedy's novel *Ironweed.*

Michael Patrick Gillespie is a professor of English at Florida International University. While at Marquette University, where he taught for twenty-nine years, Gillespie published *Reading William Kennedy* (2002), which provides an introduction, context, and analysis of Kennedy's novels. He has also written books on James Joyce and Oscar Wilde.

Paul Grondahl is Director of the New York State Writers Institute. He is an award-winning journalist and author and was a staff writer at the Albany *Times Union* from 1984 to 2017. He is the author of four books, including *I Rose Like a Rocket: The Political Education of Theodore Roosevelt* (2007), *Now Is the Time: A History of Parsons Child and Family Center 1829–2004* (2006), *That Place Called Home* (2000), and *Mayor Corning: Albany Icon, Albany Enigma* (1997).

Doris Grumbach is a novelist, memoirist, biographer, literary critic, and essayist. She was literary editor of the *New Republic* for several years and a book reviewer for *Morning Edition* on National Public Radio. She has taught at the College of Saint Rose in Albany, New York, the Iowa Writers' Workshop, and American University in Washington, DC.

Suzanne Lance served as Associate Director of the New York State Writers Institute for twenty-nine years and is now semi-retired. She was editor of *Adirondack Peeks*, the biannual magazine of the Adirondack Forty-Sixers for seventeen years, and wrote an extensive history of the organization for the club's publication *Heaven Up-h'isted-ness! The History of the Adirondack Forty-Sixers and the High Peaks of the Adirondacks* (2011).

Vivian Valvano Lynch, Professor Emerita of English at St. John's University, is the author of the book *Portraits of Artists: Warriors in the Novels of William Kennedy* (1999). She has also written numerous essays on James Joyce, contemporary Irish fiction and drama, and Irish American fiction. She was a coeditor for the *James Joyce Literary Supplement.*

Colum McCann, a native Dubliner, teaches in the MFA program at Hunter College in New York City. He has authored six novels and three collections of short stories. His most recent collection is the 2015 *Thirteen Ways of Looking* from which the short story "Sh'khol" garnered a Pushcart Prize. His novel *Let the Great World Spin* (2009) won the National Book Award and became a best-seller on four continents. He published the nonfiction book *Letters to a Young Writer* in 2017 and will bring out a new novel in 2019.

Christian Michener is a professor of English and the director of the English Honors Program at Saint Mary's University of Minnesota. His book *From Then Into Now: William Kennedy's Albany Novels* (1998) offers insights into Kennedy's use of time in each of his novels.

Donald Newlove published two novels, *Leo and Theodore* (1972) and *The Drunks* (1974), which he revised in 2014 as one book, *Sweet Adversity.* These novels and his memoir *Those Drinking Days: Myself and Other Writers* (1981) focus on the devastating effects of alcohol abuse. In his books *First Paragraphs* (1992), *Painted Paragraphs* (1993), and *Invented Voices* (1994), he offers writers and readers insights into great writers' use of openings, description, and dialogue.

Fintan O'Toole, a native of Dublin, is a novelist, historical writer, political and social affairs columnist for the *Irish Times* (since 1988), and literary critic, with frequent contributions to *The New York Review of Books*. In 2017, he received extraordinary recognition for his journalism on Brexit, winning the European Press Prize and the Orwell Prize for Journalism.

William Patrick is a poet, novelist, and nonfiction writer. His most recent book is *The Call of Nursing: Voices from the Front Lines of Health Care* (2013). He is the founder and director of the New York State Summer Young Writers Institute at Skidmore College in Saratoga Springs, New York, and is on the faculty of Fairfield University's MFA Program in Creative Writing.

Anthony P. Radford is an associate professor of voice and opera at California State University, Fresno, and the director of the voice ensemble group Fresno State Opera Theatre. Radford also writes reviews for the *Opera Journal* and has served a term on the Board of Directors for the National Opera Association.

John Sayles is an American independent film director, screenwriter, novelist, and critic. He has received Oscar nominations for Best Original Screenplay for *Passion Fish* (1992) and *Lone Star* (1996). He has written several novels, most recently *A Moment in the Sun* (2011). Like Kennedy, Sayles received a MacArthur Fellowship in 1983.

Edward Schwarzschild, fiction writer, is an associate professor of English at the University at Albany, and a fellow at the New York State Writers Institute. He is the author of the novel *Responsible Men* (2005), a *San Francisco Chronicle* Best Book of the Year, and the short story collection *The Family Diamond* (2007).

Neila C. Seshachari (1934–2002) was an English professor at Weber State University in Ogden, Utah, for three decades. She was editor of *Weber Studies: An Interdisciplinary Humanities Journal* for eleven years. In addition to writing short stories and critical essays, she edited *Conversations with William Kennedy* (1997), a series of interviews with Kennedy between 1969 and 1996.

Robert Towers (1923–1995), novelist and critic, was an English professor at Queens College and Columbia University. He was the author of three novels, *The Necklace of Kali* (1960), *The Monkey Watcher* (1964), and *The Summoning* (1983). His critical reviews of fiction and nonfiction appeared in *The New York Times Book Review* and *The New York Review of Books*.

Index

Note: Page numbers in *italics* refer to illustrations.